RACE, GENDER,
and POWER in
AMERICA

RACE, GENDER, and POWER in AMERICA

THE LEGACY OF THE HILL-THOMAS HEARINGS

Edited by

Anita Faye Hill
Emma Coleman Jordan

New York Oxford | *Oxford University Press* | *1995*

Oxford University Press

Oxford   New York
Athens   Auckland   Bangkok   Bombay
Calcutta   Cape Town   Dar es Salaam   Delhi
Florence   Hong Kong   Istanbul   Karachi
Kuala Lumpur   Madras   Madrid   Melbourne
Mexico City   Nairobi   Paris   Singapore
Taipei   Tokyo   Toronto

and associated companies in
Berlin   Ibadan

Published by Oxford University Press, Inc.
198 Madison Avenue, New York, New York 10016

Oxford is a registered trademark of Oxford University Press

Library of Congress Cataloging-in-Publication Data
Race, gender, and power in America : the legacy of the Hill-Thomas
hearing / edited by Anita Faye Hill and Emma Coleman Jordan.
p.   cm.   Includes index.
ISBN 0-19-508774-7
1. Thomas, Clarence, 1948–   .   2. Hill, Anita.   3. United States.
Supreme Court—Officials and employees—Selection and appointment.
4. Sexual harassment of women—Law and legislation—United States.
I. Hill, Anita.   II. Jordan, Emma Coleman.
KF8745.T48R32   1995   347.73'2634—dc20
[347.3073534]   95-33987

1 3 5 7 9 8 6 4 2

Printed in the United States of America
on acid-free paper

*For the Hill family,
especially Erma and Albert Hill*

*For Earl and Myrtle Coleman,
for a lifetime of support*

CONTENTS

ACKNOWLEDGMENTS

This book grew out of a conference sponsored by Georgetown University Law Center in October 1992. Both the conference and the book owe a debt to many members of the Georgetown community, especially faculty contributors Susan Deller Ross, Eleanor Holmes Norton, Mari Matsuda (for a fabulous job standing in at the last minute for bell hooks), and Charles R. Lawrence III. I appreciate the generosity of many law students who volunteered during the conference. My research assistants—Deborah "Sonni" Smith, Judith O'Sullivan, Jackie Belk, Destefano Bracey, and Geraldine Rowe—provided indispensable and loving support. The work was made easier by the Law Center's outstanding technical and secretarial support staff, especially my secretaries, Pam Irwin and Vickie White.

Joy Johannessen, our Oxford editor, showed faith, hope, and charity to us as law professors unaccustomed to superb editing.

The financial support provided by Dean Areen and the Georgetown University Law Center, Arnold and Porter, the William Penn Foundation, Nestlé Corporation of North America, the Albert and Barrie Zesiger Foundation, Ben and Jerry's Homemade, Inc., and Ms. Sallie Bingham made possible the conference that gave birth to this book. We trusted and relied on Louise Hilsen for crucial public relations guidance and fund raising during the hearings and the conference and beyond.

My public life is only possible because Don, Kristen, Allison, Damon, and Kevin fill in the private holes created by my absences.

The contributors to the book became a kind of family whose lives have been touched by the hearings and Anita Hill's testimony in many ways. I value greatly the insights we shared across several disciplines. Here we offer for a general audience a glimpse of the unruly conversation that took place at the conference.

E.C.J.

I too wish to thank the generous contributors mentioned above who made the conference and this collection possible. I especially want to thank Louise Hilsen and the former CEO of the Penn Foundation, Bernard C. Watson, whose wisdom and guidance were particularly helpful to me.

The secretarial staff at the University of Oklahoma College of Law provided invaluable support in the completion of this project. I also wish to thank my research assistants—Yolanda Johnson, Marisha Steward, and Lata Matherny—for their hard work. Rose Martinez Elugardo, my assistant, gave generously of her time and seemingly boundless energy to do research and other support work on this project as well.

I owe a debt of gratitude to the group of African American women whose November 1991 ad in various papers around the country reminded the world that the Senate dismissal of me and my statement about Clarence Thomas's behavior had tragic and historical racial and gender dimensions. In a meaningful and real way, their willingness to speak out inspired my work on the conference and on this collection.

I am grateful for the support of my colleagues at the College of Law, especially Professors Shirley Wiegand and Leisha Self, whose participation in the conference and whose comments on early drafts contributed to my essay's thoughtfulness.

Joy Johannessen, editor supreme, of Oxford University Press, has been a source of knowledge, experience, and patience. Her skillful editing improved the essays in this collection and left a positive mark on my writing for the future. Her dedication to her profession and in particular to this collection has made completion possible.

Finally, I want to thank my family, whose love, guidance, and nurturing throughout my life largely make me who I am and sustain me in good and bad times.

Any lack of clarity and/or omissions in parts of this collection for which I am responsible are my fault and should not be attributed to any of the persons mentioned in these acknowledgments.

A.F.H.

FOREWORD

The world is not a narrow moral occasion. All too often, yesterday's villains are today's heroes. When Anita Hill first raised her voice to talk about her experiences with Supreme Court Justice Clarence Thomas, most people didn't believe her. A year later, most did. Between the time Professor Hill first spoke out and the time people heard her, there was confusion, the reaction of those who hoped the world could be reduced to a sound bite or a bumper sticker. Too many people wish that events came with subtitles telling them what to think.

I don't know that Anita Hill cares what people think. Her testimony in the Clarence Thomas confirmation hearings seemed self-propelled, unconnected to the opinions that others advanced. From where I sit, Anita Hill is a woman of courage. Sexually harassed a decade earlier, she came forward with her story when approached by the Senate Judiciary Committee. Responding to speculation about her motives, she held a press conference on October 7, 1991, at the University of Oklahoma Law School, where she is a tenured professor. Subjecting herself to nearly an hour of questioning from members of the press, she discussed her reasons for coming forward, talked about the issue of sexual harassment, and maintained her composure and dignity through what must have been a difficult process.

My first awareness of Professor Hill came in the days before the October press conference. Timothy Phelps of *Newsday* reported her charges on October 5. National Public Radio correspondent Nina Totenberg mentioned her in an October 6 broadcast. By the time she came forward on Monday, October 7, my curiosity was piqued.

Denunciations and equivocations quickly followed the press conference. Arizona senator Dennis DeConcini was among the first to speak, stumbling over Professor Hill's name, describing her as "this lady, Mrs. or Miss Hill," and then suggesting that her press conference was "unfortunate for Judge Thomas." I remember marveling at Senator DeConcini's laconic choice of words. "Unfortunate" was a word of restraint, a word that suggested just a fraction of the turmoil to come when Professor Hill's allegations were explored in Senate hearings. DeConcini might have chosen a more appropriate adjective. Lamentable. Woeful. Wretched. Pathetic. Deplorable. Damned. These words more accurately describe the quasi-judicial fiasco that led to the narrow confirmation of Clarence Thomas as associate justice of the Supreme Court. These words more accurately describe the painful probing of images that took place in the wake of the Clarence Thomas–Anita Hill hearings.

Anita Hill's action has had an impact on both popular culture and public policy in the last decade of the twentieth century. She burst into national attention, and for nine days, from her press conference on October 7 until Thomas's confirmation on October 15, she fully captured our awareness. The Civil Rights Act of 1991 was passed weeks after the Thomas confirmation. The following year was described by many as "the year of the woman," with Hill's name invoked as a reason to do everything from elect candidates to form political action committees. In 1992, voters recalled her black female voice and the race and gender of her white male interrogators, and four women senators were elected because of "the Anita Hill effect." But if Carol Moseley-Braun, Patty Murray, Dianne Feinstein, and Barbara Boxer went to the Senate because of the ire that Hill's treatment had provoked among women voters, they were incapable of using that ire to secure a fair hearing for another African American woman, Lani Guinier, initially touted as an excellent nominee for assistant attorney general for civil rights, later denigrated as "loony Lani" whose views were out of sync with the so-called mainstream. Indeed, the gains yielded by "the year of the woman" were canceled by a clause in the Contract with America. If in 1994 the pendulum swung so far right as to produce the year of the Newt, imagine what would happen if there were ever a "year of the black woman."

Anita Hill's testimony did not trigger the "angry white male" backlash that has been so fully examined in the wake of the Republican electoral sweep in 1994, but her words certainly raised the hackles of the "equity feminists," who reject the notion of "woman as victim" and assert that women must take "responsibility" for the situations in which we find ourselves. Camille Paglia and Katie Roiphe have dismissed the concept of date rape as women's irresponsibility; Christine Hoff Sommers has suggested that gender feminists have gone too far in blaming men for oppression; and a coterie of columnists have called for a statute of limitations on accusations of sexual harassment, especially in the case of Oregon senator Robert Packwood. No, Anita Hill did not trigger the backlash, but some of it can certainly be interpreted as a response to the October 1991 hearings, when an African American woman making charges against a more powerful man had to be heard, if not believed.

In hindsight, it is particularly ironic to review the moment in which Clarence Thomas was able to swing the hearings in his favor, the moment when he played the most powerful card in his deck: the specter of lynching. It is incredible that the man who railed against "electronic lynching," in a clear plea for racial consideration, later wrote in *Adarand* v. *Pena* (June 12, 1995), "I believe there is a moral and constitutional equivalence between laws designed to subjugate a race and those that distribute benefits on the basis of race in order to foster some current notion of equality. Government cannot make us equal; it can only recognize, respect, and protect us as equal before the law." Thomas sought to become *more equal* with his invocation of lynching in 1991. His cries of electronic lynching have as much resonance as contemporary claims of "reverse discrimination." Both claims are made without context, as if the past were not prologue to the present, as if history has no significance and can be distorted at will.

In the years since the hearings, Clarence Thomas has retreated behind his robes, and Anita Hill, both caricatured and canonized by the press and women's groups, has become more image than individual, more noun, verb, pronoun, adjective, and catalyst than person. As uncomfortable as that may be for her, perhaps it is appropriate. In the aftermath of the Thomas confirmation, there has been conversation about race, gender, class, economic status, the law, philosophy, history, and even marital status in the context of the indirect confrontation between Thomas and Hill. Speeches have been given, books written, and the ugly underbelly of gender workplace relations—the sexual harassment complaints that more than doubled in the year after Anita Hill went public—revealed.

In a symposium held on the first anniversary of the Hill-Thomas hearings, Professor Hill took the conversation a step further. Convening a conference on race, gender, and power in America, Hill and Georgetown law professor Emma Coleman Jordan assembled a stellar group of scholars and lawyers—many of them part of Hill's legal team during the hearings—to push the issues raised in October 1991 to the edge. This volume, which grew out of the conference, examines the impact of race, gender, and power on our society, using Hill's testimony as a launching pad to ask jarring and provocative questions. Whether the questions are raised by Susan Deller Ross, who views changes in sexual harassment law as changes in our cultural construct, or by Congresswoman Eleanor Holmes Norton, who assures us that Hill has affected both political process and political culture, these essays impart the sense, notwithstanding the Contract with America, that the turgid white male political tradition is being challenged and reinterpreted.

Anna Deavere Smith's essay explores the Hill-Thomas hearings in the context of popular culture, describing them as "riveting television." Smith's layered analysis of issues of denial and pain is as much a part of this dialogue as Judge Leon Higginbotham's historical analysis of the denigration of African American women. Judith Resnik's meditation on wrongs done to women is as critical as Charles Ogletree's view of Hill's appearance before the Judiciary Committee as a case for "client-centered advocacy."

The most powerful essays in this volume take us to a place we don't visit often, a place that trains academic analysis on the status of black women and reveals, in Emma Jordan's words, "the power of false racial memory," the notion that an unwillingness to air black "dirty laundry" pushes sexual harassment under the rug and mutes questions raised about issues of gender. Jordan's theme is echoed by Robert Allen, who asks how men can be brought into the struggle against abuse and violence. He challenges men to consider power *with* women, not power *over* women, and places the issues of harassment, violence, and abuse in the broader context of sexual and racial inequality. In many ways, he takes Anita Hill's story from that of Anywoman (as DeConcini told it) to that of Everywoman, and calls on men to see mother, daughter, sister in her narrative.

Anchoring his "morality play" in the lives of male protagonists—Clarence Thomas, Mike Tyson, and William Kennedy-Smith—

Charles Lawrence probes the Everywoman notion and looks for the sister in women as dissimilar as Anita Hill, Desiree Washington, and Patricia Bowman. Lawrence captures the peculiarities of race and gender reality when he shows, in effect, how a black man who would be uncle was treated as a white man who would be judge, how a white woman who collided with a dynasty came to be judged as a black woman who would be slut, and how a black girl who accused Bigger Thomas was cast as Miss Anne. This is not about charades, but about the power of race and gender myths and the way the lens of class shades characters to accommodate the mythology. Orlando Patterson, too, uses class as a lens through which to view race and gender issues in the African American community. His unsettling essay combines history, sociology, demographics, popular culture, and psychology to probe the black gender crisis that was starkly revealed by the Hill-Thomas hearings.

Anita's Hill's testimony was not the first occasion to question the way black women are treated in public space. Remember the tear-stained face of Linda Brown, who was turned away from her high school by raging racists in Little Rock. Remember the quiet dignity of Charlayne Hunter, a freshman at the University of Georgia, who walked to class through taunts, and studied and carved out a campus life despite intense racial harassment. In the years since Anita Hill raised her voice, we've seen the capricious dismissal of Professor Guinier, and we've seen Surgeon General Joycelyn Elders skewered before and during her confirmation hearings, viciously attacked during her brief tenure in office, and then opprobriously dismissed by the Clinton administration in an attempt at political posturing. These events call to mind the words that Adele Logan Alexander takes as the title of her essay, "She's no lady, she's a nigger." In a powerful treatise that speaks to the compromised status of black women, Alexander explores the "convoluted framework of racist, sexist, and elitist assumptions that none of us can escape and that condition our responses to any such public event."

Anita Hill's own contribution to this volume raises questions not often asked about the role of marriage and patronage in assessing the status of African American women. How differently might Hill have been treated if she had had some spouse or sponsor to speak to her stability, veracity, and integrity? Would farfetched theories invoking *The Exorcist* have been verbalized had she had a husband by her side? Hill uses works like Zora Neale Hurston's *Their Eyes Were Watching God* and Simone de Beauvoir's *The Second Sex* to examine sexism and patriarchy in the African American community and in the larger society. Is single status a stigma? asks Hill. If so, since marriage rates are lower among African Americans than among other groups, are proportionately more African American women hampered by this stigma? Can black women's single status be used to muffle our outcries against workplace sexual harassment and our legitimate concerns about sexism in our community?

Sexual harassment is about people using their power to make someone else's work environment uncomfortable, even intolerable. It can involve talking, displaying photos, or touching. When bosses use lewd talk around subordinates who may jeopardize themselves by objecting to the talk, that's sexual harassment. When workplace lounges are draped with *Playboy* pictures, and when the one or two women on the job must tolerate the pictures and the banter that goes along with them, that's sexual harassment. When bosses talk to unwilling subordinates about pornographic movies and their sexual desires, that's sexual harassment.

Those on the receiving end often don't object because they don't want to be blackballed or ridiculed for "making a mountain out of a molehill." When bosses are called on their behavior, they often reply by saying that they were "joking" or that they didn't mean anything by it. But they have the power to engage in it, to make their subordinates squirm. Some women convince themselves that the squirming they do is no big thing. It's uncomfortable, it's ugly, but maybe it's the price we pay for holding a job. We convince ourselves of this because when we talk to our fathers, brothers, cousins, husbands, and lovers, they tell us that our bosses are engaging in their "male prerogative," that this kind of talk is meant to be flattering, that nothing "really" happened, that it could be worse.

In raising her voice to the Senate Judiciary Committee in October 1991, Anita Hill insisted that sexual harassment had no place in the contemporary workplace. A year later, when she and Emma Jordan gathered colleagues at Georgetown, she turned her testimony from the individual to the institutional. The essays in this volume are like the pieces of a Rubik's cube, the twisting and turning of points of view around testimony and history, race, power, and gender. They are rich, intricate explorations of matters that continue to confound our nation. They are a plea and a challenge to a judicial system too frequently defined by patriarchy and privilege. If we are indebted to Professor Anita Hill for coming forward in October 1991, we are further obliged to her for gathering these thinkers together to place her testimony in context.

The Republican revolution of 1994 and the legislation proposed by the 104th Congress have changed the political climate significantly. Between Hill's appearance before the Judiciary Committee in 1991 and the elections of 1994, there was a box-office hit, *Disclosure*, that featured a woman who harassed a man. There was a lawsuit brought by men who worked at a weight-watching franchise and claimed they had experienced "sexual harassment." There was the notion, despite the fact that men file just 10 percent of all sexual harassment cases, that women can also victimize. There was an attempt, in short, to shift the focus of the sexual harassment inquiry away from the reality of institutionalized gender discrimination, just as the affirmative action backlash attempts to shift the focus away from institutionalized racism.

Against both attempts stands the testimony of Anita Hill as an African American woman. As time passes, I am convinced of the enduring impact that her testimony has had on popular and political culture. Further, I am convinced that her appearance before the Judiciary Committee moved the awareness of sexual harassment issues from bumper-sticker simplicity to the level of complexity they deserve. Since she spoke up, we have heard of sexual harassment at Stanford Medical School, in the United States Navy, in the United States Senate, and in other lofty institutions. Her voice has been an empowering one, and if her impact has meant that some measure of patriarchal power is dismantled, then we are all enriched.

June 1995   —Julianne Malveaux

CHRONOLOGY

1991

June 27: Justice Thurgood Marshall, the first African American to serve on the Supreme Court, resigns after a twenty-four-year tenure.[1] His letter to President George Bush reads:

My Dear Mr. President:

The strenuous demands of Court work and its related duties required or expected of a justice appear at this time to be incompatible with my advancing age and medical condition.

I, therefore, retire as an Associate Justice of the Supreme Court of the United States when my successor is qualified.

Respectfully,
Thurgood Marshall.[2]

July 1: President Bush nominates Judge Clarence Thomas of the District of Columbia Circuit Court of Appeals to the Supreme Court. At a press conference held at the president's vacation home in Kennebunkport, Maine, Bush calls Thomas "the best person for this position." Thomas responds by telling the press, "In my view, only in America could this have been possible. I look forward to the confirmation process, and an opportunity to be of service once again to my country."[3]

July–August: The Alliance for Justice, a public interest watchdog coalition that tracks judicial appointments and opposes conservative nominees, learns that a former colleague of Thomas's, now a law professor in Oklahoma, told a Yale Law School classmate that she had been sexually harassed by the nominee. Putting this information together with other clues, the Alliance identifies Anita Hill.[4] The director of the Alliance tells William Corr, chief counsel to the Senate Judiciary Committee's Subcommittee on Antitrust, Monopolies, and Business Rights, what the Alliance has learned. Corr instructs Gail Laster, working for Senator Howard Metzenbaum of Ohio as counsel to the Labor Subcommittee, to look into these allegations.[5]

September 5: Laster telephones Hill and asks her if she knows anything about charges of sexual harassment at the Equal Employment Opportunity Commission (EEOC). Hill suggests that Laster pursue any leads she has.[6]

September 6: Following up on a lead she learned independently of Laster, Ricki Seidman, Senator Edward Kennedy's chief investigator for the Senate Labor and Human Resources Committee, telephones Hill and inquires whether Hill was harassed by Thomas. Hill responds that she will neither confirm nor deny the allegations.[7]

September 9: Seidman contacts Hill again. Hill indicates that she believes that Thomas behaved inappropriately toward her and agrees to provide some information about the behavior, but she stresses that to preserve her privacy she does not want the information made public. Seidman tells Hill that the Judiciary Committee can protect her confidentiality. Hill then outlines the general pattern of behavior. Seidman suggests that Hill "might be more comfortable discussing the matter" with James Brudney, Laster's immediate supervisor, with whom Hill attended Yale Law School. Hill agrees. Brudney takes Laster off the sexual harassment inquiry.[8]

September 10: The Senate Judiciary Committee begins hearings on Thomas's nomination.[9]

Brudney contacts Hill. She again expresses reservations and informs him of her desire for confidentiality. She then describes Thomas's sexual harassment of her. Brudney and several other Metzenbaum staffers inform the senator of Hill's allegations. Metzenbaum tells Brudney that if Hill wishes to pursue this issue, she must contact Senator Joseph R. Biden, Jr., Democrat of Delaware, chairman of the Judiciary Committee. Brudney informs Hill of Senator Metzenbaum's advice. Hill tells Brudney she will go forward.[10]

September 12: Hill telephones Biden aide Harriet Grant, head of the Nominations Unit for the Judiciary Committee. Hill reiterates her desire to maintain her privacy. She informs Grant of her allegations and states that in so doing she feels she has done enough and that it is up to the committee to investigate. Grant tells Hill that unless Thomas is given a chance to answer Hill's allegations, the committee cannot follow up on them. No procedure for making a formal complaint is discussed with Hill.[11]

September 13 or 16: Staffers bring Biden up to date on Grant's conversation with Hill. He agrees that the matter cannot be pursued unless Hill consents to informing Thomas of the charges.[12]

September 16: Hill contacts her corroborating witness, Susan Hoerchner, a close friend and law school classmate in whom she had confided while employed by Thomas, regarding her allegations of sexual harassment.[13]

September 17: Hoerchner contacts Grant and corroborates that Hill confided in her about Thomas's behavior. She tells Grant that because of her position as a California workers' compensation judge, she wants to maintain her confidentiality.[14]

September 18: On Brudney's advice, Hill contacts Professor Susan Deller Ross, a lawyer working at the Georgetown University Law Center Sex Discrimination Clinic, for her recommendation on how to proceed.[15]

September 19: Hill telephones Grant and requests that committee members be informed of her allegations.[16]

September 20: After consulting with Jeffrey Peck, her supervisor and Biden's staff director for the Judiciary Committee, Grant informs Hill that the next step in bringing allegations before the Judiciary Committee would be for Hill to agree to an FBI investigation. The FBI would then interview Hill, Thomas, and others with "relevant information."[17]

September 20–21: Ross contacts Carolyn Oslinik, aide to Senator Kennedy, and Judith Lichtman, president of the Women's Legal Defense Fund. Lichtman and Ross agree that Hill should prepare a written statement to avoid unfavorable construction of her comments by the FBI, and they so advise Hill.[18] Hill agrees to an FBI interview on the condition that her statement be attached to the FBI report. Grant agrees.

September 23: Hill faxes a statement describing her experiences with Thomas to Senator Biden's staff.[19] Her statement outlines a pattern of sexual harassment between 1981 and 1983 that included asking Hill out on dates and describing sexual activities:

His conversations were very vivid. He spoke about acts that he had seen in pornographic films involving such things as women having sex with animals and films involving group sex or rape scenes. . . . In January of 1983, I began to make discreet inquiries about other employment opportunities. This was difficult because I feared that if he found out that I was looking elsewhere he might make it difficult for me to find other employment. A second factor that made my search more difficult was my desire to stay in public service during a time of a governmental hiring freeze.[20]

Hill asks that her statement be distributed with the FBI report. After communication with the Justice Department and the White House, the FBI begins an investigation and interviews Hill.[21]

September 24: The FBI interviews Allyson Duncan, who worked as chief of staff for Thomas at the EEOC, and Nancy Fitch, who worked as special assistant and historian to Thomas at the EEOC.[22]

September 25: The FBI interviews Thomas,[23] and then makes its report available to the Judiciary Committee.[24] Hill asks Grant for assurance that the FBI report will be accompanied by her statement and that the statement will be given to members of the Judiciary Committee. Grant informs Hill that she cannot provide such assurance, although she indicates that the senators will learn of the issue in some form.[25]

Biden informs the Democrats on the committee of Hill's allegations and the FBI report. He also informs Senate Minority Leader Robert Dole and Senate Majority Leader George Mitchell of the allegations. Biden tells the senators that they can see Hill's statement and the FBI report if they want, but does not distribute copies.[26]

September 26: Hill calls Brudney to express her concern that her statement has not been distributed to the committee members. She telephones her friends Sonia Jarvis and Kim Taylor, both of whom have experience in Washington politics, to ask for aid in getting her statement disseminated to the committee members. Jarvis arranges a telephone interview between Hill and Democratic senator Paul Simon of Illinois. During the call, Hill suggests distributing her statement to the entire Senate.[27] Simon informs Hill, "You can't distribute it to one hundred senators and keep the thing confidential. You have to make a very difficult decision—whether to go public or not."[28] Hill decides against total dissemination. Simon reviews Hill's statement and the FBI report. Taylor and Jarvis contact Stanford classmate Charles Ogletree, professor of law at Harvard, expressing Hill's concern that her statement has not been distributed to committee members.[29]

September 27: Ogletree asks a colleague, Harvard professor Laurence Tribe, to pursue the matter. Tribe telephones Ron Klain, chief counsel to Biden on the Judiciary Committee, and informs him that " 'a group of women professors on the West Coast' are concerned that an unidentified woman's allegations of sexual harassment had not been circulated to the Committee." Klain will not discuss the matter, other than to assure Tribe that it is being pursued.[30]

Klain tells Biden about Tribe's telephone call. They decide to distribute copies of Hill's statement to the Democratic committee members in sealed envelopes labeled "Senators' Eyes Only." Democratic senator Dennis DeConcini of Arizona and Republican senator Arlen Specter of Pennsylvania review the FBI report and Hill's statement. During a meeting with Thomas, Specter talks with the nominee about Hill's allegations.[31]

The Judiciary Committee splits 7-7 on Thomas's confirmation and votes 13-1 to place the matter before the full Senate for consideration.[32]

Timothy M. Phelps, a reporter for *Newsday*, learns that the FBI is investigating "allegations of personal misconduct" against Thomas. Before September 27, Phelps had received unsubstantiated information alluding to allegations of sexual harassment against Thomas.[33] At some unknown time, Phelps learned from an anonymous source that Hill was the person alleging sexual harassment.[34]

September 28: Hill's allegations are alluded to "during at least two [Washington] dinner parties."[35] *Newsday* publishes an article by Phelps referring to the "reopening of the FBI background investigation on Thomas to check opponents' allegations of personal misconduct."[36]

October 2: Nina Totenberg, legal affairs correspondent for National Public Radio (NPR), obtains or has already obtained a copy of Hill's statement to the Judiciary Committee.[37] Totenberg is later interviewed by *Vanity Fair*, which reports that " 'as far back as July,' [according to Totenberg], 'there were sexual harassment rumors' circling the nomination of Clarence Thomas, 'but I couldn't nail them down.' [Totenberg] didn't discover Anita Hill's name until much later, 'but I knew about her before I got the affidavit [Hill's statement]. . . . For me the affidavit was the icing on the cake.' "[38]

October 3: Totenberg calls Hill. Totenberg's extensive knowledge of Hill's allegations leads Hill to believe that they can no longer be kept private. Although Hill refuses to answer Totenberg's questions, she provides Totenberg with the names of references. Hill contacts Ogletree and discusses the committee's activities thus far and Totenberg's telephone call. Ogletree advises Hill to refuse to answer any questions until Totenberg proves she has Hill's statement.[39]

October 4: Phelps calls Hill, but she refuses to comment unless he has the statement she gave to the committee. Although he demonstrates some knowledge of the statement, he does not have it.[40]

October 5: Phelps again contacts Hill. She admits that she gave an interview to the FBI. When Phelps concedes that he does not have Hill's statement, she refuses to be interviewed. Totenberg contacts Hill and reads a portion of Hill's statement over the phone. Hill agrees to a taped interview.[41]

October 6: Newsday discloses Hill's allegations. The front-page teaser for Phelps's story reads, "Sex Harassment Allegation; THE CHARGE AGAINST THOMAS; Law Prof Told FBI of EEOC Incidents."[42]

The White House issues a statement asserting that it has reviewed the FBI report and " 'determined that the allegation was unfounded.' . . . President George Bush 'continues to believe that Judge Thomas is eminently qualified to serve on the Supreme Court and expects him to be confirmed promptly.' "[43]

NPR broadcasts a radio report on Hill's allegations. The report includes a portion of the taped interview with Hill, an interview with Senator Simon, and a rundown of the incidents leading to and following from Hill's allegations.[44]

Members of the press arrive in Norman, Oklahoma, to interview Hill regarding her statement.

October 7: Hill holds a nationally televised press conference. She refutes accusations that her allegations are politically motivated and requests "official resolution," saying, "My integrity has been called into question." She challenges the White House statement that the allegations are unfounded, and faults the thoroughness of the FBI report on which that statement was based.[45]

October 8: After watching the press conference, Professor Judith Resnik of the University of Southern California Law Center decides to offer Hill her legal services and contacts Professor Emma Coleman Jordan of the Georgetown University Law Center. She asks if Jordan, president-elect of the Association of American Law Schools, can put her in contact with Hill.[46]

Republican senator John Danforth of Missouri presents to the Senate a sworn affidavit in which Thomas avers that Hill's allegations are untrue.[47]

Seven Democratic congresswomen (Louise Slaughter and Nita M. Lowey of New York, Patricia Schroeder of Colorado, Barbara Boxer of California, Jolene Unsoeld of Washington, Patsy T. Mink of Hawaii, and Eleanor Holmes Norton of the District of Columbia) attempt to enter the Capitol Room as the Democratic senators hold their regular Tuesday caucus on the day scheduled for the confirmation vote on Thomas. The women want to argue that the confirmation vote should be delayed to provide an airing of Hill's charges against Thomas, but they are not allowed in. Eventually, "an aide to Senator George J. Mitchell . . . [tells] the women that Mr. Mitchell [will] meet with them for a few moments in his office around the corner."[48]

Through Danforth, Thomas requests a delay in the Senate vote and an opportunity "to appear before the appropriate forum and clear my name." The Senate unanimously votes to delay the vote on Thomas's confirmation.[49]

Biden telephones Hill at her home to inform her that she will be subpoenaed to testify before the Judiciary Committee.

October 9: Jordan contacts Hill and inquires whether she has legal representation. Jordan begins to organize the legal team. Hill, Ogletree, Jordan, Resnik, Ross, and Michelle Roberts, a former public defender now in private practice in Washington, D.C., participate in a three-hour conference call to discuss how Hill should proceed. This group, along with John T. Frank, a former Yale Law School professor, Frank's partner Janet Napolitano, and Warner Gardner, a Washington lawyer, come to comprise the Hill legal team.[50]

Hill arrives in Washington, D.C.

October 10: The Judiciary Committee takes the statement of Angela Denise Wright, a former colleague of Thomas's at the EEOC, now a metro editor at the *Charlotte Observer*, who describes the judge's improper conduct toward her.[51]

October 11: Articles in the *Charlotte Observer* and the *Washington Times* report on Wright's statements about Thomas.[52]

The Judiciary Committee begins hearings on Hill's charge that Thomas sexually harassed her. Biden and Republican senator Strom Thurmond of South Carolina present opening remarks. At the urging of the White House the evening before, the decision as to whether Hill or Thomas will go first has been deferred to the nominee.[53] Thomas delivers a prepared statement.[54]

Republican senator Orrin G. Hatch of Utah declares his intention to make use of Hill's statement before she testifies. After some debate, Thomas is excused, and Hill, who has insisted that she be present when her statement is admitted, appears in the hearing room.[55]

After Hill delivers her statement, questioning begins. She is questioned twice by Senator Biden, four times by Senator Specter, twice by Senator Patrick Leahy, and once by Senator Howell Heflin. The senators, by agreement, limit each questioning to approximately one-half hour. Following this round of questioning, the other senators on the committee are allowed to question Hill for five minutes each.[56]

In the afternoon session, statements by the FBI agents who interviewed Hill are placed in the record. These statements, drafted in response to Hill's testimony in the morning, assert that this testimony is inconsistent with the FBI's recollection of what she said when interviewed.[57]

Thomas decides that he wishes to testify again in the evening, and Biden permits him to do so. Thomas calls the hearings "a high-tech lynching for uppity blacks who in any way deign to think for themselves, to do for themselves, to have different ideas, and it is a message that, unless you kow-tow to an old order, this is what will happen to you, you will be lynched, destroyed, caricatured by a committee of the U.S. Senate, rather than hung from a tree."[58]

October 12: Questioning of Thomas resumes. Thomas is questioned twice by Leahy and Hatch, and once by Biden, Specter, and Heflin, for roughly half an hour each time, and then by the other senators for five minutes or so each. Specter states during his questioning, "Judge Thomas, . . . it is my legal judgment, having had some experience in perjury prosecutions, that the testimony of Professor Hill in the morning was flat-out perjury."[59]

October 13: Judiciary Committee staff conduct a telephone interview of Rose Jourdain, Wright's corroborating witness.[60]

A panel of witnesses testifies for Hill. Ellen M. Wells, a project manager for the American Public Welfare Association, says that she and Hill were friends beginning in 1981, and that she knew Thomas through their mutual involvement in the Black Republican Congressional Staff Association. Wells tells the committee, "In the fall of 1982, Professor Hill shared with me, in confidence, the fact that she considered Judge Thomas' behavior toward her in the office to be inappropriate."[61]

John W. Carr, a partner in the New York law firm Simpson Thacher & Bartlett, tells the committee that in 1982 and 1983 he was socially involved with Hill, and that at the time Hill "revealed to me that her supervisor was sexually harassing her. . . . In response to my expressions of concern about her feelings, Anita Hill told me that she was upset, because her boss was making sexual advances towards her."[62]

Hoerchner testifies that she and Hill became friends at Yale Law School and both got jobs in D.C. after they graduated. She says Hill confided in her that "she was being subjected to sexual harassment from her boss, to whom she referred by name. That boss was Clarence Thomas."[63]

Joel Paul, associate professor at the Washington College of Law at American University, testifies that he met Hill at a conference in 1987 and developed a professional relationship with her. He says that he "asked Professor Hill why she had left the EEOC. . . . Professor Hill responded, reluctantly and with obvious emotion and embarrassment, that she had been sexually harassed by her supervisor at the EEOC."[64]

A panel then testifies for Thomas. J. C. Alvarez, a Chicago businesswoman, tells the committee that she was employed by Thomas at the EEOC. She says, "I know Clarence Thomas and I know Anita Hill. . . . [T]he Anita Hill that I knew and worked with . . . was a very hard, tough woman. She was opinionated. She was arrogant. She was a relentless debater. . . . She always acted as if she was a little bit superior to everyone." Alvarez characterizes Thomas as "meticulous about being sure that he retained a very serious and professional atmosphere within his office, without the slightest hint of impropriety."[65]

Nancy E. Fitch, assistant professor of African American studies at Temple University, informs the committee that she worked with Thomas at the EEOC and that "there is no way Clarence Thomas—CT—would callously venally hurt someone."[66]

Diane Holt, a management analyst for the Office of the Chairman of the EEOC, testifies that she met Thomas when he began working at the Department of Education in 1981. He employed Holt as his personal secretary. She met Hill shortly thereafter, when Hill was hired by Thomas. Holt asserts that "the Chairman Thomas that I have known for ten years is absolutely incapable of the abuses described by Professor Hill."[67]

Phyllis Berry-Myers testifies that she met Thomas in 1979 and that he hired her to work for him at the EEOC in 1982, at which time she met Hill. According to Berry-Myers, "Clarence Thomas' behavior toward Anita Hill was no more, no less than his behavior towards the rest of his staff. He was respectful, demand [sic] of excellence in our work, cordial, professional, interested in our lives and our career ambitions."[68]

The committee moves on to another panel of four witnesses testifying for Thomas.[69]

Ogletree announces to the press that Hill took a lie detector test during the afternoon and her examiner concluded that she was telling the truth. The test was administered by Paul Minor, president of the American International Security Corporation and a polygraph trainer for the FBI. Biden refuses to admit the test results into the record because "the committee had not vouched for the credentials of the examiner and had 'nothing to do' with ordering the test."[70] Test questions included "Have you deliberately lied to me about Clarence Thomas? . . . Are you fabricating the allegation that Clarence Thomas discussed pornographic material with you?" Asked if Thomas would take a lie detector test, President Bush responds, "I think it's a stupid idea. . . . [I]f the idea is challenging the word of one over another, to use a lie detector test in that way, I reject it."[71]

Except for short breaks, the committee has been in continuous session all day. Wright is waiting to testify, but Senate Republicans and Democrats agree not to call her, thus keeping her off national television.[72] Simon later characterizes this decision as motivated by time constraints and a bipartisan desire to downplay her testimony, the Republicans "for obvious reasons," and the Democrats "because she had been fired by Thomas and her motivation for testifying could be brought into question."[73] Instead, the telephone interviews of Wright and her corroborating witness Jourdain are placed in the record.[74] In her interview, Wright says that when she worked for Thomas at the EEOC, he "did consistently pressure me to date him. At one point, Clarence Thomas made comments about my anatomy. Clarence Thomas made comments about women's anatomy quite often."[75]

After the phone interviews with Wright and Jourdain are placed in the record, questioning of the second Thomas panel continues. Then a final panel of eight witnesses for Thomas is sworn in to testify. At 2:03 a.m. on October 14, the committee adjourns.[76]

October 15: The Senate votes 52-48 in favor of confirming Thomas. Protesters chanting "We'll remember in November" demonstrate against the Senate vote on the Capitol steps.[77]

October 24: The Senate passes a resolution to appoint a Temporary Special Independent Counsel "to 'conduct an investigation of any unauthorized disclosure of non-public confidential information from Senate documents' in connection with . . . the nomination of Clarence Thomas." Peter Fleming, Jr., is later appointed to this post. He is unable to identify the source of the leaks.[78]

Notes

1. Andrew Rosenthal, *Only Black Justice, After 24 Year Tenure, Leaves in Frustration*, N.Y. TIMES, June 28, 1991, at A1.
2. Thurgood Marshall, *My Dear Mr. President*, N.Y. TIMES, June 28, 1991, at A13 (article located courtesy of Professor Charles Ogletree).
3. *Excerpts from News Conference Announcing Court Nominee*, N.Y. TIMES, July 2, 1991, at A14.
4. TIMOTHY M. PHELPS & HELEN WINTERNITZ, CAPITOL GAMES: CLARENCE THOMAS, ANITA HILL, AND THE STORY OF A SUPREME COURT NOMINATION 123–24 (1992); PETER FLEMING, JR., REPORT OF TEMPORARY SPECIAL INDEPENDENT COUNSEL PURSUANT TO SENATE RESOLUTION 202, S. DOC. NO. 20, 102d Cong., 2d Sess., pt. 1, at 11 (1992) [hereinafter REPORT, pt. 1].
5. REPORT, pt. 1, *supra* note 4, at 11 & n.17; Nina Burleigh, *The Thomas Hearings: Now That It's Over—Winners and Losers in the Confirmation Process*, A.B.A.J., Jan. 1992, at 50, 52–53, *cited in* REPORT; PHELPS & WINTERNITZ, *supra* note 4, at 126.
6. REPORT, pt. 1, *supra* note 4, at 12.
7. *Id.* at 12–13.

8. *Id.*
9. *Id.* at 9 (these hearings continued on September 11–13, 16, 17, and 19, and concluded on September 20).
10. *Id.* at 13–14.
11. *Id.* at 14.
12. *Id.* (the meeting took place on either Friday, September 13, or Monday, September 16; however, no one was able to recall the exact date).
13. *Id.* at 15; *Statement of Anita F. Hill, reprinted in* PETER FLEMING, JR., REPORT OF TEMPORARY SPECIAL INDEPENDENT COUNSEL PURSUANT TO SENATE RESOLUTION 202, S. DOC. NO. 102–20, 102d Cong., 2d Sess., pt. 2, at 37 (1992) [hereinafter REPORT, pt. 2].
14. REPORT, pt. 1, *supra* note 4, at 15.
15. *Id.* at 16.
16. *Id.*
17. *Id.*
18. *Id.* at 16 & n. 54, 17.
19. *Id.* at 18.
20. REPORT, pt. 2, *supra* note 13, at 30–31.
21. REPORT, pt. 1, *supra* note 4, at 18.
22. *Id.* at 19.
23. *Id.*
24. PHELPS & WINTERNITZ, *supra* note 4, at 218.
25. REPORT, pt. 1, *supra* note 4, at 18.
26. PHELPS & WINTERNITZ, *supra* note 4, at 218–19.
27. REPORT, pt. 1, *supra* note 4, at 19–20.
28. REPORT, pt. 2, *supra* note 13, at 45.
29. REPORT, pt. 1, *supra* note 4, at 19–20.
30. *Id.* at 20.
31. *Id.* at 19–20.
32. *Id.* at 5.
33. *Id.* at 3.
34. PHELPS & WINTERNITZ, *supra* note 4, at 227.
35. REPORT, pt. 1, *supra* note 4, at 22.
36. *Id.* at 23; REPORT, pt. 2, *supra* note 13, at 39.
37. REPORT, pt. 1, *supra* note 4, at 3–4, 25–26.
38. Ann Louise Bardach, *Nina Totenberg, Queen of the Leaks*, Vanity Fair, Jan. 1992, at 48.
39. REPORT, pt. 1, *supra* note 4, at 27.
40. *Id.* at 24.
41. *Id.* at 4, 24, 30.
42. Timothy M. Phelps, *The Thomas Charge: Law Prof Told FBI He Sexually Harassed Her at EEOC*, NEWSDAY, Oct. 6., 1991, at 7, *reprinted in* REPORT, pt. 2, *supra* note 13, at 51.
43. Timothy M. Phelps, *The Thomas Charge; Law Professor Told the FBI He Sexually Harassed Her*, NEWSDAY, Home Edition, Oct. 6, 1991, at 7.

44. *Law Professor Files Affidavit Accusing Clarence Thomas of Sexual Harassment* (National Public Radio broadcast, Oct. 6, 1991), *reprinted in* REPORT, pt. 2, *supra* note 13, at 91–94.

45. *Excerpts of Hill's Remarks*, BOSTON GLOBE, Oct. 8, 1991, at National/Foreign 13.

46. Neil A. Lewis, *Hill Advisers Say They Took the Initiative to Help*, N.Y. TIMES, Oct. 15, 1991, at A19.

47. *Affidavit by Thomas*, N.Y. TIMES, Oct. 9, 1991, at A18.

48. Maureen Dowd, *7 Congresswomen March to Senate to Demand Delay in Thomas Vote*, N.Y. TIMES, Oct. 9, 1991, at A1, A19.

49. Timothy M. Phelps & Myron S. Waldman, *Delayed: Senators Delay Vote on Confirmation*, NEWSDAY, Oct. 9, 1991, at 5.

50. Lewis, *supra* note 46, at A19.

51. REPORT, pt. 1, *supra* note 4, at 49; deposition reprinted in *Nomination of Judge Clarence Thomas to Be Associate Justice of the Supreme Court of the United States, Hearings before the Committee on the Judiciary, United States Senate (Committee Print Draft)*, 102d Cong., 1st Sess. 410–79 (1991) [hererinafter *Hearings*].

52. REPORT, pt. 1, *supra* note 4, at 49.

53. PHELPS & WINTERNITZ, *supra* note 4, at 395.

54. *Hearings*, *supra* note 51, at 5–25.

55. *Id.* at 26–29.

56. *Id.* at 30–147.

57. *Id.* at 115–17.

58. *Id.* at 127, 147.

59. *Id.* at 214.

60. *Id.* at 480.

61. *Id.* at 253.

62. *Id.* at 254.

63. *Id.* at 255–56.

64. *Id.* at 257.

65. *Id.* at 311–12, 314.

66. *Id.* at 316.

67. *Id.* at 316–17.

68. *Id.* at 317–18.

69. *Id.* at 397.

70. *Hill Passes Lie Detector Test; Her Lawyer Says Senator Biden Won't Allow Results*, CHI. TRIB., Oct. 14, 1991, at 5.

71. Martin Tolchin, *Hill Said to Pass a Polygraph Test*, N.Y. TIMES, Oct. 14, 1991, at A10.

72. Douglas Frantz & Sam Fulwood III, *Senators' Private Deal Kept '2d Woman' Off TV*, L.A. TIMES, Oct. 17, 1991, at A22.

73. PAUL SIMON, ADVICE and CONSENT: CLARENCE THOMAS, ROBERT BORK, AND THE INTRIGUING HISTORY OF THE SUPREME COURT NOMINATION BATTLES 118 (1992).

74. *Hearings, supra* note 51, at 407–519.
75. *Id.* at 420.
76. Id. at 520–68.
77. Hilary MacKenzie, *Tainted Victory*, Maclean's, Oct. 28, 1991, at 24.
78. REPORT, pt. 1, *supra* note 4, at 2–4, 7.

RACE, GENDER, and POWER in AMERICA

"She's No Lady, She's a Nigger": Abuses, Stereotypes, and Realities from the Middle Passage to Capitol (and Anita) Hill

ADELE LOGAN ALEXANDER

In the early 1940s, according to an apocryphal story often told by my older relatives, Mary McLeod Bethune, a well-known educator and official in the Roosevelt administration, was traveling one day by train through the segregated South.[1] She was a very dark-skinned woman, and there was no mistaking her African American (or at that time, Negro) heritage. She dressed and groomed herself meticulously, was tightly corseted, and in public wore her ever present hat and gloves, and carried both pocketbook and umbrella, like all "respectable ladies" of the period—and much like the women with whom I grew up. Her posture was ramrod straight, and she appeared, in short, both utterly refined and indomitable.

At the time, of course, most schools, parks and playgrounds, theaters, hotels, drinking fountains, means of transportation, and other public facilities throughout the southern United States were strictly segregated both by law and in practice. But on this particular day in this particular depot in this particular unidentified southern city, the white stationmaster was stunned when Mrs. Bethune, an apparition of imperious rectitude, started to walk unswervingly across his expansive "whites only" waiting room. Feeling obligated to assert his power in order to maintain the rigidly established racial hierarchy, he called out to the elegant yet determined interloper, "Hey there! You can't do that." Mrs. Bethune lifted her chin higher but never once hesitated. "Yes, you know who I'm talkin' to, old colored woman. You can't just come marchin' through here," he shouted, waving his arms and shaking his fists. "This room's reserved for white folks." Still no response at all from Mrs. Bethune, who kept moving toward her destination. By now other travelers were staring in amazement at the drama unfolding between the increasingly frantic white male agent of authority and the well-dressed black woman blatantly flaunting established racial practices. Finally, in disbelief that his vigorous admonitions had gone unheeded, and realizing that he was unable to preserve the segregated sanctity of his waiting room, the stationmaster turned in puzzled frustration to the slack-jawed clerk standing beside him and asked, "She *is* a nigger, ain't she?"

My family relished telling that story, understanding as they did the distasteful yet ironic reality it illustrated. They knew all too well that "ladylike" behavior was totally irreconcilable with most white people's concept of black womanhood. Recognizing this demeaning perception, and determined to uphold their dignity, our women often behaved with just the kind of extraordinary hauteur Mrs. Bethune exhibited. The pleasure of the story was that at least in this rare instance one African American woman, with her unflinching display of courage and aplomb, had outmaneuvered the racist establishment and scored a small victory for us all.

To this oft-told account add a related report. "Southern Railway stations have three waiting rooms," an anonymous African American woman wrote in 1902, and "conspicuous signs tell the ignorant that this room is for 'ladies' and this is for 'gents' and that is for 'colored' people. We are neither 'ladies' nor 'gents,' but just 'colored.' "[2] As recently as the late 1960s, in many cases, white authorities even assigned single toilet facilities to black people of both sexes, thereby deliberately denying African American women the basic courtesies they unquestioningly accorded white women. Neither Mary McLeod Bethune nor the women who raised me and told stories about her would openly acknowledge that much of America never considered them "ladies" but just "colored folks," yet that is exactly how black women *were* perceived, and often still are.

Distorted images of black women as promiscuous and untrustworthy, not to be valued and respected as "ladies" (read "white ladies"), their honesty questioned and their word discounted, have prevailed throughout our past. Exceptions have been rare. Even in the late twentieth century, few Americans can move completely beyond these negative assumptions about and the dismissive treatment of African American women, any more than they can ignore, avoid, or forget the other enduring beliefs and practices—both admirable and reprehensible—that characterize our nation's historic legacy.

My purpose here is to offer a brief overview of the history of black women in the United States as a framework for understanding the origins, evolution, and persistence of some of the myths and stereotypes about them. This essay attempts to contextualize the ways in which past events and behaviors inevitably and indelibly influence the present, and in particular to show how the treatment and perceptions of African American women made it almost impossible for any of the diverse segments of our television-transfixed society to respond other than as they did when they watched and listened to Professor Anita Hill's testimony, the disparaging thrusts and parries by members of the Senate Judiciary Committee, and Judge Clarence Thomas's blustering refutation of Hill's assertions about his sexual improprieties. Our individual and collective responses to 1991's most riveting real-life drama were neither aberrant nor isolated. Rather, they reflected a great deal about our social, legal, and economic history—especially as that history has pertained to black women.

Throughout the past three and a half centuries, America's black women have been perceived primarily as sexual beings who have no modesty, virtue, or intelligence, and little claim to respect or power. Characterized by an "image of mindlessness," in the words of historian Patricia Morton, and "belonging to two groups historically labelled as intellectually inferior—women and blacks—[African American women] continue to find their intellectual capabilities doubly discredited."[3] Clearly, black women have always had to shoulder a dual load of demeaning perceptions. As the indefatigable reformer and social feminist Mary Church Terrell pointed out more than half a century ago, "A white woman has only one handicap to over-

come—that of sex. . . . Colored men have only one—that of race.
. . . I have two—both sex and race. I belong to the only group in
this country that has two such huge obstacles to surmount."[4]

Now numbering some eighteen million, America's black women,
as in the past, remain the quintessential "others," perhaps the most
consistently marginalized segment of our society. This marginality—
a function of their political and economic powerlessness, reinforced
by presumptions about their untrustworthiness and immorality—set
the stage for the hearings on the nomination of Clarence Thomas to
the United States Supreme Court. Unable to shed these commonly
held and longstanding preconceptions, the all-male, all-white Senate
Judiciary Committee, and a plethora of outside observers as well, had
difficulty granting Anita Hill any respect whatsoever or accepting the
veracity of her testimony. Centuries of disregard for black women
in America indelibly stamped the committee's treatment of Hill and
contributed to the pervasive skepticism about her.

Those official, journalistic, and public perceptions should come as
no surprise, because they are absolutely nothing new. Since the period of the initial forced deportations from Africa and the introduction of slaves into the Western Hemisphere, black women have con-
tinually been subjected to various sorts of degradation. Even during
the Middle Passage (the sea journey slave ships made with their human cargo from Africa's west coast across the Atlantic to the New
World), slave traders sought to consolidate control over their female
captives through forced sexual relations. These rapes had almost
nothing to do with sexual gratification, were far more than isolated
incidents of coercion, and really amounted to institutionalized terrorism, as political activist and Marxist academician Angela Davis, for
one, suggests.[5]

In the Republic's earliest years, noted Americans such as Thomas
Jefferson—even as he most likely pursued a prolonged sexual relationship with his slave Sally Hemings—argued that women of African ancestry were characterized by limited intellectual capacities and
a bestial sexuality (not to mention physical repulsiveness) exacerbated
by their infantile emotionality.[6] These widely accepted views, projected and then legitimized by leaders like Jefferson, reinforced perceptions of black women as subhuman, unreliable, immoral, and
clearly inconsequential.

To focus on these negative images and the deplorable maltreatment of women in bondage is not for a moment to ignore or deny that black men were routinely victimized, or that white women have been perceived and treated as white men's inferiors and sexually abused as well. In early America a small group of affluent white men who rarely hesitated to exercise their hegemony over any of the weaker segments of society held practically all political, economic, and legal power. Black women, however, were uniquely disempowered by their position at the nexus of a presumed racial *and* sexual inferiority.

In the eighteenth and nineteenth centuries black women were never seen as virtuous and deserving of respect, as were most white women. Female slaves were stripped for auction, their flesh manipulated and their body cavities eagerly explored, fueling a belief in their "primitive" nature and "insatiable" sensuality. When they were put to work in the fields, the emerging consensus about the "appropriate" sexual division of labor that circumscribed white women's lives was totally disregarded. The arduous physical demands of field work and practical accommodations to hot weather, along with the impossibility of complying with the standards of modest dress prescribed by the dominant race, all contributed to the view that female slaves were wanton.[7] The generally chivalrous treatment of white "ladies" was neither extended to black women nor protected them.

Sexual morality among women and men of African ancestry was presumed to be virtually nonexistent during America's antebellum years. And as a corollary to these generalized presumptions about the race in its entirety, black women enjoyed few of the legal protections accorded white females. At least in the slave states, where the great majority of America's black people lived, most legal statutes defined the crime of rape as an act of sexual violence perpetrated against a *white* woman.[8] Under the law, only a white woman could be raped, but she could be raped by a man of any race. Black men could be, and sometimes were, sentenced to death for the *attempted* rape of white women, even though the woman herself might claim no injury or any sexual contact whatsoever.[9] But as laws were created, codified, and revised, no such crime as the rape or attempted rape of black women existed. In 1859 a Mississippi appellate court actually overturned the conviction of a black man who had sexually violated a ten-year-old girl slave, arguing that "there is no act which embraces either the attempted or actual commission of a rape . . . on a female slave."[10] In most instances, the only legal charge that could be brought if a man—black or white, enslaved or free—forced a female slave into an unwelcome sexual act was one of trespass against or injury inflicted on her owner's property.[11]

In truth, a black woman rarely had the option of saying no and making it stick when *any* man wanted to exploit her sexually. Examples abound. Around 1870 the Georgia Supreme Court recorded the words of Louisa, a former slave, who reported that her master used to "go to her room and try to have intercourse with her." She had to "lock the door [and] nail up the windows . . . to keep [him] out." Another woman charged that the same man constantly tried to "feel her titties" and attempted to copulate with "every negro woman on the plantation." His own wife, understandably petitioning the court for a divorce, testified about one of those abused women that she "was his slave then, and had to obey his call."[12] Or as Harriet Jacobs, who was raised in slavery, put it in her autobiography, her owner "told me I was his property; that I must be subject to his will in all things."[13] In the vast majority of cases, of course, sexual congress with a slave woman was a manifestation of the man's power over her rather than an expression of affection or desire, but the central point that these women, black and white, all understood was that when a master demanded sexual compliance, a female slave usually had little choice but to "obey his call." She could look neither to black men, white women, nor the law for support or protection.

Historian Melton McLaurin tells the story of Celia, a Missouri slave who killed her master. From the day he purchased her when she was about fourteen, her owner constantly demanded her sexual services. She even bore two of his children. Finally one night she unequivocally said no, pushed him away, and repeatedly told him to stop. Celia was pregnant at the time, and when he persisted in his attempts to force her to have intercourse, she smashed his skull and then incinerated his body.[14] This story is unusual *only* because it resulted in a white man's violent death.[15] In general, black women understood that neither verbal rejection, attempted escape, nor physical resistance served any deterrent purpose, and that they sometimes had to compromise their own sexual integrity to protect their lives and the lives of loved ones. When her case went to trial, Celia could not testify that she had acted in self-defense, because by law no slave could testify in any case involving a white person. As a woman, too, her word would not have carried much weight in court. With little delay a jury of white men convicted her and sentenced her to death for murdering the man who tried to rape her yet one more time.[16]

The institution of slavery provided both a convenient venue for coerced sexual relations between white men and black women and an authoritarian environment that sanctioned and even encouraged those encounters. Many white men extended their dominance over women of African ancestry through nonconsensual sexual encroachment, thereby reinforcing the slave society's accepted and legally codified patterns of hegemony. Nonetheless, from the skewed perspective of most white people, their men remained blameless in any such instances of sexual "debauchery." It was the supposedly debased and erotically provocative nature of black women that incited the white men's promiscuity and stimulated their vilest proclivities. Even the clearest cases of sexual assault perpetrated against African American women never appeared in court since there were no legal grounds for such charges, even if the prevailing social climate had allowed or encouraged them, which it certainly did not. As the antebellum era drew to a close, one southern jurist noted that no "slave has *ever* [emphasis mine] maintained an action against the violator of his bed," and Harriet Jacobs, once enslaved herself, observed, "There is no shadow of law to protect [black women] from insult, from violence, or even from death."[17]

Inequitably contrived legal provisions in most of the antebellum South affected not only slaves but "free" women of color as well.[18] By law nonenslaved African American women could not be raped any more than slaves could—an important point that indicates the belief held by members of the dominant race that race per se, perhaps even more than slaves' debased legal status as chattel, made *all* nonwhite women essentially "unrapeable."[19] Indiscriminately, and with apparent regularity, white men sexually assaulted African American women because they considered it an inviolable privilege, and because no moral suasion or legal authority restrained them.

Questions may be raised concerning the degree of coercion such encounters involved and the extent to which white men's sexual license was so widely tolerated among all segments of the population that violence, although often present, essentially became unnecessary. One fine afternoon in 1848, for instance, an affluent Georgia planter named David Dickson simply rode up to Julia, a prepubescent thirteen-year-old slave on his plantation, swung her up onto the back of his horse, and "that was the end of that," according to her descendants. Julia never forgave him for "forcing her to have sex with him at such an early age," but she had no choice in the matter, said nothing, and became and remained her master's sexual servant.[20]

Many women of color assiduously tried to avoid or repel such unwelcome incursions, and instances of vigorous resistance were frequent. But counterviolence often endangered both the woman and her family, and it was usually ineffective besides. Even ongoing acquiescence hardly indicated complicity, because of the vast social, legal, and economic gulf between black women and white men. That unconquerable abyss always defined such sexual encounters and ensured that they would be exploitative, since they pitted a white man whose privilege and authority knew few limits against a black woman nearly powerless to resist him. In a situation so inherently unequal, force was redundant. Whether physical coercion was involved or not, the woman rarely had any real choice in the matter.[21]

Moreover, the widespread toleration of white male domination does not alone adequately explain much of the sexual abuse that occurred during the antebellum period. In the 1930s a Federal Writers Project interviewer talked with one former Georgia slave who reported that when her sister was just a girl, "they'd make her go out and lay on a table and two or three white men would have in'ercourse with her befo' they'd let her git up." Another woman recalled the slaveholder who told his sons "ter go down ter dem nigger quarters an' git me mo' slaves."[22] That is, he ordered the boys to copulate with any black woman on the plantation of childbearing age with the intent of impregnating her. This sort of exploitative behavior brutally illustrates the position of black women, who were valued only to the extent that they fulfilled their "responsibilities" not only as laborers but also as acquiescent sexual partners who would perpetuate the South's cadre of black workers. Some slave owners treated black women as animals who were expected to breed as rapidly as possible and produce new "foals" each year. Under law, of course, and regardless of who the father might be, those women's offspring always "belonged" to the master, never to the parents.

At least until general emancipation, most white Americans accepted the assumption that black women had but two significant roles: labor (production) and breeding (reproduction). In addition to their grueling field work, and especially after 1808 when federal law cut off most of the previously ample supply of new labor from Africa, black women were expected to bear children in order to replenish the enslaved work force that sustained the southern economy. This unique role made slavery a different and especially destructive experience for women, one that constantly exposed and subjected them to sexual exploitation.

Though procreation was considered an essential part of a female slave's "job," she had no official authority over her children because of her status as chattel, nor could she marry or enter into other legal contracts. Commitment, passion, mutual respect, and affection certainly characterized many resilient conjugal relationships within the black community, but in the final analysis slave "marriages" only survived through an owner's tolerance and at his convenience, and had no standing in law. America's first single black mothers hardly acquired or maintained that role by choice, or through a lack of sexual morality.[23]

Many of the abuses and inequities of the slave era survived both the Civil War and emancipation. In the early twentieth century the religious leader and educator Nannie Helen Burroughs pointed out that "when [a black woman] appears in court in defense of her virtue, she is looked upon with amused contempt." And we should remember that the first conviction of a white man for raping a black woman in the American South occurred only in the final third of this, the twentieth century, so prevalent and so long-lived has been the assumption that women of color have no virtue to defend.[24]

Negative perceptions of black women changed little during the nineteenth century, and much of America bought into them, at least to some degree. Founded in 1896, the National Association of Colored Women's Clubs adopted as its credo "Lifting As We Climb," which expressed the organization's common understanding that many African American women in fact *needed* to be "lifted" from the "sinful" lives that had been forced on them prior to general emancipation. These "colored" clubwomen accepted as one of their responsibilities the task of countering the negative assumptions and alleviating the wretched conditions created by the legacy of slavery and racism. A number of women's clubs dedicated to self-improvement and community uplift had existed in northern free black communities for decades, and reform movements of all sorts swept the country in the 1890s, but one significant proximate incident that led to the establishment and rapid expansion of a strong national network of African American women was an ugly slap at their collective morality by a white newspaperman who brashly asserted in a widely circulated article that "[Negro] women were prostitutes . . . thieves and liars."[25] Negative images of African American women remained a haunting presence even within the black community itself, and certainly, as John Dollard aptly observed in his classic *Caste and Class in a Southern Town*, most white people continued to believe that black women were "as accessible as animals in heat and always ready for sexual gratification."[26]

By the early twentieth century, although some African Americans tried to emulate the "idealized" patterns of middle-class white family life, in which wives were expected to shun the corrupting influence of the workplace, economic necessity kept the majority of black women employed outside their own homes. Many worked in menial and economically vulnerable positions, while the majority of married white women remained in their nurseries, kitchens, and parlors if financial circumstances permitted. Whether they labored in agriculture, as domestic workers, or in factories, most African American women were stuck at the bottom of the economic barrel, where they were locked into dependent relationships with employers and regularly found themselves subject to uninvited and unwanted sexual advances.[27] Rape, harassment, and other forms of personal abuse remained part and parcel of an environment that routinely and oppressively reinforced a system of racial, sexual, and economic exploitation.[28]

This is not to say that nonwhite women in the more prestigious occupations were invulnerable. Indeed they were not. Stories told by one of my aunts, Myra Logan—a physician—punctuated my childhood.[29] In the early 1930s she struggled against the prejudices she encountered as a woman ("Too fragile and emotional for scientific pursuits," or "Why does a pretty girl like you want to enter such a bloody and demanding profession?") and as a Negro ("You people just aren't intelligent or disciplined enough," or "Getting some pretty highfalutin notions about yourself, don't you think?"). She had limited choices both in seeking admission to medical school and later in obtaining a surgical internship. In addition, respected white male medical practitioners chased her around gurneys, tried to fondle her in laboratories, and then threatened *her* with demerits for improper conduct, creating further obstacles to her success.

Many black women today will recall how their mothers, in response to such improprieties, and because young African American females were so widely perceived as both vulnerable and sexually available, often acted on the assumption that the only way to protect their daughters' virtue was to repress even healthy expressions of independence and sexuality. These women, my own mother among them, insisted that their girls return home earlier at night than white girls, and wear less revealing clothes and less makeup and jewelry (no pierced ears, please, and *certainly* no ankle bracelets), lest they be considered provocative, accessible, and compliant sexual targets.

If African American women in particular have been seen as potential objects of easy sexual conquest, the struggle for equitable treatment as responsible adults in the eyes of the law and as equal and integral members of the body politic has been an arduous and still incomplete one for *all* women. Nationally, women didn't obtain the right to vote until 1920, and many states have allowed them to serve on juries only within the last quarter century. They are underrepresented in both elective and appointive public office, and their real power in American industry and finance remains insignificant.

It should therefore be easy to understand that African American women have had an even more difficult time achieving economic parity and winning respect and full political rights. In much of our country, millions of black people—male and female—were denied the franchise until after the passage of federal civil rights legislation during the mid-1960s. As Dorothy Height, president of the National Council of Negro Women, has pointed out, fifty years after women acquired the vote "it took lynching, bombing, the Civil Rights movement, and the Voting Rights Act . . . to get it for Black women."[30] Into the 1970s and beyond, they also had to fight for the right to be called by their surnames in official, social, and workplace situations. Many courts of law routinely denied them the simple courtesy of being referred to as "Miss" or "Mrs." An employer typically would be identified as "Mr. Harris," while his employee was just "Cora Mae" or "Alice," and a recent history of black female workers quotes an elderly housekeeper who complained that "the child I work for calls me 'girl.' "[31] Not so long ago, one southern politician even "joked" that the only difference he knew of between a colored woman and a cow was "the number of her tits."[32] For African American women, disrespect and denial of opportunity have always marched hand in hand.

We must also acknowledge that white men are not the only ones who have insulted and abused our women. White women and black men—even those who may otherwise merit respect—have sometimes done the same. Racism has always sullied women's reform movements. In the late nineteenth century, for example, Frances Willard, president of the Woman's Christian Temperance Union, sarcastically commented that "the colored race multiplies like the locusts of Egypt." Certain leaders of the woman's suffrage movement made similar derogatory remarks and actively discouraged the participation of nonwhite reformers in their cause.[33] Racist rhetoric and behavior have often made a mockery of the idea of interracial sisterhood. In much the same way, in the words of civil rights organizer Septima Clark, during the 1960s many black men in the movement "just thought that women were sex symbols and had no contributions to make, [and] whatever the man said would be right and the wives would have to accept it." And can we (should we) forget that despite his bravery and vision, Stokely Carmichael stated on at least one occasion that the most appropriate position for women in SNCC (the Student Nonviolent Coordinating Committee) was "prone"?[34]

Even today, although legitimate concerns about censorship may temper our criticism, we are appalled by the misogynist lyrics of some rap musicians who reduce black women to intimate body parts and urge unspeakably violent sexual acts against them. These musical representations, with their brutal portrayals of relationships between African American men and women, only serve to throw into harsh relief preexisting destructive mythologies about both race and gender, and cannot be excused by our equally appropriate outrage at the continuing racism black men encounter.[35] Historian Gerda Lerner, for one, suggests that for too long too many Americans have believed that "all black women were eager for sexual exploits, voluntarily 'loose' in their morals, and therefore, deserved none of the consideration and respect granted to white women."[36] At times, too many white women and black men have reinforced that belief.

Essayist and poet June Jordan has argued recently that "if you're not an American white man, and you travel through the traditional twistings and distortions of the white Western canon, you stand an excellent chance of ending up *nuts*: estranged if not opposed to yourself and your heritage."[37] Most assuredly, "whiteness" and "maleness" have traditionally been the standards by which every American who is neither white nor male is judged—and found wanting. These androcentric Anglo-American standards firmly position black women as our country's ultimate outsiders, even those who manage to avoid "ending up nuts." "To be in the margin," feminist scholar bell hooks writes, "is to be part of the whole but outside the main body."[38] And America's black women have always been "outside the main body." By our society's prevailing measures of success, we are most unlike and therefore most completely lacking the presumptively positive attributes of our diametric human opposites: white men. Within this framework of interwoven racism and sexism, some black men have also engaged in the same sorts of abusive behavior as those "in-charge" white guys who have held the power, written and enforced the laws, established the social standards, and controlled our country's wealth so effectively and for so long.

Coercive male sexual conduct, of course, is neither limited by race nor confined to our country's shores. Patriarchy and its attendant range of abuses have been prevalent throughout history and around the world. But here in the United States several unique and interrelated assumptions have often held sway at the intersection of sexuality and race. One is that any sexual encounter between any black man and any white woman necessarily involves some degree of coercion on the man's part, most probably physical brutality, overwhelming the woman's innate virtuous resistance. As the African American journalist and antilynching activist Ida B. Wells-Barnett said in the early years of this century, "Any *mésalliance* existing between a white woman and a colored man is a sufficient foundation for the charge of rape."[39] The white community has often used this widespread presumption, based on fear and abhorrence of black male sexuality, to justify all sorts of terrorism and lynching, from the era of slavery to the bloody surge of violence during the late nineteenth and early twentieth centuries, to the notorious Scottsboro Boys "rape" case in the 1930s, to the savage murder two decades later of a teenager named Emmett Till, who naively flirted with a white woman. Recently a group of white thugs in Brooklyn, New York, persistently but mistakenly argued that Yusef Hawkins, the African American youth whom they shot to death, had come to "their" neighborhood hoping to "socialize" with one of "their" white girlfriends.

As already noted, a second fantasy arising from our country's long heritage of slavery and racism is that sex between a black woman and a white man is almost always prompted by her insatiable sexuality. The black woman has been considered the more degraded of the "sinning" pair, her erotic proclivities presumably corrupting an innocent man who otherwise would only have had sexual relations with a white woman within the sanctioned bonds of matrimony. Women of African ancestry supposedly possessed none of the inborn modesty of white females. As the outspoken black reformer Fannie Barrier Williams stated around the turn of the century, "Slavery made [the Negro woman] the only woman in America for whom virtue was not an ornament and a necessity."[40]

In these two highly mythologized scenarios, black men and women are cast as depraved in their sexual inclinations and habits, and lacking any capacity for restraint. These distorted assumptions about interracial sex, of course, have been extremely damaging, but they are only the other side of the coin that considers virtually *any* sexual encounter between a black man and a black woman—no matter how questionable, distasteful, or even violent the circumstances—noncensurable, consensual, and frankly just "business as usual."[41]

So when Anita Hill agreed to appear before the Senate Judiciary Committee in the fall of 1991, she was heir to a plethora of malformed perceptions that almost four hundred years had created, nurtured, and then loaded onto her shoulders. Her account of Clarence Thomas's behavior challenged a complex network of racial and sexual preconceptions that many Americans still cling to, and as the country listened and watched, a majority found her testimony unbelievable and her very presence highly suspicious.

Many black people condemned her because she failed to uphold the "solidarity of the race"—a solidarity that has been crucial in the face of this country's longstanding and pervasive racism. Some African American women who knew perfectly well that the abusive behavior she described was distressingly familiar shrugged because they had experienced worse themselves. "What's all the fuss about?" they asked when her revelations threatened both a respected black man's reputation *and* the "black seat" on the Supreme Court. If Hill had been treated so egregiously, why had she remained silent for ten years? Why didn't she display the emotions of outraged virtue? Her critics failed to remember that such protestations by black women have rarely been taken seriously.[42]

Anita Hill was suspect on so many levels. Had she been too successful in her own career, possibly at the expense of black men? And why had she never married? Did all that suggest a condemnation of "the brother"? She had no children either, and so had failed to fulfill her "proper" role as a mother. Weren't African American women from Mammy right on down through the generations supposed to be our quintessential nurturers?[43]

The habit of disbelief is perniciously contagious. From the earliest days of the Republic, blacks were rarely permitted to testify in court, nor were many women granted this acknowledgment of their maturity and legal responsibility. Certainly, courts of law have long remained bastions of white male authority. When Anita Hill appeared on that "legal stage" in the now famous Senate Caucus Room in the fall of 1991, enduring assumptions about the diminished intellectual capacity and the inflated, uncontrolled emotionality of both blacks and women made it difficult for many people to believe her sworn testimony. This legacy both defined and reinforced the double load of blackness and womanhood she carried.

Then too, a person of reputation and substance stoutly contradicted her. He was also black, of course, but he was a man of authority—a judge, no less—and his credibility was not impugned by the burdens of both race and gender. When Hill detailed the unwelcome sexual advances of her employer and mentor, not only the white male panel of senators but the whole country listened and sat in judgment on her, and if the results of a phalanx of opinion polls can be believed, the majority of Americans raised a collective eyebrow.[44]

In 1920 the eminent scholar and political activist W. E. B. Du Bois wrote, "The crushing weight of slavery fell on black women. Under it there was no legal marriage, no legal family, no legal control over children." As a result of that legacy, most Americans have long believed that "out of black slavery came nothing decent in womanhood; that adultery and uncleanness were their heritage and are their continued portion." However, Du Bois continued, "the result of this history of insult and degradation has been both fearful and glorious. It has birthed the haunting prostitute, the brawler, and the beast of burden, but it has also given the world an efficient woman-hood."[45] Anita Hill's presence and demeanor refuted the negative stereotypes and simultaneously challenged the preconceived assumptions of a querulous panel of senators because she personified the unfamiliar (to them) but exceedingly "efficient womanhood" Du Bois described.

Du Bois was astutely observing and commenting on black women's often dubious heritage as well when he told the story of the white southern boy, still unschooled in the protocols of race and gender, who one day admonished a companion to "wait till the lady passes." "She's no lady, she's a nigger," promptly responded his friend, who was more sophisticated about the perversity of America's prevailing racial and sexual ideologies, and instantly dismissed the possibility that an African American woman could *ever* be a "lady" deserving of the courtesy and esteem automatically bestowed on white women.[46]

Those damning words would have been spoken more than seventy years ago, and yet, although decades of education and public performance had certainly polished their language and behavior, some of the United States senators who questioned and passed judgment on Anita Hill in 1991 transmitted a similar message. They could not see her as one of their own mothers, sisters, wives, or daughters—honest, virtuous "ladies" worthy of both protection and respect—and they could not escape the weight of centuries of assumptions about and abuse of African American women.

Today, however, we must turn to other legacies, other experiences. We must move beyond the familiar stereotypes of America's black women, be they Mammy or Prissy, Jezebel, Topsy, or Eliza, Sapphire, "red-hot mama," "tragic mulatto," "welfare queen," "superwoman," or "emasculating matriarch." We need to reclaim and recreate a more realistic and diverse picture of our past. We should look not only at strengths but at weaknesses, at instances of both wisdom and folly, at the successes and the failures as well, to understand that the history of black women is as complex, as intricately woven, and often as contradictory as that of any other group of Americans. Any serious assessment of the various roles African American women have played throughout our country's history demonstrates the futility and irrationality of trying to delineate and project a single, simplistically conceived, all-inclusive "black female experience."

Too often black women have been disregarded and demeaned, their images grotesquely distorted and reduced to cartoons. Nonetheless, the heritage of slavery and racism, as well as the injustices perpetuated against far too many women of all races, must never be forgotten or purged from our nation's memory. Entrenched historical methodologies and skewed prioritizations that deny the significance and validity of nontraditional sources have helped to create a hierarchy of authenticity and believability in which black women's experiences are misunderstood, doubted, downgraded, or ignored. Even now, African Americans and women remain noticeably underrepresented in historical literature, and frequently, when they do appear, as one group of scholars provocatively suggests, "all the women are white, all the blacks are men."[47] Because of black women's continued marginalization and the paucity of analytical materials exploring their lives, they have been largely portrayed and seen as objects rather than subjects—stereotyped, one-dimensional, peripheral players on the American scene. To move beyond this murky cavern of omission and distortion, even to approach parity in empowerment, African American women must be reclaimed from their perceived oblivion and irrelevance, and then shifted, as bell hooks says, "from margin to center."[48]

Many Americans had trouble accepting and believing Anita Hill when she came to Capitol Hill to testify because they had primarily been exposed to demeaning, trivialized, formulaic images of black women. Within that context, how could they possibly understand the deeds, words, and motivations of this complex person who fit none of the cookie-cutter molds so often used to define America's black women?

Hill's determined dignity when she appeared before the Senate Judiciary Committee reminded me of Mary McLeod Bethune's resolve as she strode across the "whites only" waiting room in the story my parents told years ago. In Hill's place, others might have acted differently, their equally valid responses emerging from their own particular experiences. They might have declined to speak out at all, succumbed to understandable tears of frustration and rage, or used the occasion as a forum to present their own political agendas.[49] Any or all of these options might have been justified, but Anita Hill approached the situation with understated courage and directness.

Everyone who watched the proceedings during the fall of 1991 not only reacted to Hill herself but also viewed the drama around her from within a convoluted framework of racist, sexist, and elitist assumptions that none of us can escape and that condition our responses to any such public event. I, for one, scarcely fault either her demeanor or her message. However, the responses of the senators who questioned her, the myriad reporters who covered and "interpreted" the proceedings, the doubters and critics—black, white, male, female, from every part of the country—were grounded in an intricate and often oppressive national history.

Seeing and hearing Anita Hill during that critical week when she first appeared on television screens across the country, I especially recalled the millions of Americans of generations past with whom she shared both race and gender. Those women—though little known, for the most part—played familiar and unexpected, varied and unique, glorious and tragic roles in our country's history. Perhaps, in light of the sometimes surprising developments that have unfolded in America since those well-publicized confirmation hearings in the United States Senate, scholar Paula Giddings' telling statement about African American women who preceded Anita Hill can now be applied to Hill herself: "In the course of defying the imposed limitations of race and sex, they loosened the chains around both."[50]

Finally, in looking back across almost four hundred years of American experience, and then again at the relatively short period of time that has passed since Hill testified (which may indeed be appropriately characterized as a defining moment in our recent history), the words of the African American educator Anna Julia Cooper inevitably come to mind. In 1892—just over one century ago—Cooper wrote, "Only the black woman can say, 'when and where I enter, in the quiet undisputed dignity of my womanhood, without violence and without suing or special patronage, then and there the whole . . . race enters with me.' "[51]

Notes

Many friends and colleagues helped to develop and refine this paper. Emma Coleman Jordan, Janet Langhart, Kent Leslie, Lillian Lewis, Carole Merritt, Brooke Stephens, Rosalyn Terborg-Penn, and Eve Wilkins deserve special mention and thanks. As I was growing up, the women in my family told the stories, set the standards, and showed me by example what being a black woman in America was about. They, too, have my enduring appreciation. My daughter Elizabeth, poet and scholar extraordinaire, has a special place as valued editor and critic. She always knew that I could work a little harder to make it a little better. My husband, Clifford, on the other hand, seems to think that anything I write is just about perfect—an absolutely untrue but marvelously reinforcing assumption.

1. For an overview of Bethune's life, see "Mary McLeod Bethune," in *Black Women in America: An Historical Encyclopedia*, ed. Darlene Clark Hine (Brooklyn: Carlson Publishers, 1993), 113–27.

2. Anonymous article, *Independent*, September 18, 1902, in *Black Women in White America*, ed. Gerda Lerner (New York: Pantheon Books, 1972), 167.

3. Patricia Morton, *Disfigured Images: The Historical Assault on Afro-American Women* (New York: Praeger, 1992), xii.

4. Quoted in Rosalyn Terborg-Penn, "Discontented Black Feminists: Prelude and Postscript to the Passage of the Nineteenth Amendment," in *Decades of Discontent: The Woman's Movement, 1920–1940*, ed. Lois Scharf and Joan M. Jensen (Westport: Greenwood Press, 1983), 275. For an overview of Terrell's life, see "Mary Church Terrell," in *Black Women in America*, 1157–59.

5. Angela Y. Davis, *Women, Race, and Class* (New York: Random House, 1981), chap. 1, "The Legacy of Slavery"; bell hooks, *Ain't I a Woman? Black Women and Feminism* (Boston: South End Press, 1981), 27. See also "Angela Davis," in *Black Women in America*, 304–6. The most complete study of slave women is Deborah Gray White, *Ar'n't I a Woman? Female Slaves in the Plantation South* (New York: W. W. Norton, 1985). For a more concise treatment, see "Slavery," in *Black Women in America*, 1045–70.

6. Fawn M. Brodie, *Thomas Jefferson: An Intimate History* (New York: W. W. Norton, 1974); "Sally Hemings," in *Black Women in America*, 554–55. In *White over Black: American Attitudes toward the Negro, 1550–1812* (New York: W. W. Norton, 1977), 168–69, Winthrop D. Jordan discusses Jefferson's views on women and blacks as expressed in his *Notes on the State of Virginia*.

7. Hooks, *Ain't I a Woman*, chap. 1, "Sexism and the Black Female Slave Experience."

8. See especially Darlene Clark Hine, "Rape and the Inner Lives of Southern Black Women: Thoughts on the Culture of Dissemblance," in *Southern Women: Histories and Identities*, ed. Virginia Bernhard et al. (Columbia: University of Missouri Press, 1992).

9. Such an incident occurred, for example, in Baldwin County, Georgia, in 1812. See Adele Logan Alexander, *Ambiguous Lives: Free Women of Color in Rural Georgia, 1789–1879* (Fayetteville: University of Arkansas Press, 1991), 35. For other accounts of male slaves accused of raping white women, see Mark Tushnet, *The American Law of Slavery, 1810–1860:*

Considerations of Humanity and Interest (Princeton: Princeton University Press, 1981), 72, 85, 128, 189.

10. Quoted in White, *Ar'n't I a Woman*, 152.

11. Tushnet, *American Law of Slavery*, 85, points out the disparities between statutory law, common law, and accepted behavior. For instance, most southern states had laws prohibiting miscegenation, but they were never enforced in the many instances when white men had intercourse with black women. A number of antebellum state statutes specified that the rape of a female slave constituted only trespass. See, for example, Ulrich B. Phillips, *Life and Labor in the Old South* (Boston: Little, Brown, 1930), 162.

12. *Odom v. Odom, Georgia Reports* 33:286–321.

13. Harriet Jacobs, *Incidents in the Life of a Slave Girl*, ed. Jean Fagan Yellin (Cambridge: Harvard University Press, 1987), 27. See also "Harriet Ann Jacobs," in *Black Women in America*, 627–29.

14. Melton McLaurin, *Celia: A Slave* (Athens: University of Georgia Press, 1991). See also the discussion of Celia's case in A. Leon Higginbotham, Jr., "The Hill-Thomas Hearings—What Took Place and What Happened," pp. 29–31 herein.

15. Susan Brownmiller, *Against Our Will: Men, Women, and Rape* (New York: Simon and Schuster, 1975), 175–76, provides other examples of slave women's ultimately futile retaliatory actions against white men.

16. One bizarre addendum to this case is that Celia was only executed *after* her pregnancy terminated in a stillbirth. She might be sentenced to death for the crime, but her unborn child was potentially valuable property that belonged to the estate of the man she killed.

17. Brownmiller, *Against Our Will*, 177, notes the irony of using the pronoun "his"; Jacobs, *Incidents in the Life of a Slave Girl*, 27.

18. For further discussion, see "Free Black Women in the Antebellum South," in *Black Women in America*, 456–62, and Alexander, *Ambiguous Lives*. The limitations on these women's freedoms were exceedingly restrictive, and their legal protections were few.

19. This is made clear, for example, in Georgia's antebellum statutes and decisions. Tushnet, *American Law of Slavery*, 151, quotes Georgia's Judge Joseph Lumpkin, who wrote that under law the free person of color was always "associated . . . with the slave in this State."

20. Virginia Kent Anderson Leslie, *Woman of Color, Daughter of Privilege: Amanda America Dickson, 1849–1893* (Athens: University of Georgia Press, 1995), 77, 139. See also "Amanda America Dickson," in *Black Women in America*, 336–37, and Georgia examples in Alexander, *Ambiguous Lives*, 64–66.

21. White, *Ar'n't I a Woman*, 152–53, 164–65; Alexander, *Ambiguous Lives*, 64–66.

22. Quoted in Alexander, *Ambiguous Lives*, 65. See "Federal Writers Project Slave Narratives," in *Black Women in America*, 416–17. White, *Ar'n't I a Woman*, 98–106, discusses the economic importance of black women as "breeders."

23. The most complete historical examination of marriage among African Americans is Herbert G. Gutman, *The Black Family in Slavery and Freedom, 1750–1925* (New York: Pantheon Books, 1976).

24. For an overview of Burroughs' life, see "Nannie Helen Burroughs," in *Black Women in America*, 201–5; Hine, "Rape and the Inner Lives of Southern Black Women," 186, and White, *Ar'n't I a Woman*, 164.

25. "National Association of Colored Women," in *Black Women in America*, 842–51, provides a good overview of the organization. For the attack on black women's morality, see Wilson Jeremiah Moses, "Domestic Feminism, Conservatism, Sex Roles, and Black Women's Clubs, 1893–1896," in *Journal of Social and Behavioral Sciences* 24, no. 4 (Fall 1987): 166–77. See also Mary Martha Thomas, *The New Woman in Alabama: Social Reforms and Suffrage, 1890–1920* (Tuscaloosa: University of Alabama Press, 1992), 70; and Hine, "Rape and the Inner Lives of Southern Black Women."

26. John Dollard, *Caste and Class in a Southern Town*, 3d ed. (Garden City, NY: Doubleday, 1957), 152.

27. See especially Hine, "Rape and the Inner Lives of Southern Black Women."

28. This concept is hardly unique, but it is well expressed in Lerner, *Black Women in White America*, 173.

29. For a look at black women in more prestigious occupations, see Bettina Aptheker's "Quest for Dignity: Black Women in the Professions, 1865–1900," in her *Woman's Legacy: Essays on Race, Sex, and Class in American History* (Amherst: University of Massachusetts Press, 1982). And see "Myra Adele Logan," in *Black Women in America*, 731.

30. Quoted in Paula Giddings, *When and Where I Enter: The Impact of Black Women on Race and Sex in America* (New York: William Morrow, 1984), 308. For information on Height, see "Dorothy Irene Height," in *Black Women in America*, 552–54.

31. Jacqueline Jones, *Labor of Love, Labor of Sorrow: Black Women, Work, and the Family from Slavery to the Present* (New York: Basic Books, 1985), 130.

32. I have been unable to pin down the source of this well-remembered political story from the 1950s.

33. Giddings, *When and Where I Enter*, 91. For a look at black women in early-twentieth-century reform movements, see Terborg-Penn, "Discontented Black Feminists," and Adele Logan Alexander, "How I Discovered My Grandmother, and the Truth about Black Women and the Suffrage Movement," *Ms.*, November 1983, 29–33.

34. "Septima Poinsette Clark," in *Black Women in America*, 249–52, provides an overview of her life. See also Anne Standley, "The Role of Black Women in the Civil Rights Movement," in *Black Women in United States History*, vol. 16, ed. Darlene Clark Hine (Brooklyn: Carlson Publishing, 1990), 183–202.

35. For a new and far-reaching discussion of the significance of rap music, including sexual connotations and behavior, see Tricia Rose, *Black Noise:*

Rap Music and Black Culture in Contemporary America (Hanover: Wesleyan University Press, 1994), especially chap. 5, "Bad Sistas: Black Women Rappers and Sexual Politics in Rap Music."

36. Lerner, *Black Women in White America*, 163.

37. June Jordan, *Technical Difficulties: African-American Notes on the State of the Union* (New York: Pantheon Books, 1992), 202. See also "June Jordan," in *Black Women in America*, 660.

38. Bell hooks, *Feminist Theory: From Margin to Center* (Boston: South End Press, 1984), preface.

39. Quoted in Lerner, *Black Women in White America*, 202. See also "Ida Bell Wells-Barnett," in *Black Women in America*, 1242–46. In his rebuttal of Anita Hill's accusations, Clarence Thomas evoked these memories with his "high-tech lynching" comment. In many cases, African American men's sexual misconduct is more likely to be retaliated against than that of white men, but this is true only in instances of *interracial*—black male/white female—sexual encounters.

40. Quoted in Lerner, *Black Women in White America*, 164. See also "Fannie Barrier Williams," in *Black Women in America*, 1259–61.

41. See, for example, White, *Ar'n't I a Woman*, 165: "Black women had almost as little recourse to justice when the perpetrator was black. When a black man raped a black woman, police consistently reported the crime as 'unfounded,' and in the relatively few cases that reached the courts, the testimony of black female victims was seldom believed by white juries."

42. Certainly, however, there was no unanimity of opinion about Anita Hill among African American women. Deserving of mention are the more than sixteen hundred women, predominantly academicians, who formed a group called African American Women in Defense of Ourselves and took out an advertisement in the *New York Times* on Sunday, November 17, 1991. It stated, in part: "We recognize that the media are now portraying the black community as prepared to tolerate both the dismantling of affirmative action and the evil of sexual harassment in order to have any black man on the Supreme Court. . . . The media have ignored or distorted many African American voices [but] we will not be silenced." An article supporting the credibility of Hill's assertions was Rosemary Bray's "Taking Sides against Ourselves," *New York Times Magazine*, November 17, 1991. For a variety of views on this controversy, see Toni Morrison, ed., *Race-ing Justice, Engendering Power: Essays on Anita Hill, Clarence Thomas, and the Construction of Social Reality* (New York: Pantheon Books, 1992), and *Black Scholar* 22, nos. 1 and 2 (Winter 1991–Spring 1992), *The Clarence Thomas Confirmation: The Black Community Responds*.

43. In a footnote to her article "Race, Gender, and Social Class in the Thomas Sexual Harassment Hearings: The Hidden Fault Lines in Political Discourse," *Harvard Women's Law Journal* 15 (Spring 1992): 9, Emma Coleman Jordan, for example, cites a letter she received from Professor Joan Williams of American University: "Single women . . . get judged by norms

that originate in domesticity. One such norm is the sense that women should not be too 'careerist' if higher values—sexual integrity or children's needs—are at stake."

44. Ibid, 2–3. Jordan attempts to analyze the meaning of these polls taken soon after the hearings in the fall of 1991. Opinion polls taken a year or more later showed a shift in sentiment. Apparently a majority of Americans came to believe Anita Hill and disbelieve Clarence Thomas.

45. W. E. B. Du Bois, "The Damnation of Women," in *Darkwater: Voices from within the Veil* (1920; reprint, New York: Schocken Books, 1969), 169, 172–73. A classically trained scholar and early NAACP leader who later became a rather doctrinaire Marxist, Du Bois consistently championed women's rights in addition to his more familiar efforts on behalf of his race.

46. Ibid., 185.

47. Gloria T. Hull, Patricia Bell Scott, and Barbara Smith, eds., *All the Women Are White, All the Blacks Are Men, but Some of Us Are Brave: Black Women's Studies* (Old Westbury, NY: Feminist Press, 1981).

48. Hooks, *Feminist Theory*, preface.

49. In "A Feminist Challenge: Must We Call Every Woman Sister?" *Black Looks: Race and Representation* (Boston: South End Press, 1992), 79–86, bell hooks takes Hill to task for failing to enunciate a clear political philosophy during her testimony.

50. Giddings, *When and Where I Enter*, 7.

51. Anna Julia Cooper, *A Voice from the South* (1892; reprint, New York: Oxford University Press, 1988), 31. Also see "Anna Julia Haywood Cooper," in *Black Women in America*, 275–81.

The Hill-Thomas Hearings—What Took Place and What Happened: White Male Domination, Black Male Domination, and the Denigration of Black Women

A. Leon Higginbotham, Jr.

I

I have a pleasant disclosure to make, and it is important to make it now, before I say anything else. I count Professor Anita Hill as a friend. She is a person of integrity and courage who made a great sacrifice in testifying before the Senate Judiciary Committee in October 1991. Therefore, I will not pretend that my commentary about the Hill-Thomas hearings begins from a blank slate. Indeed, Professor Hill is not the only participant in the October 1991 hearings with whom I can be said to have had prior communications.[1] In the past, I have been both praised and condemned for writing to and about Justice Thomas. Because of these past comments, now I often find myself in the position of being thought of as some sort of an "expert" on Justice Thomas. It is not a designation I ever asked for or even desired. In any event, in order to be able to understand the circumstances of the Hill-Thomas hearings, one needs to be more than an expert on Justice Thomas's judicial philosophy or lack of it. For example, in her introduction to *Race-ing Justice, En-gendering Power*,[2] Toni Morrison writes that while we may know what "took place" in the chambers of the Senate Judiciary Committee back in October 1991, we do not yet know "what happened, how it happened, why it happened," and that for us to know the full story of what happened, "the focus must be on the history routinely ignored or played down or unknown."

I believe that part of what Morrison meant is that if we are to know what happened during the Hill-Thomas hearings, our focus must be on the history of black women in this country. That history, which is "routinely ignored or played down or unknown," has often been marked by what I would call the precepts of slavery. Though I have discussed these precepts in far greater detail elsewhere,[3] for present purposes I need only discuss: (1) white male domination over both black and white females; (2) black male domination over black females; and (3) the persistent denigration of black women in this society. These three precepts were the unseen—though certainly not unheard—witnesses in the Hill-Thomas hearings. They drove every question, modified every answer, put a spin on every fact, and cloaked every comment made in support of or against Clarence Thomas or Anita Hill.

The purpose of this paper is to take a look at these precepts from a historical and legal perspective. For that, I will ask you to imagine the legal evidence of these precepts as a series of historical snapshots.

II

The first snapshot is Virginia, 1662. That year, the Virginia legislature passed a statute to attack the "problem" caused by women indentured servants having children out of wedlock. The statute required unmarried women to serve an additional two years of indentured servitude when they had children out of wedlock.[4] In the preamble, the legislature noted that "some dissolute masters" had "gotten their maids with child" in order to "claim the benefit of their service," and that some loose women, hoping to gain their freedom, had laid "all their bastards to their masters." Given that state of affairs, the legislature provided that any woman servant got with child by her master

"would serve an additional two years" after her indenture was scheduled to expire. She was sold, with the church wardens receiving the
funds payable in tobacco for two years. While conception of a child
required a male's active involvement (at least back in 1662), *only* the
mother had the additional burden of servitude.

Further, in the case of sexual relations between a male master and
a female servant, it is entirely possible that the female servant was
raped. In any event, even if the master did not actually rape the
servant, at the very least he voluntarily chose to enter into sexual
relations with her. That probably was not the case for the female
servant. Since the master held almost absolute power over her life,
her having sexual intercourse and bearing his child may not have
been voluntary. Nevertheless, the "church wardens" obtained the rewards from the labor of a servant for two years. The child of the
union suffered the social stigmatization of being a bastard. And the
female indentured servant gave two more years of servitude to the
state for an act that should not have been a crime on her part, in
addition to an untold number of years to a child she may not even
have wanted.

In 1662 most if not all of the indentured female servants were
white. This first snapshot gives a brief demonstration of one aspect of
precept 1: white male domination over white women. If a black female indentured servant had existed at the time, she would have
been subjected to similar denigration and exploitation for the benefit
of white males.

III

The second snapshot is also Virginia, 1662. That year, the Virginia
legislature passed a statute to address the "special" problem of sexual
relations between blacks and whites. The statute provided:

> Children got by an Englishman upon a Negro woman shall be bond
> or free according to the condition of the mother, and if any Christian
> shall commit fornication with a Negro man or woman, he shall pay
> double the fines of a former act.

"Englishman," as used in the statute, was a synonym for whites generally, or white Englishmen specifically. The fact that males were

punished with a double fine may at first glance suggest that the statute was not biased toward white males. Quite the contrary. In fact, the statute maximized the economic advantages white males stole from the bodies of black women. Prior to passage of this statute, it had been an open question as to whether the English legal doctrine that the status of a child is determined by the status of the father would apply to the children of white male masters and black female slaves. The 1662 legislature repudiated the English law concept as to the status of a child being determined by the status of the father, and instead accepted the Roman law doctrine of *partus sequitur ventrem*.[5] The consequence of the children of white Englishmen and black women taking the slave status of their mother was that white males regularly reaped the economic benefits of what was the rape of black women. The children of the white master and the black female slave became slaves themselves. The white master could then work his slave progeny to nurse his legitimate children, harvest the fields, pick the cotton, and stoke the engines of American industry. When the white master became a statesman, he could say of his slaves—regardless of their paternity—what Mr. Gholson of the Virginia Legislature said in 1831 in arguing against abolition:

> Why I really have been under the impression that I owned my slaves. I lately purchased *four women* and *ten children* in whom I thought I obtained a great bargain, for I really supposed they were *my property*, as were my *brood mares*.[6]

This snapshot is more specific evidence of another part of precept 1: white male domination over black women.[7]

IV

The third snapshot is Missouri, 1850. That year, Robert Newsom, a seventy-year-old white male, purchased Celia, a fourteen-year-old black slave girl.[8] On the way from the slave market to his farm, Newsom raped Celia for the first time. Over the next five years, he regularly visited her cabin and had sexual intercourse with her if she consented, or raped her if she did not. Newsom was the father of at least one of the two children Celia bore during that five-year period.

In 1854 Celia started a relationship with a black male slave named George, who apparently pressured her to terminate sexual relations with Newsom. In February 1855, Celia became pregnant with her third child. From that point on, she was constantly sick. She told Newsom that she would no longer have sexual relations with him and warned him that she would hurt him if he did not stop raping her. On the afternoon of June 23, 1855, Newsom told Celia that he was coming down to her cabin that night. Celia again warned Newsom that she would hurt him if he molested her. That night, when Newsom arrived at the cabin, Celia struck him in the head with a stick. Newsom apparently died instantly.

Still pregnant, Celia was brought to trial for murder in the first degree. After presentation of the evidence, Celia's court-appointed counsel requested the court to instruct the jury that the rape of a slave woman was not a property right of the master, and that if it was justifiable homicide for a white woman to kill her assailant, so too was it justifiable homicide for Celia to kill Newsom to prevent him from raping her. The trial judge rejected the requested instructions. Instead, the judge submitted to the jury the following instructions:

> If Newsom was in the habit of having intercourse with the defendant who was his slave and went to her cabin on the night he was killed to have intercourse with her or for any other purpose and while he was standing in the floor talking to her she struck him with a stick which was a dangerous weapon and knocked him down, and struck him again after he fell, and killed him by either blow, it is murder in the first degree.

The jury returned a verdict of guilty. Celia was sentenced to death. The Missouri Supreme Court refused to hear her appeal and denied her a stay of execution. Celia escaped but was quickly recaptured. The court, apparently without a trace of irony, "mercifully" delayed her execution until she could give birth to her baby, which was, after all, the slave property of Newsom's estate. The baby, we are told, was born dead. On December 13, 1855, Celia, who would forever be known as Celia, a slave with no last name, was taken from the prison gallows and "hanged until she died."

This snapshot illustrates both precepts 1 and 2. It illustrates precept 1 because Celia, in life and in death, was obviously dominated and violated by white males. But it also illustrates precept 2 because George, the black slave, in his own way exploited Celia too. George pressured Celia to break off relations with Newsom because he himself did not have the power to defend Celia. Yet George must have known full well that Celia was equally powerless to terminate the relationship. In the end, the pressure George exerted on Celia may have engendered the circumstances that led her to kill Newsom. It is true that George was charged with the unbearable burden of not being able to defend his lover. It is also true that he unjustly sought to shift the impossible weight of his burden to Celia.

V

The fourth snapshot is Mississippi, 1859. That year, the Court of Appeals of Mississippi considered the case of *George (a slave) v. The State*.[9] In that case, a black slave named George was convicted of raping a black slave girl about nine years old. On appeal, George's counsel argued before the court as follows:

> The crime of rape does not exist in this State between African Slaves. Our laws recognize no marital status as between slaves; their sexual intercourse is left to be regulated by their owners. The regulations of law, as to the white race, on the subject of sexual intercourse, do not and cannot, for obvious reasons, apply to slaves; their intercourse is promiscuous, and the violation of a female slave by a male slave would be a mere assault and battery.

The Court of Appeals of Mississippi agreed with George's counsel and reversed his conviction. The court held that under the common law and under Mississippi statutory law it was not a crime for a black man to rape a black woman or even a girl of nine. According to the court, "Masters and slaves cannot be governed by the same common system of laws: so different are their positions, rights and duties."

Of course, in stating that masters and slaves were different in their "positions," the court was not simply referring to the fact that masters were free and slaves were not, or to the fact that masters possessed full citizenship rights and slaves did not. The court was also alluding to the theory that masters and slaves were subject to different laws because masters possessed moral standards and slaves did not. Specifically, the court was alluding to the widely held theory that white women possessed moral virtues and black women did not. According to that theory, black women so totally lacked "moral virtue" that it was not within their nature to be raped. Indeed, for some time the law simply did not recognize the rape of a black woman by any man, either black or white.

The snapshot of *George (a slave) v. The State* is an example of precepts 2 and 3: the domination of black women by black men, and the persistent denigration of black women in American society.

VI

The fifth and final snapshot is Washington, D.C., October 1991, in the chambers of the Senate Judiciary Committee. Professor Anita Hill was questioned, berated, and abused by many members of an all-white and all-male Senate committee. Many senators dismissed her testimony of having been sexually harassed by Clarence Thomas with outright accusations that she was lying, and with sly innuendos that she was a scorned, vengeful, and psychotic woman. Senator Arlen Specter accused Professor Hill of perjury to Congress—a punishable federal offense—without producing the least bit of evidence to back up his charge. Senator Orrin Hatch, waving over his head a copy of *The Exorcist*, managed to suggest quite seriously that Professor Hill was as demented as the character in the novel who was possessed by the devil. Senator Simpson, recalling the McCarthy witch hunts, made the vague and sinister announcement that he had reams of compromising letters about "this woman" coming out of his every pocket. Clarence Thomas, for his part, implied that Professor Hill, a dark-skinned woman, resented him for his preference for women of "lighter complexion." Finally, Clarence Thomas closed forever any real consideration of Professor Hill's charges by protesting that Professor Hill was being used as the instrument of *his* lynching.

Clarence Thomas's charge was, of course, ridiculous. There has never been a recorded instance of a black man being lynched for abusing a black woman. More to the point, for a very long time, black men were not even prosecuted for physically abusing or raping black women. Yet as preposterous as the charge was, it was clearly effective in silencing and shaming the 1991 Senate Judiciary Committee, which was no more *gender or racially* integrated than the 1662 Virginia Assembly, which decreed that black women would be denied the legal standards of English law.

VII

The Hill-Thomas hearings represented a sequela of attitudes that in some ways were not very different from those of the antebellum "statesmen" and "judges" who regarded all women, and particularly black women, as inferior persons. *Thus, Anita Hill was treated far more harshly by the Senate committee than she would have been had she been white, and Clarence Thomas was treated far more generously than he would have been had the victim been a white woman.* This is clearly demonstrated by analyzing three theoretical scenarios, with the principal roles in the hearings recast and all other factors being the same.

Scenario 1: If the nominee had been Clarence Thomas and the victim had been a white woman, either the Judiciary Committee would have rejected Clarence Thomas unanimously, or more probably, the president would have withdrawn his name the moment the evidence was submitted.

Scenario 2: If the nominee had been a white man and the victim had been a white woman, the white nominee would have been rejected by the Judiciary Committee and would never have been confirmed. It is worth recalling that the Armed Services Committee rejected Senator John Tower's nomination as secretary of defense, even though, unlike Clarence Thomas, he would not have won a lifetime appointment. Part of the rejection was predicated on his alleged questionable relationships with white women.[10]

Scenario 3: If the nominee had been a white man and the victim Anita Hill, he would have been overwhelmingly rejected. Some of the so-called civil rights leaders who supported Clarence Thomas would have been the first to demand the rejection of a white Supreme Court nominee accused of sexually harassing an African American woman.

In the scenario that was actually played out in October 1991, of course, the nominee was a black man and the victim was a black woman. Suddenly the senators became more tolerant in evaluating the nominee.

Even before Professor Hill had completed her testimony, every member of the Judiciary Committee, those who had questioned her sanity as well as those who had failed to defend her, made sanctimonious little statements about how grateful they personally were that she had raised their consciousness on the issue of sexual harassment, and about how certain they were that history would judge her a true heroine in the fight for equal rights and equal opportunities for women in the United States. History, they seemed to be saying, would in the end treat her more kindly than they themselves had.

That many of these gentlemen made wild and unfounded statements about Professor Hill with apparent immunity says nothing about the extent of her sanity and everything about the degree of their own integrity, and about the measure of respect accorded black women in this society. However, the fact that many of the white male members of the Judiciary Committee dismissed Professor Hill's testimony by accusing her of being a liar and a delusional woman does not, in and of itself, mean that those senators are singularly dimwitted. They may or may not be. But the point here is that those senators were not the only ones who tended to doubt her testimony. After all, Clarence Thomas was confirmed to the Supreme Court precisely because the senators who voted for him had good reasons to believe that the majority of their constituents would also dismiss Professor Hill's testimony as the inexplicable ranting of a disturbed woman. In the end, therefore, Clarence Thomas's confirmation says more about how we define ourselves as a society than about the personal inclinations of the members of the Senate Judiciary Committee.

Conclusion

As I look back on the Senate Judiciary Committee hearings of October 1991, the words of Samuel Johnson in 1775 again have meaning to me: just as he said of the conduct of white colonialists, the performance of many members of the Judiciary Committee was "too foolish for buffoonery and too wild for madness." As I watched the members of the committee during the hearings, I could not help but feel that most of the "good Senators" just did not "get it." It seemed to me then, just as it seems to me today, that in focusing exclusively on the issue of sexual harassment in the "workplace," the Judiciary Committee was only interested—and only mildly so—in learning what took place between Professor Hill and Clarence Thomas. They certainly were not interested in what happened.

Had the senators been interested in the question of *why* Professor Hill was sexually harassed, they would have been forced to face immediately and directly the history of how black women have been dominated and denigrated by white males and by black males in this society. But much more than the *history* of domination and denigration of black women, these senators would have been forced to confront the *present-day reality* of how many but not all of them dominated and denigrated Professor Hill because she was a woman, and because she was a black woman. By ignoring and playing down the history and the story of black women in this country, the Senate Judiciary Committee effectively told Professor Hill and other women the same thing: that the law is the embodiment of what most senators represented and that Professor Hill's story had no place in it. With this volume, we may yet begin to tell them they were wrong.

Notes

This paper was adapted from a paper researched by myself and my former law clerk, Aderson Bellegarde Francois, J.D., NYU 1991.

1. *See* A. Leon Higginbotham, Jr., "An Open Letter to Justice Clarence Thomas from a Federal Judicial Colleague," 140 *University of Pennsylvania Law Review* 1005 (1992).
2. Toni Morrison, ed., *Race-ing Justice, En-gendering Power: Essays on Anita Hill, Clarence Thomas, and the Construction of Social Reality* (Pantheon Books, 1992).
3. In the forthcoming book *Shades of Freedom*, chapter 2, I discuss in detail "The Ten Precepts of Slavery: The Consensus That Led to the Legitimization of Slavery and Racism" (Oxford University Press).
4. For a discussion of this statute, *see* A. Leon Higginbotham, Jr., *In the Matter of Color* (Oxford University Press, 1978), p. 42.
5. "The offspring follows the mother; the brood of an animal belongs to the owner of the dam; the offspring of a slave belongs to the owner of the mother, or follows the condition of the mother. A maxim of the civil law,

which has been adopted in the law of England in regard to animals, though never allowed in the case of human beings. 2 Bl. Comm. 390, 94; Fortes. 42." *Black's Law Dictionary*, 3d ed. (West Publishing, 1933).

6. *See* A. Leon Higginbotham, Jr., "Racism and the Early American Legal Process, 1619–1896," 407 *Annals of the American Academy of Political and Social Science* 1–17 (1973) (quoting William Goodell, *The American Slave Code* (1853; reprint, New American Library, 1968), p. 36).

7. *See* Higginbotham and Kopytoff, "Property First, Humanity Second: The Recognition of the Slave's Human Nature in Virginia Civil Law," 50 *Ohio State Law Journal* 511 (1989).

8. For a more detailed discussion of Celia's case, *see* A. Leon Higginbotham, Jr., "Race, Sex, Education, and Missouri Jurisprudence: Shelley v. Kraemer in a Historical Perspective," 67 *Washington University Law Quarterly* 673 (1989).

9. 37 Miss. 316 (1859).

10. *New York Times*, May 5, 1990, p. 24; March 2, 1989, p. 27; February 25, 1989, p. 1; February 24, 1989, p. 1.

The Power of False Racial Memory
and the Metaphor of Lynching

EMMA COLEMAN JORDAN

This is a circus. It is a national disgrace. And from my standpoint as a black American, as far as I am concerned, it is a high-tech lynching for uppity blacks who in any way deign to think for themselves, to have different ideas, and it is a message that unless you kow-tow to an old order, this is what will happen to you, you will be lynched, destroyed, caricatured by a committee of the U.S. Senate, rather than hung from a tree.

CLARENCE THOMAS, October 11, 1991[1]

*E*ven now, years after the Hill-Thomas hearings, the text of Clarence Thomas's high-tech lynching speech bristles with defiant racial anger. It calls to mind the televised image of his face showing the pain of an innocent man unjustly accused. His attitude of righteous indignation, disgust, even contempt for the Senate Judiciary Committee, was powerfully displayed in every gesture. This emotional soliloquy is widely agreed to be the point at which opinion turned in his favor.[2] The phrase "high-tech lynching," while generally believed to have originated with Thomas,[3] had in fact appeared in a story in the *New York Times* in early September of 1991, after his nomination and before his confirmation. Ironically, the story was about the first white person to be executed in the United States for killing a black person in nearly fifty years and one thousand executions.[4]

Why was this rhetorical device[5] more powerful than any other deployed during that intense weekend under the klieg lights? What historical and linguistic markers are bound up in the symbolism of lynching? How much of our legacy of racial oppression returned to life during this now historic soliloquy? Did the magic of the lynching metaphor derive from its defensive power to position Thomas, an advocate of race-blind decision making, as heir to a long line of innocent black men tortured and executed by unruly mobs? Or did it work offensively because it served to re-race Anita Hill as a white woman falsely shouting "Rape!" Surely, the lynching metaphor worked on a number of levels because it offered multiple and contradictory characterizations. On one hand, Thomas could evoke sympathy in the black community and guilt among whites by recalling the horrors of "lynch law."[6] At the same time, he could remind the Senate committee subliminally that Anita Hill was no white woman on whose word a black man should be punished—in other words, like Mary McLeod Bethune in a story Adele Alexander relates, "She's no lady, she's a nigger."[7]

When Clarence Thomas asserted that he was the victim of a high-tech lynching at the hands of the all-white male Senate Judiciary Committee, he not only played the race card against whites, he trumped the gender card of a black woman's claim of intraracial sexual harassment. This metaphor gave Thomas an all-purpose substitute for a factual account of his behavior with Hill. Instead, he adopted a two-pronged strategy that consisted of categorical denial coupled with the powerful racial metaphor of lynching.

A somewhat less obvious message of the lynching comparison casts Thomas as a white man seeking solidarity with other powerful white men who might see themselves confronted with similar allegations of past sexual harassment of women employees.[8] The lynching comparison proved to be an extremely useful and pliable metaphor for the synergy between race and gender subordination. Incredibly, Thomas could claim immunity from answering the charges both as an honorary white man and as a black man, even while painting Hill with the negative characteristics of *both* white and black women.

These treacherous racial dynamics were largely invisible to most Americans, who could only see Thomas, a black man, defiantly confronting the epitome of white power: the all-male Senate Judiciary Committee. From this bipolar racial perspective, the senators were cast, like their forebears, in the role of masculine purveyors of racial hatred against a black man. This bipolar image of racial subordination thus captured the imagination and sympathy of both white and black Americans. Whites, acting from guilt, and blacks from rage, could then be counted on to assure the margin of support for the nomination, in the absence of irrefutable proof of the behavior described by Professor Hill.[9]

The Themes of the Metaphor

In the years since the hearings, Thomas's metaphor has spawned imitators and stimulated analysts to delve into the history of race, gender, and power relationships on display in the complex violence of the American institution of lynching. The brutal history of lynching shows with unique force how our collective failure to extend the dialogue about racial issues that began in the 1960s left both black and white Americans vulnerable to the kind of racial manipulation Thomas used to defend himself.[10] The hearings provide a textbook study in the manipulation of history and the presentation of false historical analogies in the national political arena of an intensely contested Supreme Court nomination. The Thomas nomination, more than any before or since, tested African American loyalties by seeking to build support based on skin color[11] for a nominee whose conservative ideology placed him far outside the mainstream of modern African American intellectual understandings on race relations.

Thomas's decision to compare the Senate inquiry into the truth of Hill's allegations to the work of nineteenth-century lynch mobs, although abjectly cynical, proved to be extraordinarily fertile, because it opened a Pandora's box of race and gender myths. Five dominant themes emerge on close analysis.

First, Thomas claimed that the hearings were consistent with the history of using lynching as a tool of terror to put "uppity blacks who deign to think for themselves" in their places. In this theme, Thomas becomes a victim of a liberal witch hunt to enforce intellectual subservience on black conservatives.

A second theme, though largely unspoken, sought to invoke the modern tolerance for interracial marriages. In this meaning of the metaphor, Thomas dared the senators to "lynch" him for being married to a white woman.[12]

The third theme of the lynching metaphor was to remind the black community of one of the ironclad conventions of black cultural life: Don't "air our dirty laundry" in public.[13] An African American woman who is the victim of sexual harassment, domestic violence, or even rape by a black man faces a Hobbesian choice between claiming individual protection as a member of her gender and race or contributing to the collective stigma upon her race if she decides to report the sexual misdeeds of a black man to white authority figures.[14] In this theme of the lynching metaphor, Hill thus stood accused of violating one of the most powerful taboos of African American survival.

Fourth, the lynching metaphor highlighted the double standard of treatment for black and white women. Unpunished, real rape was the norm for black women, who were portrayed as the sexually available property of white men during slavery and in the post-slavery narrative of black women's lives.[15] Thus, in this theme, Thomas could seek the benefit of the unwritten understanding that lynching was reserved for the violation of white women's honor. He could remind the senators that Hill was no white woman, so what was all the fuss about? It is an especially poignant irony of Thomas's lynching metaphor that it traded in this way on the traditional disrespect for black women. This theme of the metaphor relies on the ultimate conservatism: preservation of black women's disadvantaged status in society. In effect Thomas was telling the country that in the previous century, when countless innocent black men were lynched on the word of white women, Anita Hill would not have been eligible to trigger the punishment of a black man, even if her charges were true.

The historical double standard applied to the status and respective gender roles of black and white women has spawned a rich debate among feminists about essentialist models of gender equality that ignore white women's complicity in the oppression of black men and women.[16] These cross-currents of intragender tension also proved to be fertile ground for exploitation. By rekindling memories of white women's role in the lynching of innocent black men, Thomas's metaphor set up an opposition between black and white women, and this opposition became the basis for the fifth theme of the metaphor: the claim that Anita Hill was being manipulated by white feminists. In contrast to the fourth theme—in which Hill is rebuked for invoking the code of white patriarchy and asserting for herself, and for black womanhood, an entitlement to be protected from sexual imposition under that code—Hill appears here as a mere dupe. This version of Hill's agency proved to be critically disabling for many African American women who sought to interpret the meaning of Hill's historic decision to step forward and break the "dirty linen" taboo. For many black women, Hill's action could be explained most easily by accepting Thomas's characterization that she was not acting for herself but as the delusional, unwitting pawn of clever and politically sophisticated white feminists who opposed his presumed position on abortion.[17] Thus, the fifth theme of the lynching metaphor was yet another tool for dividing various constituencies in the political arena and capitalizing on intellectual disagreements and confusions to destabilize support for Hill.

In the fall of 1991, Professor Anita Hill was a talented but completely unfamiliar figure to most Americans. When she appeared in the Senate Caucus Room to face a grueling interrogation from fourteen white male senators, she became a household word, an icon, a *cause célèbre*, a symbol of the frustrations of many women. Yet the process through which she entered the repertoire of American symbols reveals more about America than it does about her. The race and gender weapons that Thomas and his supporters used in the public relations assault on Hill succeeded primarily because black men and women have never had a serious conversation about the intraracial impact of sexual subordination. Therefore, there were no conceptual guideposts, or even respected public policy analysts, to explain the mechanism by which the metaphor of a "high-tech lynching" accomplished the task of fusing Thomas's identity with the history of vigilante executions of black men.[18] This void in the public discourse has begun to be filled in the years since the hearings. However, the conversation about sensitive issues of racial solidarity and intraracial taboo is still relatively primitive. The O. J. Simpson double murder trial reveals much of the same "closing ranks" mentality as did the initial reaction of the black community to the Hill-Thomas hearings.[19]

To unravel the layers of racial nuance largely hidden in the meaning of the hearings, we must explore the race and gender history that served as the foundation upon which Clarence Thomas was able to shift the focus of the hearings away from the question of whether or not he engaged in a series of pornography-laced conversations with Professor Hill in the workplace. In the black community, the lynching metaphor succeeded in signaling a call for racial solidarity by reviving the single most painful collective racial memory other than slavery itself: the memory of vigilante violence against innocent black men.

Professor Hill's treatment by the Senate Judiciary Committee made it clear as never before that the unique history, traditions, and struggles of African American women require special focus to be fully comprehended.[20] The experience of women of color reflects the combined effects of oppression based on both race and gender. The resulting disadvantage, however, is greater than the sum of its parts. While this captures much of the reality, charges by black women against black men to white authority figures reside in a unique zone of synergistic interaction between racial taboos and gender subordination that cannot be fully understood without a historical frame of reference.[21]

Whose Lynching?

A primary source for our knowledge of lynching is the work of Ida B. Wells-Barnett, an African American journalist and daughter of slaves, who devoted more than forty years of her life to a public campaign against racism.[22] Best known for her anti-lynching crusade, she was also an early advocate of women's suffrage, fighting vigorously for the inclusion of women in the black struggle for equality, and of black women in the white-dominated suffrage movement.[23] In the 1890s she concentrated her considerable energy on the task of creating a public record of the toll of lynching in the United States. She compiled the detailed statistical and narrative records on which we rely today.[24] Recognizing that her reports alone would not be believed,[25] even though she often traveled to lynching sites, she adopted the strategy of documenting each lynching primarily from reports in southern newspapers and statistics published by the *Chicago Tribune*. "Out of their own mouths shall the murderers be condemned," she wrote.[26]

Clarence Thomas's claim that he was being "lynched" to enforce intellectual subordination resonated with African Americans because it reminded us of the primary purpose of lynching. Wells-Barnett documented an entire category of lynchings carried out because the victims had been "saucy to white people."[27] Thus, Thomas's distorted use of lynching history invited the assumption that his intellectual position was antagonistic to or disrespectful of whites. In fact his political troubles came largely from blacks who opposed the nomination and challenged his suitability to serve either because of his ideological conservatism or his undistinguished legal career.[28]

A reading of the passage from Thomas's lynching speech that opens this essay leaves unclear who Thomas perceived his antagonists to be. Several interpretations are possible. The most obvious is that the Senate Judiciary Committee itself sought to impose an intellectual orthodoxy on nominees to the Court.[29] Thomas's Senate patron, John Danforth, provides the only direct account of Thomas's perception of his treatment as a Court nominee. Danforth reports that Thomas's first reaction to the confirmation process was fear for his physical safety.

> Beginning shortly after his nomination on July 1, Clarence Thomas had the strong feeling that someone was trying to kill him. His description of his fears resembles an extended nightmare or perhaps a scene from a movie thriller. . . . The small townhouse the Thomases then owned in suburban northern Virginia had a tiny grass yard and a patio, and it was hemmed in by similar homes in the large development. . . . [Thomas] recalls peering through his window at the decks of surrounding houses to see if there was anyone there who was trying to kill him.[30]

Danforth quotes Thomas as saying, "The feeling is as though you're waiting in the wilderness for someone with guns to find you and kill you. And that's the way I felt all summer." And again: "These people are going to try to kill me. I hadn't done anything to them, but they are going to try to kill me. And so I was always waiting to be killed. I mean literally waiting to be destroyed in some way."[31] Danforth acknowledges that this statement might appear "paranoid" to the casual observer, but he attempts to place it in context.

> Concern for physical survival was not new to a black male raised in the rural Georgia of the 1950s and 1960s. As a child he had heard horrifying tales of black men who had been abducted and thrown into the

swamps, where their bodies were consumed by the crabs. . . . While he was in law school, continued concern for his childhood fears led him to literature on lynchings of southern blacks.[32]

Thomas was reported to be especially alarmed by a press conference held by black feminist Florence Kennedy, who allegedly said, "We're going to Bork him. We're going to kill him politically—this little creep. Where did he come from?"[33]

Thus, one clear referent of Thomas's use of the term "lynching" was the fiery rhetoric of his political opponents in the confirmation process. Nothwithstanding his prior extensive experience in Washington politics—as a black Reagan appointee at the Department of Education, as chairman of the Equal Employment Opportunity Commission, and as a judge on the Federal Court of Appeals for the District of Columbia—Thomas equated this rhetoric with threats to his physical safety. In his view, "physical death and destruction of his reputation were not clearly differentiated," writes Danforth, conceding that "we could fault Clarence Thomas for confusing the Florence Kennedy threat to 'Bork' or to 'kill him politically' with a threat of physical violence."[34]

In light of the insights shared by his mentor Senator Danforth, the lynching speech can be seen as an expression of Thomas's deepest fears. On Danforth's evidence, Thomas's distortion of lynching history to manipulate the sympathies of even his most ardent supporter began more than three months before the hearings on Hill's sexual harassment allegations. Thomas emerges in Danforth's account as a man who sought to convince his powerful white sponsors, including the president of the United States and a senior senator, that he feared physical violence, not from the conservative forces of the right, but from people with whom he shared skin color and the experience of racial subordination. The irony of his claim that he might be physically and politically lynched to enforce liberal political orthodoxy is that those most likely to be direct descendants of the lynch mob participants described by Ida Wells-Barnett could be found instead among his conservative supporters.

The magnitude of Thomas's distortion of history becomes clearer when the record of real lynchings is reviewed. For example, an editorial in the June 4, 1894, Memphis *Evening Scimitar* defended the use of lynching to enforce black intellectual and social subordination in this way:

Aside from the violation of white women by Negroes . . . the chief cause of trouble between the races in the South is the Negro's lack of manners. . . . he has taken up the idea that boorish insolence is independence, and the exercise of a decent degree of breeding toward white people is identical with servile submission. . . . The white people won't stand this sort of thing, and whether they be insulted as individuals are [sic] as a race, the response will be prompt and effectual. . . . It is also a remarkable and discouraging fact that the majority of such scoundrels are Negroes who have received educational advantages at the hands of the white taxpayers. They have got just enough of learning to make them realize how hopelessly their race is behind the other in everything that makes a great people, and they attempt to "get even" by insolence.[35]

Senator Danforth's disclosures about Clarence Thomas's state of mind immediately after the nomination in July make clear that the lynching metaphor was not a reaction to the intense pressure of Hill's allegations. Rather, the metaphor captures Thomas's deep paranoia about his political and personal safety. It seems likely that the power and emotional intensity we saw on display during this famous speech revealed long-held fears that predated and transcended the hastily organized Hill-Thomas hearings.

Thomas's fear of being lynched by liberal opponents of his conservative ideology, like Florence Kennedy, is less than persuasive for a number of reasons, among them the fact that the leading civil rights organizations did not forcefully oppose him. For instance, the NAACP, of which Ida Wells-Barnett was a founding member (she left the organization when the leadership refused to take a militant stand against lynching), chose to engage in a protracted and divisive internal debate that muted its participation in the confirmation hearings and effectively foreclosed any real opportunity to have a political impact on the outcome.[36]

The ideological campaign that Thomas waged to make himself an attractive Supreme Court nominee for a conservative president[37] calls to mind another era of intense internecine warfare among blacks seeking to plot a course of political, social, and economic success in America. David Levering Lewis captures well the complexity of intellectual competition and jealousy among black leaders at the turn of the century in his splendid biography of W. E. B. Du Bois.[38] The NAACP, founded in 1909, had its inception in the growing dissatisfaction of a group of intense black intellectuals led by Du Bois with the vocational-education and self-help rhetoric of Booker T. Washington.[39] For many critics of Thomas's alliance with white conservatives, his rise as a national figure places him squarely in the tradition of Washington, "the great accommodator," who counseled African Americans in his famous Atlanta Compromise speech to "cast down your buckets where you are"—the original bootstraps argument now embraced by many black conservatives like Thomas.

The Thomas nomination was only the most public display of growing confusion and political aimlessness in the ranks of traditional civil rights leaders. Anita Hill's sexual harassment allegations hit an especially tender nerve because they exposed the increasing tension between strong black feminist arguments on civil rights and the civil liberties orientation among black intellectuals.[40] This tension was largely invisible until the dispute erupted in full public view during the hearings. Thomas's nomination exposed the disarray among the intellectual and political elites in the African American community. In the absence of a respected voice among the national leadership on issues arising from sexual discrimination, many African Americans were blinded by skin color and gagged by the "dirty linen" taboo. In this atmosphere, Thomas's "high-tech lynching" speech made it all too easy for many to dismiss Anita Hill as a race-disrespecting troublemaker who did not have the backing of the black community.

Events in the years since the hearings have made the tensions between race and gender an even more urgent priority on the African American agenda. The ideological battles within the NAACP that led to the ouster of its executive director, Ben Chavis, in August 1994, were acute symptoms of the continuing aimlessness of many black intellectuals and political leaders.[41] Chavis refused to resign under pressure from the NAACP board when allegations of sexual harassment, gender-based pay discrimination, and financial irregularities were leveled against him. Strikingly, Chavis joined Clarence Thomas in relying on distorted lynching rhetoric to defend himself, telling one reporter, "The NAACP was founded to challenge lynching, to challenge injustice. . . . Yet 85 years later there's another kind of lynch mob. And unfortunately if you look at the lynch mob, you'll find persons of all colors."[42] It is hard not to read Chavis's resort to the lynching metaphor as another attempt to keep the dirty linen in the closet.[43]

Whose Dirty Linen?

Properly understood, the age-old injunction against "airing dirty linen" is in fact a call for racial loyalty, and depends upon a stratification of race and gender identities. To retain approval of the race, black women must not only excise our gender identity but must substitute the identity of black men for our own. In this unique, historically determined equation, the racial memory becomes the only memory, and the women of the race must seek comfort in the uncertain solidarity arising from this social contract.

The lynching of black men for real or imagined crimes of sexual trespass in the domain of white male ownership understandably occupies a central place in the matrix of black-white relationships. For that reason, it would be painful and wrong to deny the pull of our shared racial heritage and the power of the memory of racial violence heaped upon brother, father, husband, and son. Every African American carries the collective memory of men who were lynched for "reasons" as trivial as failing to yield a sidewalk at the demand of a white person.[44] Moreover, while black men were the primary victims of lynching, many women and children were also lynched.[45] "Lynch law" superseded the rule of law. One lynching occurred after an all-white jury rendered a verdict of not guilty in favor of a black man charged with murder. The acquitted defendant was hanged a few nights after the verdict was rendered.[46] For every African American, therefore, the image of lynched black men bears an irrefutable claim of entitlement to represent the experiences of the entire race. Unfortunately, that image has always overshadowed the equally irrefutable and equally representative experience of the sexual violation of black women.[47]

The "dirty linen" charge has special irony because it depends upon an absolute prohibition against violating the pseudo-intrafamilial expectation of private conversations about sensitive matters. But this dysfunctional pseudo-family doesn't talk about the taboo subject in private either. In reality, the subject of black male sexual imposition on black women is not discussed in uniracial company any more often than it is discussed in interracial company. Thus, the call for private discussion is best understood as a call for the race-based gagging of black women, whose injuries will be completely ignored under the rule.[48]

Ironically, too, it is the force of this expectation of silence that makes black women hesitate to bring charges of sexual harassment against black men. This source of pressure, added to the reluctance of any woman to confront a male harasser, may lead to long and otherwise inexplicable delays. If this issue were studied, it would not be surprising to find that African American women hold back or fail to report sexual harassment or other sexual impositions more than their white counterparts when the perpetrator is a member of the same race.[49]

The "dirty linen" metaphor assumes a completely segregated society in which blacks and whites inhabit vastly different worlds, but there are many cultural bridges and areas of common culture. For instance, a zone of shared experience arises from the migration of culture through television, movies, and popular music. This zone of commonality makes it impossible to keep "racial secrets."

A final force that pulls the dirty linen out of the closet is the ambition and success of members of our community. When an African American man or woman enters the arena of competition for offices once held exclusively by whites, or otherwise achieves a high national profile, he or she is necessarily exposed to intense public scrutiny. Those who claim that African American men are entitled to protection from the onslaught of racial myths called up by charges of sexual harassment must tell us what alternative avenues of discussion are available. At a minimum, those who insist on adherence to the racial etiquette while maintaining their belief in the sexual equality of women have an obligation to articulate their vision of an alternative dispute resolution mechanism that protects black women. Without this protection the call for silence is inconsistent with the call for equality.

Anita Hill's testimony set a new paradigm for understanding intraracial gender relations. The conversation has only just begun, however.[50] It is time to explore the real conditions of the lives of African American women. It is time to discard the prohibition against "airing dirty linen." Only candor will move this dysfunctional family closer to healthy functioning for all its members. Only through honest discussion of the issues, however painful, can we create new energy for change.

Notes

1. *Nomination of Judge Clarence Thomas to Be Associate Justice of the Supreme Court of the United States, Hearings before the Committee on the Judiciary*, U.S. Senate, 102d Cong., 1st Sess. 157–58 (Oct. 11, 1991).

2. Senator John Danforth describes the reaction of Thomas's closest advisers: "Standing at the back of the Caucus Room, Ken Duberstein heard the most powerful testimony he had ever heard in his life. He thought Clarence's reference to a high-tech lynching for uppity blacks was 'right on target.' . . . As we returned to our office that night, Ken and I were ecstatic. There was a general feeling among his supporters that Clarence had taken the offensive and the committee was under siege. Ken remembers telling Clarence, 'You hit a home run. In fact, you hit a grand slam.'" John C. Danforth, *Resurrection: The Confirmation of Clarence Thomas* (1994), at 148–49.

3. Senator Danforth writes: "I remember precisely where Clarence was when he first spoke what would be the most memorable words of the hearing. He was sitting in the middle of the couch on the south wall of my office, and he said, 'You know what this is, Jack? This is lynching. This is a high-tech lynching.' The idea was his. The words were his. No person put them in his mind. I said, 'Clarence, if that is how you feel, then go upstairs and say it.' I suggested that he write it down, and he did." Danforth, *supra* note 2, at 145. Danforth goes on to say that while "the word 'lynching' was rooted in his lifelong interest in the subject," Thomas's "reference to 'uppity blacks' may have had its origin in a *Wall Street Journal* editorial shown to Clarence by John Mackey in the early weeks of the confirmation process." *Id.*

4. David Margolick, "Rarity for U.S. Executions: White Dies for Killing Black," N.Y. *Times*, Sept. 7, 1991, A1, col. 1. The execution took place in South Carolina, where no white had been executed for killing a black since 1880. The term "high-tech lynching" was attributed to David Bruck, chief lawyer for the South Carolina Office of Appellate Defense and an active critic of the systemic racism on display in the application of capital punishment. The man who was executed, Donald (Peewee) Gaskins, was an avowed racist who had already been convicted of killing nine other people, all whites. In one of these cases Gaskins had been sentenced to death, but his sentence was commuted to life imprisonment. For the other eight murders he was given consecutive life sentences. Gaskins was finally executed for the murder of one of his fellow prisoners, Rudolph Tyner, a black man convicted of killing a white man whose son hired Gaskins to give Tyner a bomb disguised as a radio. Death-penalty lawyer Bruck called the contract killing by radio-bomb a "high-tech lynching" to emphasize his larger point that the South Carolina execution of a white man for killing a black was not evidence of a changing trend in carrying out the death penalty. Bruck noted sarcastically, "This is hardly evidence that South Carolina

is protecting black lives more energetically than it used to. Gaskins' crime, after all, is that he killed his black victim before the state could get around to killing him itself." The case was portrayed in a CBS made-for-television movie, *Vengeance: The Tony Cimo Story.*

5. *See* Toni Morrison, *Playing in the Dark: Whiteness and the Literary Imagination* (1990), for an exploration of the centrality of racial images in the American literary canon. Morrison powerfully describes the uses of language and literary imagery to capture the projection of deviance onto black literary characters. *See also* Robert Cover, "Violence and the Word," 95 *Yale L. J.* 1601 (1986) (arguing the centrality of violence to legal interpretation), and Cover, "The Supreme Court, 1982 Term—Forward: Nomos and Narrative," 97 *Harv. L. Rev.* 47 (1983).

6. Lynching has been so central to the racial memory of African Americans that I would guess that in most black families with a southern heritage narratives of lynching or near-lynching are part of the family lore. To test this proposition, I asked my father, who was born in Terrebone Parish, Louisiana, outside New Orleans, what he knew about lynching. He immediately told a story about a teenage cousin who was the object of a lynching attempt when "a white woman accused him of trying to look under her skirt. He denied the accusation but admitted saying, 'I sure wish I was a white man,' while smiling at the woman." The cousin was saved when his father, my paternal great-grandfather, appeared with a 30/30 Winchester rifle and "threatened to shoot the first thing that moved in the direction of his house. The would-be lynchers later gang-raped the accuser to teach her a lesson about flirting with black men." Interview by author, Berkeley, California, May 30, 1995. *And see* Ida B. Wells, *Southern Horrors: Lynch Law in All Its Phases* (1990; reprint of 1892 pamphlet, ed. William Warren Katz).

7. *See* Adele Logan Alexander, " 'She's No Lady, She's a Nigger,' " p. 18 herein.

8. Not long after the Hill-Thomas hearings ended, Senator Robert Packwood, Republican of Oregon, was accused of sexual harassment by nineteen women, some of whom were former Senate staff members and lobbyists on Capitol Hill. *See* Florence Graves and Charles E. Shepard, "Packwood Accused of Sexual Advances; Alleged Behavior Pattern Counters Image," *Wash. Post*, Nov. 22, 1992, A1.

9. As Susan Deller Ross notes, in many cases sexual harassment is inherently difficult to prove because the offensive behavior occurs in isolated or semi-isolated settings, so that the victim's recollection of events is the only account that contradicts the defendant's version. In such "he-said-she-said" cases, victims seldom have physical evidence or eyewitness corroboration of their experiences. *See* Ross, "Sexual Harassment Law in the Aftermath of the Hill-Thomas Hearings," pp. 228–241 herein.

10. *See, e.g.*, Cornel West, *Keeping Faith: Philosophy and Race in America* (1993). West decries the separation of black and white intellectuals today.

These two groups might have been expected to pursue the strands of black-white common denominators, but the "general polarization of American intellectual life," along with "heated political and cultural issues, such as the legacy of the Black Power movement, . . . have created rigid lines of demarcation and distance between black and white intellectuals." *Id.* at 69. *See also* Cornel West and Michael Lerner, *Jews and Blacks: The Hard Hunt for Common Ground* (1995).

11. Cornel West argues that the Thomas nomination hearings reveal "a crude discourse about race and gender that bespeaks a failure of nerve of black leadership. . . . Most black leaders got lost . . . in a vulgar form of racial reasoning: *black authenticity—black closing-ranks mentality—black male subordination of black women in the interests of the black community in a hostile white-racist country*" (italics in original). West, "Black Leadership and the Pitfalls of Racial Reasoning," in Toni Morrison, ed., *Race-ing Justice, En-gendering Power: Essays on Anita Hill, Clarence Thomas, and the Construction of Social Reality* (1992), 390, 392 [hereinafter Morrison].

12. At the Race, Gender, and Power in America conference in the fall of 1992, Anna Deavere Smith addressed the visual impact of Thomas's wife, Virginia Lamp Thomas, sitting behind him during the hearings. *See also* Anna Deavere Smith, "The Most Riveting Television," pp. 264–65 herein (quoting film historian Donald Bogle observing that for the conservative white senators on the committee Thomas must have seemed a ". . . friendly/conciliatory/agreeable/congenial/Uncle Tom," but "according to what Anita Hill is telling them/. . . they've got a *buck* on their hands/and *worse*/he has one of their women!"); and A. Leon Higginbotham, Jr., "An Open Letter to Justice Clarence Thomas from a Federal Judicial Colleague," 140 *Univ. of Penn. L. Rev.* 1005 (1992) (reminding Thomas that but for the civil rights struggles of African Americans, he might be jailed for violating antimiscegenation laws once in place in Virginia, where he and his wife now live).

13. *See* Paula Giddings, "The Last Taboo," in Morrison, *supra* note 11, 441–65. "For many, what was *inappropriate* was that a black woman's commitment to a gender issue superseded what was largely perceived as racial solidarity. Still others, I think, reacted to an even greater taboo, perhaps the last and most deeply set one. This was to disclose not only a gender but a sexual discourse, unmediated by the question of racism" (italics in original). *Id.* at 442. Giddings concludes that Anita Hill's testimony revealed that "black men and women have not had their own sexual revolution—the one we couldn't have before." *Id.* at 462.

14. Desiree Washington, the woman whom heavyweight champion Mike Tyson was convicted of raping, became the object of black women's contempt when her accusations were first made public. On the Tyson case, *see* Charles R. Lawrence, "The Message of the Verdict," pp. 105–28 herein.

15. *See, in general,* Paula Giddings, *When and Where I Enter: The Impact of Black Women on Race and Sex in America* (1984). *And see* the discussions of the case of Celia, a fourteen-year-old slave who was raped by her master

and killed him, in Alexander, " 'She's No Lady,' " pp. 8–9 herein, and in A. Leon Higginbotham, Jr., "The Hill-Thomas Hearings—What Took Place and What Happened," pp. 29–31 herein. Celia's trial is famous because it illustrates judicial enforcement of the proposition that under the law a slave could not be raped because she had no right to withhold her consent. *See* Melton A. McLaurin, *Celia: A Slave* (1991).

16. *See, e.g.*, Angela Harris, "Race and Essentialism in Feminist Legal Theory," 42 *Stan. L. J.* 581, 614 (1990), and Kimberlé Crenshaw, "Whose Story Is It, Anyway? Feminist and Antiracist Appropriations of Anita Hill," in Morrison, *supra* note 11, 402–40.

17. Ironically, this view was apparently shared by Senator Orrin Hatch, one of Hill's harshest interrogators on the Judiciary Committee. Senator Danforth reports that Hatch rejected the theories that Hill was a fantasizer or a liar. According to Danforth, Hatch thought that "she believed she was telling the truth but that she was under heavy pressure from interest groups and was coached by experts to make her story more vivid. Orrin believes that an 'entourage of feminist lawyers and feminist special interest groups' followed her wherever she went. In his words, 'Unethical lawyers can put words into the mouths of witnesses all the time, and they get so they think these are their own words.' " Danforth, *Resurrection, supra* note 2, at 153–54.

18. I use the term "vigilante" in this essay to designate the whole spectrum of illegal violence seeking to replace official authority. I fully recognize that although many lynch mobs were spontaneous, purely private affairs, an equally large number were assisted by law enforcement officers and/or elected officials. Some lynchings occurred when authorities simply failed to intervene to confront a building mob. All these permutations of private and state action are included in my use of the term "vigilante," which is defined in *Webster's Third New International Dictionary* (1986) in deceptively neutral terms: "vigilante: a member of a vigilance committee," which is in turn defined as "a volunteer committee of citizens for the oversight and protection of an interest; *esp:* a committee organized to suppress and punish crime summarily (as when the processes of law appear inadequate)."

19. *See, e.g.*, Kimberlé Crenshaw, "Perspective on the Simpson Case: Racism Ploy Can Only Hurt Blacks," *L.A. Times*, July 24, 1994, M1; and Glenn Frankel, "O.J., O.J., On the Wall, Who's the Most Divided, Anxious and Fearful of Them All?" *Wash. Post*, June 4, 1995, at C1.

20. *See* Anita Faye Hill, "Marriage and Patronage in the Empowerment and Disempowerment of African American Women," pp. 271–91 herein.

21. For a good discussion of this interaction in historical context, *see* Giddings, "The Last Taboo," *supra* note 13.

22. *See Crusade for Justice: The Autobiography of Ida B. Wells* (1970), edited by Alfreda M. Duster, Wells's daughter. Wells's first official confrontation with racism occurred in May 1884, when she sat in the "ladies' car" on a train to Memphis, instead of the smoking car reserved for Negroes. The

conductor asked her to leave, and when she refused, "he tried to drag me out of the seat, but the moment he caught hold of my arm I fastened my teeth in the back of his hand. I braced my feet against the seat in front and was holding to the back, and as he had already been badly bitten he didn't try it again by himself." Wells filed a suit for damages. The trial court awarded her $500. In her autobiography she recalled "the headlines in the *Memphis Appeal* announcing 'Darky Damsel Gets Damages.' " Her victory was short-lived. The Tennessee Supreme Court reversed the trial court, and Wells was forced to pay the railroad $200 in costs. *Id.* at 18–19.

23. In 1914, for example, Wells-Barnett fought against white women's efforts in the state of Illinois to exclude black women from the suffrage: "When I saw that we were likely to have a restricted suffrage, and the white women of the organization were working like beavers to bring it about, I made another effort to get our women interested." *Id.* at 345.

24. *See* Ida B. Wells-Barnett, *On Lynchings: Southern Horrors; A Red Record; Mob Rule in New Orleans* (1990; reprint of three 1890s pamphlets, ed. August Meier).

25. Like Anita Hill a century later, Wells-Barnett confronted the age-old credibility problems that have plagued black women in American society. For excellent discussions of these socially and culturally constructed problems, see Hill, "Marriage and Patronage," pp. 271–91 herein, and Alexander, " 'She's No Lady,' " pp. 3–25 herein.

26. Wells-Barnett, *On Lynchings: A Red Record, supra* note 24, at 15.

27. *Id.* at 44. In some cases, economic friction rather than "sauciness" was the immediate cause of lynchings. For example, in 1892 three young black men whom Wells-Barnett described as "peaceful, law abiding citizens and energetic businessmen" owned a prosperous grocery store in a heavily populated suburb of Memphis. After a dispute with a white competitor on the opposite corner, a mob confronted the black owners and an armed group of blacks who were prepared to defend themselves. Many of the blacks were arrested and jailed, but the president, the manager, and a clerk of the grocery store were whisked out of jail and lynched. Wells-Barnett's report of these events includes this comment: " 'The Negroes are getting too independent,' they say, 'we must teach them a lesson.' " Wells-Barnett interjects, "What lesson?" The lesson of subordination: "Kill the leaders and it will cow the Negro who dares to shoot a white man, even in self-defense." *Id.* at 19.

28. *See, e.g.*, the essays in Morrison, *supra* note 11, and in Robert Chrisman and Robert L. Allen, eds., *Court of Appeal: The Black Community Speaks Out on the Racial and Sexual Politics of Thomas vs. Hill* (1992). Taken together, these two collections provide an outstanding survey of the range of opinion on the Thomas nomination in the African American community, both before and after Anita Hill's charges became public.

29. *See* Stephen L. Carter, *The Confirmation Mess: Cleaning Up the Federal Appointments Process* (1994); Robert H. Bork, *The Tempting of America*

(1990); and Yxta Maya Murray, "The Cultural Implications of Judicial Selection" (book review of Morrison, *supra* note 11), 79 *Cornell L. Rev.* 374 (1994).

30. Danforth, *Resurrection*, *supra* note 2, at 10.
31. *Id.* at 10, 11.
32. *Id.* at 10–11.
33. *Id.* at 11.
34. *Id.*
35. Quoted in Wells, *On Lynchings: A Red Record*, *supra* note 24, at 18.
36. According to *Wall Street Journal* reporters Jane Mayer and Jill Abramson, the delayed participation of the NAACP was no accident; Bush White House strategists planned to create a "perception of indecision" (quoting black White House legislative aide Fred McClure) on the part of black leaders, and the strategy worked. Mayer and Abramson allege that Arch Parsons, a black reporter for the *Baltimore Sun* who was covering the Thomas nomination, acted as a go-between to help the White House implement this strategy by getting the NAACP to stall or avoid decisive action. Ben Hooks, then chairman of the NAACP, has vehemently denied this allegation. Mayer and Abramson, *Strange Justice: The Selling of Clarence Thomas* (1994), at 179–80.
37. Mayer and Abramson detail this campaign in *Strange Justice*, *supra* note 36, chap. 1, "The Deal," and chap. 7, "Marshall's Heir." They observe that Thomas's good reputation among conservatives was "not entirely accidental. . . . Indeed, he had long been planning for the day he would stand in front of the cameras and accept a Supreme Court nomination." They interviewed "a number of colleagues [who] recalled him setting his sights on Marshall's seat" as early as 1981, when he was only thirty years old. *Id.* at 18. Mayer and Abramson describe President Bush's objectives in nominating Thomas as follows: "In Clarence Thomas, Bush found a nominee whose personal contradictions perfectly matched his own political ones. Thomas was a black conservative who could symbolize diversity while denouncing the very concept of affirmative action." *Id.* at 170.
38. David Levering Lewis, *W. E. B. Du Bois: Biography of a Race, 1868–1919* (1993).
39. Lewis, *Du Bois*, *supra* note 38, offers a fascinating and detailed exploration of the intellectual divisions that sparked the Niagara Movement and eventually the founding of the NAACP. He describes the intense criticism that Booker T. Washington's advocacy of vocational education engendered among the black intellectual elite, also known as the "talented tenth." For instance, Edward H. Morris, philosopher and graduate of Yale and Harvard, asserted that Washington was "largely responsible for the lynching in this country." *Id.* at 275.
40. I do not mean to suggest that there is universal agreement among black feminists on the Hill-Thomas hearings (or any other issue). *See, e.g.*, bell hooks, *Black Looks: Race and Representation* (1992), at 79–86 (criticizing

Hill's conservatism and lack of feminist consciousness); *contra* Kimberlé Crenshaw, "Roundtable: Sexuality in America after Thomas/Hill,"*Tikkun*, Jan.–Feb. 1992, at 25. *See also* Crenshaw, "Demarginalizing the Intersection of Race and Gender in Antidiscrimination Law, Feminist Theory, and Antiracist Politics," 1989 *Chicago Legal Forum.*

41. *See* Cornel West, *Race Matters* (1993), chap. 3, "The Crisis of Black Leadership."

42. Quoted in David Waters, " 'Lynch Mob' Plots His Ouster, Says NAACP Chief," *Commercial Appeal*, Aug. 10, 1994, 1A. *See also* Edward Walsh, "Chavis Likens Ouster from NAACP to 'Crucifixion,' " *Wash. Post*, Aug. 21, 1994, A1.

43. *See* Emma Jordan, "Prisoners of Sex: When Will the NAACP Learn That Equality Begins at Home?" *Wash. Post*, August 20, 1994. I also discuss the dilemma of the African American community when prominent black men are accused of sexual harassment of black women, or when sexual charges surface in the context of other allegations, in "Race, Gender, and Social Class in the Thomas Sexual Harassment Hearings: The Hidden Fault Lines in Political Discourse," 15 *Harv. Women's L. J.* (comparing the reaction of African American women to the sex-related issues in the cocaine possession trial of Marion Barry, mayor of Washington, D.C., with their reaction to the Hill-Thomas hearings).

44. Wells-Barnett, *On Lynchings: A Red Record, supra* note 24, at 44.

45. *See* August Meier, Preface, *On Lynchings, supra* note 24.

46. Wells-Barnett, *On Lynchings: A Red Record, supra* note 24, at 44 (describing the case of Meredith Lewis, who was arrested, tried, and acquitted of murder in Roseland, Louisiana, in July 1893).

47. For historical examinations of the sexual violation of black women, *see* Alexander, " 'She's No Lady,' " pp. 7–16 herein; Giddings, *When and Where I Enter, supra* note 15; and bell hooks, *Ain't I a Woman? Black Women and Feminism* (1981).

48. *See* the statement of African American Women in Defense of Ourselves, *N.Y. Times*, Nov. 17, 1991. Sixteen hundred women formed this group expressly to break the deafening silence of the absent commentary of black male civil rights leaders during the hearings. Their statement said in part, "We recognize that the media are now portraying the black community as prepared to tolerate both the dismantling of affirmative action and the evil of sexual harassment in order to have any black man on the Supreme Court. [However] we will not be silenced."

49. Giddings makes this point about date rape in "The Last Taboo," *supra* note 13, at 459.

50. For the argument that the conversation is in dire trouble, *see* Orlando Patterson, "The Crisis of Gender Relations among African Americans," pp. 56–104 herein.

The Crisis of Gender Relations
among African Americans

ORLANDO PATTERSON

Introduction

Whatever misgivings Americans may hold about the Thomas-Hill hearings, there can be no doubt that one of their salutary effects was to bring to the forefront of national consciousness the critical issue of gender relations in modern America. They initiated a serious public examination of how men and women are to live with each other in a world where women strive to be equal in all areas of life, both at home and in the workplace. In this they were a watershed in American culture, and indeed in modern industrial culture.

The hearings also highlighted extraordinary changes in the position of African Americans in American society. It was of great importance that a critical *national* debate was being waged in which the two leading players were Blacks. As a student of slavery and its sociological consequences, I was perhaps struck by this fact more forcefully than most other observers. The defining quality of slavery was the natal alienation of the slave population and their descendants. The slave, quintessentially, is one who does not belong, who is seen as a perpetual outsider with whom the insider in no way identifies, especially in matters of critical personal and national import. In this respect, American society remained a slave culture long after the master-slave relationship had been legally extinguished. Hence I see the civil rights movement less as a struggle for equality—that struggle is still very much with us—than as a struggle for the final abolition of slavery, for the recognition of Blacks as constituent members of the community. In this it was mightily successful. That is what I mean when I say that the culture of slavery is now dead; which is not to say that its legacies are not very much with us.

Apart from Martin Luther King's great speech at the Capitol, there have been few defining moments in this final abolition. In my view, the Thomas-Hill hearings were one such moment. They struck me as a powerful expression of the cultural-symbolic change that has taken place in America with respect to the final acceptance of Blacks as integral—even if still greatly disadvantaged—members of the society. The most intimate problems of White men and women, how they were to conduct their gender relations in and out of the workplace, could now be seen in terms of people who happened to be African American.

Kimberlé Crenshaw claims both too little and too much when she asserts that during the hearings America "stumbled into the place where African-American women live."[1] Too little, in that what the nation stumbled on was the contradictory and unjust place where *all* women live; too much, in that the peculiar dilemmas of Black women *and men*, in their relations with each other, were never really addressed, precisely because an African American woman had emerged as a symbol for all women, including those White mothers, sisters, and daughters who up to that moment had been considered by White middle-class men as among the most privileged persons alive.

As Karen Dugger makes clear, the intersection of race and gender does indeed "produce race-specific gender effects that generate important experiential cleavages among women," and these in turn produce different identities and ideological orientations, aspects of which will be our concern below. But what her own and other empirically based work (as opposed to rhetorical outbursts) also shows is that these differences are increasingly being supplanted by the common experience of White and African American women in the two central relations of production and reproduction.[2]

I am not for a moment suggesting that the problems of racism are not still with us. Indeed, as I have argued elsewhere, the very real progress that Blacks have achieved in becoming full citizens of the society has generated a kind of homeostatic backlash of racism.[3] Precisely because Blacks are in, there are greater opportunities for nastiness and abuse. Even so, I think these hearings were a powerful symbolic confirmation of the fact that race, while still important, is of radically *changing* significance.[4] However unequal we may be, we are now very much a central part of this society, a permanent and essential shape on its cultural landscape, and an integral, if turbulent, part of its national consciousness.

But this new inclusion also creates new challenges for us. As long as African Americans remained outsiders, we were forced to concentrate on the central issue of getting in, and in the process to downplay the many problems that beset us internally. As long as we were preoccupied with the lingering effects of the slave culture, it was strategically questionable to ponder too deeply what divides us. I think the time has now come to confront these issues squarely. When we do so, we find that at the top of this internal racial agenda is the thorny, crisis-ridden, and long-closeted problem of gender relations between African American men and women. The hearings forced upon me, and on other Blacks, I hope, the need to examine this whole area more closely.

There has of course been a great deal of very angry talk among Blacks on the subject, but little conversation and even less light. People have been railing at each other, both between and within genders (not to mention differences between groups with separate sexual orientations and feminist ideologies), as the debates surrounding Ntozake Shange's play *For Colored Girls Who Have Considered Suicide* and Michele Wallace's book *Black Macho and the Myth of the Superwoman* amply demonstrate.[5] In spite of what bell hooks calls "the liberatory pedagogy" of contemporary African American feminist thought, it has had, as she acknowledges, little impact on African American political thinking.[6] Worse, it has badly obscured our understanding of gender relations. This failure to explore and communicate is found not only in the popular discourse but in academia, as reflected in the paucity of academic works directly focused on the subject of Black gender relations.[7]

One major factor accounting for the failure of communication on this most urgent of problems among African Americans is the tendency of Black feminists, who dominate the discourse, to confound issues of gender—which concern males and females *both* in their relations with each other—with women's issues, or when they do consider relational problems, to privilege the standpoint of women on the assumption that they are always the victims of the interaction. Black men have as much at stake as Black women in understanding, and resolving, the terrible crisis in their gender relations. Perhaps more, for as I hope to show, Black men suffer great trauma and unhappiness, and literally die horrible and premature deaths, as a direct result of this crisis. When the full range of gender roles and their implied relations is considered—sons/daughters, brothers/sisters, fathers/mothers, male kinsmen/female kinsmen, husbands/wives, boyfriends/girlfriends, "mack-men"/"nasty-girls," pimps/whores, the lot—it is not at all clear whether either sex can claim the dubious privilege of being the greater victim or carrying the greater burden.

The Double Burden: Myth, Reality, or Confusion?

It has become almost a truism in discussions of Black gender relations that African American women are uniquely oppressed with a "double burden," a sociological trope originated in 1857 by Harriet A. Jacobs, the ancestor of all modern bourgeois Black feminists, when she wrote, "Superadded to the burden common to all, *they* have wrongs, and sufferings, and mortifications peculiarly their own."[8] In today's term, added to the burden of racism is the "double jeopardy" of mainstream gender discrimination. Following the Thomas-Hill hearings, in which an African American woman was pitted against an African American man, and the subsequent dismay over the fact that at the time of the hearings (although no longer so) most Americans, white *and* African American, believed Judge Thomas's version of what had transpired, many commentators and analysts emphasized yet a third burden experienced by African American women: that of gender prejudice and exploitation from African American men, which, according to Crenshaw, intersect with the traditional double burden in ways that limit "the means available to relate and conceptualize our experiences as black women."[9]

I think the double burden argument, while not strictly incorrect, obscures more than it illuminates. One way of getting at the real issues is to begin by putting it to rest. This is best done by asking two questions. First, how does the double burden thesis square with the facts, especially the facts of more recent African American male experience? Second, how do the facts relate to the admittedly serious, indeed grievous, problem of African American male attitudes and behavior toward African American women?[10]

As to the facts, there can be no denying what has come to be called the feminization of poverty. There is such an abundance of economic and sociological evidence that women—and children—now bear the major burden of poverty in this society that it is hardly necessary to offer further data here.[11] However, it is equally true that this is not a peculiarly African American problem, although it weighs disproportionately on African American women when compared with White women and men.

Although there is no denying the misogynistic irresponsibility of many underclass African American men, few responsible analysts hold them solely accountable for this problem. There is now no question that single parenting by premature, "never married" women is a major correlate, and perhaps cause, of poverty and its feminization: half of all families headed by such women are in poverty, and three quarters of poor African American families are headed by them, in striking contrast to the absolutely and relatively improving situation of African American families headed by married couples, who as of 1990 were on the verge of catching up with their White counterparts (i.e., they earned $40,040 per annum compared with the White figure of $47,250, a stunning relative improvement over the figures even two decades ago). Whatever the attitude of young African American men toward parenting, the fact remains that it takes two to bring a child into the world, and it is patronizing and sexist to place greater blame for high-risk parenting on African American fathers than on mothers.[12] What is more, as numerous studies have shown, lower-class African American youths, even if willing to help support their children, are in no position to do so.[13]

It is when we compare the life chances and actual experience of African American men and women in recent years that we are forced to question the conventional wisdom that African American women are somehow more destructively burdened by the system than their male counterparts. The social statistics on young African American men are simply frightening.[14] On almost every indicator they are not only far behind their White male counterparts but also significantly worse off than African American women. They die of natural causes and epidemics such as AIDS at a higher rate; they are far more likely to be the victims of homicide at each other's hands; they are incarcerated and addicted and drop out of high school at considerably greater rates than women. Most ominous, African American men not only perform far more poorly than African American women at all levels of the educational system, but they are now to be found in substantially lower and declining numbers at the tertiary levels so crucial for any kind of success in the wider society.

I won't cite all the dismal data, but three sets of statistics are extremely telling. In 1976, 563,114 African American women were enrolled in institutions of higher learning compared with only 469,881 African American men; and of these figures, 38,336 African American women were in graduate studies, compared with 27,016 men. That disparity was already troubling enough. However, by 1984 the number of African American men in higher education had *declined* to 434,515, compared with an *increase* in the number of African American women to 635,370; and there were over 65 percent more African American women in graduate studies than African American men: 32,873 compared with 19,961.

A second important statistic has to do with the earnings of African American women. While their median income is still lower than that of African American men, it is noteworthy that African American women get much higher returns from each increment of education, and that African American women with four years of college now earn more than White women. Since this educated group is perhaps the most influential in the African American community, it is significant that they not only far outnumber African American men but do so at increasing rates.

Finally, there is the tragic record of suicide. No other statistic is more reflective of despair and anguish, and as Emile Durkheim taught us long ago, no data are more indicative of social disorganization and anomie. It is therefore enormously significant that young African American men between the ages of fifteen and twenty-four commit suicide at a rate almost five times greater than African American women of the same age group (11.2 per 100,000 compared with

2.4 for women). As grim as these figures are, it is likely that the situation is actually much worse, not only because of underreporting for African American youth, which according to Gibbs and Hines may be as high as 82 percent,[15] but because of the masking effect of what Seiden calls "victim precipitated" homicide, in which young African American men commit suicide the "macho" way by inciting violence against themselves.[16] The gender difference, according to specialists on the subject, stems from the much greater involvement of women with institutions in the African American community, such as the extended family, church organizations, and other support networks. Indeed, the suicide rate for African American women is among the lowest in the nation; the rate is twice as high for White women and over nine times higher for White men.

I have said enough to pose the really crucial question that concerns me, which is simply this: If African American women continue to suffer the double or triple burden we so often hear about, how do we reconcile this with their relatively better position on these important indicators in comparison with African American men? Why, in particular, are African American women now poised to assume leadership in almost all areas of the African American community, and to outperform African American men at middle- and upper-middle-class levels of the wider society and economy, if they have been so overwhelmingly burdened compared with men? Is the double burden thesis a myth?[17]

In attempting to answer this question, we come to the heart of the problem of gender relations between African American men and women. I think that it is not a myth that African American women have been more burdened than African American men, but it is perhaps time to think again, more carefully, about the nature of the burdens that each gender has had to face. Being burdened, having to work harder than others, is not in itself a necessarily bad thing. From the days of the Puritan founders, Americans have always prided themselves on being hardworking; people competed with each other for the privilege of being burdened with great responsibilities and with the necessity to work "while their companions slept." Some burdens, in other words, we not only welcome but consider generative and empowering.

Without in any way underplaying the enormous problems that poor African American women face, I want to suggest that the burdens of poor African American men have always been oppressive, dispiriting, demoralizing, and soul-killing, whereas those of women have always been at least *partly* generative, empowering, and humanizing.

In the first place, it should be noted that while slavery viciously undermined the two most important male gender roles, father and husband, it simply could not destroy the role of mother. As Deborah Gray White demonstrates in her splendid study of the female slave, "Giving birth was a life-affirming action. It was, ironically, an act of defiance, a signal to the slave owner that no matter how cruel and inhumane his actions, African Americans would not be utterly subjected or destroyed."[18] Indeed, given the peculiar demographic demands of American slave society, the role of mother was valued and reinforced by the vast majority of slaveholders. True, the slave woman was doubly burdened with the tasks of being both reproducer and worker, not to mention "the malevolence that flowed from both racism and sexism."[19] However, with regard to her role as worker, while it was exploitative, as it was for African American men, it is a mistake to argue, as Horton and others have done, that it "affronted [the] femininity" of the African American woman. In the West African cultures from which all African Americans came, women did most of the agricultural field work; the plantation emphasis on the woman as field worker merely reinforced a preexisting pattern of work and gender roles. The opposite was true of African American men, who experienced a sharp and utterly devastating break with preexisting patterns of work and gender roles.[20] The recent revisionist literature that attempts to underplay the destructive impact of slavery on male gender roles, even while continuing to denounce the sociological horrors of slavery, is not just contradictory but incredible, and cannot be taken seriously by a student of slavery.[21]

As for the role of mother, it was an added burden that provided its own partial relief, its own special rewards, and its own opportunities. Since "many slave mothers adhered to mores that made motherhood almost sacred, mores rooted in the black woman's African past,"[22] the slaveholder's emphasis on childbearing unwittingly reinforced the link with Africa. The slave woman had the love and support of her children and was more intimately tied into her network of kinsmen than the male slave, who had no rights whatever to his children, and in the final analysis no authority or recognized role as father, son, or provider (which is not to say that these roles were not informally pursued and defiantly sanctioned within the slave community itself). We continue to live with the consequences of this differential effect of slavery on gender roles, and I will return to the subject later.

Second, the African American woman has always had greater access to the wider, dominant White world in her roles as domestic, nanny, nurse, and clerk. As Fran Sanders has written, with little exaggeration, "For two hundred years it was she who initiated the dialogue between the White world and the African American."[23] Today we despise the job of domestic, but it is clearly wrong to project such attitudes onto the past. In spite of its unpleasant association with slavery and the often exploitative terms of employment, what African American and White domestics always hated was not the job itself but live-in domestic work. When done on a regular basis with civilized employers and a decent wage in both kind and money, it was a modestly secure job in which the African American woman, unlike her male counterpart in the fields or factories, "wielded an informal power that directly affected the basic human services provided within the White households."[24]

Domestic and other employment in the service sector also brought the African American woman into direct contact with the most intimate areas of the dominant culture. This intimacy was sometimes deepened by another factor peculiar to women: that in America, as in most human societies, women of different statuses and races can and often do establish close relationships, where men so separated cannot or will not. The knowledge thus acquired was valuable cultural capital, a point explicitly stated by many of the domestics interviewed by Bonnie Thornton Dill; these women "saw work as an ability rather than a burden. Work was a means for attaining [the domestic's] goals; it provided her with the money she needed to be an independent person, and it exposed her and her children to 'good' things—values and a style of life which she considered important."[25]

However, I strongly suspect that this cultural capital was selectively transmitted only to daughters and not to sons, for reasons that are complex but may have to do with the differing expectations Black mothers had of their daughters and sons. The less successful daughter could be expected to pursue a job as a domestic; the more successful daughter was expected to become a schoolteacher or nurse. In both cases, the cultural skills acquired from the dominant culture would be an asset. No such transmissions were considered important for lower-class boys, who were expected to do manual work. More research needs to be done on this subject, but there is some evidence that the same pattern continues today among the lower classes.[26]

It should also be noted, of course, that the dominant culture has always been more willing to accept Black women than Black men. Greater fear of Black men, induced by racist sexual attitudes,[27] and greater familiarity with Black women in the course of growing up, made it much easier for Black women to find jobs in clerical and later in professional White settings.

I think these attitudes and expectations still persist. Indeed, they may well be interacting with affirmative action to reinforce this traditional bias toward Black women. It is not simply that firms under pressure to meet affirmative action guidelines achieve both gender and racial targets when they employ Black women. Even more important, it has been found that in the professional and corporate world the intersection of race and gender benefits Black career women, compared not only with Black men but with White women. Corporate White men are less inclined to view Black women as sex objects, as women "out to get a husband," or indeed as women at all, and are therefore more inclined to take them seriously as fellow professionals. The highly successful Black women interviewed by Epstein almost all agreed that being female "reduced the effect of the racial taboo" against Blacks in corporate positions, and that the combination of being Black, female, and educated created a unique social space for them, enhancing their self-confidence and motivation.[28] Thus, ironically, when feminist academic bell hooks writes of Black women that it is "crucial to explore marginal locations as spaces where we can best become whatever we want to be," she is describing not only that which "pleasures, delights and fulfills [the] desire" of the radical professional Black woman but equally of her conservative bourgeois sisters in the interstices of the corporate structure.[29] Alas, it is precisely in those marginal locations that Black professional men tend to get crushed.

The Social Sources of the Gender Crisis among the Lower Class and the Underclass

While there is a gender crisis among all African Americans, we must clearly distinguish between the middle and working classes, on the one hand, and the underclass and disorganized lower class on the other. The crisis takes different forms and has different social sources in these two broad categories of African Americans.

Socialization patterns obviously play some part in explaining the growing discrepancy in male and female achievement, and especially the prevalence of self-destructive behavior among lower-class male adolescents. It defies good sense to argue, as such scholars as E. J. Smith[30] rather too oversensitively do, that there is no gender bias against males in the lower-class socialization process. The statistical evidence in regard to male child abuse in the Black underclass and lower class suggests the contrary.[31] In a recent study based on over six years of close participant observations, Carl H. Nightingale takes issue with the current conventional wisdom among sociologists and social psychologists that minimizes the importance of family background in explaining male youth violence in the ghetto. Nightingale agrees that there has been an overemphasis on household type as an explanatory factor. This variable indeed explains little, he correctly notes, and to emphasize it is to miss the main point: that the parenting of boys in the Black lower classes has become increasingly abusive. "Almost without exception," he writes, "parents have seen severe punishments—like prolonged isolation from friends, beatings, and other uses of force—as the best means to educate kids in values of social responsibility and respect for parents."[32] This tendency, he points out, is reinforced and legitimized by the traditional fundamentalist reluctance to spare the rod and spoil the child, by law enforcement agencies, by the courts and the prison system, and by primitive mainstream law-and-order rhetoric. The result is parental behavior that leaves boys with "hurtful and even traumatic memories."[33]

In contrast, mothers often have much warmer relations with their daughters, treating them as friends and helpmates and projecting onto them many of their unrealized ambitions. "The girl's instrumental role within the household," writes Lee Rainwater, "is an important part of her growing sense of identity as a woman-to-be. As her ability to function effectively increases, the recognition her mother gives her in this identity becomes more and more important to her. . . . Mothers generally seem to prefer their girls, in the sense that they have closer and more taken-for-granted relationships with them." Boys, on the other hand, "live in a more anxious and ambiguous situation. . . . their sense of solidarity with their mothers is not strong, and they do not acquire the girls' feeling that a recognized and valued identity is coming into being."[34]

The murderous aggressiveness and self-destructive violence of a disproportionate number of under- and lower-class Black men,[35] their hyperkinetic posturing and braggadocio, their misogynistic abuse of women and identification of manliness with impregnation and the abandonment of mothers,[36] are the modernized "cool pose" version of a brutal behavior complex going back to slavery.[37] It is of course exacerbated by the horribly depressed conditions of the ghetto. What's more, it is a pattern that darkly mirrors and is legitimized by the mainstream culture, not simply, as Paul Peterson thinks, because of declining mainstream support for familial, communal, and religious values,[38] but more paradoxically, as Nightingale brilliantly shows, precisely because of the mass media's glorification of the very *traditional* mainstream values of violence (cowboys?), sexuality (Madonna?), and cutthroat greed (Wall Street?).[39] As I have said, this behavior complex is not new, even if in certain of the larger, more media-saturated urban ghettos it is getting worse. Tragically, it is an inherited pattern, and like all behaviors transmitted from one generation to the next, it is reproduced through processes of socialization, through boys' experience growing up with mothers (and sporadic fathers) who are desperately overstressed, poverty-stricken, and physically overburdened, and whose childrearing behavior oscillates between seductive overindulgence and brutal abuse.

The other side of the coin is the effect on Black women, who, if they do not escape this horrendous cycle of socialization and male misogyny, adapt to it by developing childrearing attitudes that simply reproduce the entire disastrous course of mutual gender exploitation and violence. The violence of the mother toward her son is displaced in the violence of the son toward women, which is then reproduced in the violence of these women toward the sons they begin to generate while they are still children themselves, under the powerful influence of their own mothers.

The street culture and the home mutually reinforce and reproduce each other. As David A. Schulz observed, "A woman's experience of being exploited by men influences her attitude toward her son."[40] As a result, "in the ghetto the sexes are pitted against each other from an early age," and "mistrust is built into the socialization process very early in a child's life."[41] Carol B. Stack found that "many women tend to debase men and especially young boys, regarding them as inherently 'bad,' more susceptible to sin, drinking, going around with women."[42] This view is shared by the African American sociologist Charles Willie, who finds a fear of trust in the lower-class family, where there is "fierce loyalty" between mothers and offspring but "little love."[43] Not only are Black boys given conflicting messages about women, but as G. I. Joseph and other researchers have pointed out, so too are Black girls about men.[44]

One revealing finding from recent studies of young Black street-gang members is that they are attracted to these gangs because gang leaders become parent substitutes, providing them with the security, and sometimes care, they feel their mothers have failed to give them. This is forcefully demonstrated by the case of Terence, second child of LaJoe, the mother of the Chicago ghetto family so movingly portrayed by Alex Kotlowitz. Terence dearly loved LaJoe when he was young, and felt deeply betrayed and abandoned when she went on to have six more children. This was no ordinary case of sibling rivalry, for Terence saw clearly the implications of his mother's irresponsible childbearing: that she would have less time and energy to love him. When he left home at the age of ten to join a gang, LaJoe confronted the gang leader: " 'I want my son,' she told him. 'Terence is my son. He belongs to me,' Charles replied." Equally poignant was the case of Bird Leg, who, "his mother suspects, sought protection from the gang in the same way he sought love from his dogs."[45]

What is true of Chicago holds equally for Milwaukee. When Tony, a member of the Four Corner Hustlers, was asked, "What does being in a gang mean to you?" he replied, "Being in a gang to me means if I didn't have no family I'll think that's where I'd be. To me it's like community help without all the community. They'll understand better than my mother and father."[46]

The research on the role of gangs in the socialization of Black males dovetails with an intriguing finding recently reported by Bruce R. Hare. In his study of self-esteem among boys and girls, he found that unlike White youths, "Black boys scored significantly lower than their female counterparts in mathematics ability and achievement orientation and displayed a trend toward lower school self-esteem." The one area in which Black boys scored higher than girls, indeed on a par with White boys, was "non-school social abilities and higher peer self-esteem." In other words, young Black males felt good about themselves, in spite of their poor performance in school, not only because school meant little to them, but because they were much more concerned with developing their social abilities and because their really important significant others were not their mothers or teachers but their peer gang members.

Black underclass and marginal working-class girls, on the other hand, developed such enormous self-confidence from their socialization that they both performed better and realistically rated their school self-esteem higher than Black boys. What's more, their self-esteem, both in social abilities and in school-related activities, was higher than that of the White girls, who were in fact performing far better in school. Hare could only explain this difference in terms of the boost to their self-confidence the lower-class Black girls derived from so persistently outperforming their male counterparts. He further attributes this striking discrepancy not simply to the input of the school environment but to the "consequences of differentiated sex socialization within Black families."[47]

Another important difference concerns the obvious but infrequently recognized fact that during the tumultuous period of adolescence, girls' delinquent behavior is invariably rewarded by a closer, even more intimate bonding with the mother and other female relatives, not to mention the financial support of welfare payments, with their symbolic confirmation of adult status,[48] whereas boys' delinquent behavior results all too often in parental rejection and a jail term. We should not let our sympathy for the plight of the teenage mother, and especially of her infant, blind us to the fact that such practices are grossly delinquent acts, *and are so considered by lower-class Black adults*. Their long-term destructive consequences are far greater than the typical "cool pose" delinquencies of Black boys. Teenage childbearing is usually catastrophic for the life chances not only of the teenage mother, but for her own mother, who is further burdened just when she begins to look forward to relief from the trials of childrearing under poverty; for younger siblings of the teenage mother, who receive even less attention as their already burdened mother now takes on the role of grandmother;[49] but above all, for the unfortunate children teenage mothers bring into the world. Recent research demonstrates that the children of adolescent mothers are far more likely to have lower intelligence, to show poorer academic performance, and to drop out of school, and "are at greater risk of social impairment (e.g., poor control of anger, feelings of inferiority, fearfulness, etc.) and mild behavior disorders." Further, the sons of teenage mothers are more likely to be violent, to abuse drugs, and to engage in early sexual activity. Worst of all, the children of adolescent mothers are far more likely to become adolescent mothers themselves, thus perpetuating the pattern of poverty and destructive gender and parenting behavior.[50] This may be the single most important cause of chronic poverty among Blacks.[51]

We should also take account of two kinds of double messages that young Black men receive from women in their roles as mothers and mates, according to sociologists and psychologists. Phyllis Harrison-Ross and Barbara Wyden argue that lower-class Black women have an understandable ambivalence toward sex and men, which leads to abusive overreaction to normal displays of "healthy aggression" by their sons. At the same time, these mothers urge their sons to regard themselves as the "man of the house" from too early an age, thus pushing them to a premature sense of sexual maturity. "One part of [the double message] is: 'You hurry and grow up and take care of me the way your father never did. Be the man of the house.' And the other part is: 'You better grow up gentle and obedient and do everything I tell you.' " This double message generates enormous tension and produces feelings of both dependency and aggression, as well as excessive attraction to and repulsion from women.[52]

In the street culture men confront another double message from women. Kochman found that "rapping to a woman is a colorful way of 'asking for some pussy.' " The "mack man" who is good at "pimp talk" is a "person of considerable status in the street hierarchy."[53] Two other students of the street culture, Majors and Billson, also report that while Black lower-class women may declare that they dislike the cool style, they persistently send a double message to Black men by rewarding coolness.

> Black females are sometimes turned on by or attracted to Black males who act and look cool. Those males who do not act cool may suffer a heavy penalty of rejection. Some women are attracted to the urbane, emotionless, smooth, fearless, aloof, apparently masculine qualities of cool pose.[54]

The result is a marked absence of intimacy in gender relations.

For Black women who wish to develop intimate relationships with Black men who act and look cool, it is the cool pose that attracts them. Ultimately, these cool behaviors may prevent couples from establishing strong, committed, and authentic relationships. The games and masks, the highly stylized expression of self that makes the cool male attractive, are the very same artifices that inhibit intimacy and genuine companionship. [55]

Nightingale also informs us that while predatory sexuality is "distinctly gender specific" and is not required by young women for their feminine identity, they nonetheless "often take pride in their 'attitude.' " "Round-the-way" and other kinds of "nasty" girls not only fight rivals and goad men into violence but "pride themselves on sexual adventure and their ability to manipulate men." [56]

The childhood experiences of lower-class men, their chronic ambivalence and predatory attitudes toward women, and the pattern of mutual cynicism and distrust between the sexes are given full expression in the popular culture of lower-class Blacks, especially in the "verbal art" of signifying. [57] It is not accidental that one of the most commonly used terms in this culture, both in and out of ritual situations, is "motherfucker." Now, while I fully agree with my colleague Henry L. Gates that past interpreters have given undue attention to insult rituals, and that these constitute one form subsumed under the more general cultural style of signifying, [58] the fact remains that this particular ritual form is perhaps the most frequently enacted in the urban ghettos today, and the most distinctively African American. I know of no other cultural tradition outside the African American lower class where the trope "motherfucker" is so inscribed, not even the closely related Afro-Caribbean lower-class cultures, which have many similar insult rituals directed at the mother. [59] Further, we have it on Gates's authority that "Your Mamma" jokes "abound in black discourse, all the way from the field and the street to Langston Hughes." [60] The misogyny evident in the sexual style of contemporary ghetto youth and in rap music has deep roots in the traditional culture, as Lawrence Levine has shown. [61]

Consider the following from the St. Louis ghetto of the late sixties.

> I was walking in the jungle
> With my dick in my hand

I was the baddest mother fucker
In the jungle land.
I looked up in the tree
And what did I see?
Your little black mamma
Trying to piss on me.
I picked up a rock
And hit her in the cock
And knocked that bitch
A half a block.[62]

One could write a whole volume of interpretation on this single verse. What, for example, is the significance of the fact that in this, as in many other "joaning" and "dozens" rhymes, the mother has a "cock"? It is now *de rigueur* to deny that the antimaternal verbal content of the dozens and other Black tropes is in any way connected to problems in the actual mother-son relationship. I find this politically correct denial simply preposterous.[63] Recognizing the cultural assumptions of Freudian theory (as Freud, incidentally, did) does not commit one to the aridity of relativism. As Peter Blos has recently pointed out, Freud's real insight concerning the mother-son relationship lay in his emphasis on the problem of attachment and the need to overcome it; ironically, what makes Freud important here is less the Oedipal complex (which may well be a largely Euro-American bourgeois phenomenon) than his recognition of "the need of the growing [male] child to distance himself from the central female care person."[64] In every culture boys must find ways of resisting the pull of maternal dependency, and lower-class Black youth are no exception, any more, for example, than privileged Japanese youth who have reacted to the commuting father's vanishing role, and the resulting excessive dependence on and "psychological presence" of the mother, by taking to a pattern of juvenile delinquency with a pathological focus on mother beating and even matricide.[65]

What all the sociological and psychological research makes clear is that there is no provision within the lower-class pattern of child-rearing for the separation of the son from the mother. Those who deny that there is a serious problem here often make reference to extended networks of kinsmen and friends, but when the ethnographies are closely examined, we find that even when men, including natural fathers, attempt to help, they tend to do so through their own female relatives. It is the father's female kin who activate and assert paternal rights, if and when these rights are claimed: "Mothers expect little from the father; they just hope that he will help out. But they do expect something from his kin, especially his mother and sisters."[66] The prevailing dogma that effective father substitutes exist in the network of support that poor Black women mobilize to raise their male children is pure Afrocentric myth, as is the twin dogma that father absence does not matter anyway. Even in the stable working class Scanzoni was unable to find these consistent father substitutes among the small minority of his respondents with single-parent backgrounds: "either the father was not there, or if a father substitute was used by the child, he participated only minimally in these particular phases of the child's socialization."[67]

The lower-class male child of a single woman, then, has no assistance, no ally within the family, in his struggle to separate from his mother. The neglected clinical literature has documented the serious psychological consequences of this failure to separate, especially when the mother is neglectful or abusive. The case of Virgil, a troubled, anxious five-year-old analyzed by Meers, illustrates the problem.

> . . . he turns his aggression back on himself in a range of accidents and provoked punishments. . . . Virgil's masculinity has a profound sadistic base, and his compensating defenses have led to regressive, passive, effeminate accommodation. Virgil's dominant fears *are of his painful, emerging fantasies and dreams of being a girl.* Such passivity and effeminate inclinations, however, outrage his self-esteem, and his acting out appears as a chronic need to reestablish his sense of masculinity.[68]

It is thus easy to see the powerful attraction of the street gang and "cool pose" culture for under- and lower-class youth. The antimaternal abuse and promiscuous sexual and physical violence of the street culture act as a belated but savagely effective means of breaking with the mother. The androgynous figure in the dozens gives expression to the mother with the "cock" who also fathers, who claims to love the son yet debases the man he will become, who nurtures and brutally disciplines. At the same time, in its antimaternal misogyny, the street culture clobbers into deep repression the painful transsexual fantasies generated by the mother who is at once loved and feared, and whose psychological presence is overwhelming. The result is the "b-boy" (baad-boy) masculinity that brooks no "dissing," that "links gender identity with predatory violence" against women and seeks respect through murder and suicide.[69] The murder of fellow Black males, it should be further noted, is a pathologically gratifying way of gaining the approval of the internalized mother who reviles "rotten, no-good, 'motherfucking' men." And suicide is the ultimate high, especially in its "macho" guise, for in one fell swoop it wins the respect of peers, since the victim appears to have gone down gunning; it satisfies the internal impulse to be punished, as the inner mother dictates; it compels the attention and love of the outer mother, who recognizes at last what she has lost, even as it punishes her through the grief it is bound to cause; and not least, it expresses the frustrating self-loathing, sense of meaninglessness and worthlessness, and utter nihilism of growing up desperately poor, Black, brutalized, and neglected in late-twentieth-century America.

The disastrous, and rapid, social consequences of this psychocultural pattern are reflected daily in the newspapers, where we read the fate of all the little Virgils of the ghettos. Consider the recent case of Robert Sandifer, alias "Yummy," an underweight eleven-year-old boy from the South Side of Chicago, whose story could still shock a nearly jaded nation. He had been so severely beaten and burned with cigarette butts by his drug-addicted mother, who had had the first of seven children at the age of fifteen, that he had been taken from her by the Illinois Department of Children and Family Services and placed in the custody of his maternal grandmother, who had several minor children of her own and simply neglected him. He began accumulating a police record from the age of six and was already a hardened criminal and gang member by the age of ten. In mid-August 1994, Yummy, who once told a psychologist that life was like "serving time," emotionally exploded. He gave away his horde of stolen teddy bears to his siblings, got himself a gun, and two weeks later went on a shooting spree that resulted in the death of a fifteen-year-old girl and the wounding of two other teenagers. Several days later he was found dead, shot in the head by his fellow gang members, who feared that he would squeal on them if caught. Yummy's case is not an isolated one. Within days of his execution, another eleven-year-old Chicagoan was charged with the brutal murder of an old lady the previous year, when he was only ten. Since 1990, thirty-four children under fourteen, six of them between eleven and twelve, have been charged with homicide in Chicago alone. But one detail in the profile the police sent out on Yummy during their manhunt for him is as poignant as it is revealing. On the frail arm of this paternally abandoned and maternally abused child were tattooed the words "I LOVE MOMMY."

The Social Sources of the Gender Crisis among the Working and Middle Classes

It must be emphasized that the situation I have just described applies primarily to the bottom 30 percent or so of underclass and lower-class African Americans, though obviously not to all persons belonging to these groups.[70] I suspect that it also applies, to some extent, to marginal working-class people, and thus embraces perhaps some 35 percent of the Black population. The vast majority of middle-class and stable working-class African Americans themselves come from secure working-class or middle-class homes.[71]

Studies of the more prosperous segments of the Black population suggest that families function well in socializing children and indeed make extraordinary sacrifices to ensure their success in the wider society. Scanzoni, like Billingsley[72] before him, found no evidence of "female dominance" in these families. Nor did he find the slightest trace of a distinctively African American "ethnic family form." The middle-class and stable working-class Black family functions, in most respects, very much like its White counterpart, except that it is under greater financial strain, and must socialize its offspring to cope with the social and psychological cancer of racism.[73] McAdoo's study of middle- and lower-middle-class parenting styles among African Americans in the Baltimore-Washington area, for example, found that relations between mothers and children were "warm . . . loving and devoid of conflict," and that the children had high self-esteem.[74] And in a major comparative study of family dynamics in Black and White middle-class and secure working-class families in the Chicago area, Walter Allen found few really sharp differences between the races. Black mothers tended to occupy a more central position in their families, and their sons tended to identify strongly with them, even though they considered them somewhat less approving than White sons considered their mothers. However, this seems to have been good for the Black sons, who generally "sensed themselves to be in greater control of their lives" than White sons.[75] Middle- and working-class African American fathers also seem to be no less effective than their White counterparts in the socialization of their children, and one study even suggests that African American fathers behave in a manner that tends to make their daughters very independent,[76] though as we will see later, for reasons that are rather complex.

But the research also suggests that adult gender relations, including marriage, are far more problematic. Most middle- and working-class Blacks seem to view gender relations as fragile at best. In a study of 256 mainly working- and lower-middle-class African American students at Temple University, Cazenave and Smith asked respondents for their views on Michele Wallace's assertion that there was "distrust, even hatred, between Black men and women." Only 34 percent of the men and 26 percent of the women disagreed with this statement. What is more, the majority of respondents, men and women, agreed that "Black women seem to have many more opportunities than Black men."[77] Nor is this an isolated study. The Turners, for example, in their study of Black evaluations of future marital relations, found that most African American women considered most men less responsible, reliable, trustworthy, and happy. And while most Black men considered Black women "trustworthy," the researchers were forced to conclude that "Black females' views of relationships with Black men were laced with the anticipation of disappointment."[78]

Such attitudes are reflected in the serious deterioration of the institution of marriage among middle-class African Americans. An unusually large number of these marriages end in divorce, and even when they do not, there is evidence of an extraordinary degree of marital discord and dissatisfaction, especially among wives. One major study reported that the majority of residents of a solidly middle-class African American neighborhood in Atlanta described their marriages as "weak."[79] Black marriages are twice as likely to end in divorce as White marriages; indeed, Black divorce rates are the highest in the nation, and among the highest in the world. The racial difference is not explained by the greater proportion of African Americans in lower-class occupations, and only partly explained by differences in income distribution. Black men are still more than twice as likely to be divorced as White men when we control for educational attainment. And while there is a significant reduction in the racial difference when we control for income distribution, it is still substantial: 20 percent of all black men between the ages of thirty-five and forty-four have been divorced, compared with 11 percent of White males. The differences in divorce rates, controlling for education, are even greater when White and Black women are compared.[80] Clearly, there is a serious problem here that cannot be explained in terms of relative class and educational differences.

The findings of these various studies fit with what is, after all, the best evidence of what people actually think about marriage, namely, their willingness to practice it. It is hard to believe now, but in 1940 there were more married Black men between the ages of twenty-four and twenty-nine than married White men in the same age group (59 percent vs. 56 percent). By 1985–87 the proportion of married White men had declined by only four points, to 52 percent, while the figure for Black men had fallen to 35 percent.[81] The drop was almost as great for Black women. Mare and Winship have shown that diminished employment prospects for Black men can explain only 20 percent of this dramatic change, and growing school enrollment of Black men not a great deal more.[82] As Jencks points out, if the unavailability of steady jobs was the main factor in declining marriage rates among Black men, then we ought to expect no decline in the case of mature Black men with steady jobs, and if anything, an increase, since their marriageability should have been greatly enhanced. Yet we find just the opposite trend, the marriage rate of such men falling from 75 percent to 58 percent between 1960 and 1980.[83] Clearly, then, from what African Americans report about their attitudes, from their unwillingness to marry, and from the fragility of their unions when they do get married, it must be concluded that the institution is in serious trouble among all classes of Black people, especially the middle class, where it was always of far greater economic, social, and emotional significance.

What accounts for the relatively high rate of marital instability and dissatisfaction among middle-class Blacks? Two important structural factors recently emphasized are the increased economic independence of Black women and the scarcity of marriageable men.[84] It has long been established that divorce rates rise with the growing economic independence of women, and Black middle-class wives have always worked to a greater degree than their White counterparts. For married middle-class Black men, the large pool of marriageable women (the obverse of the female "marriage squeeze," there being only 772 men for every 1,000 middle-class Black women) is not only a constant source of temptation but heightens the probability that when discord arises in a marriage, as it inevitably does, men will leave their current wives for other women. This cry for help from a distraught wife, recently published in the *Essence* advice column of African American psychologist Dr. Gwen Goldsby Grant, may not be uncommon: "My husband is a successful attorney who is constantly the object of sexual advances from women who find him attractive. I get angry and feel totally out of control. How can I learn to handle my jealousy?"[85]

The tendency of Black men to divorce is intensified by the fact that so many middle-class Black women not only work full-time but often earn incomes much closer to the median male income than White women do. Consequently, the economic cost of divorce—traditionally a major disincentive—is likely to be much lower for middle-class Black men than for their White counterparts. Where, for example, the typical middle-class White male loses his home and all its comforts upon divorce, and must start all over again, the middle-class Black male divorcee can usually walk straight into the welcoming home of his career-established second wife-to-be. Black men between thirty-five and forty-four in fact remain divorced, widowed, or separated at a substantially lower rate than Black women of the same age group: only 25 percent, compared with 38 percent for Black women in 1980.[86]

Structural factors alone cannot explain these high rates of marital discord and dissolution. To understand more fully what is going on, we must take a closer look at attitudes toward, and the actual distribution of power in, interpersonal relations among African American couples, focusing on attitudes and behavior in three areas: the division of conjugal and familial tasks; the nature of sex-role differentiation, that is, stereotypes about traits that define maleness and femaleness; and views about the reasons for getting, and staying, married.

Nearly all studies on the subject report highly egalitarian attitudes toward the division of family tasks between husband and wife among both male and female respondents.[87] Closer examination of these attitudes, however, reveals a more complex pattern, fraught with conflict. In an excellent study of modes of interaction between Black lower- and middle-class couples in Los Angeles, DeJarnett and Raven paid special attention to the degree and *kind* of power sharing taking place among their respondents.[88] They confirmed previous findings that overall Black couples do indeed tend to be highly egalitarian in their interactions, and that in this regard there was little difference between lower- and middle-class Blacks. However, their highly sophisticated scales uncovered levels of tension not detected in earlier, less probing studies.

First, while there was a balance of authority between couples, this balance, contrary to what other surveys have found, rested on clearly demarcated spheres of authority in which each sex exercised complete control. To put it another way, there was a high level of sex segregation in which power was distributed separately but equally.

Second, when the researchers examined the nature and operation of male dominance ideology, they came up with a startling contradiction. They found that Black men of both classes, but especially the middle class, continued to hold highly sexist views about male dominance and women's place in the home and society at large. Seventy-one percent of middle-class Black men believed that husbands should have the final say in all matters, and 42 percent held the highly reactionary view that the idea of "women in authority" is "against human nature." On both scores, Black women strongly rejected these sexist views.

These responses point to a severe gender gap in the attitudes of middle-class Black men and women. There is a sharp contradiction between male dominance ideology and the egalitarian power relations Black husbands are actually obliged to live by. Indeed, the contradiction is even greater than it appears. DeJarnett and Raven found a significant relationship between male dominance ideology and the distribution of power in couples, but to the researchers' great surprise the relationship was *negative*. In other words, the stronger their commitment to male dominance ideology, the less power middle-class men actually had in their relations with their spouses.

DeJarnett and Raven were at a loss to explain this extraordinary finding. They concluded, rather cautiously, "It does suggest that there is indeed a discrepancy between how partners in Black couples influence one another and the ideal way in which they should influence one another." This is putting it very mildly. It seems to me that what we have here is evidence of severe tension between Black men and women, reflected in the very high rate of marital dissolution. Confirmation of this is found in Hatchett's study, which indicated that in spite of highly egalitarian attitudes, "marriages were also unstable if Black men felt their wives had equal power in the family."[89] Willie is right, then, that African American women may well be among the most ideologically liberated groups of women in America (except in one important area to be discussed shortly). What he fails to note is that middle-class Black men remain among the most traditionalist on gender matters. However, unlike White men, Black men have been prevented from actualizing their male dominance ideology by their determinedly emancipated spouses.

In combination with recent efforts to alleviate the racist past, racial discrimination, by imposing its added burden on Black women historically, has produced among them a strong sense of their own worth and capacities. The result has not been what used to be called, insultingly, Black "matriarchy" (there is no such thing, and it is doubtful whether a matriarchy ever existed anywhere) but Black female autonomy. In an exquisite Rousseauean twist, racism and class oppression have forced Black women to be free. Of course, they are yet to be fully free and equal in the society and economy at large, but their existentially generated ideology of liberation, along with their relatively greater labor force participation, has created a situation in which they can at least insist on equality within their own homes. Alas, they do so at a price.

As is well known, the same hostile forces that drove Black women to liberate themselves constrained Black men horribly. The civil rights and Black identity struggles did have a major impact on Black men's *racial* self-esteem, and some effect on their labor force participation, although gains in the latter eroded badly during the 1980s. Unfortunately, there is little evidence that these important struggles had much of an impact on Black men's personal self-esteem and gender attitudes. Indeed, one study came up with the disturbing finding that there is actually a negative relationship between Black ego development and Black racial identity, a finding that so distressed the researcher, who had been expecting just the opposite, that she promptly turned on her own fundamental concepts, condemning them as the racist product of a "White frame of reference."[90]

Nor did the Black civil rights and liberation movement influence Black male dominance ideology in a positive way. As bell hooks contends, Black political radicals, by equating their oppression with castration and emasculation, also came to identify freedom with manhood and sexual domination. In the process they took over the sexual metaphor of freedom from the very oppressors they claimed to be fighting, forging a bond with them: "They shared the patriarchal belief that revolutionary struggle was really about the erect phallus."[91] Hooks' argument is potent stuff, but not entirely ill-conceived. The most militant group of Black men, those belonging to the Black Muslims, openly acknowledge an extreme sexist view, and have persuaded Black Muslim women that this is in the best interest of the race, as the extraordinary recent diatribe by Shahrazadi Ali demonstrates.[92] But in a less overt way, and to varying degrees, the ideology of male dominance seems to prevail among many, perhaps most, middle-class Black men.

Moving next to the subject of sex-role differentiation, we again find severe conflict beneath an outwardly progressive pattern. In a probing study of upwardly mobile Blacks and Whites in Houston, Jim Millham and Lynette Smith found, overall, a much greater tendency among Blacks to minimize sex-role differentiation.[93] The White men and women differentiated between male- and female-specific gender traits to a considerable degree, both sexes agreeing on a large number of traits as being peculiarly masculine or feminine. Remarkably, apart from the tautologous choice of the words "masculine" and "feminine" as being appropriate to men and women, the Black respondents could only agree *together* on two traits as appropriate to a particular sex: they agreed that "bold" and "rugged" are appropriately masculine. Beyond that, there was no significant agreement between Black men and women concerning appropriately male or female traits, whether "aggressive," "businesslike," "cries without shame," "independent," "glamorous," or "helpless." But along with this welcome expression of Black female self-confidence, the researchers found two disquieting patterns in Black male attitudes. The first was that Black men identified twice as many traits as Black women "as being valued significantly more highly for one sex than the other." This is a major ethnic difference from Whites, who are in much closer agreement about gender-specific traits. However, when the sex-stereotyping traits of Black men are examined more closely, they turn out to be extremely conservative. For while their beliefs concerning gender equality were not highly interrelated,[94] what did emerge was a clearly defined dimension of attitudes about gender that described the wife's proper role "as bearer of her husband's children, as under his protection, and as an extension of his identity by taking his name."

The authors, then, would seem to misinterpret their own data—the only flaw in an otherwise cogent analysis—when they declare somewhat optimistically, "Black society seems to have developed a trait value system that permits and encourages more flexibility in the sharing and distribution of the economic and the nurturing dimensions of family life." Nothing of the sort. It is not "Black society" but Black *women* who have developed this flexibility, and it is their strong rejection of gender stereotyping that yields the high overall progressive Black score.

This is borne out by the other extraordinary finding on Black male gender attitudes. White men and women, both together and separately, tended to view "socially undesirable characteristics as more negative when possessed by a man than by a woman." It was quite different among Blacks. Black women, like White men and women, did not consider undesirable traits less offensive when found in men. Black men, however, held firmly to an egregious double standard, believing that undesirable behaviors were to be judged less harshly when practiced by men. The authors' comments on this double standard are so forcefully on the mark that they are worth quoting at length.

Thus within the present sample of Black Americans, men set lower standards of behavior for themselves than they set for women, *and lower standards than women set for men.* If these results are shown subsequently to have a broad generalizability across Black American culture, they indicate potential conflict for Black men between behavior and performance influenced by their value standards, and between the standards set for them by Black women and by the majority White society. . . . To the extent that other Black men ratify his perception of the seriousness of his behavioral transgression, [the Black man] may develop . . . *a view of women as inappropriately harsh or negative in their evaluation of him.* In a like manner, to the extent that many of these negative characteristics (e.g., cynical, forgetful, obstinate, over-confident, rebellious, suspicious, tactless, secretive) are focused upon in the economic and vocational sphere, the Black man may find himself angry about what he views as inappropriate and unduly harsh censure for negative behavior.[95]

Given their very modern (some might even say radical) rejection of gender stereotyping, there is one finding about Black middle-class women's attitudes (which they share with working-class Black women) that is initially quite puzzling. The National Survey of Blacks, in keeping with several other studies, found that for most Black women "being a mother and raising children is the most fulfilling experience a woman can have." Eighty-seven percent of all Black women held this view, a figure 5 percent greater than for their otherwise far more traditionalist male counterparts.[96] This closet of maternalism in a highly liberated structure of beliefs is a peculiarly African American complex that only the past can explain. I will return to it shortly.

Before I do, it is important to explore the reasons Black men and women give for living together, for here we come upon another contradiction. To a far greater degree than women, Black men feel that raising children, a good love life, and companionship are the main reasons for living together; women are more likely to mention financial security and other instrumental factors. It is striking that in Hatchett's study more than two and a half times as many men as women gave companionship as the main reason for having a relationship: 49 percent as against 19 percent. "All in all," comments Hatchett, "Black women seem to value the instrumental aspects of marriage—particularly financial security—more than Black men. Black men . . . place more emphasis on the socio-emotional aspects of living with the opposite sex."[97] Hatchett emphasizes one sociological "contradiction" or "lack of fit" in this disparity in attitudes: the fact that it exacerbates the "marriage squeeze," or the pool-of-marriageable-males problem.

One solution to this problem, of course, would be for Black women to marry less materially successful but stable and emotionally supportive working-class men "for love" and companionship. This is not an impractical or unusual occurrence in other ethnic groups and societies. For example, it was (and still is) a common practice among upwardly mobile women who remained in the mining towns of Wales and England, where there was also something of a middle-class marriage squeeze, to marry less educated miners and laborers. These women—schoolteachers, civil servants, postmistresses, and the like—came up through the educational system from the stable working class, and as such are directly analogous to recently upwardly mobile Black middle-class women. Basically, they chose to marry men who were like their fathers. (In fairness, I should add that not all these marriages achieved happiness, as the fictive biography of D. H. Lawrence, *Sons and Lovers*, graphically demonstrates.)

Why won't Black middle-class women consider marrying men who are like their fathers: those stable, economically secure paragons of hard work and paternal virtue, according to a long line of recent Black sociologists (almost all male with working-class backgrounds, it should be noted)? The answer lies in part in one of the most remarkable findings reported by John Scanzoni in his meticulous study of the family among stable working- and middle-class Blacks in Indianapolis. It concerns the identification of his respondents with their fathers. First, he found that only a minority of men (36 percent) and women (29 percent) from stable two-parent families positively identified with their fathers. A similar proportion of men (36 percent) and women (37 percent) negatively identified with their fathers: that is, the father was rejected as an ideal, becoming a counter-model, the kind of person they emphatically did not want to be. Scanzoni concurs with a tradition of social psychology that argues that there is nothing necessarily problematic in this, that indeed, in some cases, such negative identification may even be healthy. However, what is quite extraordinary about middle-class Blacks—and in this respect they are unique among American ethnic groups—is a related finding: that there was a positive relationship between rejection of the father and socioeconomic success. The relationship was very strong, and held even when Scanzoni controlled for class background, family composition, education, and—most puzzling of all—parental resources and support. That is, all other factors being constant, middle-class African Americans were more likely to succeed if they rejected their fathers during adolescence than if they identified with them under circumstances in which the father provided the warmest and most generous support the family could afford.[98]

I want to stress that this does not mean that women and men who identified with their fathers, or were indifferent to them, did not succeed. What it does mean is that the most successful women and men were those who had rejected their fathers as adolescents. To explain why this is so would involve an excursion into developmental psychology. It is enough to point out here that for whatever psychological reasons, there are especially strong factors working against the "marrying-down" solution to the "marriage-squeeze" problem facing middle-class Black women. The great majority of middle-class Black women, and especially the most successful, have rejected their fathers, and presumably would not want to marry men who remotely reminded them of this kind of male.

But there is a deeper problem. For even when Black middle-class women do find husbands from their own class, there is still the dilemma that the typical Black man yearns for companionship, emotional bonding, and support from his conjugal relationships, while the typical Black woman instrumentally searches for financial and other forms of security, a stark reversal of what one tends to find among White middle-class couples. And it is all the more peculiar when it is recalled that the one set of attitudes on which Black women consistently score more conservatively than Black men, or White women, concerns their views on mothering.

The Origins of the Crisis: Bringing Slavery Back In

Behind these curious sociological findings lies the deepest historical tragedy of Black men and women. In explaining them, we return to the centuries-long holocaust of slavery and its most devastating impact: the ethnocidal assault on gender roles and relations between Black men and women.

During the 1970s, a revisionist literature emerged in reaction to the earlier scholarship on slavery, which had emphasized the destructive impact of the institution on Black life. In its laudable attempt to demonstrate that the slaves, in spite of their condition, did develop their own unique patterns of culture and social organization, the revisionists went to the opposite extreme, creating what Peter Parish calls a "historiographical hornet's nest" that "came dangerously close to writing the slaveholder out of the story completely." Or as Peter Kolchin more bluntly puts it, the old myth of decimated Sambos and Aunt Jemimas with no social structures of their own was replaced by a new myth: "that of the utopian slave community." More recently, the excesses of this revisionist literature on slavery have been sharply challenged by a younger generation of counter-revisionists, most of whom, significantly, are feminist women scholars. These scholars have questioned not only the methodological flaws of the revisionists—such as the bias of their sources toward the atypical large plantations; the overemphasis on the nuclear household type; the relative neglect of the distribution of children across household types and the nature of their socialization; the failure to take account of the abundant evidence of violence and compensating patriarchalism in gender relations among slaves and freedmen; and the underplaying of the negative impact of the slaveholder class—but also what Susan Lebsock rightly condemns as the "conventional, androcentric value judgment" implicit in the revisionist assumption that female-headed families are inherently unhealthy.[99]

In light of these more recent studies, we can now make the following generalizations about the impact of slavery on gender roles and relations among African Americans. The slavemaster, while forcing Black women to be self-sufficient, attempted to reduce the Black male to the role of stud and worker. To be sure, it was in the interest of the slaveholder that couples stayed together, since this not only increased the fertility rate but acted as a powerful brake on the urge to resist or run away. But slaveholders thought nothing of treating men who were "fine and stout" as "stockmen" and "breeding niggers." There was certainly strong cultural resistance to these vile indignities from the great majority of slaves, and the evidence from interviews with ex-slaves, along with demographic data analyzed by cliometricians, strongly suggests that they did everything possible to maintain familial and kinship ties.[100] The result was that the majority of living units under slavery had an adult couple present, and such couples did have an impact on their children's quality of life. However, it must be emphasized that where the man was present, his role was always provisional, de facto, weak, and subject to sudden rupture. Against the Whites he could offer his children and his cohabitor no protection, no security, no status, no name, no identity. While this male vulnerability did not lead to "matriarchy," it did enhance the status of women in relation to their men, a change already set in motion by the peculiar circumstances of socialization on the plantation, where "most slave girls grew up believing that boys and girls were equal."[101]

What is extraordinary about the quantitative studies of slave families and unions is that they suggest a distribution very similar to what prevails today: that is, roughly two thirds of all family units had two parents present, exactly two thirds of ex-slave interviewees born before 1851 were "married," and about the same proportion of children grew up in these two-adult households.[102] Revisionist historians have concentrated on the two-thirds majority who stubbornly held on to familial and kinship ties, thus providing a degree of stability and cultural autonomy within the overarching, will-killing horror of the slave system. However, we need to know much more about the neglected bottom third of the slave population who were not in these more stable structures. This other group was also the concern of Du Bois and Frazier in their dual-family view of slavery, a view that the revisionists attacked but the most recent work on slavery seems to support.[103]

It is indeed remarkable how rapidly working- and middle-class Blacks overcame the worst aspects of slavery's familial and gender ethnocide. As early as 1937, on the basis of his detailed psycho-ethnographic studies of a typical southern town, psychologist John Dollard could write:

> It is unmistakable that middle-class Negroes have different conceptions of their roles from lower-class Negroes, and that these conceptions are nearer to the dominant American middle-class pattern. . . . However it may be among lower-class Negroes, in the life histories of the middle-class group the father plays a considerable role and the mother does not seem to play a disproportionately important one. The father seems to appear regularly as disciplinarian and as one who stresses restrictive aspects of the culture. It is very likely that families whose children emerge into the middle class have already a tradition and discipline which is superior to the mine run of lower-class Negroes, and, further, that the family form tends to approximate the white patriarchal type.[104]

In this passage we read a world of progress and effort, but we also detect the lingering shadows of the past. Black men reacted in two ways to the sociological mutilation of slavery. The lower-class reaction, which Dollard clearly distinguished and delineated in the thirties, and which is still very much with us, was to embrace, both defiantly and tomishly, the very role the White aggressor had forced upon them. The resulting anger and self-loathing found expression inwardly in the high incidence of depression among lower-class Black men, both in the rural South and in the modern ghetto,[105] and outwardly in violence against other Black men as well as sexual aggression against women. Significantly, the sexual aggression against women did not stop at mere compulsive sexuality; rather, we find throughout the decades of the rural South, and throughout the underclass today, the vicious desire to impregnate and abandon women, as if Black men were unable to shake off the one role of value (to the master) thrust upon them during slavery, that of breeders. Dollard, so much closer to the period of slavery than we are, was in no doubt that the aggressive and "disproportionate" sexuality of the lower-class blacks he observed and interviewed in the South was "a feature of [their] permissive slave culture."[106]

Recent historical work supports Dollard's viewpoint. In her detailed study of the slave family in Louisiana, Ann Patton Malone found frequent "reports of domestic violence in planters' records involving slave men against their wives," and attributed this violence to the "overwhelming sense of powerlessness and impotence which threatened the male's concept of his manhood and fatherhood."[107] A simpler explanation is the brutality and pervasive violence of slavery itself, which corroded all human relations, especially those between physically stronger and weaker persons. Tragically, this pattern of violence against the more vulnerable extended to children, as Brenda Stevenson notes.

> The violence and brutality that whites imposed on their slaves undoubtedly influenced the ways in which bondsmen and bondswomen reared their own children. The ability to beat someone, to hold that kind of physical control over another human, was a sadistic expression of power that blacks learned repeatedly from their interaction with, and observation of, white authority figures.[108]

The beatings, she adds, were meant to show the children just who was in control, and thus could be seen as a pathetic defiance of White authority. The same held for spousal abuse by men. This chain of violence, according to the testimony of the slaves, extended right down the pecking order to children themselves, who in their games often simulated, and sometimes actually performed, the whipping of playmates, girls no doubt getting the bitter end of the stick, like their adult counterparts.[109]

Today one sees exactly the same pattern of violence in the households and streets of any ghetto. The underclass male is not a Don Juan but a stud, exactly like his slave ancestor. His behavior, reproduced in socialization, is a collective psychosis, a historical addiction to a collective racial trauma, similar in origin to the counterphobic attraction of a drug addict to the drug he once deeply feared and loathed. As Kohut writes, "He cannot overcome the original fear, and so he continuously covers it up, to himself and to the judging social surrounding, by proving not only that he is not afraid of it but that, on the contrary, he loves it. Little Hans has become a jockey."[110] The under- and lower-class Black man now idealizes what once dehumanized him, internalizes what once externalized him as a mere sexual object, invests his manhood in the very thing that once emasculated him. Little Sambo has become a badass dude.

But middle-class Blacks did not escape unscathed, and no amount of celebration of the strength and resilience of Black marriages and families is going to hide the cracks left by the seismic shocks of slavery and racial oppression. From Dollard's observations in the thirties, it was already obvious what one of the problems inherited from the past would be: Black male dominance ideology. Where the lower-class Black reacted to the trauma of the past by pathologically internalizing the perverse role assigned him, with all its destructive consequences, the middle-class Black reacted in two ways. One was a healthy venting of his anger against the White oppressor in social and political action, on both the individual and collective levels, often at great risk to himself since he was always outnumbered and outgunned. Black radicalism and the achievement of civil rights, full citizenship, and racial dignity against all odds, a struggle fought by women as well as men, must rank as one of the greatest episodes in the modern history of freedom.

The other kind of reaction was more problematic. In casting off the hateful gender role assigned the Black man, middle-class Blacks both positively and negatively identified with the White paternalistic aggressor. The more conservative, positive identification took the form of an internalization of the White oppressor's own male ideal in his relationship with White women. The middle-class Black strove to outdo the "best" that White elite men had to offer their own women. That "best" ideology, of course, was to spell trouble for Black women, as it had for southern elite White women, for it was nothing other than the courtly tradition of genteel male dominance. The Black woman was to be protected, to be cherished, even to be placed on a pedestal; and Black men could graciously pay lip service to equality (as they have in superficial telephone surveys) as long as women knew and kept their place in the exercise of power both in and out of the household. But as we have seen, unlike White women, Black women refused to conform to this genteel paternalistic tradition either in their attitudes or in their behavior.

It is remarkable that this pattern of imitative patriarchal behavior was already well formed among the free northern Blacks of the early nineteenth century. As Horton shows, Black women were systematically excluded from the public spheres of politics and religious leadership by their Black male counterparts, and gender attitudes were slavishly modeled on White bourgeois norms. As with the majority White group, "manhood and freedom were tied to personal power," which within the household meant power over spouses who were expected to be models of female rectitude.

All women were expected to defer to men, but for black women deference was a racial imperative. Slavery and racism sought the emasculation of black men. Black people sought to counter such effect. Part of the responsibility of black men was to "act like a man," and part of the responsibility of black women was to "encourage and support the manhood of our men. . . . never intimidate him [the black man] with her knowledge or common sense, let him feel stable and dominant." [111]

Then as now, gender realities were inconsistent with these patriarchal ideals. Not only did early-nineteenth-century Black women vigorously protest their exclusion from positions of public leadership, but their relatively greater economic independence meant that they could effectively prevent men from actualizing their gender stereotypes. To the degree that women conformed to the role expectations of the times, they did so largely of their own choosing, and one wonders how emotionally attached they were to these outward shows of bourgeois female behavior.

But there was also a negative assimilation of the White oppressor's gender ideal. Here the middle-class Black man angrily rejected the White gender ideal as a model, claiming that nothing good could come from an oppressor so vile. What replaced the White paternalistic ideal, however, was not a counter-ideal of genuine gender equality but the male dominance ideology discussed earlier. Sometimes male dominance has been rationalized as part of a nationalist ideology of "nigrescence" or Africanness, sometimes as a dangerous pseudo-radical expression of unity with the lower-class brothers through a glorification of their pathological hip-hop sexuality. This tragic embourgeoisement of lower-class promiscuity has been encouraged, on the one hand, by the fact that many of the leading figures in the Black radical movement themselves came up from the lower classes, Eldridge Cleaver and his execrable *Soul on Ice* being the most notorious case in point; and on the other hand, by Black race-leaders of middle- or solidly working-class backgrounds who in their partly guilt-driven, partly self-interested desire for solidarity with the most oppressed Blacks found it psychologically only too easy to reject the courtly paternalism of their own fathers. Whatever its source, this ideology of masculinity spelled even more trouble and contradiction for middle-class Black women.

But the problems of coming to terms with the tragic legacy of slavery were not confined to Black men. We also see the footprints of the past in the contradictions in Black women's gender attitudes and behavior. It was during the period of slavery that the egalitarianism of the modern middle-class Black family and the autonomy of Black women were fashioned, as Deborah White convincingly argues.

> The nature of plantation life required that marital relationships allow slave women a large degree of autonomy. Marriage did not bring the traditional benefits to female slaves. As we have seen, slave women could not depend on their husbands for protection against whipping or sexual exploitation. Slave couples had no property to share, and essential needs like food, clothing, and shelter were not provided by slave husbands. Thus slave men could not use the provision of subsistence goods as leverage in the exercise of authority over women. In almost all societies where men consistently dominate women, their control is

based on male ownership and distribution of property and/or control of certain culturally valued subsistence goods. The absence of such mechanisms in slave society probably contributed to female slave independence from slave men.[112]

Black women's unexpected valorization of mothering as the most fulfilling role for women, so seemingly out of tune with their other, highly modern gender views, can only be explained in terms of the long years of struggle during slavery and its aftermath. The heroic commitment to the preservation of the race, both culturally and socially, entailed an extreme valorization of mothering and security, independent of any support from the dishonored roles of "husband" and "father." While slave families "were egalitarian," White concludes, "relationships between mother and child still superseded those between husband and wife. Slaveholder practices encouraged the primacy of the mother-child relationship, and in the mores of the slave community motherhood ranked above marriage."[113] And she shows too that it was under the impact of slavery that romance, though cherished, as often as not had to give way to "pragmatic considerations."[114]

It is remarkable that the set of attitudes sociologists have identified among modern middle-class Black women is already fully evident in the life of slave, freedom fighter, and feminist Harriet Jacobs. Jacobs (Linda, in her *Incidents in the Life of a Slave Girl*) never sexually consummated her relationship with her only "love-dream," the free-born "young colored carpenter" who courted her, but instead established a companionless concubinage of convenience with the White attorney Samuel Tredwell Sawyer (Mr. Sands), by whom she had two children, expecting "security" for them and the ultimate "boon" of freedom. Her epic struggle for freedom, first for herself, then for her children and for all Blacks, was counterpoised by her deep filial love for her mother substitute—she was "grandmother's child"—and her devotion to her children, especially her daughter, Louisa Matilda. An intelligent, beautiful woman who must have had many suitors, Jacobs never married, even though she was freed at the age of thirty-nine and lived for another forty-five years; it is also noteworthy that in sharp contrast to her strong lifelong bond with Louisa Matilda, both her brother, Joseph, and her son of the same name were lost to the family.

In this regard, Jacobs was not unusual. There was already a "marriage squeeze" for free middle-class Black women in both the South and the North in the early nineteenth century. For the Black women of Petersburg, "it was not unusual to refrain from marriage, thereby retaining their legal autonomy," quite apart from the shortage of free Black men with adequate incomes. Those who did marry often regretted doing so. "There was a relatively high degree of open antagonism between the sexes," writes Lebsock. "Free black women had relatively little cause to defer to their men, and the result may have been a substantial amount of conjugal conflict." One husband terminated an argument over who should preside at the table by hitting his wife over the head with an iron bar.[115] In the North during this same period, according to Horton, "many black women remained single or postponed marriage while they pursued a career in business or reform." Middle-class Black aunts, in sharp contrast with their White counterparts, rather than cajoling their nieces into marriage, would condemn the institution as "a waste of time." And those nieces who did marry were sometimes bitter about their lot, one of them complaining about the "grievous trials" and "painful results" of her mistake.[116] Harriet Jacobs, then, like her counterparts today, had good reason to remain single.

Conclusion: The Gendered Burden of History

This, then, is what we have inherited: a lower class with gender attitudes and behaviors that are emotionally and socially brutalizing and physically self-destructive; the posturing, pathological narcissism of "cool pose" masculinity, with its predatory, antimaternal sexuality, soul-numbing addictions, and murderous, self-loathing displacements; the daily and nightly carnage on the streets of the inner cities; the grim statistics on child and spousal abuse, rape, poverty, illiteracy, and suicide. These are the gruesome manifestations of this historically, sociologically, and psychologically en-gendered crisis between lower-class Black men and women.

And this: a middle class with one of the most contradictory and incompatible sets of gender attitudes, both within and between the sexes, anywhere on earth; the mismatch between the most liberated and autonomous of women and some of the most sexist and self-excusing of men; women in search of security frustrated by men wanting indulgence for their insecurities and female compensation for the daily wounds of being male, bourgeois, and Black; the dismal marriage market that confronts middle-class Black women, and the exceedingly high rates of marital discord, dissatisfaction, and dissolution if and when they do get married; the anger, the excuses, the betrayals, the denials. These are the painful consequences of this tragically conflicted set of gender relations and attitudes.

In closing, let me stress that nothing I have said should be taken to imply a conservative approach to social policies. Americans of all ideological persuasions now seem to insist on a monolithic approach to the resolution of social issues. Any demand for a universal welfare state immediately provokes neoconservative rhetoric about the neglect of individual agency. On the other hand, any reference to the ways in which dysfunctional parenting and childrearing practices are generative of Black poverty and self-destruction immediately elicits the Black and White liberal charge of "blaming the victim."

It is time we rid ourselves of this either-or dogma. Changes are essential on both the structural and policy level and on the individual and cultural level. While all these levels always have to be taken into account, the one we emphasize will depend on the nature of the problem we are addressing. In regard to the problem of gender relations, there can be no doubt that change in such an intimate, complex, and ideologically fraught area of Black life must emphasize behavioral factors, individual will, and cultural, moral, and attitudinal transformations. Needless to say, such transformations in no way assume as a model traditional bourgeois norms and ideals, which are themselves in a state of disarray, as Edward M. Levine has recently observed.[117] I share Na'im Akbar's skepticism of the "Eurocentric model," of gender relations, although his suggestion of a "new man" based on the "African traditional healer—herbalist, griot and psychic"–is not only Afrocentric mumbo-jumbo but dangerous talk in light of the devastating AIDS epidemic that traditional African male sexual mores have inflicted on the continent.[118] And while it is true that we must work from present realities and present gender and familial patterns, it is perhaps defensive and counterproductive to emphasize the "resilience" and "strength" of "the black family" and gender relations at a time such as this.[119]

What Toni Cade wrote some twenty-five years ago, drawing on the social psychology of Frantz Fanon, is still powerfully relevant today.

> Revolution begins with the self, in the self. The individual, the basic revolutionary unit, must be purged of poison and lies that assault the ego and threaten the heart, that hazard the next larger unit—the couple or pair—that jeopardize the still larger unit—the family or cell—that put the entire movement at peril.[120]

Black men and women of all classes have a poisoned relationship. Slavery and the system of racial oppression brewed and injected that poison, and poverty and racism sustain it. But blaming these injustices alone will get us nowhere. Not only because it is we who now inject the poison in our own mis-gendered souls, through the ways we bring up our children, through the ways we relate, or fail to relate, to each other, through the values we cherish and the ones we choose to spurn, but because only we as individual men and women can find the antidote and heal ourselves. We can only reclaim ourselves by first reclaiming our past, individually and collectively. And we can only reclaim our past by returning to its traumatic source, and in an orphic grasp of self-liberation come to say, as the widow of Malcolm X said recently at Harvard, that everything we are, and have been, is all "because of us."

If I am correct in thinking that a full recognition of the Black gender crisis, and its promotion to the top of the agenda of issues for dispassionate study, public discourse, and change, have been another consequence of the Thomas-Hill hearings, it would indeed be these hearings' most significant legacy to the communities of Black people in America.

Notes

1. Crenshaw, "Whose Story Is It, Anyway?" in Toni Morrison, ed., *Race-ing Justice, En-gendering Power* (New York: Pantheon, 1992), 403.
2. Dugger, "Social Location and Gender-Role Attitudes: A Comparison of Black and White Women," in Judith Lorber and Susan A. Farrell, eds., *The Social Construction of Gender* (Newbury Park, Calif.: Sage, 1991), 38–59.

3. Orlando Patterson, "Toward a Study of Black America: Notes on the Culture of Racism," *Dissent*, Fall 1989, 476–86.

4. It may even be, as William Julius Wilson claims, of declining significance for some Blacks, and it is certainly true that White attitudes toward Blacks have changed dramatically over recent decades. Yet racism is still too pervasive to proclaim its decline, even if Wilson's main point is granted, that for the mass of Black poor the fundamental problem is their economic irrelevance in a structurally changed economy. See Wilson, *The Declining Significance of Race* (Chicago: Univ. of Chicago Press, 1978); see also Thomas Pettigrew, "Race and Class in the 1980s: An Interactive View," *Daedalus* 110 (Spring 1981).

5. Wallace, *Black Macho and the Myth of the Superwoman* (New York: Dial Press, 1978). See also Robert Staples, "The Myth of Black Macho: A Response to Angry Black Feminists," *Black Scholar*, March–April 1979, 24–32; and the special issue of the *Black Scholar*, "Black Male/Female Relationships," May–June 1979, 14–67.

6. Bell hooks, *Yearning: Race, Gender, and Cultural Politics* (Boston: South End Press, 1990), 5, 17.

7. There is, of course, a vast and growing body of academic studies of the African American family, as well as more specific works on sex roles and self-esteem, upon which I draw in what follows. However, while many of these works refer to the problem of gender relations, surprisingly few are exclusively or even primarily concerned with this problem. A major academic study of Black gender relations that also takes account of class and regional variations in the population is yet to be written.

8. Jacobs, *Incidents in the Life of a Slave Girl, Written by Herself* (Cambridge: Harvard Univ. Press, 1987), 77. Cf. Frances Beale, "Double Jeopardy: To Be Black and Female," in Toni Cade, ed., *The Black Woman* (New York: New American Library, 1970), 90–100; hooks, *Yearning*, 101–2; and Pamela J. Smith, "All-Male Black Schools and the Equal Protection Clause: A Step Forward toward Education," *Tulane Law Review* 66, no. 6 (1992): 2025–27.

9. Crenshaw, "Whose Story," 404.

10. On these attitudes, see Elijah Anderson, *Streetwise* (Chicago: Univ. of Chicago Press, 1990), chap. 4; and Richard Majors and Janet Mancini Billson, *Cool Pose: The Dilemmas of Black Manhood in America* (Lexington, Mass.: Lexington Books, 1992), 93–95.

11. See Irwin Garfinkel and Sara S. McLanahan, *Single Mothers and Their Children: The New American Dilemma* (Washington, D.C.: Urban Institute Press, 1986); National Research Council, *Risking the Future: Adolescent Sexuality, Pregnancy, and Childbearing* (Washington, D.C.: National Academy Press, 1987); Diane Pearce, "The Feminization of Poverty: Women, Work and Welfare," *Urban and Social Change Review* 11, nos. 1/2 (1978): 28–36.

12. Research on the degree to which nonmarital childbearing has become nor-

mative among lower-class African American adolescents yields conflicting results. Furstenberg found that the great majority of adolescent girls and their mothers viewed such childbearing negatively, but his data come from the mid-seventies: *Unplanned Parenthood: The Social Consequences of Teenage Childbearing* (New York: Free Press, 1976). Other, more recent research suggests a growing acceptance and positive desire for children at an early age. See National Research Council, *Risking the Future*, 117–18; Garfinkel and McLanahan, *Single Mothers*, 79–85; and Lena Wright Myers, *Black Women: Do They Cope Better?* (Englewood Cliffs: Prentice Hall, 1980), 39–40.

13. W. J. Wilson and K. M. Neckerman, "Poverty and Family Structure: The Widening Gap between Evidence and Public Policy Issues," in W. J. Wilson, *The Truly Disadvantaged* (Chicago: Univ. of Chicago Press, 1987), 83–92.

14. Jewelle Taylor Gibbs, ed., *Young, Black, and Male in America: An Endangered Species* (New York: Auburn House, 1988); Wilson, *The Truly Disadvantaged*, chap. 2; Richard B. Freeman, "Employment and Earnings of Disadvantaged Young Men in a Labor Shortage Economy," in Christopher Jencks and Paul E. Peterson, eds., *The Urban Underclass* (Washington, D.C.: Brookings Institution, 1991), 103–21; Majors and Billson, *Cool Pose*, chap. 2.

15. J. T. Gibbs and A. M. Hines, "Factors Related to Sex Differences in Suicidal Behavior among African-American Youth," *Journal of Adolescent Research* 4, no. 2, 152–72.

16. R. H. Seiden, "We're Driving Young Blacks to Suicide," *Psychology Today* 4 (1970): 24–28.

17. The discrepancy has not gone unnoticed by all Black women, as Pamela Smith's paper (see note 8 above) clearly indicates. In a personal communication after a lecture based on an earlier draft of this paper, Professor Smith said, "I do not, however, believe that the Black community should put the Black female on hold forever." I go further: the Black woman cannot and should not be placed "on hold" for anyone, at any time. Gender problems in the Black community can only be solved simultaneously for both sexes.

18. White, *Ar'n't I a Woman?* (New York: Norton, 1985), 110. This excellent study brings a badly needed womanist perspective to American slave studies, and is sharply critical of the paternalistic bias in recent revisionist works. For further evidence of the matrifocality of the slave family, even where the two-parent pattern was technically present, see Cheryll Ann Cody, "Naming, Kinship, and Estate Dispersal: Notes on Slave Family Life on a South Carolina Plantation, 1786 to 1833," *William and Mary Quarterly* 39 (1982), esp. 208–11; and Thomas Webber, *Deep Like the Rivers* (New York: Norton, 1978), 159–65.

19. White, *Ar'n't I a Woman*, 161.

20. See James Oliver Horton, "Freedom's Yoke: Gender Conventions among Antebellum Free Blacks," *Feminist Studies* 12, no. 1 (Spring 1986): 53 (an

otherwise excellent paper); cf. Jacqueline Jones, "My Mother Was Much of a Woman: Black Women, Work, and the Family Under Slavery," *Feminist Studies* 8 (Summer 1982): 235–69. On the role of women in the traditional West African societies from which the American slaves came, see Melville J. Herskovits, *The Myth of the Negro Past* (Boston: Beacon Press, 1958), 167–86.

21. This wholly misguided revisionist literature commits what I have called the fallacy of demographic reification—confusing the mere demographic presence of the male progenitor (not infrequently forced upon the woman by the master) with the father-husband role. The contemporary literary data and a vast body of interviews with ex-slaves leave us in no doubt about the ethnocidal impact of slavery on the meaning and roles of father and husband, and fully support the classic interpretation of Franklin E. Frazier's *The Negro Family in the United States* (Chicago: Univ. of Chicago Press, 1939). For the standard revisionist study, see Herbert G. Gutman, *The Black Family in Slavery and Freedom, 1750–1925* (New York: Pantheon, 1976). Even so distinguished a scholar as Frank Furstenberg, with no expertise on the subject of slavery, has joined ranks with this academic travesty. See Furstenberg et al., "The Origins of the Female-Headed Black Family: The Impact of the Urban Experience," *Journal of Interdisciplinary History* 6, no. 2 (1975): 211–33. On the recent counter-revisionist literature, see note 99 below.

22. White, *Ar'n't I a Woman*, 68–69, 106.

23. Sanders, "Dear Black Man," in Cade, *The Black Woman*, 73.

24. Jacqueline Jones, *Labor of Love, Labor of Sorrow* (New York: Basic Books, 1985), 134.

25. Dill, " 'The Means to Put My Children Through': Child-Rearing Goals and Strategies among Black Female Domestic Servants," in La Frances Rodgers-Rose, ed., *The Black Woman* (Beverly Hills: Sage, 1980), 115.

26. See P. J. Bowman and C. Howard, "Race-related Socialization, Motivation, and Academic Achievement: A Study of Black Youths in Three-generation Families," *Journal of the American Academy of Child Psychiatry* 24, no. 2 (1985): 131–41. Diane K. Lewis admits that there was a strong preference for and greater tendency to promote girls in the past, but speculates that with growing economic opportunities for men this should change: "The Black Family: Socialization and Sex Roles," *Phylon* 36, no. 3 (1975): 221–31. Recent developments have not supported her prediction.

27. For the classic exploration of such racist fears and fantasies about Black men, see John Dollard, *Caste and Class in a Southern Town* (New York: Doubleday Anchor, 1949), 160–63, and more generally, chaps. 15–16.

28. Cynthia F. Epstein, "Positive Effects of the Multiple Negatives: Explaining the Success of Black Professional Women," *American Journal of Sociology* 78 (1973): 912–35.

29. Hooks, *Yearning*, 20, 153.

30. Smith, "The Black Female Adolescent: A Review of the Education, Career,

and Psychological Literature," *Psychology of Women Quarterly* 6, no. 3, 261–88.

31. See Robert L. Hampton, ed., *Violence in the Black Family: Correlates and Consequences* (Lexington, Mass.: Lexington Books, 1987); Richard Dembo, "Delinquency and Black Male Youth," in Gibbs, *Young, Black, and Male*, 140–42, 152–53. See also E. M. Kinard and L. V. Klerman, "Teenage Parenting and Child Abuse: Are They Related?" *American Journal of Orthopsychiatry* 59, no. 3 (1980).

32. Nightingale, *On the Edge: A History of Poor Black Kids and Their American Dreams* (New York: Basic Books, 1993), 76.

33. Ibid., 77.

34. Rainwater, *Behind Ghetto Walls* (Chicago: Aldine, 1970), 221.

35. See, especially, Gibbs, *Young, Black, and Male*, chaps. 4 and 8.

36. Jo-Ellen Asbury reports that the incidence of wife abuse among Blacks is four times greater than for any other ethnic group, although she correctly points out that poverty explains a good deal of this abuse: "Black Women in Violent Relationships," in Hampton, *Violence in the Black Family*, 89–105.

37. On the "cool pose" culture today, see Majors and Billson, *Cool Pose*, esp. chaps. 2–3; and Anderson, *Streetwise*, chap. 5. On the history of underclass violence, see Roger Lane, *Roots of Violence in Black Philadelphia, 1860–1900* (Cambridge: Harvard Univ. Press, 1986), esp. chaps. 4–6. On the tradition of "bad men and bandits" in lower-class Black culture, see Lawrence Levine, *Black Culture and Black Consciousness* (New York: Oxford Univ. Press, 1979), 407–20.

38. Paul E. Peterson, "The Urban Underclass and the Poverty Paradox," in Peterson and Jencks, *The Urban Underclass*, 19.

39. Nightingale, *On the Edge*, esp. chaps. 5–6. The point is also made by Mitchell Dunier, *Slim's Table: Race, Respectability, and Masculinity* (Chicago: Univ. of Chicago Press, 1992), 127.

40. Schulz, *Coming Up Black* (Englewood Cliffs: Prentice Hall, 1969), 64.

41. Ibid., 175–80.

42. Stack, *All Our Kin* (New York: Harper and Row, 1974), 111.

43. Willie, "The Black Family and Social Class," in Robert Staples, *The Black Family: Essays and Studies* (Belmont, Calif.: Wadsworth, 1978), 240.

44. Joseph, "Black Mothers and Daughters: Traditional and New Populations," *Sage: A Scholarly Journal on Black Women* 1, 2 (1984): 17–21.

45. Alex Kotlowitz, *There Are No Children Here* (New York: Doubleday, 1991), 85.

46. John M. Hagedorn, *People and Folks: Gangs, Crime, and the Underclass in a Rustbelt City* (Chicago: Lakeview Press, 1988), 131.

47. Hare, "Reexamining the Achievement Central Tendency: Sex Differences within Race and Class Differences within Sex," in Harriette Pipes McAdoo and John McAdoo, *Black Children: Social, Educational, and Parental Environments* (Beverly Hills: Sage, 1985), 139–55.

48. On which, see F. F. Furstenberg, "Burden and Benefit: The Impact of Early Childbearing on the Family," *Journal of Social Issues* 36, no. 1 (1980): 64–87. Cf. C. J. Poole, M. S. Smith, and M. Hoffman, "Mothers of Adolescent Mothers," *Journal of Adolescent Health* 3 (1982): 28–31.

49. Roger Rubin's work carefully demonstrates that while the lower-class single-mother Black family can be very supportive for the child under certain circumstances, the crowding of the household with too many family members has immediate damaging effects on the personality development of younger children. See his *Matricentric Family Structure and the Self-Attributes of Negro Children* (San Francisco: R & E Research Associates, 1976).

50. National Research Council, *Risking the Future*, 134–38.

51. Let me be clear on this matter. The issue is *not* high fertility, for if anything, this rate is stable generally, and declining precipitously among middle-class Blacks. Nor is the issue that of out-of-wedlock marriages, since the increasing proportion of out-of-wedlock births in the Black population is accounted for almost entirely by the decline in birth rate among married Blacks and the increase among Blacks of the category of "never married" women.

52. Harrison-Ross and Wyden, *The Black Child: A Parent's Guide* (New York: Peter Wyden, 1973), 237.

53. Thomas Kochman, "Toward an Ethnography of Black American Speech Behavior," in Thomas Kochman, ed., *Rappin' and Stylin' Out: Communication in Urban Black America* (Urbana: Univ. of Illinois Press, 1972), 243.

54. Majors and Billson, *Cool Pose*, 43.

55. Ibid.

56. Nightingale, *On the Edge*, 31.

57. Claudia Mitchell-Kernan, "Signifying, Loud-talking, and Marking," in Kochman, *Rappin' and Stylin' Out*, 315–35. See also the classic study by Roger D. Williams, *Deep Down in the Jungle: Negro Narrative Folklore from the Streets of Philadelphia* (Hartboro, Pa.: Folklore Associates, 1964).

58. Gates, *The Signifying Monkey: A Theory of African American Literary Criticism* (New York: Oxford Univ. Press, 1988), 80–81.

59. On which, see Roger Abrahams, "Joking: The Training of the Man of Words in Talking Broad," in Kochman, *Rappin' and Stylin' Out*, 215–40.

60. Gates, *The Signifying Monkey*, 66.

61. Levine, *Black Culture and Black Consciousness*, 347. Levine notes that the mother is "a favorite though not invariable target."

62. Cited in Rainwater, *Behind Ghetto Walls*, 278. Majors and Billson, who also cite this rhyme, fail to note that it was "joaned" to the researcher by a girl. However, this is consistent with the second kind of double message I have discussed, which they themselves report.

63. Not all students of the subject have buckled under the pressure to conform to the dogma that father absence means nothing. See, for example, J. Badaines, "Identification, Imitation, and Sex-role Preference in Father-present

and Father-absent Black and Chicano Boys," *Journal of Psychology* 92 (1976): 15–24; and L. L. Hunt and J. G. Hunt, "Race and Father-Son Connection: The Conditional Relevance of Father Absence for the . . . Identity of Adolescent Boys," *Social Problems* 23, no. 1 (1975): 35–52.

64. Blos, "Freud and the Father Complex," *Psychoanalytic Study of the Child* 42 (1978): 425–41.

65. Kosuke Yamazaki et al., "Self Expression, Interpersonal Relations, and Juvenile Delinquency in Japan," in Charles M. Super, ed., *The Role of Culture in Developmental Disorder* (New York: Academic Press, 1987), 197–201.

66. Stack, *All Our Kin*, 52–53.

67. John H. Scanzoni, *The Black Family in Modern Society* (Boston: Allyn and Bacon, 1971), 93.

68. Dale R. Meers, "Psychoanalytic Research and Intellectual Functioning of Ghetto-reared Black Children," *Psychoanalytic Study of the Child* 28 (1973): 411 (emphasis added).

69. Nightingale, *On the Edge*, 15–49.

70. There is a long tradition of studies of these distinctions. See Allison Davis, *Children of Bondage* (New York: Harper and Row, 1940); Charles Willie, *A New Look at Black Families* (Bayside, N.Y.: General Hall, 1976). On the vexed question of the size of the underclass and its relation to the larger Black lower and working classes, see Jencks and Peterson, *The Urban Underclass*, especially the chapters by Jencks, Peterson, and Duncan.

71. Scanzoni, *The Black Family in Modern Society*, 36–39; Harriette Pipes McAdoo, "Upward Mobility and Parenting in Middle-Income Black Families," *Journal of Black Psychology* 8, no. 1 (1981): 12.

72. A. Billingsley, *Black Families in White America* (Englewood Cliffs: Prentice Hall, 1968).

73. Scanzoni, *The Black Family in Modern Society*, 93–98.

74. John L. McAdoo, "Parenting Styles: Mother-Child Interactions and Self-Esteem in Young Black Children," in Constance Obudho, ed., *Black Marriage and Family Therapy* (Westport, Conn.: Greenwood Press, 1983), 135–50.

75. Allen, "Race, Income, and Family Dynamics," in M. B. Spencer et al., *Beginnings: The Social and Psychological Development of Black Children* (Hillsdale, N.J: L. Erlbaum, 1985).

76. John McAdoo, "The Roles of Black Fathers in the Socialization of Black Children," in Harriette Pipes McAdoo, ed., *Black Families* (Newbury Park, Calif.: Sage, 1988), 257–69.

77. Noel A. Cazenave and Rita Smith, "Gender Differences in the Perception of Black Male-Female Relationships and Stereotypes," in Harold E. Cheatham and James B. Stewart, eds., *Black Families: Interdisciplinary Perspectives* (New Brunswick, N.J.: Transaction Books, 1991).

78. Castellano Turner and Barbara Turner, "Black Families, Social Evaluations, and Future Marital Relations," in Obudho, *Black Marriage and*

Family Therapy, 23–37. This finding, however, has been contested by Lynette Smith and Jim Millham, "Sex Role Stereotypes amongst Blacks and Whites," *Journal of Black Psychology* 6, no. 1 (1979): 1–6.

79. Annie S. Banes, "Black Husbands and Wives: An Account of Marital Roles in a Middle-Class Neighborhood," in Obudho, *Black Marriage and Family Therapy*, 55–73.

80. Gerald D. Jaynes and Robin M. Williams, Jr., eds., *A Common Destiny: Blacks and American Society* (Washington, D.C.: National Academy Press, 1989), 529–30.

81. Robert D. Mare and Christopher Winship, "Socioeconomic Change and the Decline of Marriage for Blacks and Whites," in Jencks and Peterson, *The Urban Underclass*, 182–87.

82. Ibid., 176–77.

83. Jencks, "Is the American Underclass Growing?" in Jencks and Peterson, *The Urban Underclass*, 89.

84. Jaynes and Williams, *A Common Destiny*, 534–40.

85. *Essence*, August 1993, 30. I found it odd that Dr. Grant, in her response, addressed only the woman's jealousy and advised her to fix herself, with the aid of professional help if necessary. The problem causing the jealousy was assumed to be either a fantasy or a fact of life over which the woman had no control.

86. Jaynes and Williams, *A Common Destiny*, 530.

87. See, for example, Shirley J. Hatchett, "Women and Men," in James S. Jackson, ed., *Life in Black America* (Newbury Park, Calif.: Sage, 1991), 90.

88. Sandra DeJarnett and Bertram H. Raven, "The Balance, Bases, and Modes of Interpersonal Power in Black Couples: The Role of Sex and Socio-Economic Circumstances," *Journal of Black Psychology* 7, no. 2 (1981): 51–66.

89. Hatchett, "Women and Men," 103.

90. Jacqueline Looney, "Ego Development and Black Identity," *Journal of Black Psychology* 5, no. 1 (1988): 52.

91. Hooks, *Yearning*, 58.

92. Ali, *The Blackman's Guide to Understanding the Blackwoman* (Philadelphia: Civilized Publications, 1989).

93. Millham and Smith, "Sex-role Differentiation among Black and White Americans: A Comparative Study," *Journal of Black Psychology* 7, no. 2 (1981): 77–79.

94. There was only one attitude set with significant factor loading for at least five belief statements.

95. Millham and Smith, "Sex-role Differentiation," 85 (emphasis added).

96. Hatchett, "Women and Men," 90.

97. Ibid., 99.

98. Scanzoni, *The Black Family in Modern Society*, 176–90; see also chap. 4.

99. Parish, *Slavery: History and Historians* (New York: Harper and Row, 1989), 76; Kolchin, "Reevaluating the Antebellum Slave Community: A Com-

parative Perspective," *Journal of American History* 70, no.3 (December 1983): 581. Among the best of the counter-revisionists, see, in addition to White, *Ar'n't I a Woman*, Brenda Stevenson, "Distress and Discord in Virginia Slave Families, 1830–1860," in Carol Blesser, ed., *In Joy and in Sorrow: Women, Family, and Marriage in the Victorian South, 1830–1900* (New York: Oxford Univ. Press, 1991), 103–24; Ann Patton Malone, *Sweet Chariot* (Chapel Hill: Univ. of North Carolina Press, 1992), esp. chaps. 7 and 8; Susan Lebsock, *The Free Women of Petersburg: Status and Culture in a Southern Town, 1784–1860* (New York: Norton, 1984); Horton, "Freedom's Yoke"; and Elizabeth Fox-Genovese, *Within the Plantation Household: Black and White Women of the Old South* (Chapel Hill: Univ. of North Carolina Press, 1989).

100. Paul D. Scott, *Slavery Remembered: A Record of Twentieth-Century Slave Narratives* (Chapel Hill: Univ. of North Carolina Press, 1979), 44–53; Stephen C. Crawford, "Quantified Memory: A Study of WPA and Fisk University Slave Narrative Collections" (Ph.D. diss., Univ. of Chicago, 1980), chaps. 5–6.

101. White, *Ar'n't I a Woman*, 118.

102. Scott, *Slavery Remembered*, 44; Crawford, *Quantified Memory*, chap. 5.

103. W. E. B. Du Bois, *The Negro American Family* (Cambridge: MIT Press, 1970); E. Franklin Frazier, *The Negro Family in the United States* (Chicago: Univ. of Chicago Press, 1939). For recent though qualified support of the Du Bois–Frazier dual-family thesis, see White, *Ar'n't I a Woman*, and Robert Fogel, *Without Consent or Contract: The Rise and Fall of American Slavery* (New York: Norton, 1989), 164–86.

104. Dollard, *Caste and Class in a Southern Town* (Garden City, N.Y.: Doubleday Anchor, 1949), 450–51.

105. On the South, see Florence Halpern, *Survival: Black/White* (Elmsford, N.Y.: Pergamon, 1973), 126–36, 145; on the urban North, see Adelbert H. Jenkins, *The Psychology of the Afro-American* (New York: Pergamon, 1982), 158–59, 179–80.

106. Dollard, *Caste and Class in a Southern Town*, 420. In the mid-thirties, when Dollard carried out his research, a great number of his middle-aged respondents would have been children of persons born in slavery.

107. Malone, *Sweet Chariot*, 229.

108. Stevenson, "Distress and Discord in Virginia Slave Families," 115.

109. Webber, *Deep Like the Rivers*, 165–66. In Jamaica the pecking order of violence extended down to animals, the smallest slave children being notorious for their cruelty to young domestic animals. See Orlando Patterson, *The Sociology of Slavery* (London: McGibbon and Kee, 1967).

110. The counterphobic theory of drug addiction is that of Thomas S. Szasz. The quotation here is from a summary by Heinz Kohut in his not uncritical comment on it. See Kohut, "The Role of the Counterphobic Mechanism in Addiction, by Thomas S. Szasz," in Paul H. Ornstein, ed., *The*

Search for the Self: Selected Writings of Heinz Kohut: 1950–1978 (New York: International Universities Press, 1978), vol. 1, 201–3.

111. Horton, "Freedom's Yoke," 70.
112. White, *Ar'n't I a Woman*, 153.
113. Ibid., 159.
114. Ibid., 150.
115. Lebsock, *Free Women of Petersburg*, 104–9.
116. Horton, "Freedom's Yoke," 67–68.
117. Levine, "The Middle Class Family and Middle Class Adolescents in a State of Disarray: A Social-Psychiatric Analysis," *Psychiatry* 47, no. 1 (1984): 152–61.
118. Akbar, "Our Destiny: Anthems of a Scientific Revolution," in McAdoo and McAdoo, *Black Children*, 29–30.
119. For the most extreme recent statement of this view, see Andrew Billingsley, *Climbing Jacob's Ladder: The Enduring Legacy of Black Families* (New York: Simon and Schuster, 1992).
120. Toni Cade, "On the Issue of Roles," in Cade, *The Black Woman*, 109.

The Message of the Verdict: A Three-Act Morality Play Starring Clarence Thomas, Willie Smith, and Mike Tyson

CHARLES R. LAWRENCE III

Americans are obsessed with sex and fearful of black sexuality. The obsession has to do with a search for stimulation and meaning in a fast-paced, market driven culture; the fear is rooted in visceral feelings about black bodies fueled by sexual myths of black women and men. . . .

Yet the paradox of the sexual politics of race in America is that, behind closed doors, the dirty, disgusting, and funky sex associated with black people is often perceived to be more intriguing and interesting, while in public spaces talk about black sexuality is virtually taboo. Everyone knows it is virtually impossible to talk candidly about race without talking about sex.

CORNEL WEST, *Race Matters*

Introduction

This is an essay about racism, sexism, and black sexuality. It is a part of my own effort to understand how the American mythology of black sexuality is related to the mutually reinforcing ideologies and systems of white supremacy and patriarchy. The roles assigned to black women and men in the black sexuality myth define and limit our humanity. They turn us against one another. They inhibit our creative definition of ourselves.

I want to explore the ways in which we are creatures of and captives to these roles. I want to understand how we internalize the myth even as we resist it, and in so doing aid the cause of our oppressors. I want to break the taboo against public talk of black sexuality and begin to speak honestly with my brothers and sisters about what it means to be black men and women. I want to ask my brother wearing the "Free Mike Tyson" T-shirt to think about how his sister Anita Hill's struggle against sexism is related to his own liberation, his own freedom to define himself as a man. I want to ask my sisters to see how Mike Tyson is a victim of patriarchy, and why his victimization makes it all the more important to hold him and other men responsible for their participation in sexism and misogyny.

These are lofty ambitions. The essay itself is a modest beginning. It examines three very public legal proceedings involving charges of sexual harassment and assault, and seeks to understand the stories told in these legal dramas in the context of a larger cultural story of race, class, and sexuality. It looks for emerging themes that we can begin to make the subject of candid discussions among black men, between black men and women, and across lines of race and class.

The narrative that begins the essay was written four months after the Senate's confirmation of Supreme Court Justice Clarence Thomas. It opens with the announcement of the rape conviction of ex–heavyweight champion Mike Tyson. But the story's chronology and the essay's conceptual and emotional origins begin in the midst of the Senate Judiciary Committee hearings into Professor Anita Hill's sexual harassment charges against Supreme Court nominee Clarence Thomas.

During these hearings black sexuality took center stage in the most public of spaces. Millions of Americans watched this televised real-life drama with a fascination usually reserved for daytime soaps. The story of any Supreme Court nominee's sexual harassment of a professional colleague might well have captured the American imagination, but both the nominee and the professor were black, and that made their story part of a much older story about race and sex in this country, a story deeply embedded in the American psyche.

The taboos surrounding black sexuality, of which Cornel West speaks, are strong. There was little acknowledgment or discussion of what was on everybody's mind as we watched the Hill-Thomas hearings. Many black Americans, including some who believed her story, accused Professor Hill of "airing dirty laundry." All of us knew that white America would hear this story not just as a lesson about the ubiquity of sexual harassment in the workplace but as a story about oversexed black men.

There was another part of the story of black sexuality that all of us heard but few of us acknowledged: the story of the "unchaste" black woman who has no right to refuse the sexual advances of any man. When Senator Orrin Hatch charged that Professor Hill's experience was the sexual fantasy of a spurned woman, he was evoking this myth. When he implied that she tried to seduce Thomas by inviting him into her apartment, and when he read the most lurid language from her testimony over and over again, all the while protesting his disgust, he was conjuring up these same racist images of the wanton black woman.

The myth of black sexuality was everywhere but it was never named. We never challenged white folks to speak aloud the images, words, and feelings that made this televised drama a story about every black man and woman. Nor did we admit to each other that when we sat watching the hearings in the company of whites, we were cringing at what we knew must be on their minds. Our fear of perpetuating racist sexual stereotypes made us complicit in the enforcement of the taboo against naming them. We were made silent witnesses to the nominee's and the Judiciary Committee's abuse of Professor Hill, and our silence rendered us ineffective in our opposition to a man who will do great damage to the cause of human liberation during his term on the Supreme Court. Perhaps most importantly, we did not use this opportunity to talk with one another about how the myth of black sexuality, and the taboo against talk about it, undermines our opposition to racism, sexism, homophobia, and class oppression within our own communities as well as in American culture as a whole.[1]

The Master Narrative

"TYSON VERDICT SENDS A MESSAGE." These were the words that greeted me on the front of the sports section of my morning *L.A. Times* on February 11, 1992. The subhead read, "Some say conviction on rape charge shows athletes are not above the law."[2] I suppose it was a headline I might have expected on the sports page, but it was hardly the message that was screaming in my head. I was hearing another message, one about racism and patriarchy in America. It was a message I had been anticipating from the moment I first learned that this troubled young black man had been charged with rape.

The Tyson trial was the final act of a three-act American morality play. The play had begun in Washington, D.C., in the fall of 1991, with the Senate confirmation hearings of Supreme Court nominee Clarence Thomas. The second act was set in Florida, at the trial of William Kennedy-Smith, who was charged with raping a woman at the Kennedy family estate in Palm Beach in March 1991. And now, in Indianapolis, the curtain had come down on act three. A more complex and deeply textured message of the Tyson verdict is contained in the social text of this three-act play; and the message of and the meaning of this dramatic trilogy can only be understood within the context of a historical meta-story, or Master Narrative, about race, gender, and sex in America.[3]

It was early the previous evening that I first learned of the verdict in the Tyson rape trial. I was watching a college basketball game on ESPN, the sports channel. The game was interrupted by a news bulletin. After ten hours of deliberation, a jury had found Mike Tyson guilty of rape and two counts of "deviate sexual conduct." Now two white male reporters appeared on the screen standing outside the Indianapolis courtroom. In a dramatic tone indistinguishable from that used by sportscasters covering a heavyweight championship bout, one of the reporters recounted the events of the past several minutes. A brief video clip showed Tyson leaving the courtroom flanked by two policemen and trailed by his entourage of attorneys and handlers. Prominent among them was Don King, the flamboyant promoter.[4]

It was July 1991 when I first heard that Desiree Washington, a contestant in the Miss Teenage Black America pageant, had reported being raped by Mike Tyson. I had every reason to believe this young woman's account of Tyson's assault on her. Tyson, like Kennedy-Smith, had a history of similar behavior.[5] He was accustomed to having his way with women. But I was just as certain that unlike the Kennedy brat and Thomas, Tyson would pay for his misdeed. His conviction was inevitable. This was not because his jurors were racists, though their roles in this play were determined in part by our culture's racism.[6] It was because the Master Narrative called for a third act to this play, which had begun the previous September with the confirmation hearings—a third act in which we were told that truth and justice prevail in the American legal system, and in which we learned that "good girls" will be protected from the unwanted advances of "bad men."

"Why was this case different from Willie Smith's rape trial?" the ESPN anchor was asking the reporter who had witnessed the Tyson trial.[7] The reporter's answer was given in the manner of a knowledgeable sports commentator asked to compare the relative merits of Larry Bird and Michael Jordan. Kennedy-Smith was a much stronger witness, he said. He was attractive, likable, and well spoken on the stand. He remembered details about the evening. His accuser was confused. She couldn't remember details. She was a much less credible witness than Tyson's victim, who was articulate and poised throughout the trial and had a clear and consistent memory of the details of that evening. Tyson's testimony, by contrast to Kennedy-Smith's, was vague. He was inarticulate, brutish, and altogether an unattractive witness. In short, the Indianapolis prosecution simply had a better case. The reporter concluded by saying, "The jury usually gets these things right." In other words, the difference between the William Kennedy-Smith trial and the Tyson trial was that Tyson was a rapist and Kennedy-Smith wasn't.

The message of the Tyson verdict was clear. The system works. We know a rapist when we see one. And *this* is what a rapist looks like. He is big and burly and black and inarticulate. He hangs around with guys with weird hairdos and questionable reputations. He is not attractive and well spoken. He is not William Kennedy-Smith, medical student from a good family.[8] He is not Clarence Thomas, Supreme Court nominee, with nuns and law school deans to testify to his impeccable character.[9] He is not the white-haired Harvard graduate whose adult daughter tells her therapist she was the victim of incest as a child.[10] We do not believe the victims of these men because we know what a rapist looks like. He looks like Mike Tyson.

"JUDGMENT DAY: Payback Comes to Sexual Predator," screamed the headline in *People* magazine.

After the Clarence Thomas hearings and the William Kennedy-Smith trial, it was beginning to seem as if a woman might never win a round in the he-said-she-said battle of the sexes. This time, though, a panel of 12 jurors chose to believe the accuser.[11]

Helen Neuborne, executive director of the National Organization for Women, called the jury's decision "an important victory," and Miami law professor Mary Coombs agreed that the Tyson case "may mitigate the public image that there's no point in bringing accusations (of date or acquaintance rape)."[12] The rape counselor for Patricia Bowman, Smith's victim, said, "This sends a message that there is a chance that justice will prevail and that a woman will be believed by a jury."[13]

The editorial and opinion page of the *L.A. Times* two days after the Tyson verdict was also proclaiming a victory for the cause of women's liberation. "RECLAIMING THE MEANING OF THE WORD 'NO': Tyson Verdict a Clarifying Moment for America," trumpeted the headline of the paper's editorial. And under the subhead "Direct Message" the editorial announced:

> Tyson's conviction . . . has been hailed as a victory for all acquaintance rape victims who might have been afraid to come forward because they feared that they would not be believed.
>
> Now slowly but surely American society seems to be coming to accept that when a woman says "no" to sex it should be assumed that "no" is what she means.
>
> . . . the most enduring—and positive—result from this verdict is that the word "no" may have regained its true meaning as, in this kind of case, the very last word.[14]

On the next page an opinion piece titled "Sexist Myths Take a Beating," written by an activist woman lawyer, closed with these lines: "Women everywhere should be encouraged by the verdict. The system has shown itself willing to believe rape survivors, at least some of the time, and even against the word of a powerful man."[15]

Did sexist myths really take a beating in this case? Should potential victims of acquaintance rape feel more secure? Are victims more likely to be believed? The system has always been willing to believe rape survivors *some* of the time. When black men have raped white women, and often when they haven't, women have been believed.[16]

When poor men have raped rich women, women have been be-lieved.[17] But the Thomas/Kennedy-Smith/Tyson trilogy of cases is not a simple matter of "One out of three ain't bad" or "This last case shows things are getting better." Women, and men who support feminism, would do well to ask whether the *some* of the time that women are believed is evidence of the continuing vitality of patriar-chy rather than of its demise. We should ask ourselves whether the story told by these cases is the same old story white males have always told and too many of us have believed.

My point here is not to justify or defend Tyson's behavior or to claim that he is the innocent victim of racism. Nor am I arguing that laws punishing violence against women should not be enforced until we are prepared to enforce them against all. I believe that Tyson was guilty and that he deserved to be punished for his crime. I grieve for his victim, Desiree Washington. I admire her bravery and wish I could find a way to ease her pain. My concern here is with the message of the Tyson verdict, the story it tells, not with the result. I am troubled that too many of us, including many feminists, do not see how sexism and racism intersect in this three-act play to create cultural meanings that reinforce the structures of our subordination. I am worried about the continued mystifying power of the Master Narrative.

What is the story contained in this trio of sexual assault trials that captured the imagination of America? What is the historical meta-story that gives this story context, that transforms it into a morality play? The larger story is a story of stereotypes about race, sex, and class that are deeply embedded in the American psyche.[18] It is a story of oversexed black men and wanton black women, of violence motivated and justified by these sexual stereotypes.[19] It is a history of black men lynched and castrated in the name of "protecting white womanhood," of black women raped as an expression of male sexual attitudes bred in a culture both racist and patriarchal.[20] It is also a story about class, a story where powerful men relegated their wives and daughters to a pedestal of asexual purity and made servant girls their sexual prey.[21] Our three-act play is cast with contemporary characters. It is set in a post–civil rights, post–women's movement era. The lines have been changed so that the language will not seem archaic, but the story is the same.

Act I: The Senate Judiciary Hearings: Wherein the "House Slave" Reminds the Master of Their Deal

When Judge Clarence Thomas called the Judiciary Committee's inquiry into Professor Anita Hill's charges of sexual harassment a "high-tech lynching of an uppity black man," declaring himself the victim of "racial attitudes about black men and their views of sex," he invoked the most vivid symbol of racial oppression, the lynch mob.[22] Thomas spoke to his white male panel of interrogators in language that resonated with the Master Narrative of our national history. His claim was that they were using false charges of sexual harassment in the same way that their grandfathers had used false charges of rape: to raise the specter of black sexuality in order to keep black men out of public life and maintain the racial hierarchy in the public transactions of men.[23]

Of course there was a perverse irony in this scene. This would-be victim was the same Clarence Thomas who had scolded fellow African Americans for complaining about racism.[24] This was the man who had invoked the racist stereotype of the black welfare queen to slander his own sister.[25] The same man who had proven himself the paradigmatic assimilationist accommodationist, the ultimate house slave,[26] had cast himself in the role of "uppity black man." And yet this miscast theater of the absurd got rave reviews in the Senate and was a hit in living rooms across the nation.[27]

Clarence Thomas's resort to the lynching metaphor was successful in part because of the power of the history he evoked. For African Americans the memory of Emmett Till[28] and the Scottsboro Boys[29] is all too fresh. The modern-day lynch mobs of Howard Beach[30] and Bensonhurst[31] remind us that the story of vigilante justice is told in the present as well as the past tense. No matter that Judge Thomas had little concern for the legal lynchings of his brothers and sisters in a racist criminal justice system.[32] No matter that he had shuffled and grinned his way through two weeks of testimony.[33] The visual image of the lone black man facing a white male panel of inquisitors (the mob) caused African Americans to reach out instinctively in a protective embrace.[34] There were some of us who quickly recognized this calculated appeal to the memory of our shared horror for what it was, but all of us experienced a brief moment of terror and kinship. Such was the power of the image and the narrative it evoked.

Of course Judge Thomas had no interest in calling up the image of the parallel history of terrorism through rape that was visited upon black women in the service of the same institutions of racism and patriarchy served by the lynch mob.[35] This story is excluded from the Master Narrative. It is a story all too often omitted from the counter-narratives of the civil rights and women's movements.[36] When Anita Hill spoke of her victimization, there were few in her audience who saw the legions of her sisters violated and silenced, with no one to tell of their horrific pain and degradation.[37] Ida Wells, Elsa Brown, Zora Hurston, Alice Walker, Paula Giddings, Toni Morrison, Nell Painter, Angela Davis, Patricia Williams, Kimberlé Crenshaw, and many others have struggled mightily to give these violated sisters voice, but their story remained a whisper in the Senate hearing room, drowned out by the roar of stories told by men.

Thomas's story reminded the senators and the nation that in principle we no longer tolerate lynching. His tale invoked a more recent chapter of the Master Narrative, the story of racial progress and reform. "Remember, black men are no longer treated this way" was a prominent subtext of his lynching metaphor. This story of racial reform is a gendered story. In saying this I mean something more than "There were sexists in the civil rights movement" or "Black men are sexists." I mean that the quest for racial equality in America has been a quest after a patriarchal grail. When African Americans demanded equality, we sought an equal place within a legal system dominated by men.[38] When we were given the right to vote under the Fifteenth Amendment, it was the male franchise that was granted.[39] When we demanded an end to segregated schools, jobs, and housing, we sought entry into schools that taught boys to look down on girls and into a world where men went to work and women were kept at home to cook dinner and raise the kids. When young black men seek to express their manhood by carrying guns, wearing gold, and "dissing" their sisters, they are emulating Clint Eastwood, Donald Trump, and Hugh Hefner.

There was a final message in Thomas's lynch mob scene, a message central to the larger tale. Judge Thomas was reminding the senators of a bargain they had struck, an unspoken gentleman's agreement that should not be broken. Historically, white men had denied black men the patriarchal authority to "protect their women."[40] White men's rape of black women was a way of delivering this message of domination from one man to another. But these same white men had allowed black men to inflict abuse on black women.[41] Now Thomas was calling in his chips on this historical deal that put whatever went on between him and Anita Hill outside the white man's law.[42]

Act II: *The William Kennedy-Smith Trial: Wherein the Master Visits the Slave Quarters*

White men have said over and over—and we have believed it because it was repeated so often—that not only was there no such thing as a chaste Negro woman—but that a Negro woman could not be assaulted, that it was never against her will.[43]

JESSIE DANIEL AMES (1936)

Historian Jacquelyn Dowd Hall has called the sexual access of white men to black women "a cornerstone of patriarchal power in the South." The rationale for the absence of laws protecting a black woman from rape was based in part on her status as property and on the economic purpose she served by replenishing the slave supply, but it was also justified by reference to the innate lasciviousness of black women.[44] Hall notes the process by which Victorian views of the female as passionless replaced an older notion of women's dangerous sexual power: "In the United States, the fear and fascination of female sexuality was projected onto black women; the passionless lady arose in symbiosis with the primitively sexual slave."[45] In the Master Narrative the aristocratic planter's son who visited the slave quarters was merely sowing wild oats with an eager sexual partner.[46]

This story of interracial rape so central to our history is but one version of an even older story of sexuality and patriarchal hegemony. The noble's sexual access to the serf's daughter and the lord's dalliance with the downstairs maid are also stories of the rape of powerless women by powerful men, justified by the portrayal of the victim as wanton and unchaste, without any wish, much less any right, to say no.[47]

This was the story that William Kennedy-Smith's defense attorneys relied upon so successfully. Smith is cast in the role of the gentleman's son. He is a clean-cut, upstanding young man from a prominent family. He enjoys a good party, but doesn't every red-blooded wealthy white boy? He does not deny that he had sex with his victim, but he reminds us that she's the tramp from the other side of the tracks. Doesn't the young master get to try out his stuff on the lusty servant girl? The lawyers representing William Kennedy-Smith painted his victim, Patricia Bowman, as promiscuous and sexually aggressive. She had worn a black dress and fancy undergarments, and had canceled a date with another man when Kennedy-Smith became available.[48] In the context of the Master Narrative, Bowman becomes the slave girl. Her role in the black sexuality myth is no longer that of the presumptively chaste white woman who must be believed. By portraying her as sexually aggressive, the defense transforms her from the white woman on the pedestal to the fallen white woman, no better than the inherently unchaste black woman whose veracity is always to be questioned.[49] Patricia Bowman, the gentleman's victim, is even rendered invisible by CNN's device of the face-obliterating dark spot.[50] In the Master Narrative there is no such thing as rape in the slave quarters. It is never against her will.

Act III: The Trial in Indianapolis: Wherein the True Identity of the Rapist Is Revealed and We Learn That in the New "Color-Blind" World Even a Black Girl Can Be "Miss Anne"

In the final act of this play "evil" is brought to "justice." The placement of this act at the end is critical because it gives meaning to the two stories that have gone before. The imagery is stark. Mike Tyson is the brute valued by the master only for the strength of his back and arms. He is white America's worst/favorite nightmare.[51]

Tyson could not have been more perfectly cast for the role of the rapist. He fit all the time-honored stereotypes of the violent, sexual, savage, unintelligent, irresponsible, scary black male.[52] The *Sports Illustrated* cover story on the trial described Tyson as "a single-purpose organism, bred for bad intentions and well maintained for its unique ability to enact violent public spectacle, but entirely unsuited for real life."[53] Before he was twenty his extraordinary physical prowess and rage were harnessed and commodified for an American public fascinated and titillated by the sight of raw violence. "You can't look away from a Tyson fight, because you know that at any moment something terrible is going to happen," said Jimmy Jacobs, one of Tyson's former co-managers.[54] And a *Washington Post colum-nist admitted:*

> I have this terrible conflict about Tyson. I was never so thrilled by an athlete as I was by him. I never found anything in sports as heart-stopping, as nerve-tingling as watching Tyson . . . race furiously across the ring at the sound of the opening bell, bent on dismantling his opponent. I saw in him a nobility of effort, a profound commitment to courage, a bright and shining honor.[55]

Feminist theorists will recognize in the vicarious pleasure that men derive from watching Tyson the same elements that make pornography a multimillion-dollar business.[56] The fascination of hearing about Tyson the rapist is not so different from the thrill derived from seeing him in the ring. A woman friend of mine wondered aloud about the fact that the Tyson trial was reported mostly on the sports pages. "Does this mean that rape has become a sport?" she said.[57]

"PERFECT VICTIM," read the *Newsweek* headline.

> Unlike Patricia Bowman, who lost her date rape case against William Kennedy-Smith, Tyson's accuser came across on the stand as the per-fect victim. Now a scholarship student at a Roman Catholic college, she was barely 18 when she arrived at the beauty pageant. Growing up in Rhode Island, she was apparently the all-American girl: She played softball, ushered at her church and volunteered as a Big Sister. The court heard about her high school days as a varsity cheerleader, class president and most-outstanding sophomore.[58]

During the trial Desiree Washington "spoke in a high pitched, almost childlike voice, used words like 'neat' and 'yucky' and admitted to being star struck." Prosecutor Greg Garrison said the jury was sold on "that beautiful 18-year-old kid with a pure heart. . . . this is a very very special young woman."[59] If Desiree Washington is the "perfect victim," who are the not so perfect victims? Are they the prostitutes found raped and dead whose cases are never investigated? Are they women like Anita Hill who are strong, intelligent, aggres-sive, and ambitious, who do not know their place?

Garrison is quoted as saying, "If Tyson had been a kid from the projects this trial would have been over in two days."[60] He meant this not as an admission that poor kids don't get a fair shake but as further evidence that the system will protect women even when their rapists are rich and powerful. But what if Desiree Washington had been a kid from the projects? What if she had been the not so perfect victim? Would her rapist ever have been brought to trial? If we are to believe the statistics, the chances are slim to none. These statistics suggest that African American women are most likely to be raped and least likely to believed. When their rapists are convicted, they do less time. A study in Dallas revealed that the average prison term for a man convicted of raping a black woman was two years. Where the victims were white the sentence was ten years.[61]

The Tyson guilty verdict was an exception to the rule. It was an aberration in a system that devalues the bodies and lives of women of color, an anomaly necessitated by the need to shore up the story that tells us we are ever closer to the achievement of equal justice under law.[62] Ms. Washington is allowed to play "Miss Anne,"[63] the perfect victim, so that women can be told that men have heard them, so that we can all be convinced that any woman can say no and be taken seriously. But my sister Desiree is no safer today than she was before Mike Tyson's conviction, and that is the tragedy.

The message of the Tyson verdict, like the message of the Master Narrative of which it is a part, is intended to mystify and mislead. It should not be a cause for celebration. It should be a call to continue the fight.

Conclusion

The cultural story about race and gender and sexuality that I have called the Master Narrative shapes our images of self and others, and in so doing helps to maintain the mutually reinforcing systems of white supremacy, patriarchy, and class oppression. It is a powerful story because it is so deeply rooted in our history and cultural consciousness. It has been told so often that it is sometimes hard for us to see that it is just a story. Much of the Master Narrative's power comes from the taboo against talk about it, against naming it and speaking of its origins and purposes. First we must break the taboo. We must talk candidly to one another about black sexuality. We must speak forthrightly and honestly about the distortions of the myth *and* the realities of sexism and misogyny within our community. This talk is necessary for the liberation of black men as well as black women. It is necessary for the deconstruction of the Master Narrative. It is necessary for the reconstruction of a new, more liberating story of our own.

Notes

1. Many African American women spoke with passion and force about these issues both during and after the hearings, but few were given access to the mainstream media. Black men's voices on the subject of sexism and sexuality were notably absent during the hearings. A small but significant number of male African American scholars did speak to these issues. *See generally* Toni Morrison, ed., RACE-ING JUSTICE, EN-GENDERING POWER: ESSAYS ON ANITA HILL, CLARENCE THOMAS, AND THE CONSTRUCTION OF SOCIAL REALITY (1992); and Robert Chrisman and Robert L. Allen, eds., COURT OF APPEAL: THE BLACK COMMUNITY SPEAKS OUT ON THE RACIAL AND SEXUAL POLITICS OF THOMAS VS. HILL (1992). This essay is in part a response to the ongoing challenge of my sister critical race theorists to bring a thoughtful black male perspective to the discussion.

2. Julie Cart and Maryann Hudson, *Tyson Verdict Sends a Message*, L.A. TIMES, Feb. 11, 1992 (Sports), at C1.

3. In using the term "Master Narrative," I do not wish to imbue the words with an overly deterministic meaning; the "mastery" of the Master Narrative may not be as complete as the term suggests. I refer here to the narrative of American society in which the subordination of certain groups has been structured along race and gender lines. As with all narrative accounts of the past, the retelling of the Thomas/Kennedy-Smith/Tyson stories cannot escape the cluster of epistemological and interpretive issues that arise whenever reality is represented in a textual domain. As Kendall Thomas states in his historiographical remembrance of the *Herndon v. Lowry case*: "The claim that history is a kind of writing—that its textual representations are not identical to the lived historical reality of which they purport to give an account—raises important questions about the status of narrative tradition in historiography. Most notably, it challenges the notion that the historical text is or can be a faithful retelling of what 'actually' took place in the past. . . . What these narrative forms obscure, however, is the possibility that the same event or set of events might be viewed in radically different ways. For example, from the vantage point of the vanquished rather than of the victor, the 'epic' of Manifest Destiny might be the 'tragedy' of the extermi-

nation of the Indian nations. The point to be emphasized here is that the narrative form in which a historical account is modeled is not neutral or innocent." Kendall Thomas, *Rouge et Noir Reread: A Popular Constitutional History of the Angelo Herndon Case*, 65 S. CAL. L. REV. 2599, 2658–59 (1992). W. E. B. Du Bois, in criticizing the writing of history solely from the perspective of those with power, called for a study of American history "from below." *Id.* at 2604.

4. Don King is routinely characterized by the news media as flamboyant, outrageous, gangsterlike. Newspaper accounts typically portray him as a living parody of a professional businessman: "Don King is one of the craftiest self-creations in history." Rick Kogan, *Only in America; 'Frontline' Portrays Boxing's King as a Menace in an Unsavory World*, CHICAGO TRIBUNE, Nov. 5, 1991 (Tempo), at C7; "He [Don King] thrives as a sports mogul and media manipulator. See him any time globbing on the glitz. . . . Just like Zsa Zsa, he's cute, funny and outrageous. Oh so outrageous. Just look at the picture: King flashing white teeth while playfully lecturing the press nonstop before one of his fights, his famous Brillo hair brushed forward so that it adds eight inches to his height. 'If Don King were a city, he would be Las Vegas—flamboyant, awake 24 hours a day, driven by money, rooted in gambling and the mob.' So says veteran investigative reporter Jack Newfield in 'Don King, Unauthorized.' " Howard Rosenberg, *Don King Takes Some Punches*, L. A. TIMES, Nov. 4, 1991 (Entertainment), at F1; "He is considered manipulative, brilliant, egocentric, tireless, greedy, and ruthless." Jack Saraceno, *A Hair-Raising Round*, USA TODAY, April 5, 1990 (Sports), at 1C.

   Don King's hair is often the object of ridicule in the press; it has been called the "electric-shock hair-do," among other descriptions. Ed Schuyler, Jr., *Ali's Act Will Be Very Tough to Follow for Tyson's World Tour*, CHICAGO TRIBUNE, Feb. 12, 1988 (Sports), at C3.

5. On February 20, 1986, Mike Tyson allegedly propositioned a female sales clerk. He became violent when she rejected him. Later that night, he was ejected from a movie theater after another such incident. Tyson was charged with misdemeanor assault and battery and assault with a deadly weapon after a parking lot attendant alleged that Tyson tried to kiss a female employee and hit the male attendant. Tyson paid $105,000 to settle the case out of court. Other victims of his alleged violence include tennis players Lori McNeil and Sandra Miller, whom he allegedly grabbed, propositioned, and insulted on December 15, 1988, while at a Manhattan nightclub, and Lori Davis, whom he allegedly grabbed while at the same nightclub on the same night. Cart and Hudson, *supra* note 2.

6. I have discussed elsewhere the dynamics and unacknowledged impact of racism on the law and our lives. *See* Charles R. Lawrence III, *The Id, the Ego, and Equal Protection: Reckoning with Unconscious Racism*, 39 STAN. L. REV. 317 (1987). *See also* Derrick Bell, RACE, RACISM AND AMERICAN LAW (2d ed. 1980).

7. ESPN was unable to provide a transcript of their news broadcast of February 10, 1992. Thus, this paragraph represents my rough recollection in response to the ESPN broadcast of the Tyson verdict, not a verbatim description of the broadcast.

8. William Kennedy-Smith is the grandson of Joseph Kennedy and the second son of Jean Kennedy-Smith. His uncle is Senator Ted Kennedy. *See* Paula Chin et al., *Camelot after Dark*, PEOPLE, May 27, 1991, at 58.

9. Among those who helped Judge Thomas during the hearings on his nomination were White House counsel C. Boyden Gray, J. Michael Luttig of the Justice Department, and Vice President Dan Quayle. N.Y. TIMES, Oct. 14, 1991, at A1, A11. Guido Calabresi, dean of the Yale Law School, was also among Thomas's supporters, as was Sister Mary Virgilius Reidy, a Franciscan nun who taught Judge Thomas in the eighth grade and testified in his favor. Neal Lewis, *Thomas Is Called Unworthy to Succeed Marshall*, N.Y. TIMES, Sept. 18, 1991.

10. See Janet Hawkins, *Rowers on the River Styx*, HARVARD MAGAZINE, March–April 1991, at 43.

11. PEOPLE, February 24, 1992, at 36.

12. Quoted in Barbara Novovitch, *Tyson Rape Conviction May Aid Date Rape Victims*, REUTERS, Feb. 11, 1992.

13. *Id.*

14. *Reclaiming the Meaning of the Word "No,"* L.A. TIMES, Feb. 12, 1992, at B6.

15. Gloria Allred, *Sexist Myths Take a Beating*, L.A. TIMES, Feb. 12, 1992, at B7.

16. The presumption was held, not only by whites generally, but by the law as well, that any white woman who had intercourse with a black man had been raped. On this presumption "untold men were lynched or legally executed." Jacquelyn Dowd Hall, REVOLT AGAINST CHIVALRY: JESSIE DANIEL AMES AND THE WOMEN'S CAMPAIGN AGAINST LYNCHING, 154 (1979).

17. The sexualized representation of blacks, regardless of class, is connected to the stereotyping of both the poor and blacks. "Over and over in European imaginations, the poor epitomize unfettered sexuality, and this convention has come to serve in the United States as well. American writing not only echoes the sexualization of the poor . . . but, reflecting a history in which masses of workers were enslaved, also adds the ingredient of race." Nell Irvin Painter, *Hill, Thomas, and the Use of Racial Stereotype*, in Morrison, *supra* note 1, at 206–7.

18. *See generally* Lawrence, *supra* note 6; John Hope Franklin, FROM SLAVERY TO FREEDOM (5th ed. 1980); Joel Kovel, WHITE RACISM: A PSYCHOHISTORY (1970). A number of race/gender/class stereotypes are deployed within this network of sexual assault cases. For the Thomas-Hill hearings, Thomas appropriated the figure of the lynch victim and (unwittingly) conjured up the image of the "black-beast-rapist." Simultaneously,

Anita Hill was cast as "black-woman-as-traitor-to-the-race" and was also associated with the "oversexed-black-Jezebel." Painter, *supra* note 17, at 204–10. Similarly, Patricia Bowman, the alleged victim of William Kennedy-Smith, evoked the image of a servant girl and the associated sexual imagery surrounding the working class. Mike Tyson, already presented to the public as the violent black man, immediately connoted the "black-beast-rapist" and the "oversexed black man." For example, Larry Merchant, a television boxing commentator, said, "It's been fairly obvious for a long time that he's been dysfunctional as far as women are concerned. . . . My take on it is that Tyson is an adult and he's the one responsible. He was a young man trying to make it in a world he was unfamiliar with. The people who formerly managed him were not 100% successful in taming his *wilder instincts.* . . . He went to Don King because that's what he wanted. *He wanted not to be controlled*" (emphasis added). Quoted in Cart and Hudson, *supra* note 2.

19. Historically, black women have been viewed as lascivious or oversexed. Jacquelyn Dowd Hall, *The Mind That Burns in Each Body: Women, Rape, and Racial Violence,* SOUTHERN EXPOSURE, Nov.–Dec. 1984, at 63. Such myths have been used to justify rape and other sexual abuses. Kimberlé Crenshaw, *Whose Story Is It, Anyway? Feminist and Antiracist Appropriations of Anita Hill,* in Morrison, *supra* note 1, at 411. Black men typically have been portrayed as rapists or violent beings. *See, e.g.,* Kovel, *supra* note 18; W. Grier and P. Cobbs, BLACK RAGE (1968); Oliver Cox, CASTE, CLASS AND RACE (1948).

20. The protection of white womanhood was a central concern of racist ideology and was often used as a rationale for lynching in the late nineteenth century. Jennifer Wriggins, *Rape, Racism, and the Law,* 6 HAR. WOMEN'S L. J. 103, 108 (1983); Hall, *Mind That Burns, supra* note 19, at 64. In the antebellum South, white men had virtually unlimited access to black women. *Id.* at 63.

21. "The connotations of wealth and family background attached to the position of the lady in the antebellum South faded in the twentieth century, but the power of ladyhood as a value construct remained. The term denoted chastity, frailty, and graciousness." Hall, *Mind That Burns, supra* note 19, at 64.

22. Text of Thomas's Reply to Charges Made by Anita Hill, REUTERS, Oct. 11, 1991. Lynching served as a powerful tool to intimidate and terrorize African Americans. Between 1882 and 1946 almost five thousand people died by lynching. Lynching peaked during the Reconstruction period and the Populist revolt. Reports of lynching, which grew in vividness with the development of communications and photographic technologies, served to intimidate every African American who saw or heard about them. As a result, during the late nineteenth and early twentieth centuries, lynching remained a highly effective and visible method of dominating and terrorizing African Americans. Hall, *Mind That Burns, supra* note 19, at 63–65.

See generally Hall, REVOLT, *supra* note 16; Mildred I. Thompson, IDA B. WELLS-BARNETT (1990); John Hope Franklin, FROM SLAVERY TO FREEDOM: A HISTORY OF NEGRO AMERICANS, 439–44 (1967).

23. Accusations of rape against African American men depend on stereotypes of black men as rapists in order to maintain their potency. *See supra* note 19. For most white Americans in the 1920s and 1930s the association between lynching and rape invoked this image of the black rapist. Lynching served as one mechanism among many to maintain white patriarchal domination over black men. Hall, *Mind That Burns, supra* note 19, at 61–65.

24. Nell Irvin Painter has also commented on the irony of Thomas's use of racial stereotypes. She writes: "Once a black woman accused him of abusing his power as a man and as an employer, he quickly slipped into the most familiar role in the American iconography of race: that of the victim. . . . Thomas appropriated the figure of the lynch victim despite glaring dissimilarities between himself and the thousands of poor unfortunates who, unprotected by white patrons in the White House or the United States Senate or by the law, perished at the hands of white southern mobs." Painter, *supra* note 17, at 203–4, 208. *See also* Scott Shepard, *The Supreme Court Showdown: The Long Day; Racism Charge Called Phony,* ATLANTA J. CONST., Oct. 16, 1991, at A10.

25. *See, e.g., Sister of High Court Nominee Traveled Different Road,* L.A. TIMES, July 5, 1991, at A4.

26. Large plantations generally had at least two groups of slaves, house slaves and field slaves. House slaves, as the name suggests, worked in the house, cooking meals, driving carriages, and performing other work required from personal servants. Favored house slaves sometimes enjoyed advantages in food, clothing, and education denied other slaves. Franklin, *supra* note 22, at 191. The term "house slave" has taken on the pejorative meaning of an African American who identifies with and serves the interests of powerful whites to the detriment of the condition of his or her own people. As Malcolm X said, reminding his audience of the historical origins of black militancy and black accommodation: "There were two kinds of slaves, the house Negro and the field Negro. The house Negroes—they lived in the house with master, they dressed pretty good, they ate good because they ate his food—what he left. They lived in the attic or the basement, but still they lived near the master; and they loved the master more than the master loved himself. They would give their life to save the master's house—quicker than the master would. . . . If the master got sick, the house Negro would say, 'What's the matter, boss, *we* sick?' We sick! He identified himself with his master, more than the master identified with himself. And if you came to the house Negro and said, 'Let's run away, let's escape, let's separate,' the house Negro would look at you and say, 'Man, you crazy. What you mean, separate? Where is there a better house than this? Where can I wear better clothes than this? Where can I eat better food than this?' That was the house Negro." MALCOLM X SPEAKS, 10–11 (1965).

27. The Thomas hearings have been described as "high drama, creating a media event that was part political convention, part heavyweight championship fight." *Outside the Hearing, It Was Cheers, Jeers; Thomas's Supporters Were Most Vocal, Visible,* WASH. POST, Oct. 12, 1991, at A9.

28. Thomas's use of the lynching image trivialized the real-life lynchings of innumerable African American men. Emmett Till, a fourteen-year-old boy from Chicago, allegedly whistled at a young white woman who worked in a drugstore where he had gone to buy gum while visiting relatives in Mississippi. That night, two white men, one of them the white woman's husband, came armed with a gun and took the boy away for "questioning." Till's naked body was discovered two days later floating in the Tallahatchie River. He had been bludgeoned and shot in the head. A few weeks later, an all-white Tallahatchie County jury acquitted the two white men charged with his murder. Kendall Thomas, *Strange Fruit,* in Morrison, *supra* note 1, at 367. *See also* Stephen Whitfield, A DEATH IN THE DELTA: THE STORY OF EMMETT TILL (1988).

29. Nine teenage black boys (one as young as thirteen, another fourteen) were arrested in Scottsboro, Alabama, and charged with the rape of two white girls on March 25, 1931. No attorney was formally appointed to represent them, although a number of lawyers were in the courtroom at the time. In one day, eight of the black defendants were convicted and sentenced to death. The Supreme Court later overturned the convictions on the ground of inadequate legal representation for the defendants. *Lawyers for Death Row,* WASH. POST, Jan. 11, 1988, at A10. Five of the Scottsboro boys were retried and served prison terms. *Obituaries,* UPI, Oct. 19, 1982. After a lengthy appeal process, all the defendants in the Scottsboro case, after having spent a combined 104 years in prison, were released. Wriggins, *supra* note 20, at 110.

30. In the Howard Beach slaying of December 22, 1986, three white teenagers allegedly chased and beat three black men. One of the black men escaped after receiving a single blow from a bat. Another man was beaten severely, and the third was beaten severely and was struck and killed by a car as he tried to run away. Robert McFadden, *3 Youths Are Held on Murder Counts in Queens Attack,* N.Y. TIMES, Dec. 23, 1986, at A1.

31. The Yusef Hawkins murder is another example of a contemporary lynching. Four black teenagers were attacked by ten to thirty young white men in the Bensonhurst section of Brooklyn. The white youths believed, mistakenly, that one of the black teenagers was dating a white girl from Bensonhurst. Yusef Hawkins, a sixteen-year-old, one of the black youths, was shot to death. Anthony Lewis, *On Our Conscience?* N.Y. TIMES, Aug. 31, 1989, at A25.

32. *See* Shepard, *supra* note 24.

33. Two particular photographs of Clarence Thomas at the time of the hearings project the image of a man who enjoys being "in the presence of power and [is] comforted by it." Wahneema Lubiano, *Black Ladies, Welfare Queens,*

and State Minstrels: Ideological War by Narrative Means, in Morrison, *supra* note 1, at 355–58.

34. *See, e.g.,* Clarence Page, *Clarence Thomas Feeds Blacks' Conspiracy Fears,* CHI. TRIB., Oct. 16, 1991, at 19. Julianne Malveaux has related an experience she had with other African American women in a candle shop run by a friend of hers. She was very angry about the treatment of Professor Hill by the Senate Judiciary Committee and expected the other women to share her feelings. "I expected solidarity, sisterhood among my women friends, but it was not there. . . . [One woman] launched into a tirade about one black person tearing another down. . . . 'She should have known better,' said one woman. 'If he talked dirty to her, why did she follow him from one place to another,' said a third woman. The woman who owned the shop is as smooth as icing on cake, she doesn't say anything, just smiles and moves her customers out of the store. But in this space there is no kind word, no empathy for Anita Hill." Julianne Malveaux, *No Peace in a Sisterly Space,* in Chrisman and Allen, *supra* note 1, at 143–44.

35. During slavery, the rape of African American women by white or black men was legal, and rape was used as a tool to maintain white supremacy. Even after the Civil War, the legal system treated the rape of African American women virtually the same way as before. The Ku Klux Klan used rape to inflict terror during Reconstruction. *Wriggins, supra* note 20, at 106–7, 118–19. The access of white men to black slave women strengthened white patriarchal power in the South as well and reasserted white dominance in the private sphere. Hall, *Mind That Burns, supra* note 19, at 62–63. Numerous authors have commented upon the image held by the white populace that black females were innately lascivious, so much so that they could not be raped. This image retained its force well after Reconstruction. *See, e.g.,* Angela Y. Davis, WOMEN, RACE AND CLASS (1981); Paula Giddings, WHEN AND WHERE I ENTER: THE IMPACT OF BLACK WOMEN ON RACE AND SEX IN AMERICA (1984); bell hooks, BLACK LOOKS: RACE AND REPRESENTATION, 62–66 (1992); Rickie Solinger, WAKE UP LITTLE SUSIE: SINGLE PREGNANCY AND RACE BEFORE ROE V. WADE, 42–45 (1992).

36. The counter-narratives of the civil rights and women's movements have usually focused on either race or gender without attempting to link them. As a result, the issues that affect black women and other women of color, the injuries and interests that arise at the intersection of race and gender, are not addressed. *See* Kimberlé Crenshaw, *Race, Gender, and Sexual Harassment,* 65 STAN. L. REV. 1467, 1468 (1992) (analyzing the complex of issues from the perspective of those who experience subordination as a result of their race and gender or as a result of their situation within the two intersecting systems of race (racism) and gender (sexism)). *See also* Angela Harris, *Race and Essentialism in Feminist Legal Theory,* 42 STAN. L. REV. 581 (1990); Judy Scales-Trent, *Black Women and the Constitution: Find-*

ing Our Place, Asserting Our Rights, 24 HAR. C. R. C. L. REV. 9 (1989).

37. *See* Rosemary L. Bray, *Taking Sides against Ourselves,* N.Y. TIMES, Nov. 17, 1991, at 56. *See also* Vicki Crawford, *On the Clarence Thomas Hearings,* in Chrisman and Allen, *supra* note 1, at 56–58; Beverly Guy-Sheftal, *Breaking the Silence: A Black Feminist Response to the Thomas/Hill Hearings* (for Audre Lorde), in *id.* at 73–77.

38. The Fourteenth Amendment's guarantee of equal protection was designed to protect the rights of black men, exclusive of the rights of black women. "Racial inequality was [the Fourteenth Amendment's] crucible, its paridigm, its target, and its subtext. Sex-based denials of equal protection were not covered." Catharine A. MacKinnon, *Reflections on Sex Equality under Law,* 100 YALE L. J. 1281, 1283 (1991). In the congressional debates over whether the Fourteenth Amendment's protection extended to black women, given its use of the word "persons," Senator Howard commented, "I believe Mr. Madison was old enough and wise enough to take it for granted that there was such a thing as the law of nature which has a certain influence even in political affairs, and that by that law women and children were not regarded as equals to men." *Id.* at n. 12 (quoting CONG. GLOBE. 39th Cong. 1st Sess. 2767 (1866)).

39. The Fifteenth Amendment, securing voting rights for black men, was passed in 1870. The Nineteenth Amendment, securing voting rights for women, was passed in 1920. Daniel A. Farber and Suzanna Sherry, A HISTORY OF THE AMERICAN CONSTITUTION, 411 (1990).

40. Hall, *Mind That Burns, supra* note 19, at 63.

41. "The legal system rendered the rape of black women by any man, white or black, invisible." Wriggins, *supra* note 20, at 118.

42. "Today black women continue to suffer rape in disproportionate numbers, while the criminal justice system still takes the claims of black rape victims less seriously than the claims of white victims." *Id.* at 123. A 1968 study of rape sentencing in Maryland found that in all fifty-five cases where the death penalty was imposed the victim was white, while 47 percent of all black men convicted of criminal assaults on black women between 1960 and 1967 were immediately released on probation. *Id.* at 121, n. 113 (citing Howard, *Racial Discrimination in Sentencing,* 59 JURISDICTURE 121, 123 (1975)).

43. Quoted in Hall, *Mind That Burns, supra* note 19, at 62.

44. *Id.* at 62–63. *See also* bell hooks, AIN'T I A WOMAN: BLACK WOMEN AND FEMINISM 52 (1981); Crenshaw, *Whose Story, supra* note 19, at 411; Painter, *supra* note 17, at 204–10.

45. Hall, *Mind That Burns, supra* note 19, at 63.

46. *See supra* note 17. In nineteenth-century England, bills to raise the age of consent from thirteen to sixteen were opposed in the House of Lords because members wanted their young lower-class servant girls to remain sexually available to themselves and their sons. Fran Olsen, *Statutory Rape: A*

Feminist Critique of Rights Analysis, 63 TEX. L. REV. 387, 402 (1984). *See also* Linda Gordon, HEROES OF THEIR OWN LIVES: THE POLITICS AND HISTORY OF FAMILY VIOLENCE, BOSTON 1880–1960 (1989), describing the treatment of women among the immigrant poor in Boston in the early twentieth century.

47. *Id.*

48. The lead lawyer for Kennedy-Smith, Roy Black, emphasized these details. John T. Litman, *The Prosecutor Rushed in Where the Defense Had Feared to Tread*, AM. LAW., April 1992, at 9. Black depicted another witness, Bowman's friend Anne Mercer, as a thief. On the second day of the trial, he produced a vase Mercer had taken from the Kennedy estate the night of the alleged rape and put it in front of her while she testified. As one commentator noted, "That vase said 'thief' every time the six jurors and two alternates looked over at Mercer." Steven Brill, *How the Willie Smith Show Changed America*, AM. LAW., Jan.–Feb. 1992, at 3.

49. "Historically Black women's words were not taken as true. In our own legal system, a connection was once drawn between lack of chastity and lack of veracity. In other words, a woman who was likely to have sex was not likely to tell the truth. Judges were known to instruct juries to take a Black woman's word with a grain of salt. One judge warned jurors that the general presumption of chastity applicable to white women did not apply to Black women." Crenshaw, *Race, Gender, and Sexual Harassment*, *supra* note 36, at 1470.

50. During the trial, Patricia Bowman's face was obscured by a blue dot on the CNN broadcast. John Carmody, WASH. POST, Dec. 17, 1991 (Style), at B6.

51. During the 1988 presidential race, the Bush campaign used sensationalist television advertisements to focus the public's attention on the case of Willie Horton, a black convict who raped a white woman while he was on leave from a Massachusetts prison. The polls indicated that the tactic was very effective in damaging the image of Michael Dukakis, Bush's opponent. Susan Estrich, campaign manager for Dukakis, said, "There is no stronger metaphor for racial hatred in our country than a black man raping a white woman." Andrew Rosenthal, *Foes Accuse Bush Campaign of Inflaming Racial Tension*, N.Y. TIMES, Oct. 24, 1988, at A1.

52. *See In Judgment of Iron Mike; Mike Tyson's Dark Past Is on Trial, and So Is the Popular Suspicion of Women Who Charge Famous Men with Rape*, TIME, Feb. 10, 1992, at 77. *And see supra* note 18.

53. Richard Hoffer, *Destined to Fall; The Same Fury That Drove Mike Tyson to Glory in the Ring Brought Him Shame Out of It*, SPORTS ILLUSTRATED, Feb. 17, 1992, at 24, 25.

54. Quoted in Tony Kornheisher, *Ex-Champ Down for the Count*, WASH. POST, Feb. 11, 1992, at C1.

55. *Id.*

56. Feminist legal scholars have argued that pornography is what pornography

does. As Catharine MacKinnon has written: "Women in pornography are bound, battered, tortured, humiliated, and killed. Or, to be fair to the soft core, merely taken and used. This is being done to real women now. It is being done for a reason: it gives sexual pleasure to its consumers and therefore profits to its providers. But to the women and children who are the victims of its making or use, it means being bound, battered and tortured, humiliated, and killed—or merely taken and used, until they are used up or can get out. It is done for a reason: because someone with more power than they have gets pleasure from seeing it, or doing it, or seeing it as a form of doing it." Catharine MacKinnon, FEMINISM UNMODIFIED: DISCOURSE ON LIFE AND LAW (1987). *See also* Catharine MacKinnon, ONLY WORDS (1993).

57. As of July 22, 1993, a search of the MAJPAP file (which includes a compilation of stories from thirty-four major papers around the country) of NEXIS revealed that of approximately three thousand stories about Mike Tyson and rape (3,106), approximately two thousand (1,906) appeared in the sports section. The same search conducted in the *New York Times* file of NEXIS found that of 221 references to Tyson and rape, 154 of them appeared in the sports section.

58. Todd Barrett, *He Started Laughing, Like It Was a Game*, NEWSWEEK, Feb. 10, 1992, at 30.

59. Stan Hochman, *Iron Mike, Iron Bars*, CALGARY HERALD, Feb. 23, 1992, at C9.

60. *Id.*

61. Studies indicate that "black women are much more likely to be victims of a rape than are white women." The average sentence received by black men, excluding cases involving life imprisonment or death, was 4.2 years if the victim was black, 16.4 years if the victim was white. Wriggins, *supra* note 20, at 121, n. 113. *See also supra* note 42.

62. *See* Derrick Bell, AND WE ARE NOT SAVED: THE ELUSIVE QUEST FOR RACIAL JUSTICE (1987); Alan Freeman, *Legitimizing Racism Through Anti-discrimination Law: A Critical Review of Supreme Court Doctrine*, 62 MINN. L. REV. 1049 (1978) (documenting how civil rights law, while appearing to advance the cause of minorities, bolsters an ideology that promotes racist and class-based structures and has served more to rationalize the continued effects of racial discrimination than to promote any genuine liberation from a history of oppression).

63. The term "Miss Anne" is an African American colloquialism originating during slavery. African American slaves were required to address the master and mistress of the plantation and all other white adults and children by the titles "Master" and "Mistress." "Mr. Charlie" (as in Baldwin's *Blues for Mr. Charlie*) and "Miss Anne" were and are used within the African American community as a generic, usually mocking reference to all white men and women, particularly those in positions of power. "Miss Anne" is pejorative in the sense that it conveys the message that this woman is given a

respectful title only by virtue of her position in a white supremist system. Catharine MacKinnon has been critical of the use of the term "Miss Anne." She argues that its identification of white women as oppressors discounts their oppression as women. Catharine MacKinnon, *From Practice to Theory, or What Is a White Woman Anyway?* 4 YALE J. L. AND FEMINISM 13 (1991). For a thoughtful response to MacKinnon, *see* Martha Mahoney, *Whiteness and Women, in Practice and Theory: A Reply to Catharine MacKinnon,* 5 YALE J. L. AND FEMINISM 217 (1993).

Stopping Sexual Harassment:
A Challenge for
Community Education

ROBERT L. ALLEN

*T*here can be little doubt that an important outcome of the 1991 Senate Judiciary Committee hearings has been growing public recognition of sexual harassment as a major social problem. Virtually the entire nation has engaged in the public discourse around this issue, and this engagement is to be welcomed.

Like many men in the aftermath of Anita Hill's testimony, I found myself hearing harrowing reports of sexual harassment from women relatives and friends who had previously felt constrained to remain silent. They told me of awful things that had been said or done to them, on the job or in the streets, sometimes recently and sometimes years ago. They spoke of their anger and humiliation, of their shame and feelings of self-blame, of their fear of the consequences of speaking out or rebuking their harassers. They experienced sexual harassment—the imposition of unwanted sexual attention—as a violation of their human dignity.

I listened and shared their outrage—but I also found myself recalling things I had said or done to women in the recent or distant past, and the recollections were sometimes distinctly discomforting. I think an important value of these exchanges was the opportunity for men to learn from the personal testimony of women they love and respect how widespread sexual harassment is. At the same time, the self-reflection and discussions among men that were sometimes provoked by the women's stories offered an opportunity for men to recognize that harassing behavior is not simply an aberration, nor is it exclusively the province of macho males; on the contrary, harassing behavior is something that many of us men have engaged in at some point, if not on the job, then on the streets or on campus or even in our homes. We knew what we were doing, because we knew the women involved were made to feel uncomfortable or humiliated by our words or actions.

Why did we do it? Why do men harass women? Why, until recently, was such behavior generally acceptable in our culture—that is, acceptable to men? Aside from punishment, what can be done to stop harassing behavior?

In this essay I want to raise two points for consideration as part of the discourse on sexual harassment.

First, sexual harassment should not be dismissed as aberrant behavior, as the macho mentality gone wild, or as the result of male biology or uncontrollable sexual desire. Sexual harassment, like child abuse and domestic violence, is an outgrowth of socialization into male and female gender roles in a sexist society. It is learned behavior.

Second, if harassment, abuse, and violence are forms of learned behavior, they can also be unlearned. I therefore argue that in addition to legal or punitive approaches to sexual harassment, it is imperative to adopt a preventive approach through community education. We must create an environment, not only in the workplace but in our communities generally, in which harassment, abuse, and violence are no longer tolerated because men and women understand the damage such behavior does to all of us. That means adopting a social change perspective critical of the values of the dominant culture, a culture that is premised on inequality.

Gender roles are not foreordained by our biology or our genes. We learn gender roles as part of our socialization into the culture. When a child is born, the first question inevitably asked is "Boy or girl?" Our response to the child is then mediated by our knowledge of its genitals, and it is *our* actions that tell the child its gender identity and the behavior appropriate to that identity.

In California I work with an organization called the Oakland

Men's Project (OMP). Formed in 1979, OMP is a nonprofit multira-
cial organization of men and women devoted to community education around issues of male violence, sexism, racism, and homophobia. Over the years we have worked with thousands of boys and men
(and girls and women) in high schools, church groups, colleges, pris-
ons, community groups, and rehabilitation programs. We conduct
workshops that involve interactive role playing and discussions that
allow men and women to examine gender roles and the social training we get in this culture.

In our workshops we ask young people what they think it means to
be a man or a woman. It is remarkable how consistently they express
the same set of expectations about appropriate male and female behavior. Men are expected to be in control, tough, aggressive, independent,
competitive, and emotionally unexpressive (with the exception of anger
and sexual desire, which are allowable emotions for men). Women, on
the other hand, are expected to be polite, dependent, emotional, and
sexy, to take care of others, and not to be too smart or pushy. In recent
years we have noticed that sometimes girls will challenge these role expectations and occasionally even a boy will object, but for the most part
they remain widely accepted. Paul Kivel, who has summed up the experience of the Oakland Men's Project in his *Men's Work: How to Stop
the Violence That Tears Our Lives Apart*, refers to these as "core expectations" that we all have, especially men, regarding appropriate male
and female behavior.

How do young men learn these expectations? At OMP, to illustrate
the socialization process, we use what we call role plays that drama-
tize common situations most boys and men have experienced. One
of these involves an interaction between a father and his ten-year-old
son, both played by facilitators. The son is sitting at home watching
television when the father comes in from work, orders the boy to
turn off the TV, and berates him for the messiness of the room.
When the boy tries to explain that he was going to clean up later,
the father tells him to shut up and stop making excuses. Then he
shoves the son's report card in his face and demands to know why he
got a D in math. The boy says he did the best he could. The father
shames the son, telling him that he is stupid and that D stands for
"dummy." The boy says that's not fair and begins to stand up. The
father shoves him down, saying, "Don't you dare get up in my face,
I didn't say you could go anyplace!" The boy is visibly upset and

begins to cry. The father gets even more angry: "Now what? You're crying? You little mama's boy! You sissy! You make me sick. When are you going to grow up and start acting like a man?" The father storms out of the room.

When we do this role play, it gets the undivided attention of everyone in the room, especially the boys. Almost every young person has had the experience of being scolded and shamed by an adult. Most boys have had the experience of being humiliated by an older male and being told that they are not acting like men.

When we stop the role play, we ask the boys how it made them feel to witness this scene between the father and son. There may be a moment of embarassed silence, but then the boys speak up and say it made them mad, upset, sad, etc. Often this is the first time they have articulated the feelings brought up by such an encounter, which sadly often replicates their own experience. Indeed, the power of this role play is that it is so familiar.

We ask the boys what messages such encounters send. They say things like, "A man is tough. A man is in control. A man doesn't cry. It's okay for a man to yell at someone. A man can take it. A man is responsible. A man is competent. A man doesn't take crap from anyone else." As they speak, we write their comments on a blackboard. Then we draw a box around the comments and label it the "Act Like a Man" box. Most males in this culture are socialized to stay in the box. We learn this from our fathers, older brothers, guys on the street, television, sports, movies, and so on. We may also learn it from our mothers and grandmothers, or from the reactions of girls in school. The fact is that this notion of manhood is so pervasive in our culture that everyone knows the role and anyone can teach it to a boy.

We ask the boys what happens if you step out of the box, if you stop acting tough enough or man enough. They reply that you get called names: sissy, wimp, nerd, fag, queer, mama's boy, punk, girl, loser, fairy. And what is the point of the name calling? The boys say that it is a challenge and you're expected to fight to prove that you're not what they called you. In other words, if challenged, boys are expected to fight to prove that they're in the box—that they're tough and not gay or effeminate. Homophobia and fear of being identified with women in any way are strong messages boys receive from an early age.

We also ask about expectations of female behavior. The young people say things like, "A girl should be polite and clean, she shouldn't argue, she's pretty, she doesn't fight or act too smart, she helps others, she's emotional." We ask what happens when a girl refuses to be submissive and dependent, when she's assertive and smart and doesn't kowtow to the boys. Again the reply is that she will be called names: bitch, tomboy, dyke, whore, ball-breaker, cunt. And what is the point of the name calling? To tell the girl she'd better start "acting right." In other words, the name calling is like a slap in the face, reducing the girl to a despised sexual object, with the purpose of humiliating her and intimidating her into resuming "acceptable" behavior. If a girl fights when called names, she may emerge the victor, but her very success raises questions about her femininity.

Though our forays into junior highs and high schools hardly constitute systematic research, again and again we find the same core expectations of acceptable male and female behavior among young people. As I have said, there is a growing tendency to question these expectations, especially among young women, but the grip of traditional roles remains very strong.

Our work at OMP involves challenging role expectations by showing that male and female behaviors are neither biologically determined nor a function of "human nature" but are learned from our interactions with significant others and from the culture at large. Our workshops and role plays give boys and girls and men and women a way of analyzing social roles, not abstractly, but by drawing insights from their own experiences. Moreover, we show that social interactions involve making choices, and that we can break free of old roles by supporting each other in changing our choices.

An important component of our work is to look at structural relationships of power and inequality in our society. We ask workshop participants to think about their experiences with different social groups and to tell us which groups they think are more powerful and which are less powerful. Most often this elicits statements to the effect that men as a group are more powerful than women as a group, whites more powerful than people of color, parents more powerful than children, teachers more powerful than pupils, the rich more powerful than the poor, straights more powerful than gays, bosses more powerful than workers, and so on. If we ask how these inequalities are maintained, we are told that it is done through laws, through rules and regulations, through discrimination and stereotypes, and ultimately through force and violence. Thus, despite our country's rhetoric of equality, experience teaches us that people are not treated equally, that we all have assigned places in the social hierarchy, and that violence is used to keep less powerful groups "in their place."

This violence takes many forms and is often legitimized through the process of blaming the victim. Consider the Rodney King case, in which the jury was told that the police officers thought he was dangerous because he was high on drugs and "out of control," and at the same time was persuaded that he was actually "in control," deliberately taunting and manipulating the officers. Either way, the message of this incredible argument was that Rodney King "deserved" the brutal beating he received and the policemen could be acquitted. Blaming victims for their own victimization is a widely employed means of justifying abuse and violence of all kinds.

Sexual harassment plays a part in reinforcing the power differential between men and women in our society, and that distinguishes it from flirtation or a simple mistake in judgment. For example, a man may harass a woman when she steps out of the role he expects her to play. In the workplace, "uppity" women who hold jobs traditionally held by men, or who are regarded as "too" assertive, competent, competitive, or emotionally reserved, are likely targets of harassment. Men may also harass women who are not "uppity" as a kind of ritual that confirms male dominance and female submissiveness. Thus, the female secretary or domestic worker may be "teased" or pinched or subjected to sexual remarks that serve to remind her of her low status and her vulnerability to men. She is expected to acquiesce in this treatment by laughing or otherwise acting as if the harassment is okay, thereby reaffirming the male's superior status and power. A woman worker may also be harassed by a male worker who is angry at the boss but fearful of the boss's power, and seeks to regain a sense of his own power by humiliating her.

Whether in the workplace or on the street, the purpose of sexual harassment is to reduce women to objects sexually vulnerable to men, and to reestablish the traditional power relationship between men and women. Indeed, women's sexual vulnerability to men is a key locus of male power, something men learn to expect. As boys we learn it from stories of sexual "conquest" we hear from older males;

we learn it from films, magazines, pornography, advertising. We live in a capitalist culture that promises women's sexual availability as a reward to the male consumer of everything from cars to cigarettes. It is not surprising, then, that men come to believe that every woman should be sexually available to any man. Sexual harassment is both a manifestation and a reinforcement of an exploitive system in which men are socialized collectively and individually to expect to have power over women collectively and individually.

Moreover, of the thousands of women who experience sexual harassment every day, a great many of them are women of color and poor women employed in the jobs that racist and sexist discrimination forces them to take—as domestics, clerical workers, farm workers, sweatshop and factory workers. Not only are these women especially vulnerable to sexual harassment, they also have less access to the levers of power needed to seek redress. Often they do not report harassment because they fear revenge from their employers or know their complaints will be dismissed. They are doubly oppressed: subjected to abuse and then constrained to remain silent about it.

The nature of sexual harassment is such that it is particularly easy to blame the victims. Often there is a suggestion that the woman somehow provoked or invited the objectionable behavior by something she said or did, or simply the way she was dressed. And if she did not protest the behavior immediately, it is insinuated that she must have enjoyed it, and any subsequent protests are suspect. In any case, the female victim's character is called into question and the male harasser is conveniently let off the hook, again reinforcing male dominance.

Of course, all men don't engage in sexual harassment, but we must ask why men who witness it often fail to intervene. One reason is obvious: male bonding to maintain male dominance. Men who would not engage in harassing behavior themselves may condone it in others because they agree that women must be "kept in their place." A second reason is more hidden: men's fear of being shamed or even attacked by other men.

As boys, most men learn that other men are dangerous. How many of us were called names or beaten up by other males when we were young? How many of us were ridiculed and humiliated by fathers or older brothers or coaches or teachers? How many were sexually assaulted by another male? We protected ourselves in various ways. Some of us withdrew into the private world of our fantasies. Some of us became bullies. Some of us became alcoholics and addicts so we wouldn't have to feel the pain and fear. Most of us learned to camouflage ourselves: we took on the coloration of the men we feared, and we hoped that no one would challenge us. We never talked about our fear because that in itself was dangerous and could mark us as targets of ridicule or violence from other men.

Instead we learned to keep our fear inside, a secret. In fact, we learned to keep most of our emotions bottled up inside because any sincere expression of emotion in front of other men was risky business that set you up to be put down. Only one emotion was considered manly: anger. Some of us learned to take other feelings—pain, grief, sadness, shame, loneliness, depression, jealousy, helplessness, fearfulness—and translate them into anger, and then pass them on to someone weaker in the form of physical or psychological violence. The humiliation we experienced at work, the fear we experienced when hassled by cops, the grief we felt when a relationship ended, the helplessness we felt when we lost a job—we learned to take these feelings, roll them into a heavy fist of rage, and slam it into our wives, our children, our lovers, women on the job or on the streets, less powerful men.

Thus, women and children often live in fear of men, and men frequently live in fear of each other. Most of us men won't admit this, but deep inside we recognize that harassment, abuse, rape, and violence are not simply "women's issues"—they're our issues as well. We know, but seldom admit, that if we didn't constantly protect ourselves, other men would do to us what we all too often do to women and children—as men who have been imprisoned can attest. So those of us who are not abusers or harassers sometimes wear the camouflage suits, we try to be "one of the boys." We present a front of manly power and control no matter what we may be feeling inside. We jostle and joke and push and shove, we make cracks about women and boast of our conquests, and we haze any guy who is different. We go along with harassers so as not to expose our own vulnerability, our fear of being shamed by other men—the weak point in our male armor.

Nevertheless, men have a stake in challenging sexual harassment, abuse, violence, and the sexist role training that underpins these behaviors. In the first place, men are not unconnected to women. We form a community of men and women—and children—together. A woman who suffers harassment might be my mother, my sister, my niece. She might be your daughter or your sister or your wife. A woman who is harassed, abused, or raped is part of a community that includes male relatives, lovers, and friends who are also hurt by the injury done to her. Men have a stake in stopping the abuse because it is directed against women we love and cherish.

I would argue that men have a further stake in challenging sexual abuse and the sexism on which it is based. Men are also damaged by sexism. A system that requires us to act as though we are always in control and to repress our emotions takes a heavy toll. It undermines our sense of authenticity. It results in a loss of intimacy with women and children. It conceals but does not change our fear of other men. It produces stress that is hazardous to our health and shortens our life spans. It makes us sick in our souls and bodies, and it turns us into enemies of those we love and of ourselves.

Historically, Black men and women in America have been victims of especially brutal and systematic violence. In the past our community has been terrorized by the lynching (and castration) of thousands of Black men by white men, and the rape (and lynching) of thousands of Black women by white men. Today white mob violence and police brutality continue unabated. African American men know intimately the violent capabilities of other men. It is a tragedy that many of us have internalized the violence of this oppressive system and brought it into our communities and our homes. The injuries done by racism to Black men's self-esteem are sometimes devastating, but the expectations of manhood we have learned block us from revealing or acknowledging our pain. Instead, we too often transform it into rage and violence against those we love. This must stop. African American men, as frequent victims of white male violence, have a particular stake in standing with women and children against all forms of violence.

How can men of all races be brought into the struggle against harassment, abuse, and violence? That is the question we have been seeking to answer through our work at the Oakland Men's Project. We have learned that it is extremely important for men to begin talking with each other about these issues. In our experience we have seen that there are growing numbers of men who are critical of sexism. All too often, however, these men as individuals are isolated and fearful of raising their concerns with other men. It is time for men who want to stop the violence to reach out to other men and break through the barrier of fear that has silenced us.

This is not an easy task, but as we have learned at OMP, it can be done. The male sex role, with its insistence on emotional "coolness" and reserve, makes open and honest communication from the heart difficult between men. We can begin to break through this isolation by sharing the often painful and humiliating ways we were socialized into the male role as young boys. At OMP we have found that workshops using interactive role plays, like the father-son encounter described earlier, are an effective method of opening up communication between men. Such techniques enable us to examine how the male sex role often sets men up to be dominating, controlling, and abusive. In another role play we watch a bully harassing the new boy at school. We discuss what the bully gains or fails to gain by bullying. For example, the bully may be seeking to compel respect from the victim, but what the victim often feels is contempt. At the same time, the bully models abusive behavior for the victim. He fails to get what he wants, but he may teach the victim how to bully someone else.

Through role plays like these, we look at how men are trained to take the hurt that has been done to them, translate it into anger, and direct the anger at a weaker person in the form of violence. This is the cycle of violence. We see it, for example, in the fact that the great majority of child abusers were themselves abused as children.

Another role play we use recreates a high school dating scene in which a boy and his girlfriend are sitting in his car in a secluded spot at night. We recruit two students from the audience to play the roles. We tell them that the boy wants to have sex that night but the girl, although she likes him, does not. Then we ask them to play out the scene. Sometimes the two actors work out a resolution acceptable to both. Sometimes the girl gets out of the car and walks away. But often the tension simply builds as the boy attempts to dominate and get his way while the girl tries to be responsive without giving in to his demands. We stop the role play and talk with the actors about the pressures they felt to behave as they did in the situation. We relate these pressures to the male and female role expectations discussed earlier. We also talk about the risk of the situation escalating into violence and rape, and the need to recognize danger signs to prevent this from happening. (For other examples of role plays and antiviolence exercises for teens, see *Helping Teens Stop Violence*, by Allan Creighton and Paul Kivel.)

Interrupting the cycle of violence requires that we unlearn sex roles that set us up to be perpetrators and victims of abuse. I am not talking only about men who are harassers or batterers, or women who have been abused. I believe that in this culture most of us are at risk for abusive behavior because most of us have been socialized into traditional sex roles. The cycle of abuse and violence can be broken at its root by challenging those roles and the institutions that support them—that is, through a process of community education and social change.

It is important for men of all races to become involved in this process. Men can take responsibility for stopping the cycle of violence and offering alternatives to violence. Men working with boys can model supportive ways of interacting and constructive methods of using anger to bring about change. All of us constantly make choices about how we relate to others, and in the power of choice is the power of change, for we are not simply passive victims of our socialization. For African American men there is a special urgency to this work. Our sons are dying in record numbers, often at each other's hands in angry acts of violence whose goal is to prove their manhood. We need to be clear that anger itself is not the problem. In a racist society Black people and other people of color have good reason to be angry. The problem lies in how the anger is expressed. Turning the anger against ourselves or others in acts of abuse and violence is self-destructive. Using righteous anger to challenge racist and oppressive institutions empowers individuals and communities, creates the possibility of real change, and builds self-esteem. Black men's orgnizations such as Simba, the Omega Boys' Club, and 100 Black Men of America are helping to develop new models of manhood among teenage Black males. We need organizations like these in every city.

Equally important, men working together can model a new version of power—*power with* others to make change, as opposed to *power over* others to perpetuate domination. In our society power generally means the ability to control others directly, with violence as the ultimate means of control. Men are socialized to exercise this form of power in all their relationships. Women sometimes learn to do the same. But this kind of power necessarily sets up conflicts with others—those we seek to control—and is alienating and isolating for the individual power holder. Power *with* others breaks down the isolation we feel and makes it possible to relate as allies rather than as competitors or opponents. It allows us to recognize that we are a community of people—men, women, and children—who are interdependent.

All of us have had the experience of powerlessness, for all of us have been children. As children we learned what it meant to be controlled by others, and often we learned what it meant to be humiliated and shamed by others. Such experiences are painful, and we may prefer to forget them, but ironically, by "owning" them, we create the possibility of empowerment through establishing our connection with others who have had similar experiences. In this way it becomes possible for men to become allies of women and children, not out of guilt, but through insight into their own lives.

Harassment, abuse, and violence arise from a system of sexual and racial inequality. To stop them we must challenge the gender roles, institutions, and power structures upon which sexism and racism stand. This is a big task, but it is one each of us can undertake in small ways—in our homes, in our schools, in our communities. We can educate ourselves and offer our children new models of male and female behavior. We can support each other in finding healing responses to the pain and hurt we have suffered. We can insist that the schools educate young people about empowering ways to counter sexism and racism. We can confront institutionalized oppression and violence. We can support movements and organizations that work for progressive social change. In sum, working together with others as allies, we can build community responses to the system of inequality and the cycle of violence that blight our lives.

References

Beneke, Timothy. *Men on Rape: What They Have to Say about Sexual Violence.* New York: St. Martin's Press, 1982.

Bravo, Ellen, and Ellen Cassedy. *The 9 to 5 Guide to Combatting Sexual Harassment.* New York: John Wiley and Sons, 1992.

Chrisman, Robert, and Robert L. Allen, eds. *Court of Appeal: The Black Community Speaks Out on the Racial and Sexual Politics of Thomas vs. Hill.* New York: Ballantine Books, 1992.

Creighton, Allan, with Paul Kivel. *Helping Teens Stop Violence: A Practical Guide for Parents, Counselors, and Educators.* Alameda, Calif.: Hunter House, 1992.

Hagan, Kay Leigh, ed. *Women Respond to the Men's Movement.* San Francisco: HarperCollins, 1992.

Hemphill, Essex, ed. *Brother to Brother: New Writings by Black Gay Men.* Boston: Alyson Publications, 1991.

Jackson, Walter H. *Sporting the Right Attitude: Surviving Family Violence.* Los Angeles: Self Expansion, 1992.

Kaufman, Michael, ed. *Beyond Patriarchy: Essays by Men on Pleasure, Power, and Change.* New York: Oxford University Press, 1987.

Kimmel, Michael S., ed. *Men Confront Pornography.* New York: Meridian, 1990.

Kivel, Paul. *Men's Work: How to Stop the Violence That Tears Our Lives Apart.* Center City, Minn.: Hazelden, 1992.

Kunjufu, Jawanza. *Countering the Conspiracy to Destroy Black Boys.* Chicago: African American Images, 1985.

Lewis, Michael. *Shame: The Exposed Self.* New York: Free Press, 1992.

Madhubuti, Haki. *Black Men: Obsolete, Single, Dangerous?* Chicago: Third World Press, 1990.

Majors, Richard, and Janet Mancini Billson. *Cool Pose: The Dilemmas of Black Manhood in America.* New York: Lexington Books, 1992.

McGill, Michael E. *The McGill Report on Male Intimacy.* New York: Harper and Row, 1985.

Miedzian, Myriam. *Boys Will Be Boys: Breaking the Link between Masculinity and Violence.* New York: Doubleday, 1991.

Staples, Robert, ed. *The Black Family: Essays and Studies.* 4th ed. Belmont, Calif.: Wadsworth, 1991.

Strauss, Susan, with Pamela Espeland. *Sexual Harassment and Teens: A Program for Positive Change.* Minneapolis: Free Spirit Publishing, 1992.

Wilkinson, Doris Y., and Ronald L. Taylor, eds. *The Black Male in America: Perspectives on His Status in Contemporary Society.* Chicago: Nelson-Hall, 1977.

The People vs. Anita Hill: A Case for Client-Centered Advocacy

CHARLES J. OGLETREE, JR.

Professor Anita Hill's dramatic appearance before the United States Senate Judiciary Committee on Friday, October 11, 1991, sent shock waves across the country. Although there have been other controversial confirmation hearings for Supreme Court nominees, as well as nominees for other confirmable positions,[1] few have generated such intense scrutiny of the nominee, of witnesses, or of a range of sensitive public issues.

The hearings and their aftermath have deservedly prompted many analyses, most of which have focused on the confirmation process in general or on the broader dynamics of race, gender, and/or sexual harassment in American life.[2] This essay will discuss the hearings from the point of view of one of the lawyers who served as counsel for Professor Hill during that demanding week in October 1991. Along with an abbreviated narrative of the hearings, I will present three conclusions. First, that procedural flaws in the conception and execution of the hearings combined with the political intentions of those conducting them to create what was less an investigation of the truth of Professor Hill's allegations than a trial of Professor Hill. Second, that counsel for Professor Hill attempted at all times to follow the familiar model of client-centered representation, protecting her autonomy rather than serving "third parties" or interest groups. Third, that the "fake trial" of Professor Hill[3] can teach us specific lessons, not only about how public interest lawyers should strive to represent their clients, but also about the process by which political and procedural rules are made. The essay concludes by recommending new rules for Senate hearings when those hearings are likely to be adversarial—rules that might prevent a similar drama of injustice if and when another witness comes forward to accuse another high-level nominee of ignominious behavior.

I

Although Professor Hill was told that she would be treated fairly by the Senate Judiciary Committee, events before, during, and after her testimony suggested otherwise. The series of attacks on Anita Hill's veracity and on her perceived motives did not begin when she appeared before the committee on October 11; from the moment her allegations surfaced in the press on October 6, some senators were publicly declaring that Professor Hill could not be trusted and that her last-minute revelations were part of a sinister plot to prevent Judge Thomas from being confirmed. This view surfaced on the Senate floor during the unruly October 8 debate over whether to postpone the confirmation vote and reopen the hearings. For example, Senator Jake Garn of Utah said:

> These latest charges are obviously serious. But where was this woman in his other confirmation processes; where has she been the last 10 years with these charges? It looks to me like part of a plot to get Clarence, delay, and bring her out of the woodwork 10 years later to make some charges that the FBI has already investigated.[4]

Senator Alan Simpson of Wyoming implied on October 8 that Professor Hill's allegations were not worth looking into, and went on to proclaim that a second round of hearings would demean and torment her. As Senator Simpson sat (and still sits) on the Judiciary Committee, he was in a position to make his words come true; those words, certainly in retrospect, seem less a disinterested warning than a threat.

> . . . I think it is a cruel thing we are witnessing. It is a harsh thing, a very sad and harsh thing, and Anita Hill will be sucked right into the

maw, the very thing she wanted to avoid most. She will be injured and destroyed and belittled and hounded and harassed—real harassment, different from the sexual kind, just plain old Washington variety harassment, which is pretty demeaning in itself.[5]

Senator Orrin Hatch of Utah—who was soon to be one of the four senators designated by the Judiciary Committee to question Professor Hill—expressed his consternation that the Democrats on the committee had known of her allegations on September 27, when the members voted 7–7 on the nomination and referred it to the full Senate, but had not asked for a delay and further investigation at that time.[6] Senator Hatch himself, however, had already made up his mind on October 8 that Judge Thomas was telling the truth.

> My conclusion is that I question [her] truthfulness. But I question it on the facts and from a personal knowledge of Judge Thomas. I know that what she said is not true because I know the man personally. I know his wife personally. . . . Is he perfect? No. But neither is anybody else.[7]

Thus, before Professor Hill had even testified, two members of the Senate Judiciary Committee had already expressed their support for Judge Thomas and their apparent hostility toward Professor Hill.

Many senators, including Patrick Leahy of the Judiciary Committee (who had already come out against Thomas), spoke in favor of a second round of hearings, but the only comprehensive and insightful objection that day to the *manner* in which the allegations had been handled so far came from Barbara Mikulski of Maryland, one of only two women then in the Senate.

> . . . what disturbs me as much as the allegations themselves is that the Senate appears not to take the charge of sexual harassment seriously. We've indicated that it was not serious enough to be raised as a question in the Judiciary Committee. We do not think it is serious enough to apprise Senators themselves that there was an allegation.
> . . . If you talk to victims of abuse the way I have, they will tell you they are often doubly victimized by both the event in which they are abused and then subsequently by the way the system treats them. To say these charges could not be taken seriously enough to be brought to our attention has consequences, as I said, for both Professor Hill and

for Judge Thomas. But let me tell you about the other consequences to the people of the United States. . . .

To anybody out there who wants to be a whistle blower, the message is, "Don't blow that whistle because you will be left out there by yourself." To any victim of sexual harassment, or sexual abuse or sexual violence, either in the street or even in his or her own home, the message is, "Nobody is going to take you seriously, not in the U.S. Senate." To the private sector, which now has to enforce these laws on sexual harassment . . . the message to the private sector is, "Cool it. Even the Senate takes a walk on this one."[8]

Finally, after a chaotic day of angry speeches, condemnations, and tangled parliamentary procedure, all one hundred senators agreed on October 8 to delay the confirmation vote and hold new hearings so that Professor Hill's charges could be investigated. John Danforth of Missouri, Judge Thomas's Senate sponsor, asked for hearings and a confirmation vote within forty-eight hours. Thomas's opponents wanted two weeks to investigate the charges.[9] The Senate compromised and scheduled the testimony of Professor Hill and Judge Thomas for Friday, October 11.

With the unanimous Senate vote of October 8, the stage was set for the dramatic confrontation between Professor Anita Hill of the University of Oklahoma Law School and Judge Clarence Thomas of the United States Court of Appeals for the D.C. Circuit. The hearings will be remembered for their value as riveting television and for the advances they have apparently achieved in the public perception of sexual harassment. But the events that led up to the hearings, as well as the hearings themselves, also demonstrate the need among public interest lawyers for sustained attention to the individual client at hand, rather than simply to the cause that client represents.

II

After the Senate decided on Tuesday evening to hold additional hearings on Friday, Professor Hill was told that she would be subpoenaed to appear before the committee and discuss her allegations under oath. At the time she was contacted, she was not represented by counsel. Once it became apparent that Professor Hill would testify, several friends called her to discuss the necessity for counsel at the hearings and to offer their support. A number of lawyers agreed to provide assistance, and discussed the roles they would play at the hearings.[10] Among them were Professor Emma Coleman Jordan, then president of the American Association of Law Schools, who knew Professor Hill and had worked with her in the association's commercial law section; Professor Judith Resnik of the University of Southern California Law Center; myself; Professor Susan Deller Ross, a sex discrimination expert at Georgetown Law Center; and Professor Kim Taylor Thompson of Stanford Law School, a close friend of Professor Hill's. Others who volunteered to assist included John Frank, a former law professor who has written extensively about judicial confirmation hearings; Janet Napolitano, a partner of John Frank's; and Michelle Roberts, a veteran criminal defense lawyer in the District of Columbia.

The legal team assembled in Washington, D.C., on Thursday, October 10, the day before the new round of hearings, and less than forty-eight hours after the Senate announced that Professor Hill would be called as a witness. The rapid pace of events left little time for extensive legal research. Members of the team met with the Senate Judiciary Committee staff to discuss procedures for the hearings. We contacted experts on the psychology of sexual harassment; Professor Louise Fitzgerald of the University of Illinois actually came to Washington. (We let Senator Biden and the committee staff know that she was willing and waiting to testify, but the committee decided to call no expert witnesses.)

The legal team's chief concern was preparing Professor Hill for the weekend's hearings, guarding her privacy, and serving her interests. This mission meant not only preparing her to rebut the allegations and insinuations Thomas's defenders would and did deliver but also protecting her from reporters and political pressure groups. Public interest in Professor Hill's story was widespread and intense: Senator Paul Simon reported receiving about 19,600 letters on the subject, compared to 15,700 on the Gulf war.[11] The televised hearings had more viewers than the NFL games that competed with them.[12]

It was obvious during Judge Thomas's first confirmation hearing in September that many groups and individuals were determined to find some basis for declaring him unfit to serve on the Supreme Court. Other groups were equally determined that he be confirmed. Daily articles in every major national and international English-language newspaper tracked the progress of the Thomas nomination in advance of the hearings. All the political organizations that had already taken a stand during the first round of hearings on Judge Thomas now had an obvious stake in the second round. Professor Hill's legal team therefore had both to prepare her to face whatever case the administration and the pro-Thomas senators might lay out and to protect her from the crush of public and third-party attention.

When Angela Wright, a North Carolina journalist who had worked for Judge Thomas in the early 1980s, said on October 10 that Thomas had also behaved inappropriately toward her, the Senate subpoenaed her, and a multimedia battalion beat a path to her door, as it had to Anita Hill's.[13] When Wright, who was not represented by counsel at that time, flew from Charlotte to Washington on the first day of the hearings, crowds gathered at the airport boarding gate to cheer and boo her. A mob of reporters pushed her into a wall in the terminal, and more than a few pursued her onto the airplane. In Washington, a television camera crew followed her automobile from the airport down the George Washington Parkway.[14] Part of our job as Anita Hill's legal team was to help her avoid similar occurrences.

In all our actions on behalf of Professor Hill, we were guided by the theory of client-centered representation, as implied in the American Bar Association (ABA) Model Code of Professional Responsibility.

> The professional judgement of a lawyer should be exercised, within the bounds of the law, solely for the benefit of his client and free of compromising influences and loyalties. Neither his personal interests, the interests of other clients, nor the desires of third persons should be permitted to dilute his loyalty to his client.[15]

As her legal advisers, we made every effort to adhere to our client's wishes. Our client, Anita Hill, did not want to be a figurehead for women's issues or for a national movement to oppose Clarence Thomas. As one member of our team said:

> Everyone wanted a piece of this woman. . . . There were people who thought she should be out there as a spokeswoman for women or whatever. Well, that is not what she wanted to do. That is not who she is. She did *not* want to be the Rosa Parks of sexual harassment.[16]

Or as a book on the hearings later put it:

> Hovering around her were feminists who wanted to make sexual harass-
> ment the issue, or diehard Thomas opponents who wanted to make
> him the issue. Hill's concern was simply that she have the opportunity
> to say what she wanted to say and survive to teach another day.[17]

Her friend Shirley Wiegand, also a law professor at the University of
Oklahoma, told journalists afterward that Hill's decision to come
forward

> was not taken with the advice of any of the interest groups. . . . we
> felt it was very dangerous to accept help from them. That was not what
> she had in mind. Later, when the folks [from interest groups] started
> trying to get involved, she made it very clear that she didn't want them
> involved. She knew that would be misinterpreted. She doesn't align
> herself with political factions. She still doesn't call herself a feminist.[18]

In coming forth with allegations of sexual harassment against Clarence Thomas, Professor Hill simply intended to lay bare information
pertinent to his fitness for the Supreme Court. To the extent that she
"came forth" as the result of a leak of those allegations to the press,
the third-party interests we were trying to protect her from were responsible for the hearings in the first place. The leak "has been described in several places as an act of courage, but it wasn't that at
all," Stephen Carter writes. "It was, rather, a splendid example of
what John le Carré has referred to as 'the selfless and devoted way in
which we sacrifice other people.' "[19]

Anita Hill's legal team tried to help her negotiate a space within
which her allegations could be fairly examined. We tried to respond
to her individual needs, rather than those of the larger forces working
to defeat Clarence Thomas. This approach to legal representation is
the one advanced by Derrick Bell, who argues, "It is essential that
lawyers 'lawyer' and not attempt to lead clients and class."[20] Advocates of client-centered representation are critical of public interest
attorneys whose focus on a broader cause often leads them to over-
look the specific needs of their clients. Deploring the lack of focus
on clients in school desegregation suits, Bell writes, "Except in rare
instances, policy decisions were made by the attorneys, often in con-
junction with the organizational leadership [of the NAACP] and
without consultation with the client."[21]

Effective lawyering, to be worthy of the name, must be "effective" in advancing the client's interests as the client defines them. Professor Hill made her interests and her goals clear to anyone who listened.

> I declined any comment to newspapers, but later when Senate staff asked me about these matters, I felt that I had a duty to report. I have no personal vendetta against Clarence Thomas. I seek only to provide the committee with information which it may regard as relevant.
>
> It would have been more comfortable to remain silent. I took no initiative to inform anyone. But when I was asked by a representative of this committee to report my experience I felt that I had to tell the truth. [22]

"Like a friend," Charles Fried has written, a lawyer "acts in your interests, not his own; or rather he adopts your interests as his own." [23] In tumultuous situations such as those surrounding the Senate hearings, this notion of the lawyer as friend must and should extend beyond the bounds of assistance in a set of formal proceedings to the broader personal and emotional goals of the client herself. [24]

A central justification of the attorney-client relationship is its power to preserve the client's individual autonomy, her or his freedom of will and action in the confusing and complicated world of the legal system [25]—a world that includes not only prosecutors and judges but hostile senators with the power to issue subpoenas.

> [Fried] notes that social institutions are so complex that without the assistance of an expert adviser, an ordinary lay person cannot exercise the personal autonomy to which he or she is morally and legally entitled within the system. [26]

As Anita Hill's lawyers, our goals were and had to be her goals: not to advance any larger cause for its own sake, but to allow her to have her fair and unobstructed say.

III

In the days leading up to the hearings, the members of our hastily assembled legal team made an enormous effort to practice client-centered advocacy. During the hearings themselves, the effort required would be greater still. The White House and the Justice Department were using the hours and days between October 8 and October 11 to prepare their case against Hill. The timing and the machinery of government created a familiar imbalance before the lopsided procedures for the hearings were even announced. As another legal team member, Judith Resnik, put it, "The televised inequalities were amplified by a lack of parity behind the scenes."[27] Several aspects of the hearings were simply beyond our control, having been determined more or less unilaterally by the Senate itself. The rules and the coverage of the hearings provided no protection for Professor Hill as a witness and alleged victim of sexual harassment. Only the senators could introduce evidence, question witnesses, and raise objections. Since there were no limits set in advance on what could be asked or said, any hope of a fair proceeding from Professor Hill's point of view would have to depend either on the pro-Thomas senators' internal sense of fair play or, more realistically, on the willingness of the other senators to object to unfair questions and statements and to press for fair procedures.

The procedures that governed the hearings, as it turned out, were anything but fair. To take one example, in his first of three appearances, on October 11, preceding Professor Hill, Judge Thomas angrily denied her charges—charges the committee had not yet formally heard. In no other juridical, quasi-judicial, or investigative procedure of which I am aware are witnesses or (ostensible) defendants permitted to rebut under oath the charges against them before those charges are even made.[28]

Just as exceptional, and just as alien to fairness, was the repeated use by Senator Specter and Senator Simpson of affidavits not introduced into evidence and witnesses (such as John Doggett III and Harry Singleton) not scheduled by the committee, witnesses whose allegations Professor Hill had had no chance to anticipate, let alone to answer. Objecting to the introduction of John Doggett's affidavit, Senator Leahy said:

> How fair can it be to either Professor Hill or any other witness if any of us can sit up here and say, "I have this stack of affidavits, and in affidavit No. 5 in the third paragraph somebody says such-and-such. What do you have to say about that?"
>
> I mean, at the very least, at the very least they ought to be able to see these affidavits. At the very least, they ought to have some idea of

who the person is and if they are credible. Otherwise you go down through a whole list and say, "Ah, affidavit No. 29, the second sentence, they say that you were living in Japan at the time. Can you prove that you weren't?" I mean, this doesn't make much sense.[29]

Because the "ground rules" laid out in advance proved simply insufficient to prevent such tactics, Professor Hill was denied the opportunity to tell her story clearly and without interference. The chairman, Senator Biden of Delaware, was ultimately able to bar the introduction of further affidavits, but the damage had been done. His attempts to impose some order on October 11 failed to untangle the improprieties, and amounted to an admission that no one was really in charge.

> It is very easy for me to insist on the committee rules being followed, but you and her other counsel may rightly conclude that Senator Simpson is correct, it will mean that this affidavit will be sitting out there for 2, 4, 6, 8 hours unresponded to. That is not a judgment I, since it is not a court of law, I am not prepared to make the judgment whether or not Professor Hill having gotten in this situation is prejudiced by the fact that she cannot respond. That is why the chair is not going to rule that the committee rules must be adhered to. And they are not the committee rules, they are the ground rules laid down in what is obviously an extraordinary, unusual, and unprecedented hearing.[30]

The committee itself had developed these procedures, which the committee's chairman found himself unable to enforce. There was then no one in a position to rule that the rules should rule: to distinguish good behavior, or manners, from unbreakable regulations, and to decide on penalties should the latter be violated.

The "game" of the hearings had started before the senators reached any effective agreement on the rules, or on enforcement mechanisms should those rules be broken. Senator Leahy explained that the senators were trying to apply what they had hurriedly written only days ago.

> I know that we have tried, in fairness to everybody involved, the administration, Judge Thomas, Professor Hill and everybody else, we have worked out ground rules that you and Senator Thurmond and the rest of the committee have agreed to. And we have all had to develop whatever we were going to do within those ground rules.[31]

In Leahy's view, the affidavits violated those "ground rules." Specter's behavior forced Biden to enunciate a new "ground rule" about affidavits during the course of the hearings, thus mixing the process of rulemaking with the process of concrete application. Biden's remarks in introducing the new rule suggested that there was something of the fanciful in the way the senators had chosen to proceed.

> So you can ask anything you want. You can ask her what Santa Claus said or didn't say, whether she spoke to him or not, but it is inappropriate to introduce an affidavit from Santa Claus prior to every member on this committee having an opportunity to check it out, for the following reason: We may find out that Santa Claus is not real.[32]

Framers of constitutions, writers of canons of professional ethics, and makers of trial procedures can construct, if not "neutral," then relatively fair or balanced rules when one of two conditions obtains: either all relevant interests are given equal weight and advocates for each interest have equal power; or the rules are made "blind"—no framer knows which side she will be on when the rules come to affect her life. The first condition rarely exists: two or more parties who have already taken sides in a specific dispute do not often have exactly equal power. (Government regulation of contract talks between unions and management, two players that seldom switch sides or interests, might be seen as an attempt to make fair industrial contracts possible by imposing the first condition on the negotiators.) Most instances of even arguably fair procedural rulemaking are the result of the second, "blind" condition, which is, of course, the "original position" put forward in a much broader context by John Rawls in his classic *A Theory of Justice.*

> . . . if a man knew that he was wealthy, he might find it rational to advance the principle that various taxes for welfare measures be counted unjust; if he knew that he was poor, he would most likely propose the contrary principle. To represent the desired restrictions one imagines a situation in which everyone is deprived of this sort of information. One excludes the knowledge of those contingencies which sets men at odds and allows them to be guided by their prejudices.[33]
>
> The original position is defined in such a way that it is a status quo in which any agreements reached are fair. It is a state of affairs in which the parties are equally represented as moral persons and the outcome is

not conditioned by arbitrary contingencies or the relative balance of social forces.[34]

No adult decisionmaker, of course, is ever quite in Rawls's original position of total ignorance of his or her own interests.[35] However, in the case of rules that are to be used over and over again (Parcheesi, a constitution, a criminal code), the rulemakers' status can sometimes approximate a Rawlsian original position in that they do not know what their interests will be each and every time the rules apply to them. In other words, the condition of repetitive use can sometimes lead rulemakers to something like Rawls's original position because fair rules applied repeatedly will sometimes aid one cause and sometimes its opposite. If the Senate's rules of procedure mean that a bill to curtail the death penalty cannot be reported out of committee on Tuesday, they may mean that a bill to expand it is similarly stifled on Wednesday.

In their adversarial and accusatory nature, the hearings of October 11–13 were substantially unlike any other recent confirmation hearing, and bore few parallels to any recent Senate hearing at all. New rules had to be constructed overnight. In Andrew Ross's analysis:

> What this debate exposed to view were the actual political decisions that go into creating a consensus about internal rules. As a result, the crucial distinction between internally accepted rules—formally neutral—and externally imposed rules—politically motivated—was inoperative from the get-go.[36]

Since the rules would be applied only once, and applied, furthermore, by the rulemakers, the senators who established them—both formally, through political bargaining (in the case of the speaking order), and silently and informally (in the case of what was a permissible question)—had no incentive to agree to restraints unhelpful to their respective sides. The pro-Thomas senators had no incentive to make the process fair; their only interests were particular ones. They had nothing to lose by introducing irrelevant affidavits, for example, or by reading newspaper articles into the record. Moreover, some have argued that the Democratic senators, most of whom voted against Thomas, nevertheless had an incentive to keep Professor Hill's charges from being thoroughly aired, and therefore to agree to rules unfair to her: since the Democrats had known about Professor Hill's charges and had sat on them, the more serious her accusations looked, the more serious the misconduct with which the Democrats could be charged.

> The Democrats on the committee had their own conflicts of interest. They had known all about Hill's charges, and had done nothing: to champion Hill's case now would be to demonstrate how wrong they had been earlier. Biden in particular, and the Democrats in general, had an interest in an inconclusive outcome. This caution on the part of the senators leached down to the level of the staff, where the real work of the Senate was done. The net result was that no senator in the Caucus Room defended Anita Hill. The role of judge was acted by Biden, that of the jury by the committee, and that of the prosecutor by the combination of Specter and Hatch.[37]

Not only in asking the questions, but in agreeing on what could be asked, in setting the order of witnesses, and in deciding whom to call, no senator on the committee had any stake either in making the procedure a fair and reusable one or in acting to "champion" Anita Hill. That procedure was almost guaranteed to be compromised, and to produce the painful embarassment of October 11–13, 1991, because Professor Hill's interest was less strongly represented among the senators than was Judge Thomas's, and because the rules for the "Thomas-Hill hearings" would not be used again elsewhere. The ad hoc nature of the hearings combined with the circumstances of the fight over Judge Thomas to ensure that Professor Hill would not receive a fair hearing. In effect, then, our job as her legal team was to provide client-centered advocacy in a process stacked against our client.

IV

In opening the hearings, Senator Biden seemed to express a desire that they not be adversarial at all. He explained how he expected the committee to operate.

> Those watching these proceedings will see witnesses being sworn and testifying pursuant to a subpoena. But I want to emphasize that this is

not a trial, this is not a court room. At the end of our proceedings, there will be no formal verdict of guilt or innocence, nor any finding of civil liability.

Because this is not a trial, the proceedings will not be conducted the way in which a sexual harassment trial would be handled in a court of law. . . . Thus, evidence and questions that would not be permitted in the court of law must, under Senate rules, be allowed here.

This is a factfinding hearing. . . . We are not here, or at least I am not here to be an advocate to one side or the other with respect to the specific allegations which we will review, and it is my hope and belief that my colleagues here today share that view.[38]

Biden added that he as chair had the power to rule out of order any questions on matters

simply irrelevant to the issue of harassment, namely the private conduct out of the workplace relationships, and intimate lives and practices of Judge Thomas, Professor Hill and any other witness that comes before us.[39]

In fact, Senator Biden never ruled *any* question out of order during Professor Hill's appearance. In what turned out to be an ironic comment, Senator Strom Thurmond of South Carolina indicated his view of the hearings as they opened.

Both Judge Thomas and Professor Hill find themselves in the unenviable position of having to discuss very personal matters in a very public forum. I want to assure them at the outset that they will be dealt with fairly. This will be an exceedingly uncomfortable process for us all, but a great deal hangs in the balance and our duty is clear, we must find the truth.[40]

Senator Thurmond here implied that the hearings, unlike a trial, would be a shared effort to "find the truth," a fact-finding inquiry like a normal legislative committee hearing, with experts and statistics. Like Biden, Thurmond had to deny that the hearing was a "trial" precisely because it looked so much like one: taken together, their introductory speeches suggested that the nontrial hearing would combine the judicial legitimacy of a trial with the nonpartisan quest for truth that presumably animates legislative inquiries.

In fact, the hearing offered just the reverse—the adversarial passions of a criminal trial without the institutional protections. The leading questions and bizarre speculations about Professor Hill showed that the "fake trial" had the distorting aspects of criminal procedure without the mandated limits that can correct distortions in real trials.

> Nor were matters helped by the committee members' repeated caveat that "this is not a trial," and that "this is not a courtroom." Such warnings cast as much dizzying doubt upon the procedural logic of the hearings as Magritte's painting *This Is Not a Pipe* had cast upon the rules for representing a pipe.[41]

In welcoming Judge Thomas to the hearing room, Senator Biden repeated his declaration: "It is my job, as chairman, to insure as best as I possibly can fair treatment. . . . The committee is not here to put Judge Thomas or Professor Hill on trial."[42] As the hearing developed, Biden's mantra—his reminder that the committee was not going to "put" either Thomas or Hill "on trial"—took on a second, more ominous meaning: the Senate Judiciary Comittee could not and would not serve as a trier of fact because it had collectively and tacitly adopted the role of prosecutor. Rather than investigating Professor Hill's charges against Judge Thomas, the committee seemed largely interested in bringing its own charges, in securing a conviction of some sort in the surprising and very public case of *The People v. Anita Hill*.

Under the rubric of investigating her charges, the committee's procedures allowed several senators to bring an array of allegations against Professor Hill. She could be accused of anything by any witness, by any senator questioning her, or by any senator in the course of questioning another witness. In general, the Democrats—far less pro-Hill than they had previously been anti-Thomas—could be counted on not to object. (Senator Biden's blistering last-minute refutation of the redoubtable John Doggett III was the exception that proved the rule: one would have to be a Doggett to excite the Democrats into effective cross-examination.) Professor Kim Taylor, one of Professor Hill's legal advisers during the hearings, later offered these observations:

The senators on the Judiciary Committee simply ignored their obligation to provide a process which could have explored the troubling issues which her allegations raised. These men, who appeared completely unconcerned about the impact of their demeaning treatment, could not begin to comprehend the dual impact of racism and sexism on African American women in the workplace. Yet, as factfinders in this process, they had an obligation to keep open minds about experiences which they obviously knew little about, at least from the perspective of a victim. As officials entrusted with the task of evaluating this evidence, they had an obligation to elevate the discussion above titillating images and to provide a regulated process for analyzing the substance of these allegations. And yet they never did.[43]

No existing precedents governed the committee in its choice of format for the hearings.

Indeed, the Committee had an infinite variety of models from which to choose. It could have established a nonconfrontational setting, gathering facts through the presentation of statements and clarifying issues with open-ended questions. Or, the Committee could have borrowed roles and rules from litigation: It could have assigned advocates to Professor Hill and Clarence Thomas, and allowed them to conduct cross-examinations, raise objections, and present arguments about inferences to be drawn from the evidence.[44]

In the jury-rigged model the committee selected, witnesses gave statements and answered questions put in turn by the sometimes hostile senators. Two senators from each political party were selected as the designated questioners for Professor Hill, and two others from each party for Judge Thomas. Counsel for witnesses and for Professor Hill could be present at the hearings but could not ask questions, nor could anyone but a senator on the Judiciary Committee take any formal action, raise objections, or make procedural inquiries. The rules of evidence, the order of witnesses, and the allowable arguments gave immeasurable advantage to the pro-Thomas "prosecutors" and their case, and the Democratic senators effectively failed to function at all in their assigned role of "defense" for Professor Hill.[45]

Dennis Curtis has analyzed the hearings as a "fake trial":

. . . there was a "petit jury," close in size to the traditional body of twelve, composed of the fourteen white men who make up the Senate Judiciary Committee. This body looked like a jury, and made noises that its job was to get to the bottom of the accusation. There were witnesses. . . . There were "defense" lawyers, Senators Hatch and Specter (taken from the ranks of the "jurors," to be sure, but no less aggressive for that), who attacked the credibility of Anita Hill and of the witnesses who testified on her behalf. Another of the "jurors," Senator Biden, played the part of "judge" or at least a quasi-judge, who ruled on objections, appeared to set the ground rules, and kept the proceedings moving. One might have remarked upon the absence of a traditional prosecutor, but two other members of the "jury," Senators Heflin and Leahy, had been designated to ask questions of the accused, and did so, albeit gingerly.[46]

Curtis makes many telling points, but from my perspective as one of Professor Hill's attorneys, it was she who became the "defendant" in the "fake trial." As Carolyn Heilbrun put it, "As in rape cases, you try the victim."[47] When those deciding to try the victim are also the "triers of fact," a miscarriage of justice is sure to ensue.

The chief "trier" of Professor Hill was a former real-life prosecutor, Senator Arlen Specter of Pennsylvania. Again, Kim Taylor's summary is apt.

In the absence of rules governing the proceedings, Senator Specter's background as a prosecutor enabled him to slide into and out of the roles of prosecutor and judge whenever doing so served his purpose. For example, Senator Specter posed a series of questions [to Thomas] that he believed demonstrated that Professor Hill had perjured herself. He then shed the role of examiner, assumed the position of arbiter of the facts, and expressed his judgement that her testimony amounted to "flat out perjury."[48]

The series of questions at issue when Senator Specter accused Professor Hill of perjury concerned a USA Today article that had appeared on October 8, 1991. Professor Hill had never seen the article, nor was she the source of it or quoted in it; nonetheless, Senator Specter continued to cross-examine her on it as if she had made statements in the article. Although Specter declared that his only purpose was "to find out what happened,"[49] it seems clear that his efforts were in keeping with a White House agenda to discredit Professor Hill and imply that she might have a political motive for coming forward with her charges.

One of Senator Specter's more startling and aggressive tactics was to question Professor Hill about a report the FBI had prepared based on its initial interview with her. This report had been made available to the Judiciary Committee but not to Professor Hill herself. Senator Specter had already asked several questions about the FBI report when Senator Biden interrupted him.

> The CHAIRMAN. Will the Senator yield for one moment for a point of clarification?
>
> Senator SPECTER. I would rather not.
>
> The CHAIRMAN. To determine whether or not the witness ever saw the FBI report. Does she know what was stated by the FBI about her comments?
>
> Senator SPECTER. Well, Mr. Chairman, I am asking her about what she said to the FBI.
>
> The CHAIRMAN. I understand. I am just asking that. Have you ever seen the FBI report?
>
> Ms. HILL. No, I have not.
>
> The CHAIRMAN. Would you like to take a few moments and look at it now?
>
> Ms. HILL. Yes, I would.[50]

Senator Specter had planned to keep interrogating Professor Hill about a document she had never seen or signed. Moreover, his main point was that the FBI report did not contain the explicit language Professor Hill had told the senators Thomas had used. The FBI report, however, was neither a statement by Professor Hill nor a transcript of what she told the FBI but only a *summary* of her interview with that agency (as Senator Biden was eventually roused to point out). Even had she told the FBI about Thomas's indelicate language, that language might well not have appeared in the report. Senator Specter's strategy was disingenuous, characteristic not of a fact finder but of an especially impassioned cross-examiner.

In general, Senator Specter's questions to Professor Hill sounded like nothing so much as a cross-examination. Sometimes his phraseology seemed addressed to the television audience's idea of a jury.

Isn't the long and short of it, Professor Hill, that when you spoke to
the Kansas City Star reporter, that you were saying, at one point in his
career he [Thomas] would have been okay for the Supreme Court?[51]

Senator Specter's consistent willingness to play the role of an aggressive prosecutor was instrumental in turning the hearings into a "fake
trial" of Professor Hill. Almost every sequence of questions from him
displays his prosecutorial orientation, his determination to shape the
hearings into an attack on Professor Hill. In another exchange, Specter grilled Professor Hill about why she did not report Judge Thomas's
offensive behavior when it took place. Because of the fear involved
in going public with harassment allegations, because such allegations
are often not believed, and because of the real danger of reprisals at
work, women probably fail to report harassment more often than they
report it. Yet Senator Specter persisted in condemning Professor Hill
for what he, as a former district attorney, should have known was
simply ordinary conduct for a woman employee faced with verbal
sexual harassment.[52]

Shortly after the hearings ended, Professor Laurence Tribe called
them "a tragicomedy of procedural errors."[53] As Stephen Carter has
written:

> The hearings themselves were grotesque. It is true that the Senate oper-
> ates outside the standard rules of evidence, but in the hearings the
> Judiciary Committee appeared to operate outside the standard rules of
> fairness. The procedure seemed to be this: in questioning Hill, or in
> indirectly challenging her while questioning another witness, the mem-
> bers could rely on any hearsay, innuendo or anonymous allegation that
> they wanted. They were free to manufacture theories about her mental
> state on the spot, and to elicit further speculation from nonexpert wit-
> nesses. In questioning Thomas, however, the members were permitted
> to ask nothing of substance.[54]

The committee's "ground rules" ended up shielding Thomas from
penetrating questions while allowing any charge to be leveled at Hill
on the basis of any imaginable evidence, or none at all. The committee in effect denied Professor Hill the equal protection of the laws,
for she testified under what turned out to be an entirely different set
of rules from those that governed the questioning of Judge Thomas.

When Judge Thomas appeared before the committee as its first witness, he adamantly denied all of Professor Hill's allegations and expressed his outrage that he even had to address them.

> I am not going to allow myself to be further humiliated in order to be confirmed. I am here specifically to respond to allegations of sex harassment in the work place. . . . I will not allow this committee or anyone else to probe into my private life. . . .
>
> I will not provide the rope for my own lynching or for further humiliation. I am not going to engage in discussions, nor will I submit to roving questions of what goes on in the most intimate parts of my private life or the sanctity of my bedroom. These are the most intimate parts of my privacy, and they will remain just that, private.[55]

Judge Thomas's dramatic and defensive denial opened the hearings on an oddly prophetic note: the format in fact left Judge Thomas and the "most intimate parts" of his life far more privacy than was accorded Anita Hill. Professor Hill got the third degree from the Republican senators and a series of hesitant questions from the presumably supportive Democrats. But the Republican encomiasts who dominated Thomas's initial appearance made his testimony seem more like an awards ceremony than a "lynching."

> Senator HATCH. . . . I don't blame you for being mad.
>
> Judge THOMAS. Senator, I have worked with hundreds of women in different capacities. I have promoted and mentored dozens. I will put my record against any member of this committee in promoting and mentoring women.
>
> Senator HATCH. I will put your record against anybody in the whole Congress.
>
> Judge THOMAS. And I think that if you really want to be fair, you parade every single one before you and you ask them, in their relationships with me, whether or not any of this nonsense, this garbage, trash that you siphoned out of the sewers against me, whether any of it is true. Ask them. . . .
>
> Senator HATCH. Well, I think we should do that.[56]

The Senate's hybrid rules permitted such a colloquy; a real trial, of course, would not have. No Democratic senator was willing to stand up for Professor Hill in the same way, or to toss her a Hatchian series of supportive nonquestions. Thomas was celebrated on camera at least as often as he was accused, while Professor Hill seemed to be the one on trial.

The committee's procedures permitted a whole landscape of unfair conduct. Senator Simpson was able to proclaim that he had "stuff coming over the transom" attacking Professor Hill's credibility, but none of this "stuff" ever materialized, nor was Simpson ever asked to produce it.[57] The committee failed to call Angela Wright, contenting itself on Sunday night with admitting her written affidavit into the record.[58] The committee did not hear expert testimony on sexual harassment, despite the obvious need for guidance as to whether the alleged behavior patterns were plausible, and if plausible, common. The committee also ruled evidence of Judge Thomas's alleged taste for pornography inadmissible, even though the ordinary rules of evidence did not apply to the Senate, and even though such evidence might have demonstrated, for example, whether he would have been likely to know of Long Dong Silver. Yet Senator Hatch was permitted to speculate on *no* evidence that Professor Hill had dredged up the oversized porn star from an obscure Tenth Circuit harassment case.[59]

While the Republicans on the committee pulled out all the stops in their attempt to impeach Professor Hill's testimony, the Democrats consistently failed to protest outlandish pro-Thomas speculation, or even to try to impeach the procession of pro-Thomas witnesses.

> Even a basic understanding of cross-examination would require that the biases of witnesses be exposed, yet the Democrats were incapable of carrying out this elementary task. For example, Nancy Fitch, who testified on the first panel of witnesses called on behalf of Thomas, was never questioned about the fact that she was in the process of writing a biography of Thomas.[60]

Outside the hearing room, Professor Hill had our legal team to help her, and Thomas had the legal resources of the executive branch of the federal government. Inside, the only people who could function as lawyers do at an actual trial, who could ask questions and raise objections, were those who had been "admitted to the bar" of the United States Senate. Judge Thomas had his senatorial defenders: Specter, Hatch, Simpson. Professor Hill had the Democrats. "One side had advocates, the other side did not, and that skewed the final result," as Senator Simon somewhat ruefully put it.[61] We, her law-yers—none of us senators—seemed to be the only ones in Washing-ton dedicated to her interests; and we were not asking the questions.

V

The widespread revulsion at the tactics pursued by the pro-Thomas side—revulsion heard as far away as London, where the *Independent* reported, "Rules of evidence and basic fairness have been trampled. . . . Smear begets smear"[62]—may have been instrumental in raising the national consciousness about issues of sexual harassment and gender fairness; the nationwide reaction to the hearings was certainly instrumental in electing a record number of women to the Senate in 1992. Professor Hill's legal team, however, was concerned not first with the national consciousness or with national politics, but with Professor Hill's interests and wishes.

It had been implied on Friday afternoon, during the spat over the Doggett affidavit, that Professor Hill would return to testify again after other witnesses had spoken. By Sunday, however, it was clear that the pro-Thomas members of the committee were willing to make and would be permitted to make an unlimited series of unfounded allegations, and that no senator would rise to stop irrelevant or de-famatory questions from being put to Professor Hill on national tele-vision. Angela Wright—the second woman to complain of unwanted sexual overtures from Judge Thomas—was waiting in Washington and expected to testify after midnight on Sunday, but the tired sena-tors had struck a bargain: her sworn affidavit was introduced into evidence, but she was prevented from appearing in person. I was stunned that the senators did not plan to hear this crucial witness when they had already found time for the parade of pro-Thomas witnesses who marched through the committee room on Sunday night. Clearly, the attempt to preserve even a semblance of fair legal procedure had collapsed.

Senator Biden called Professor Hill at her hotel and woke her up late Sunday night to ask her to come back before the committee.[63] It was her decision that she not testify again. In her judgment, which I supported, we had already achieved all we could given the process, the personnel, and the politics involved. Professor Hill had told her story and had been supported by four credible witnesses and by the government's leading expert in polygraph testing.[64] Her own credibility was such that many of the senators who voted to confirm Thomas on Tuesday, October 15, justified their votes by asserting not that Professor Hill had lied but that she had somehow imagined her story, which they admitted she believed.[65] Other senators who supported Thomas said they did so reluctantly or "without enthusiasm," as J. James Exon of Nebraska put it.[66] Senator Dixon of Illinois said he voted for Thomas only because he believed the applicable standard to be that of proof "beyond a reasonable doubt"—an argument that conflicted with the "this is not a trial" mantra, and (as Senator Byrd, among others, pointed out) with the purpose of a confirmation hearing.[67] The senators' need to resort to such explanations demonstrates what we were able to accomplish.

Some observers were suprised that Professor Hill did not choose to testify again on Monday. Given the chance—hard to measure, but real—that one or more senators might have been swayed by whatever she said in the committee room that day, why did we as her legal counsel support her decision not to return to the hearings? The answer, of course, is that her interests, her autonomy, and her well-being took and had to take precedence over the political consequences of her actions. Our client was not the coalition of forces whose goal was to defeat Judge Thomas; our client was Anita Hill. Neither to her nor to us did the possible positive political effect of testifying again outweigh the negative personal effects of another grilling on Monday.

In making this decision, we as her counsel were guided by the principles of client-centered representation; these principles, as I have argued above, demanded that her interests come first. The issue of third-party demands on counsel in politically charged cases has been addressed by the Supreme Court's ruling in *NAACP v. Button*, which held that a group interest represented through litigation is a "form of political expression" protected by the First Amendment.[68] While *Button* recognizes free speech rights for the public interest attorney, it does not go far enough in ensuring that the interests of individual class members will be safeguarded in instances where larger social goals inform a lawyer's strategy.[69] The ABA Code of Professional Responsibility also fails to protect adequately clients whose lawyers' allegiances to social movements may raise third-party conflicts.

Derrick Bell has harshly criticized the elements of *Button* that suggest that public interest lawyers have no obligation to be client centered.

> A majority of the Supreme Court . . . [created in *Button*] constitutional protection for conduct that, under other circumstances, would contravene basic precepts of professional behavior. The potential for ethical problems in these constitutionally protected lawyer-client relationships was recognized by the American Bar Association *Code of Professional Responsibility*, but it is difficult to provide standards for the attorney and protection for the client where the source of the conflict is the attorney's ideals.[70]

Bell points out that while the ABA Code responds to third-party conflicts in commercial settings, it does not adequately address conflicts that may arise between public interest lawyers and their clients. In Bell's words, "Idealism, though perhaps rarer than greed, is harder to control."[71] Even where the code recognizes that some of the "economic, political, or social pressures" are subtle, the suggested remedy is for the lawyer to withdraw from representation of the client—hardly a desirable remedy for clients with limited resources and few alternatives.[72]

More relevant for public interest attorneys and their clients are two other provisions of the ABA Code. One admonishes the lawyer not to make any important decisions without consulting the client. The other urges that the client be fully informed of all relevant considerations.[73] Even these provisions may be of limited use, however, in the case of third-party conflicts in the public interest context. As Bell contends, "The magnitude of the difficulty is more accurately gauged in a much older code that warns: 'No servant can serve two masters: for either he will hate the one, and love the other; or else he will hold to one, and despise the other.' "[74]

Congressional hearings are far more susceptible to interest group politics than are judicial fora, and lack the procedural safeguards of real courts. The Hill-Thomas hearings demonstrate that witnesses will have a difficult time establishing credibility unless they rely on one of the traditional political support systems to which Washington is accustomed. Professor Hill has written:

> As . . . I prepared for the "fact-finding" hearing, my counsel and I did not focus on getting a key senator to act as my advocate; instead we relied on the weight of my testimony and the fairness of the process as we thought it should be. [Thus] I unwittingly denied the patronage system, which is an entrenched part of Washington's political culture. In refusing to rely on this system, I implicitly questioned it and posed a challenge to those invested in it. The response was to strike back at me, the challenger.[75]

Since she lacked an actual patron, the public assigned her one; it cast Anita Hill as a radical feminist or as a tool of various anti-Thomas forces in order to fit its expectations of how the political process works. Thomas's supporters, as well as many of his critics and much of the press, were simply unable to apprehend the distinction between, on the one hand, the coalition of interest groups that had opposed Judge Thomas from the beginning, and on the other hand, Professor Hill, whose interests were not always theirs, even though her story became a powerful weapon for them. Our job as Professor Hill's legal team was to keep that distinction firmly in mind.

VI

The Constitution provides specifically that "each house may determine the rules of its proceedings."[76] The Senate Judiciary Committee is a standing committee of the Senate. Standing committees are established through the standing rules of each house. The Senate's standing rules briefly establish the jurisdiction of the various standing committees and give them broad authority to hold hearings, subpoena witnesses, compel production of documents, and make investigations. Each standing committee is also required to make its own rules and to publish those rules annually.[77] Very few provisions in the standing rules of the Senate deal explicitly with how hearings should be conducted. The rules of the Committee on the Judiciary take up only two columns in the *Congressional Record*: six sections covering meetings, quorums, proxies, voting, subcommittees, and attendance.[78]

It was this paucity of existing rules that forced the Judiciary Committee to cobble together the unworkable, unenforceable (as in the matter of the affidavits), and clearly unfair "ground rules" that governed the hearings of October 11–13, 1991. Those hearings failed to provide Professor Hill with a fair or balanced forum; in their disregard for truth and impartiality, they made ordinary courtrooms look very good by comparison. The hearings' failure demonstrated, among many other propositions, the failure of nonanticipatory rulemaking. As long as the Senate must come up with rules *de novo* for each politically and personally volatile question of character and fact, those rules will seem, and will probably be, unfair, and the proceedings themselves will not get much respect.[79]

One effect of the ad hoc procedures, and of the individual senators' behavior in invoking or ignoring those procedures, was to make both the Senate and the legal system look compromised—incapable, as presently constituted, of fundamental fairness. But as Andrew Ross has written,

> it would be all too easy to conclude that the hearings vividly demonstrated how law, and everything pertaining to the law, is simply politics by other means. Those devoted to demystifying the authority of the law might well have applauded the whole farce as a job well done: the emperor's clothes were undone, revealing long dong and all. . . . It is the conservatives who are now on the Supreme Court who have argued that law should not be in the business of politics. It is in their interests that the law, as we have understood it until recently, should be delegitimized, thereby reining in the power of the courts.[80]

If I understand this provocative passage correctly, Ross is not saying that the proceedings were a flat-out conservative conspiracy to undermine the legal system. Rather, he is suggesting that a side-effect of the behavior of the pro-Thomas senators was to foster disrespect for the traditional distinction between internal and external rules, between political bargaining and the legal system. Since a common conservative claim during the 1980s was that the Warren Court had already made the legal system too political to be just, to flout rules and standards of fairness during the hearings, to behave as Senator Hatch or Specter or Simpson did, was to promote that claim. The logic goes something like this: if the Hill-Thomas hearing was like a trial and the hearing was a farce, then a trial is a farce; if a trial is a farce, then the law as it operates now is a farce; and if the law as it operates now is a farce, then the law needs to be overhauled and the "original intent" of the Framers restored. Democratic senators, who presumably did not share the hypothesized conservative agenda of delegitimizing the judicial system, would have felt more constrained in what questions they could ask, what kinds of speeches they could make, and what they could allege about the pro-Thomas witnesses.

The conduct of the Senate Judiciary Committee outraged many veteran trial lawyers.

> Several lawyers suggested [in spite of the obstacles faced by the Senators] that through a series of patient, incremental questions—of a sort perhaps alien to politicians—an effective Democratic cross-examiner could simultaneously have chipped away at Thomas' credibility and buttressed Professor Hill's. . . . With each missed opportunity, with each failed follow-through, these lawyers grew convinced that the firm of Biden, Metzenbaum, Heflin and Kennedy had fools for clients. . . . Don Reuben, a prominent litigator in Chicago, [would have asked Thomas] " 'Did you think she was a good-looking woman?' What's he going to say? No or yes, he's dead either way."[81]

Other attorneys have also criticized in print the Democrats' performance.[82] One commentator suggested, rather improbably, an investigation into whether perjury was committed during the hearings.[83] The *Atlanta Journal-Constitution* reported nearly universal assent among the senators themselves in the aftermath of the hearings that some form of change in "the process" was needed, though not surprisingly, no specific changes were suggested.[84] As Charles Tiefer has written, "The primary concern of Members [of Congress] is politics, not procedure."[85]

A full evaluation of the entire confirmation process is beyond the scope of this essay.[86] I will instead confine myself to a few suggested remedies should a situation, like the one Professor Hill faced, again arise. What should be done when Senate confirmation hearings become or ought to become adversarial, when a Senate committee needs to become in effect a trier of fact? Senator Paul Simon, in *Advice and Consent*, makes four suggestions for altering the process:

1. When an unproven charge is made that is serious in nature, the Judiciary Committee should either hold a non-public hearing, or give the nominee the option of doing that.

2. When a sexual harassment charge is made, the Committee should first hear from experts on the patterns of conduct of those subjected to harassment.
3. When a serious charge is made about a Supreme Court nominee, Committee hearings should not be rushed.
4. In this type of procedure, the Committee would have been better served by getting professional counsel on each side who would ask questions, with less time allowed for questioning by the Senators.[87]

Senator Simon's recommendations point in the right direction, though some doubt remains as to the possibility and efficacy of closing controversial hearings. In the 1970s, reacting to the excessive secrecy of the Watergate era, the Senate and House adopted "sunshine rules" that limited the circumstances under which hearings could be closed to the public. In general, these rules prescribed that hearings could be closed only if national security issues might arise or if the testimony to be heard might be defamatory.[88] The hearings of October 11–13 certainly fell into the second category, and some have argued that they should therefore have been closed to the press and to the public. However, the degree of publicity that surrounded Professor Hill's charges from the moment they became known probably made a closed hearing a political impossibility. Stephen Carter has described the dilemma.

> Why, both sets of partisans asked, should our friend be smeared (as each side separately saw it) on national television? The answer, of course, was that once the accusations became public knowledge, the accuser and the accused both, in a sense, became public property— and the public would not have stood for closed hearings. But in another sense, this was to the good; no matter what the outcome, had the hearings been held behind closed doors, supporters of the losing side would have been certain that the fix was in.[89]

Note that Professor Carter here fails to distinguish between Professor Hill's own interests and the interests of the anti-Thomas "side"—a distinction crucial to ethical public interest representation, as I have argued above. One can wonder whether public opinion would have condemned closed hearings as vehemently as the votes in the 1992 Senate and House elections served to condemn the senators' conduct; on the other hand, of course, had the hearings been closed, the offending senators might have behaved even more irresponsibly and the voters could not easily have held them accountable.

Senator Simon's recommendation that professional counsel be brought in when confirmation hearings become adversarial is one I endorse.[90] When "sides" develop in a confirmation hearing such that the senators are obliged to sit as triers of fact, professional counsel for the parties involved should be given a principal role in asking questions and in cross-examining witnesses. Professional counsel must also be allowed to raise objections in accordance with invariant ground rules of relevance laid out in advance.

Counsel for each side should have some role in deciding who will be called to testify at a hearing of this sort, and should be able to call a limited number of witnesses: any witness whom *either* the counsel for any "side" *or* the senators wish to hear should be heard. To give counsel sole power to call witnesses would have the effect of blocking witnesses whose testimony would reflect badly on all parties, even if those witnesses could provide information the Senate needs; but to give the senators sole power to decide whom they will hear in an effectively adversarial proceeding means that the truth can be held hostage to political bargaining or to senatorial fatigue, as when the Judiciary Committee failed to call Angela Wright.

To put in place these changes, the Senate would have to adopt a new set of rules governing the conduct of specifically adversarial confirmation hearings. The procedure that produced the spectacle of *The People vs. Anita Hill* was predestined to be unfair because it was a procedure constructed on the spot by senators obliged to heed only the specific interests and circumstances of the moment, circumstances in which Professor Hill herself could not have been fairly and powerfully represented. The only way to make adversarial confirmation hearings fair is for the Senate to adopt a standard set of rules to be used over and over again in all such hearings.

The Senate should write such rules now. These rules would "kick in" whenever hearings on a serious matter regarding a nominee's conduct cast the Senate as a trier of fact, as determined either by the committee chairman or by some plurality of its members. Besides the expanded role for professional counsel outlined above, these special and invariant rules might govern what kinds of testimony could be heard, what kinds of expert testimony *had* to be heard, how long the hearings would last, when each witness would testify, when and for how long the senators themselves would ask questions, make speeches, or deliver opening and closing arguments, and perhaps whether and when to close or partly close hearings, and whether and how to admit affidavits—a principal topic of debate during Professor Hill's testimony. What exactly these rules are is less important than that they be invariant and made in advance.

Given fair procedures, the committee members will be much more likely to abide by them. Given fair procedures, any future confirmation hearings that go forward after accusations of the kind Professor Hill made will be much more likely to uncover something resembling the truth, something the Senate and the public can believe. Given fair procedures, vigorous client-centered advocates, of the kind we on Professor Hill's legal team strove to be, will find it much easier to serve their clients effectively. And given fair procedures, those clients will be much more likely to receive a fair hearing.

Notes

1. See, e.g., Joseph P. Harris, *Advice and Consent of the Senate* (1953) (describing the Senate's historic role in confirmation hearings).
2. Two of the best are Toni Morrison, ed., *Race-ing Justice, En-gendering Power* (1992), and the twenty-six essays collected under the heading Gender, Race, and the Politics of Supreme Court Appointments, 65 *S. Cal. L. Rev.* (1992).
3. See Dennis E. Curtis, "The Fake Trial," 65 *S. Cal. L. Rev.* (1992). For more on Curtis's analysis, see *infra*, pt. 4.
4. *Cong. Rec.*, Senate 14520, October 8, 1991.
5. *Id.* at 14545–46.
6. *Id.* at 14520–21.
7. *Id.* at 14524.
8. *Id.* at 14508.
9. See Timothy Phelps and Helen Winternitz, *Capitol Games* (1992) at 274 ("Senator Danforth must have known that it would be impossible to hold a hearing in 48 hours. But by fighting for two days he was able to hold the delay down to a week. . . . Senator Biden had wanted a two-week postponement in order to have time for fair hearings on the controversy. But even that would have been too short a time to get to the bottom of allega-

tions about sensitive events that may have occurred so long ago. When Senator Danforth and his fellow Republicans backed Senator Mitchell and the Democrats into a postponement of a week, the fate of Anita Hill was essentially sealed once again.").

10. See also Gay Jervey, "Tree Time," *American Lawyer*, December 1991, and *New York Times*, October 17, 1991.

11. Paul Simon, *Advice and Consent* (1992) at 122.

12. *Id.* at 124.

13. See Phelps and Winternitz, *supra* note 9, at 285 ("[Wright] was shocked. 'When they told me about the subpoena I figured it was the price I was going to pay for daring to say something against a Supreme Court nominee. . . . I felt like I had been transported to a foreign country.' Hardly had she put down the telephone when she saw herself on television being named as 'the other woman'—a label she did not think was appropriate. Then her phone started to ring incessantly; reporters were calling her number nonstop, just as they had four days earlier with Anita Hill's. She ignored the calls. People were knocking on her door. She ignored them too. When her sister arrived to help, she asked Wright why she had not let in the federal marshals, who had been standing on her doorstep for nearly half an hour.").

14. *Id.* at 313.

15. ABA Model Code of Professional Responsibility (1981) at EC 5–1.

16. Jervey, *supra* note 10, at 50.

17. Phelps and Winternitz, *supra* note 9, at 305.

18. Shirley Wiegand, quoted in *id.* at 216.

19. Stephen Carter, *The Confirmation Mess* (1994) at 138.

20. Derrick A. Bell, Jr., "Serving Two Masters: Integration Ideals and Client Interests in School Desegregation Litigation," 86 *Yale L. J.* 378, 512.

21. *Id.* at 500. For a model of the client-centered approach outside the school desegregation context, see Sandra Day O'Connor, "Thurgood Marshall: The Influence of a Raconteur," 44 *Stanford L. R.* 1217 (Summer 1992) ("His was the eye of a lawyer who saw the deepest wounds in the social fabric and used law to help heal them. His was the ear of a counselor who understood the vulnerabilities of the accused and established safeguards for their protection.").

22. U.S. Senate Committee on the Judiciary, *Hearings on the Nomination of Clarence Thomas to Be Associate Justice of the Supreme Court*, 102d Cong., 1st Sess. (Committee Print Draft), October 11–13, 1991, at 38 [hereinafter *Hearings*].

23. Charles Fried, "The Lawyer as Friend: The Moral Foundations of the Lawyer-Client Relation," 85 *Yale L. J.* 1060, 1074 (1976). For criticism of Fried's well-known model, see Edward Dauer and Arthur Leff, correspondence, 86 *Yale L. J.* 573, 578 (1977); Sanford Levinson, "Testimonial Privileges and the Preferences of Friendship," *Duke L. J.* 631, 640 (1984); Michael K. McChrystal, "Lawyers and Loyalty," 33 *Wm. and Mary L. Rev.*

367, 392 (1992); and David Luban, *Lawyers and Justice: An Ethical Study* (1988) at 84.

24. For the same point in a criminal defense context, see Charles Ogletree, "Beyond Justifications: Seeking Motivations to Sustain Public Defenders," 106 *Harv. L. Rev.* 1239, 1272–74 (1993).

25. See, for example (in addition to Fried, *supra* note 23, Bell, *supra* note 20, and Freedman, *infra* note 26), Stephen Ellman, "Manipulation by Client and Context," 34 *UCLA L. Rev.* 1003 (1986).

26. Monroe Freedman, *Understanding Lawyers' Ethics* (1990) at 47.

27. Judith Resnik, "Hearing Women," 65 *S. Cal. L. Rev.* 1333, 1335 (1992).

28. For why Clarence Thomas was not really the "defendant" in the quasi-judicial hearings, see my discussion *infra*, pt. 4.

29. *Hearings, supra* note 22, at 94.

30. *Id.* at 89.

31. *Id.* at 88.

32. *Id.* at 94–95.

33. John Rawls, *A Theory of Justice* (1972) at 18–19.

34. *Id.* at 120.

35. *Id.* ("It is clear, then, that the original position is a purely hypothetical situation. Nothing resembling it need ever take place.").

36. Andrew Ross, "The Private Parts of Justice," in Morrison, *supra* note 2, at 52.

37. Phelps and Winternitz, *supra* note 9, at 395. Biden's effectiveness in directing the proceedings may have been further impaired by the emergency root canal surgery he underwent at 2:00 a.m. on Saturday, October 12; he was seen to clutch his jaw in pain repeatedly during the rest of the hearings (Phelps and Winternitz at 347).

38. *Hearings, supra* note 22, at 2.

39. *Id.*

40. *Id.* at 4.

41. Ross, *supra* note 36, at 52.

42. *Hearings, supra* note 22, at 2–3.

43. Kim Taylor, "Invisible Woman: Reflections on the Clarence Thomas Confirmation Hearing," 45 *Stanford L. Rev.* 443, 444 (1993).

44. *Id.* at 445.

45. See also Simon, *supra* note 11, at 112.

46. Curtis, *supra* note 3, at 1523.

47. Carolyn Heilbrun, "The Thomas Confirmation Hearings, or, How Being a Humanist Prepares You For Right-Wing Politics," 65 *S. Cal. L. Rev.* 1569, 1571 (1992).

48. Taylor, *supra* note 43, at 446.

49. *Hearings, supra* note 22, at 55.

50. *Id.* at 59.

51. *Id.* at 73.

52. *Id.* at 63–64. Senator Specter's very lengthy question here was the last one asked before the lunch recess on Friday, and thus became a prosecutorial "closing argument" as well.

53. Quoted in Renee Toth, "Judging the Process," *Boston Globe*, October 20, 1991, at A25.

54. Stephen Carter, "The Candidate," *New Republic*, February 22, 1993, at 29.

55. *Hearings, supra* note 22, at 8–9.

56. *Id.* at 154–55.

57. *Id.* at 235. This speech deserves a closer look. For one thing, Simpson's proclaiming that his very *pockets* were full of information damaging to Hill must have reminded many observers of the "lists of Communists" Senator Joseph McCarthy once pulled from *his* pockets. For another, one definition of "transom" is "the horizontal beam on a cross or gallows." Could Simpson have been picking up on Thomas's "lynching" speech, suggesting that the hearings' imaginary gallows were covered with (imaginary) charges against Professor Hill? For more on the sources of this "stuff" and the carefully orchestrated effort to discredit Anita Hill, see Jane Mayer and Jill Abramson, *Strange Justice: The Selling of Clarence Thomas* (1994) at 301–20.

58. Simon, *supra* note 11, at 118 ("In retrospect we made a mistake in not hearing her. Had I read her testimony—as well as that of a corroborating witness—in advance, I would have favored calling her as a witness, even at 1:00 in the morning.").

59. *Hearings, supra* note 22, at 189–90.

60. Taylor, *supra* note 43, at 448.

61. Simon, *supra* note 11, at 112.

62. John Lichfield, "New Brutality Takes over the Thomas Drama," *Independent*, October 14, 1991, at 12.

63. Gloria Borger and Ted Guest, "The Untold Story," *U.S. News and World Report*, October 12, 1992, at 37.

64. Paul Minor, who had spent ten years performing lie detector tests for the FBI, gave Professor Hill a polygraph test on Sunday, October 13, asking her, "Have you deliberately lied to me about Clarence Thomas?"; "Are you fabricating the allegations that Clarence Thomas discussed pornographic material with you?"; and "Are you lying to me about the various topics that Clarence Thomas mentioned to you regarding specific sexual acts?" Minor found "no evidence of deception," and we announced his unsurprising results at a press conference that afternoon. The polygraph test results were never introduced into evidence by the Judiciary Committee, apparently on the grounds that polygraph tests are not admissible as evidence in real trials. For more discussion of the polygraph test and the committee's reaction, see Carter, *supra* note 19, at 141.

65. For a discussion of this assertion, see David B. Wilkins, "Presumed Crazy: The Structure of Argument in the Hill/Thomas Hearings," 65 *S. Cal. L.*

Rev. 1517, 1519 (1992) ("Thus supporters of Judge Thomas may simply contend that Professor Hill's allegations should be rejected on the ground that, although she believes them to be true, she suffers from delusions or fantasies and therefore is incapable of telling the truth. It is this argument that I implore the Senate to purge from the debate over this nomination. This explanation conveniently sidesteps such potentially troubling questions as why she could be so convincing in her testimony before the committee, pass a polygraph test, and seem to have no apparent motivation for fabricating the charges.").

66. Phelps and Winternitz, *supra* note 9, at 406.

67. Senator Dixon went on to lose the Illinois Democratic primary to Carol Moseley-Braun, who became the first African American woman senator; the primary was fought in part over Dixon's vote to confirm Thomas.

68. 371 U.S. 415 (1963).

69. See the discussion in Bell, *supra* note 20, at 495–502.

70. *Id.* at 472.

71. *Id.* at 503.

72. EC 5–21, cited in *id.* at 503, n. 107.

73. EC 7–7, EC 7–8, cited in *id.* at 504, n. 112, n. 113.

74. *Id.* at 472.

75. Anita Faye Hill, "Marriage and Patronage in the Empowerment and Disempowerment of African American Women," p. 280 herein.

76. U.S. Const., Art. I, sec. 7, cl. 2.

77. See Standing Rules of the Senate, Sen. Doc. 102–25, July 27, 1992, at 24, 37.

78. *Cong. Rec.*, February 16, 1993, at S1645.

79. Ross, *supra* note 36, at 53, makes a similar point when he argues that the hearings "looked something like the Janus face of the state, exercising power in a way that is usually not exposed to public view, because the state is supposed to be composed of separated powers, just as the legitimacy of the law depends upon its claim to be independent of state power."

80. *Id.*

81. David Margolick, "Thomas Hearings Frustrated Veteran Trial Lawyers," October 21, 1991, at 7.

82. See F. Lee Bailey, "Where Was the Crucible?: The Cross-Examination That Wasn't," *A.B.A. J.*, January 1992, at 46; and Stuart Lefstein, "It's Not Too Late for the Crucible: Question of Perjury in Thomas Hearings Will Not Go Away," *A.B.A. J.*, May 1992, at 115.

83. Lefstein, *supra* note 82.

84. "Senators Agree: Have to Change Process," *Atlanta Journal-Constitution*, October 16, 1991, at A11.

85. Charles Tiefer, *Congressional Practice and Procedure* (1989).

86. Several interesting (and often conflicting) approaches to confirmation reform in general are: Carter, *supra* note 19, chaps. 6, 7 (many different suggestions, culminating in the thesis that attitudes, not rules, are what

need to change, and that we should pay attention to "qualifications rather than disqualifications"); Glenn Harlan Reynolds, "Taking Advice Seriously: An Immodest Proposal for Reforming the Confirmation Process," 65 *S. Cal. L. Rev.* 1577 (1992) (the Senate should give the president a list of Court nominees it would support, and the president could get an expedited confirmation by choosing to nominate from that list); Michael J. Gerhardt, "Divided Justice," 60 *G. W. L. Rev.* 969 (1992) (the White House needs to look the for best-qualified candidate or messy fights will be inevitable); Erwin Chemerinsky, "October Tragedy," 65 *S. Cal. L. Rev.* 1497 (1992) (one of many who argue that the Senate should simply be more willing to reject Court nominees on the basis of policy disagreements).

87. Simon, *supra* note 11, at 303–6.
88. Standing Rules at 161.
89. Carter, *supra* note 19, at 194.
90. See also the suggestion made by journalist Haynes Johnson, "Pluses, Minuses, and Equals," *Washington Post*, October 18, 1991, at A2 ("In the future let a distinguished chief counsel of impeccable independent reputation ask the main questions of witnesses at confirmation hearings and conduct the cross-examination, as was done in the hearings by Sen. Estes Kefauver on organized crime, and in the Army-McCarthy and Watergate hearings").

From the Senate Judiciary Committee to the Country Courthouse: The Relevance of Gender, Race, and Ethnicity to Adjudication

Judith Resnik

For insight into the complicated and complicating events that the confirmation of Clarence Thomas became, one needs perspective, not attitudes; context, not anecdotes; analyses, not postures. For any kind of lasting illumination the focus must be on the history routinely ignored or played down or unknown.

TONI MORRISON, *"Friday on the Potomac"*

On Monday, October 7, 1991, the press reported that Anita Hill (a name few then knew), a law professor at the University of Oklahoma and a former employee of the Equal Employment Opportunities Commission (EEOC), had made accusations of sexual harassment against Clarence Thomas.[1] Many responded to these allegations with apparent disinterest; such information was not the stuff to stand in the way of the vote scheduled for October 8 on Clarence Thomas's nomination as an associate justice of the United States Supreme Court. The popular wisdom was that he had the job and that it would become official the next day.

But on that Monday, many people also felt a need to "do some-thing"—and across the country, "we" did. Within ten hours, some 120 women law professors had signed a letter to the Senate Judiciary Committee. We urged that the vote be postponed, that the Senate take the matter seriously and begin a full investigation.[2] Early the next day, an additional 170 law professors added their names to the roster, appealing to the Senate "to delay action . . . until it could make a fully informed and considered appraisal of Professor Hill's allegations."[3] A chorus of other groups and individuals joined in pe-titioning Congress. One image the newspapers gave us was of seven congresswomen marching up the steps to the ninety-eight-man, two-woman Senate and demanding a delay.[4]

Outrage mounted as the Senate appeared willing to ignore claims that a person who as chief of the EEOC had been in charge of the nation's sexual harassment policies was himself a sexual harasser. On Tuesday, October 8, the vote on the confirmation was delayed one week until October 15. Also announced was a plan to hold a "hear-ing," to start on Friday, October 11, the beginning of the Columbus Day weekend. On Thursday, October 10, the day before that "hear-ing" was to begin, Anita Hill met for the first time with the small group of volunteer lawyers who had assembled over the preceding few days.[5] The next day, she went before the Senate and, via the televised proceedings, the nation.

I have begun this commentary with the details of what occurred on October 7, 1991, because of the importance of remembering that on that date, Congress did not want to pause to think about the state-ments of Anita Hill. But for the public disclosure and the collective political pressure that resulted, the vote would have occurred on Oc-tober 8, presumably with a confirmation tally of 58 to 42. Therefore, to understand the meaning of the week of October 7, 1991, we must explore not only the proceedings and the subsequent confirmation but also the delay—the moment in which, ostensibly, reconsidera-tion of the nomination was on the agenda.

That delay was evidence of women's newfound powers. Although members of the Senate did not initially acknowledge it, the questions posed by Anita Hill's experiences were not trivial. Across the country, people marshalled their political wherewithal to force the Senate into begrudging recognition of the necessity of taking testimony. Those people worked against a backdrop of two decades in which "women's issues" were making their way from invisibility to plain view, a trajectory I sketch below from two vantage points, the highest and lowest courts in the country.

Records of confirmation hearings to the highest court in the United States have not before been used to explore the role of women's equality in this country's political life. The Senate's initial disinterest in Anita Hill's information was a vivid reminder that not long ago, disinterest in women's rights was the norm. Not until the 1970s were questions posed about a Supreme Court nominee's attitude toward women's rights. During the decades that followed, one can find markers of change. Questions about a nominee's views about women's equality became routine. By the late 1980s, not only were such questions asked but nominees also found it necessary to profess their commitment to equal rights for women.

The ability to obtain a delay in the Thomas confirmation was thus a culmination of efforts to make the equality of women an issue on the national agenda; the delay itself demonstrates the changing significance attached to accusations that judicial nominees (and implicitly other political appointees and office seekers) have either been opposed to or violated women's rights. Yet it was still news to the Senate in 1991 that Hill's information might matter. It is news no longer.

Just as the delay marked the political force of women's equality, that delay also illustrated the limits of the political power displayed. The brevity of the postponement and the minimal role women played in shaping the subsequent proceedings (which in many ways did not deserve the appellation "hearing") underscore the narrow range of power wielded by the women and men who were troubled by the disclosures. The fumbled and inadequate investigation and proceedings, ending in the confirmation of Clarence Thomas, expose difficulties endemic to contemporary judicial processes.

Toni Morrison's injunction to search for "lasting illumination" therefore requires placement of the extraordinary spectacle of the exchanges constituting "Hill-Thomas" not only in the context of prior Supreme Court nominations (at the apex of the United States justice system) but also in the context of the ordinary—the routine decisions made by judges and jurors around the country in courtroom adjudi-

cation at the lower end of the judicial spectrum. After mapping concern about women's rights in the dialogues between the Senate and
Supreme Court nominees, I chart the creation in the 1980s of court-
sponsored task forces on gender, racial, and ethnic bias. Across the
country, judiciaries have commissioned such task forces to explore
whether and how the judicial system itself discriminates on the basis
of gender, race, and ethnicity.

The reports of those task forces echo the Senate Judiciary Committee proceedings. The problems that haunted decision making in Hill-
Thomas are mirrored in many courtrooms. A review of the images
of justice and injustice displayed via the televised Hill-Thomas hearings offers a glimpse of scenes never broadcast but part of daily life.[6]
Unraveling the Hill-Thomas pseudo-trial brings both the promises
and failures of ordinary judicial processes into view.

Below, these three threads—the Thomas proceedings, women's
rights in Supreme Court confirmation hearings, and task force reports
on gender, racial, and ethnic bias—are interwoven. First I move back
in time, from Thomas's nomination to those that preceded it, to understand when and how women's rights became salient to the process. Returning to the Thomas proceedings themselves, I examine
the role played by gender and racial stereotyping. Thereafter I move
from those broadcast images, available to all with televisions, to the
less easily accessible data about the effects of gender and race on
adjudication in both state and federal courts. "Lasting illumination"
flows in both directions. The Thomas proceedings have much to
teach us about the "routinely ignored or played down or unknown,"
the commonplace exchanges in cases that fill the lower courts. Ordinary adjudication in turn enables "insight into the complicated and
complicating events that the confirmation of Clarence Thomas
became."[7]

The "Women's Issue"
in Supreme Court Nominations

What role did women's rights play in nominations before that of
Clarence Thomas? Exploring these precedents reveals how the official criteria for high-visibility presidential appointments has changed.
Not long ago, it was permissible in politics, law, and the popular
press to trivialize women and the problems they face. What today is

sexual harassment was just "the way it was." The "it" here refers to many facets of women's lives, at work, at home, and in between. The terms and conditions of life for many women have included, at the least, a verbal barrage of sexual comments, and at the worst, physical and mental assault. As Adele Alexander has shown, women of color stood specially degraded, with no legally recognized claim of ownership to their own bodies.[8] The unwillingness to count women's pain as injury is slowly being challenged. The results can be seen in many forums, as the "it" has become "sexual harassment," "violence against women," "date rape," "discrimination," and a host of other terms that have helped to name experiences and to link these so-called private moments of discomfort, distress, and terror to discrete political and legal wrongs.

Asking the Question

The idea that nominees to high office should be accountable for their interest (or lack thereof) in women's rights is one marker of changing attitudes. The hearings on nominations to the United States Supreme Court over the past thirty years provide one chart on which to map that change. It was not until 1970 that a nominee, George Harrold Carswell, was questioned about his attitudes toward women.[9] The two women who raised this issue were Patsy Mink, congresswoman from Hawaii, and Betty Friedan, then president of the National Organization for Women (NOW). Friedan was informed that she was "the first woman representing an organization devoted to women's rights who has ever testified about the nomination of a Supreme Court justice."[10]

Patsy Mink called the nomination of Carswell "an affront to the women of America"; she cited his role in a case upholding the refusal to employ women with children of pre-school age, although men with children of pre-school age were so employed.[11] When Senator Birch Bayh of Indiana asked Judge Carswell to address "the impression that [Carswell was] not in favor of equal rights for women," Carswell responded that he was committed to the enforcement of the "law of the land."[12]

The Carswell nomination was rejected, but not because of Carswell's views on women's role in society.[13] The following year, when William Rehnquist and Lewis Powell were nominated to be associate justices, several witnesses objected to both nominees' attitudes toward women's rights.[14] Wilma Scott Heide, then president of NOW, called for a change in criteria "to disqualify sexists and sexism" and argued that both Rehnquist and Powell should be rejected because of "their acts of commission and omission."[15] While such testimony prompted Senator Bayh to ask Rehnquist about his views on equal rights for women,[16] no such questions were addressed to Powell.[17] Attitudes toward women played a minor role in the hearings and were not the subject of analysis by those commenting on the nomination process.[18]

In addition to Carswell, Rehnquist, and Powell, NOW opposed the appointment of Justice Stevens (1975) and Justice Scalia (1986), as well as the elevation of Justice Rehnquist to chief justice (1986). At each hearing, witnesses on behalf of NOW offered evidence of disinterest in or hostility to women's rights.[19] The nominees did not respond with detailed defenses or point to their efforts to enhance women's participation in the political, economic, and social life of the country. Indeed, Justice Scalia defended his membership in an all-male club on the grounds that although the club did discriminate by excluding women, that form of discrimination was not "invidious."[20]

Until the debates about Robert Bork's nomination in 1987, a nominee's demonstrable lack of interest in or commitment to women's rights did not much matter. The Bork hearings were the first in this century in which women's issues moved to center stage and were relevant to the outcome.[21] Feminist voices were heard repeatedly during the proceedings.[22] Many witnesses questioned Bork's interpretations of constitutional doctrine to exclude women from heightened protection under the Fourteenth Amendment,[23] as well as his decisions in nonconstitutional cases. Bork's opinions caused concern about his capacity to appreciate problems from the perspective of women litigants.[24] While many factors contributed to Bork's rejection, his belief that discrimination against women was not directly prohibited by the equal protection clause of the Fourteenth Amendment,[25] his opposition to the Equal Rights Amendment,[26] and his narrow construction of statutory rights for women played an important part.

The effects were visible three months later, when Anthony Kennedy was before the Senate seeking confirmation to the seat denied Judge Bork. The discussion of women's concerns took a notably different turn. Kennedy made a point of affirming his commitment to women's rights. He explained in some detail his growing understanding of the issue; he described his unsuccessful efforts to change the policy of the all-male club to which he had belonged and his subsequent resignation.[27] As he put it, "Over the years, I have tried to become more sensitive to the existence of subtle barriers to the advancement of women and minorities in society. This was an issue on which I was continuing to educate myself."[28] Similarly, in 1990, when David Souter was questioned by the Senate Judiciary Committee about sex discrimination, he rejected the application of only a rational basis test to sex discrimination, and he noted the "difficulty" with the "looseness" of the standard of "heightened scrutiny" applied to discrimination on the basis of sex.[29]

With this review of questions put to Supreme Court nominees over the past two decades, one can trace the evolution of a discussion about women's issues. Initially absent, women's rights are subsequently introduced into the conversation (but as a minor footnote, polite and unimportant to the outcome) and then become something more. During the 1970s, women's groups made a place for women on the list of questions posed to Supreme Court nominees. By the late 1980s, nominees in turn made a point of portraying themselves as concerned about fair treatment for women.

Clarence Thomas could thus easily have anticipated that he too would be asked the "women's question" and that his response might matter. The confirmation proceedings predating disclosure of Anita Hill's statements make plain Thomas's understanding of the need to espouse commitment to women's equality. Thomas spoke of inequality ("There is discrimination. There is sex discrimination in this society") and of his record of promoting women to senior roles on his staff.[30] Further, and in marked contrast to Robert Bork, Thomas expressed openness, when women claimed discrimination, to the judiciary's reliance on a "more exacting standard" than the current rule of "heightened scrutiny."[31]

The Meaning of the Question

But before I sound too celebratory about the inclusion of women's rights as a topic of questioning, let me explore the limitations of making it "onto the list." While being in the picture is better than being absent, implicit in the inquiry are the facts that virtually all the nominees are men, that the need to ask is itself acknowledgment of women's "otherness," and that the questions asked are neither infused by an understanding of the problem of stereotypes nor reflective of how women's lives are shaped not only by gender but by other intersecting markers of identity. In the very questioning about women's rights comes evidence both of women's less than equal status and of the possibility that a nominee might view women's rights with disinterest. In contrast, men (implicitly white) are assumed to have the status of rights holders rather than to need recognition from others in order to be rights holders.

That sense of entitlement, of being rights holders and rights givers, is evident in the questions posed by senators to Thurgood Marshall, the first person of color to be nominated to the Supreme Court. As commentators on those events have explained, the major confirmation battle occurred not when Marshall was nominated to the Supreme Court in 1967, but when he was first nominated to be on the Court of Appeals for the Second Circuit in 1961. While few believed that his nomination would be blocked, Professors Richard Revesz and Mark Tushnet detail the repeated delays and differential treatment accorded Marshall as contrasted with other nominees. Marshall faced a battery of questions not asked of other nominees. As Revesz summarizes it, "The confirmation hearings of all nineteen of [President] Kennedy's other nominees were completed in a single day; in Marshall's case, they took place over six separate days spread out over almost four months."[32]

As I read the transcript of Marshall's Supreme Court nomination hearings, I find little evidence of challenges to Marshall based on anxiety about his possible lack of fairness toward white men. Given Marshall's place as one of the few blacks holding federal office, it might not have occurred to those senators unfriendly to integration that the rare appointment of a man of color would much affect their authority. Presumably, the detailed questioning to which Marshall was subjected, an uncommon experience in those days for intermediate appellate and Supreme Court nominees, was not an uncommon experience for Marshall.[33] The petty delays were a form of harassment familiar to members of the African American community. That the senators did not evidence much fear of Marshall was congruent with their privileged position and with his role as a token.

Concern about erosion of power came more into focus in the following decades, as the legal debates moved from anti-desegregation
efforts to affirmative action, from lowering barriers to so-called reverse discrimination. By 1981, when Sandra Day O'Connor became
the first woman nominated to serve on the Supreme Court,[34] the
conversation was just beginning to reflect a realization that major
reallocations of power and position could be at stake.

One theme that appears occasionally in the transcripts of the
O'Connor hearings is that Sandra Day O'Connor, as a woman, was
(in a term familiar in feminist literature) "other." Even while claiming the irrelevance of her gender, witnesses and members of Congress
could not avoid talking about it. References were made to the fact
that O'Connor was a woman, a wife, and a mother, and it was said
that she would add warmth and beauty to the Court.[35] As Arizona
State Representative Tony West put it, "With the exception of Sandra's obvious aesthetic beauty and her very feminine qualities, in the
future it will be difficult at best to determine any gender by the reading . . . of her decisions."[36]

But the praise of her "womanly virtues" was tempered with some
anxiety. A few senators hinted at concerns that because she was a
woman, O'Connor might be too favorable toward women's rights.
They asked her about abortion, women in combat, and her efforts as
a state legislator to obtain equal pay for women.[37] A subtext of suspicion lurked, as if she might do special favors for members of her own
sex. O'Connor assuaged such concerns by not complaining much
about her treatment as a woman. Responding to Senator Edward
Kennedy's question about her experiences of gender discrimination,
O'Connor explained, "I do not know that I have experienced much
in the way of discrimination. . . . I graduated from law school at
Stanford in 1952. . . . I was not successful in finding employment
. . . in any of the major firms. . . . However, I did find employment in the public sector. . . . It was a happy resolution for me.
. . . [T]hat start turned out to be very beneficial."[38]

In contrast to this questioning of O'Connor, male nominees have
not been examined about their possible partiality toward their own
gender, but rather about their possible disregard of women's rights.
Moreover, the "women's question" is almost always asked in the context of men's attitudes toward women; less explored are women's attitudes toward other women and men of all races.[39] And what is ob-

scured is the complexity of the question about "women," who are not a singular set but come with identities shaped not only by gender but also by race, ethnicity, age, class, sexual orientation, religion, and physical capacities.

Of course, the sample size of Supreme Court nominees is very small, and readings of what Mark Tushnet has called the "political theater"[40] of the nomination process are complex. As is familiar, with the sole exceptions of two white women, Sandra Day O'Connor and Ruth Bader Ginsburg, all the nominees to the Supreme Court have been men, and except for Thurgood Marshall and Clarence Thomas, white men. Further, each nomination needs to be considered within the context of its contemporary political struggles, between Congress and the presidency and about particular issues such as racial discrimination, abortion, and affirmative action. The hearings vary in terms of the degree and kind of controversy and its relationship to the gender and/or race of a nominee. Many social histories are to be written of Supreme Court nominations; this is but one, with a particular limited focus. (Another would be to examine the relationship between what nominees say, when before the Senate, and what they do, when justices).

With these caveats, a review of the past two decades of Supreme Court confirmation hearings demonstrates that within this political theater, women's rights had no role initially, then moved on stage only as a "bit player," and finally emerged to the extent that every nominee since 1987 has expressed commitment to the constitutionalization of women's rights. While all the nominees have thus learned to speak a language of equality, the decisions and actions that flow from those words vary enormously.

The hearings on nominations after Thomas display related but distinct elements.[41] Of course, it was the pre-Thomas hearings that provided the context for how questions of gender were raised, heard, and answered in the fall of 1991. It is that context that illuminates why Thomas's commentary on his sister, Emma Mae Martin, did not become a subject of widespread senatorial concern during the first part of the confirmation proceedings. In the early 1980s, the press had reported that Thomas described his sister as getting "mad when the mailman is late with her welfare check."[42] As reporters later detailed, Martin worked two minimum-wage jobs until her aunt had a stroke; thereafter, she left paid work to care for her aunt and then received welfare support. Subsequently, Martin returned to the work-force as a cook on a hospital's night shift.[43]

Some, but not all, feminists recognized Thomas's discussion of his sister as evidence of his views on women's rights. Kimberlé Crenshaw insightfully read Thomas's description of Martin as an effort to "capi-talize upon existing beliefs about the poor, about Blacks, and about women—all of which come together in the image of the Black wel-fare queen whose plight is solely rooted in her dependence on the state."[44] Both Professor Patricia King of Georgetown University Law Center and Molly Yard, NOW's president, testified before the Senate Judiciary Committee about Thomas's misuse of events in his own sister's life in order to vilify poor women.[45] But the Senate did not respond to this testimony by pursuing the relationship between Thomas's views on women's equality and his dismissive discussion of his sister. That lack of response was evocative of the pre-1987 nomi-nations, when testimony about a nominee's views on women's equal-ity was not translated into senatorial concern.

Part of the ease the senators had in "missing the issue" comes from the ways in which the women's rights question had been framed dur-ing the preceding two decades of Supreme Court nomination de-bates. "Women," for purposes of the question, were an unnuanced collective entitled to legal rights. As a consequence, in Christine Stansell's words, "Martin, the poor black woman, did not altogether register on public consciousness as a 'woman.' . . . In contrast to debates over welfare, the discourse of sexual harassment calls up the figure of a victim who is only a woman, nothing else."[46]

The Nature and Quality of the Inquiry

Had the Thomas nomination proceedings closed on October 7, 1991, his willingness to invoke racial and gender stereotyping would have remained little challenged. While careful readers of the record might have garnered insight into the relationship between stereotyp-ing and adjudicatory judgment, public attention only turned to these issues during the vivid exchanges that formed the subsequent course of the Thomas nomination. What became evident nationwide, when the Senate Judiciary Committee conducted an inquiry into what had happened between Anita Hill and Clarence Thomas, parallels problems faced by women of all colors and men of color in litigation as it occurs in courthouses across this country. Before I draw those parallels, however, some important differences between trials in courts and the Thomas proceedings need be marked.

Most trials occur with more than seven days' notice. I spoke earlier of a "victory" to mark: the delay of the confirmation vote in order to hold a "hearing." But that victory was profoundly undercut the moment it was announced, by the terms of the senatorial deal that gave but one week's delay. It takes no special training to understand that seven days (most of them over a holiday weekend) foreclosed the investigation and preparation essential to many lawsuits. This was the "speedy trial" impulse gone wild, and the limited time frame forecast the outcome.

Of equal import, as Dennis Curtis has written, the event called a "hearing" was in many respects more aptly styled "the fake trial."[47] While the senators repeatedly invoked a due process model (with much discussion of the "burden of proof" and "fairness"[48]), none of the formal trappings of a trial were in fact present.[49] Throughout the process, two members of the Senate Judiciary Committee (Senators Orrin Hatch and Arlen Specter) acted in many respects as lawyers *for* Clarence Thomas. No member of the committee took a comparable role to represent Anita Hill. The Thomas "defense lawyers" then turned into "jurors," voting to acquit Thomas. Senator Biden cast himself as "judge," but the real guiding force behind the proceedings was a series of deals between Democratic and Republican senators who made up and then renegotiated the "rules" as the proceedings unfolded.[50]

The members of the Senate Judiciary Committee were not judges but combatants, struggling to project an image of impartiality as they assumed many postures at once. While real judges are sometimes faced with litigants who can marshal imposing resources, such judges use preexisting rules to structure the litigation and to enhance their authority over the process. In the Thomas proceedings, no predetermined rules and no judge-imposed constraints. Working on behalf of Thomas were the Republican senators, the White House, the Department of Justice, and scores of others. Working on behalf of Hill was a small crew of volunteers scrambling to find phones, fax machines, and information.[51] While the Democratic members of the Judiciary Committee aspired to an image of disengagement, the strategically advantaged Republicans used resources, timing, and hostility to overwhelm the Democrats. Members of the Judiciary Committee invoked the language of the courtroom in the hope of creating an image of fairness, fashioned to cloak a deeply flawed proceeding.

Although the Hill-Thomas proceedings were a "fake trial" in these respects, elements were all too true to regular courthouse life. The resource imbalance between Hill and Thomas mirrored the imbalance in many cases in which sexual harassment is charged. He, the "employer," had resources, authority, and access to power; she, the "employee," had far fewer resources upon which to call. Economic advantage affects fair proceedings in many kinds of cases. But additional pressures, in real courts, wear thin the appearance of equal treatment of women and men of color and of white women. It was not only the asymmetry of resources that made the Hill-Thomas proceedings distressingly trial-like. Other aspects of those extraordinary proceedings echoed the ordinary moments of trials.

The Faces of Justice

Recall the picture of the Senate Judiciary Committee during the 1991 proceedings: fourteen men, all white, surrounded by aides, a few of them women, again mostly white. That image, with only slight modification, fit the reality of many federal and state courts. As of 1991, the 94 federal trial courts had some 740 sitting life-tenured judges; 49 (7 percent) of these judges were women.[52] Four of the 13 federal appellate courts then had no women appellate judges.[53] On more than eighty occasions between 1930 and 1991, the United States Supreme Court appointed special masters (who sit as ad hoc adjudicators in particular cases and make findings for the Court); not a single one was a woman.[54]

The numbers of judges of color in the federal judiciary are similarly small. As of 1992, of 837 active judges sitting on the trial and appellate courts of the federal system, 5.1 percent were African American, 3.7 percent Hispanic American, and 0.7 percent Asian American.[55] According to Judge Leon Higginbotham, of 115 appointments to the appellate courts by Presidents Bush and Reagan over twelve years, "only two were African-American."[56]

Were I compiling these data rather than reporting them, I would not describe women or men as a unitary category, without mention of race and ethnicity. Unfortunately, until 1993, categories established by the Equal Employment Office of the United States Courts described federal employees as either "men" and "women" *or* "White," "Black," "Hispanic," "Asian," "American Indian," and "Handicapped."[57] As a consequence, I cannot report how many persons have combinations of gender and race that make them distinctive minorities within the federal judiciary.[58]

While contemporary critics of the federal judicial appointment process are concerned that confirmation hearings draw too much and the wrong kind of attention, the demographic data on the lower federal courts suggest another problem: that until recently too little attention has been paid to nominees at these echelons of the judiciary. The Supreme Court, while powerful and able to do much harm or good, is only one locus of federal adjudication; it issues fewer than 150 opinions a year.[59] In contrast, intermediate appellate judges entertain some 45,000 appeals annually, and the federal trial courts hear more than 250,000 civil and criminal actions yearly.[60] The caseload grows even larger as one turns from the life-tenured federal judiciary to the work of federal bankruptcy and magistrate judges, who are appointed for statutory terms, rather than given the life tenure enjoyed by district, appellate, and Supreme Court judges and justices. More than 600 of these judges preside over a large proportion of federal judicial business;[61] for example, in 1991 more than 910,000 bankruptcies were filed.[62] As of 1991, about 17 percent of the federal bankruptcy judges and magistrate judges were women.[63]

But before reading these statistics to suggest that the lower the judicial level, the more women, consider yet another adjudicative layer—federal agencies. As of 1991, some 1,050 administrative law judges (ALJs) worked in the Social Security Administration, dealing with claims of wrongfully terminated welfare and disability benefits; fewer than 5 percent were women,[64] in part because of an affirmative action program (the "veteran's preference") that continues to favor veterans seeking to become ALJs.

The picture of the judiciaries of the state courts is not much different. In 1991, some 9 percent of more than 28,000 judges were women.[65] Women of color were scarce. The Task Force on Racial and Ethnic Bias in Florida found that 1 percent of all the judges in Florida were women of color, none of whom sat on appellate courts.[66] By 1993, nationwide, fewer than ten women described as members of "minorities" sat on the highest court of their jurisdictions.[67]

The general inattention paid to court appointees at levels below the Supreme Court has particular resonance in the context of the Thomas proceedings. Clarence Thomas was not a newcomer to the judicial nomination process when he appeared before the Senate in the fall of 1991. He had been nominated before, to be a judge on the Court of Appeals for the District of Columbia Circuit. Although a few protested that nomination,[68] others thought that while Thomas's record did not commend him as a jurist, the position was not important enough to warrant energetic opposition to his confirmation. That was a mistake, not only in retrospect but also at the time. The inattention devalued the daily experiences of litigants whose cases are decided not by the Supreme Court but by judges of the lower federal courts. Who becomes a judge is not only of moment when one of the nine positions on the United States Supreme Court is at stake; judges at every level of the hierarchy exercise powers affecting individuals. With or without life tenure, their appointments merit our attention.

Unmasking Court-Based Inequalities

The Thomas proceedings in the fall of 1991 were not the first occasion on which to notice who holds the power to judge. While those proceedings brought national publicity to the effects of gender, race, and class on processes of judgment, that inquiry has a long and distinguished pedigree. For decades, gender, ethnic, and racial stereotyping has been the subject of historical and literary accounts[69] as well as litigation battles.[70] But as antidiscrimination lawyers went to court during the 1960s and early 1970s seeking justice, they found that courts were not only places for hearing such claims but also places *of* discrimination.

In 1980, the NOW Legal Defense and Education Fund created the National Judicial Education Program (NJEP) to educate judges about their own discriminatory assumptions.[71] Working with the National Association of Women Judges (NAWJ), NJEP pressed for inquiry into "gender bias in the courts."[72] In 1982, the chief justice of the New Jersey Supreme Court launched the first gender bias task force.[73] In 1985, New Jersey also led the way by creating the first task force on "Minority Concerns."[74] In 1988, the chief justices of all the state courts signed a resolution calling for "positive action by every chief justice to address gender bias and minority concerns in the state courts."[75] While the federal courts were slower to take on the issue of discrimination from within,[76] in 1990 they too began to focus on the topic, as the Court of Appeals for the District of Columbia appointed a committee to explore gender and racial and ethnic bias[77] and the Judicial Conference of the Ninth Circuit (encompassing nine western states) authorized a study of the impact of gender on the federal courts.[78] By the time Anita Hill and Clarence Thomas appeared before the Senate Judiciary Committee, more than thirty states had put gender bias on their agendas,[79] and more than a dozen jurisdictions were considering racial and ethnic bias in the courts.[80]

A thick literature now documents what these task forces have found. As of 1994, thirty-two jurisdictions—including California, New York, Michigan, and the federal courts for the Ninth and the D.C. Circuits—had published reports on gender,[81] and ten had issued reports on race and ethnic bias. The events of the fall of 1991 can thus be read not only in terms of other Supreme Court nomination hearings, but also in the context of courthouses across the country, in which color, ethnicity, and gender create obstacles to belief and affect judgments about the fairness of the process.

First, recall watching and listening to the Thomas proceedings. Toni Morrison describes with painful clarity how the language of race and gender was deployed to belittle. Clarence Thomas was praised for his "laugh" and commended because "the object of his laughter is most often himself."[82] Morrison explains, "Every black person who heard those words understood. How necessary, how reassuring were both the grin and its being summoned for display."[83] Thomas's sister, Emma Mae Martin, was cast in the role of welfare-dependent black woman, despite evidence that she had provided for family members, had worked outside the home, and by those actions undermined assumptions about the futility of government assistance.[84] Anita Hill, who in Morrison's words was "an *intellectual* daughter of black *farmers*; a *black female* taking *offense*,"[85] was far afield from the stereotyped roles assigned to black women.[86] However, her departures from these imprisoning expectations did not break through racial and gender stereotyping: the inquiry centered on whether he was a "savage" or she a "vamp."[87]

Transfer the terms of discussion from Hill and Thomas to the ordinary litigants who appear in the nation's courthouses. If Hill and Thomas could not pierce the veil of racial and gender stereotypes, how do these other litigants fare? Consider the conclusion of the New York State Task Force Report on Women in the Courts.

> Cultural stereotypes of women's role in marriage and in society daily distort courts' application of substantive law. Women uniquely, disproportionately, and with unacceptable frequency must endure a climate of condescension, indifference, and hostility.[88]

Read also New York's report on the experiences of people of color.

> Reduced to their essence, the numerous complaints, testimony and comments received by the Commission reflect the perception that minorities are stripped of their human dignity, their individuality and their identity in their encounters with the court system.[89]

The findings of task forces on racial and ethnic bias point to a range of inequities. Washington State's minority task force concluded that in criminal processes, people of color are "more likely to be held in custody pending sentencing than whites."[90] Michigan's task force reported that in "the 83 counties in Michigan there are 2 majority female Prosecutors and no minority Prosecutors," and that such employment patterns leave "informal discretion" about prosecutorial decisions "almost exclusively in the hands of white males."[91] On the civil side, Washington's task force reviewed outcomes in personal injury litigation about asbestos injuries; after controlling for age, type of disease, and workplace, that task force concluded that "minorities had a statistically lower average settlement [$74,350] than non-minorities [$119,560]."[92]

What task force after task force has found is that the majority of women and men responding to surveys about their courtroom experiences report different understandings and experiences. Take, for example, the survey data from the Ninth Circuit's work on the effects of gender in courts. Male lawyers (more than 90 percent white) repeatedly described promotions and advancement as related to merit;

in their view, little or no gender bias occurs in courts, law firms, and other professional settings in which they operate.[93] One male respondent disavowed the existence of gender bias, imputed a belief in such bias to the survey questionnaire, and explained, "One of us, either you or I, is living in Disneyland."[94] In contrast, women lawyers and judges repeatedly report that gender counts, that gender bias exists, and that it affects both adjudication and their working environment.[95]

Recent data from the District of Columbia's federal courts make the next essential point: gender is not the only variable of relevance. Some 1,700 lawyers responded to a question about whether, within the last five years, a federal judge had either questioned that they were lawyers or assumed that they were not lawyers. One percent of the white men reported having had that experience. About 10 percent of both white women and men of color stated that they had that experience. About a third of the women of color responded that their status as lawyers had been so questioned.[96]

Thus, in general, task forces have documented that perceptions of the relevance of gender, race, and ethnicity vary by gender, race, and ethnicity. That is, women lawyers and judges report gender to be more relevant in courtrooms than do men lawyers and judges; minority lawyers and judges report minority status to affect proceedings more than do majority members. The Michigan Task Force on Racial/Ethnic Issues put it succinctly: "Majority males were less likely than any other sub-group to see instances of unfair or insensitive treatment resulting in the disparate treatment of litigants."[97]

In this society, in which gender, race, and ethnicity have such saliency, these cumulative interjurisdictional findings are hardly surprising. Perhaps what should be surprising—and surely what is moving—is the persistence of the aspiration to judgment free of assumptions derived from litigants' gender, race, class, sexual orientation, nationality, religion. This hope for equal treatment laces the work of those involved in task forces on racial, ethnic, and gender bias. The purpose is to uncover prejudices so as to redress them, to hold courts to their promise of fairness. Across the country, these projects have titles that include the words "equality," "fairness," "justice," "equity"—unlike parallel work in Canada, styled "An Inquiry into Systemic Racism in the Criminal Justice System in Ontario."[98]

Despite their aspirational tone, projects in the United States about the effects of gender on courts are often separated from parallel inquiries on race and ethnicity. The new prominence of women's issues has not, until recently, been accompanied by a nuanced understanding of the category "women." While women of different colors, classes, religions, and sexual identities have begun to learn not to equate their own experiences with those of all women, they have been less successful in translating that understanding into effective political action, whether in debates about Supreme Court nominees, in task forces investigating bias in the courts, or elsewhere. In the controversy over Robert Bork, "women" and "blacks" were allied, and women of color faced few conflicts of identification. The political power that emerged from that alliance was critical to the outcome.[99] In the debate over Clarence Thomas, no such coalition operated; no longstanding political organization links race and gender and is dedicated to understanding what Kimberlé Crenshaw calls their "intersectionalities."[100] Indeed, the opposite problem exists: both legal and popular culture continue to inscribe a disjuncture between gender and race. Accepted parlance relies on the phrase "women and minorities," erasing women who are minorities[101] and reminding us of the continuing saliency of the book title *All the Women Are White, All the Men Are Black, but Some of Us Are Brave.*[102]

Even as court systems commit themselves by creating special task forces to examine forms of discrimination, the topics of race and gender bias are often conceived as discrete rather than overlapping categories. In theory, beginning a discussion of discrimination by using either category might not be problematic. Were the intersection of race and gender understood as framing all of our experiences, attention would be paid to women and men of different races and to differences of gender within racial categories, regardless of whether the issue is cast as one of "race" or one of "gender."

Unfortunately, in practice, gender and race are often seen as exclusive categories, and the effects of color on gender or gender on color have not (with some recent exceptions) become a focus of either inquiry.[103] Most judicial task force reports are either about race *or* about gender; few address both topics or consider white women and men, and women and men of color, as categories of analysis.[104] Similarly, senators' questions to Supreme Court nominees are about either "women" or "minorities," once again missing the interrelationships. The inadequacies of such an approach were vivid during the

Hill-Thomas proceedings. The fourteen senators (race: white; gender: male) addressed and sat in judgment of two principal witnesses, one a black male and one a black female. Race and gender framed, or haunted, or informed (depending on one's interpretation) what transpired. Both categories demand analysis, but so do their interaction. The Hill-Thomas proceedings demonstrated the incompleteness of any inquiry that does not simultaneously ask about race and gender, and as Charles Lawrence illuminates, about class and sexual orientation as well.[105] The phrase "women and minorities" limits our vision and hampers our work.

Incredible Answers and Complex Questions

In the end, the Supreme Court nomination process, the Thomas proceedings, and the task force reports teach complex lessons, mixing progress with pain. Organizations devoted to women's rights and to racial and ethnic equality have succeeded in demonstrating instances of institutionalized discrimination and requiring that attention be paid. They have licensed thousands of conversations within the halls of government about the inequalities that frame the lives of many in the United States. But the past decade of that conversation has not focused official consideration on the diversity among women and men nor insisted on the required but difficult exploration of prejudices that know no political, racial, or gendered boundaries.

There has been much discussion about the credibility of both Anita Hill and Clarence Thomas.[106] The question has often been framed not as "Which of them did you believe?" but as "Did you believe her?" As Adele Alexander details, that focus echoes the challenge women witnesses in general and women of color in particular have long faced.[107] Almost all the reports on gender bias in the courts consider the problem of women's credibility. The assessment is uniform: women's credibility is readily challenged, and disbelief a constant problem.[108]

But while credibility is an important topic, there is a risk of becoming overly preoccupied with it and treating it as *the* issue. To say that people did not believe Anita Hill is too easy an answer to "what happened" in October 1991. Easy, because if she was not believed, the problem of action was solved: there was nothing to do. But the

Senate's reaction to Anita Hill's testimony, like responses to women litigants across the country, was not simply one of disbelief but also one of unwillingness to name insult and aggression as injury, and then to act upon that knowledge by sanctioning the wrongdoer.

Whatever the philosophical possibilities about the meaning of belief, in practice the question of belief in courts always entails the question of the consequences of belief.[109] This aspect of assessing credibility (that whether in courts or in the Senate, credibility implicates action) helps to explain the polls in 1992, a year later, in which larger percentages of respondents reported believing Anita Hill than had the year before.[110] Such belief is easier to entertain in retrospect, when holding that belief requires no action affecting Thomas's career.

Credibility thus serves as the proverbial red herring that distracts us from the underlying dynamics of the Hill-Thomas proceedings. For some senators, credibility was a safe harbor that buffered the more disturbing possibilities and realities: that one could believe Anita Hill but either not care or not care enough to be moved to action—not care based on a variety of formulations, such as that sexualized aggression is neither uncommon nor normatively impermissible, or that the recipient was a woman of some privilege, or that the recipient was a black woman, or that because the aggressor was also black, this was but a dispute between "others" and did not implicate oneself, the relevant "one" here being white.[111]

In my view, most senators believed Anita Hill and knew that she spoke truth. What was revealed there—and what is repeated daily throughout the country in courts at all levels, as documented by task forces on race, ethnic, and gender bias—was the problem of action. In October 1991, we watched senators silently say that these events were not "injuries" in a sense that requires redress, not cognizable harms, not harms to which attention must be paid, and certainly not the basis for rejecting a Supreme Court appointment.[112]

Facing Justice's Shifting Images

The problem of action is not limited to the Senate as it voted in 1991 on Thomas's confirmation. Task forces on gender, racial, and ethnic bias face similar problems. While it has taken two decades to make plain the story of exclusion, of the absence of women of all colors and men of color from judiciaries, in retrospect that story is the relatively easy one to tell. Not long ago, the jury was closed to men of color and to all women. The legal profession was closed. The judiciary, from high to low positions, was closed.

Over these past two decades, questions of equality have become a subject of discussion from Supreme Court nominations to the lower courts. The demography of the judiciary came clearly in view, as did the obvious remedial response of diversifying that workforce so that those who sit in judgment reflect the characteristics of those whom they judge. It is not that the struggle for what Judge Leon Higginbotham calls "judicial pluralism"[113] has been won or that affirmative efforts to do so are popular but rather that some success has been achieved in making implausible overt hostility to pluralism. Whether from the left or the right, political parties speak of the need for inclusion and prominently display individuals of both sexes and of a variety of races and ethnicities (but not of sexual orientations) as emblems of their commitment to inclusion. But inclusion is a goal very different from either diversification or transformation. Inclusion of "others" within the current framework may not entail acknowledgment that those others have different visions, requiring more than replication.

What has also become plain, from the Supreme Court to daily life in the courts, is that such inclusion (the addition of "women and minorities" to the bench) does not respond sufficiently to another lesson of the Thomas proceeding—the limits of identity politics. As Judge Higginbotham has so eloquently written, Clarence Thomas is no Thurgood Marshall.[114] Filling a seat with a black man has not installed a person responsive to many forms of racial and gender inequality in this society. As Emma Coleman Jordan has explained, concern for racial equality is not always linked to commitment to gender equality.[115] White feminists, like black feminists, have a history of experiencing gender-based exclusion from political activities ostensibly framed by commitments to equality.[116] For white feminists, the task of naming that problem is relatively easier, for when they publicly explore the sexism they encounter in their white male counterparts, they have no fear of unleashing prejudices that women of color understand flow from public exploration of unfair treatment of women by men of color.[117]

Being a member of a community of color and being a woman may well give one firsthand understanding of the pain inflicted by those of other colors or of another gender. But color and gender alone do not mean that such experiences will animate one to work toward righting such injuries. Despite Thomas's status as a victim of racial tropes, he willingly deployed them, invoking the language of "lynching" and helping to paint his sister as a "welfare mother."[118] Living within the framework of current social structures, many who share markers of subordination aspire to escape rather than to remake the meaning of those markers. Thus, while battles about exclusion have been hard fought and are hardly won, ours is the era in which we must acknowledge that inclusion alone of women and men of all colors in the judicial system is both necessary and plainly insufficient.

Just as downplaying Anita Hill's testimony avoided the necessity of action, the temptation to avert one's eyes from seeing the ways in which gender, race, ethnicity, class, and sexual orientation frame judgments is powerful; the difficulties that result from recognizing these effects feel at times overwhelming. What does one do in the face of pervasive gendered and racialized interpretations of fact, of credibility, and of legal doctrine? How does one run a court system? Or vote on nominations to the Supreme Court?[119] Is banning discrimination on the basis of gender and race in jury selection sufficient? Or should we ban all challenges to jurors not based on cause, on the theory that some form of stereotyped judgment must underlie every peremptory challenge? Should we take a different route, and insist on inclusion of women and men of a variety of colors and life experiences on every jury? Require three judges rather than a single judge, to increase the range of views represented in every trial court decision? Attempt to prohibit lawyers, judges, jurors, witnesses, and court personnel from engaging in biased behavior?[120] Or attempt to delineate when race, gender, or ethnicity might be relevant to adjudication and specify under what conditions?[121] These are the questions that must occupy us as the century closes.

Conclusion

Some read the events of the week of October 7, 1991, as a testimony to power and resources. Judge Thomas is now Justice Thomas. Furthermore, as has been demonstrated time and again by the bias task forces, the language of fairness and due process does not ensure that courts are free of acts of discrimination. But there is more to be seen in those seven days than the power of resources, and more in the task force reports than the bases for despair. The power and the hopes of the relatively less privileged are also impressive.[122]

Prompted by Anita Hill's statements, and despite the holiday weekend and the efforts of Thomas supporters to chill vocal support of Hill, six senators "got it"—saw that they were obliged to name the wrong done and then act in response to the recognition of injury. These senators did change their votes, giving Thomas the narrowest confirmation victory in this century and more negative votes than any Supreme Court nominee has ever received.[123] Think how far that ninety-eight-man, two-woman Senate would have to have traveled to perceive the injury done to Anita Hill and then to decide that Thomas's responses were disqualifying. The fact that six men were moved in seven days should be understood as a moment of empowerment.[124]

In the face of attempts by Thomas supporters to smear Anita Hill,[125] truth was acknowledged by many people, who speak of a new awareness of the problems faced by women, and that those problems are not uniform but vary with race, class, and sexual orientation. In many quarters, Anita Hill has been honored,[126] while some of her accusers have been called on to defend their behavior.[127] The testimony of Anita Hill is replayed not only by that retelling but in the words of other women who describe their own experiences of sexual harassment and injuries, at times suffered in silence but now named as wrong.

The unfolding work of the gender, race, and ethnic bias task forces has followed a parallel route. The distance traveled within a few years is also grounds for optimism. In the late 1980s, the federal judiciary evinced little interest in taking up questions of discriminatory behavior within its halls. While acknowledging that such problems existed in the state judiciaries, in 1990 a federally chartered special committee thought them to be at "a minimum" in the federal courts and in need of no special study.[128] By 1994, two federal task force reports had been filed on gender bias,[129] and more than half the federal courts of the nation had undertaken inquiries.[130] Moreover, the initial failure to focus on the intersections of race and gender had given way to some extent as task forces began to call attention to the distinctive experiences among women and men.

As the century ends, we should celebrate such activity, even as we understand that we are leaving behind the "easy" answers of prohibiting discriminatory exclusions [131] and calling for inclusion. We have moved beyond discussions of women and men as unitary categories; we have learned to understand the concept of intersectionality. But we have neither faced nor resolved the painful difficulties every day more apparent. Marking intersections neither instructs us on how to negotiate them nor permits escape from evidence that conflicts of race and gender *cross* lines of race and gender. [132]

Contemporary feminist theory and critical race theory know well these painful problems. Guided by what is often called "standpoint theory," we have learned that perspective informs judgment, that problems must be understood not only from the posture of privilege but from the point of view of the displaced, and that the displaced do not themselves all share the same point of view. [133] Legal theory has also long known these issues; in 1921, Benjamin Cardozo wrote that "we can never see . . . with any eyes except our own." [134] In 1992, Catharine Wells and other pragmatists called for "situated judging." [135]

But we are less confident now than Cardozo was in 1921 about what it means to have one's own eyes. Clarence Thomas reminds us that the formation of a human being is a many-layered phenomenon; he brings the perspective not only of the black child brought up in a small town in Georgia but also of the black man welcomed by a group of conservatives because of his willingness to embrace their values. Toni Morrison linked Thomas to the character Friday in the novel *Robinson Crusoe* and concluded that both Friday and Thomas were called on "first to mimic, then to internalize and adore, but never to utter one single sentence understood to be beneficial to their original culture." [136]

Those who are chosen, as was Clarence Thomas, by a power structure very different from their own background have what Morrison calls "the problem of debt." [137] It is that burden that obscures the utility of judicial pluralism. As long as the integraters—the Clarence Thomases, the Anita Hills, the Sandra Day O'Connors, the Ruth Ginsburgs, and the Thurgood Marshalls—are there as tokens, and are selected by a very nonpluralistic power structure, their identity as exemplars of inclusion frames them. What would Clarence Thomas have done, who would he be, were his identity not forged in pursuit of approval from a structure that had excluded him? Were he one of many, not one of a few, who not only made it into the halls of power but also had the power to construct new buildings?

Notes

My thanks to Dennis Curtis, John Frank, Anita Hill, Vicki Jackson, Emma Coleman Jordan, Mark Tushnet, Catharine Wells, Christine Carr, Veronica Gentilli, Gregory Porter, Steven Vaughan, and members of the USC Law Library staff for thinking with me about this essay, and to those who helped me with a related essay, *Hearing Women*, 65 S. CAL. L. REV. 1333 (1992), published in the symposium *Gender, Race, and the Politics of Supreme Court Appointments: The Import of the Anita Hill/Clarence Thomas Hearings*, 65 S. CAL. L. REV. 1279 (1992).

1. Neil A. Lewis, *Law Professor Accuses Thomas of Sexual Harassment in 1980's*, N.Y. TIMES (Oct. 7, 1991) at 1. A good deal of subsequent discussion focused on how Professor Hill's information was brought to light; for one review of the events leading up to the press disclosures, see REPORT OF THE TEMPORARY SPECIAL INDEPENDENT COUNSEL PURSUANT TO SENATE RESOLUTION 202, Gov't Doc. 102–20, part I at 3 (May 13, 1992) (concluding that it could not "identify any source" of disclosures from the Senate). See also JANE MAYER AND JILL ABRAMSON, STRANGE JUSTICE: THE SELLING OF CLARENCE THOMAS 221–57 (1994) (describing the growing circle of people who had heard allegations of sexual harassment involving Thomas).
2. Letter from women law professors to the Senate, October 7, 1991 (on file with author). *See also* Maureen Dowd, *The Thomas Nomination: The Senate and Sexism*, N.Y. TIMES, Oct. 8, 1991, at A1, col. 4 (Duke law professor Katharine Bartlett sent the letter to the "Senate leadership . . . calling on them to . . . 'fully and publicly' investigate [the] accusations").
3. Law professor letter of October 8, 1991 (organized under the leadership of Professors Norman Dorsen and Frank Michelman) (on file with author).
4. Maureen Dowd, *The Thomas Nomination: 7 Congresswomen March to Senate to Demand Delay in Thomas Vote*, N.Y. TIMES, Oct. 9, 1991, at A1, col. 4. The congresswomen were Barbara Boxer (California), Nita M. Lowey (New York), Patsy T. Mink (Hawaii), Eleanor Holmes Norton (nonvoting delegate, District of Columbia), Patricia Schroeder (Colorado), Louise Slaughter (New York), and Jolene Unsoeld (Washington).
5. *See* Marianne Lavelle, *Legal Counsel for Anita Hill Had Uphill Battle*, NAT'L L. J., Oct. 28, 1991, at 22.
6. *See* JUDITH N. SKLAR, THE FACES OF INJUSTICE (1990); Dennis E. Curtis and Judith Resnik, *The Images of Justice*, 96 YALE L. J. 1727 (1986).

The relatively recent advent of televised "real" trials offers another set of images, but those selected for broadcasting are the high-profile cases which, like the Thomas proceedings, attract the press's attention. The burden of task forces, in contrast, is to probe the routine events often unreported by the media.

7. TONI MORRISON, *Introduction: Friday on the Potomac*, RACE-ING JUSTICE. EN-GENDERING POWER: ESSAYS ON ANITA HILL, CLARENCE THOMAS, AND THE CONSTRUCTION OF SOCIAL REALITY, at xi (1992) [hereinafter MORRISON].

8. *See* Adele Logan Alexander, " 'She's No Lady, She's a Nigger,' " pp. 3–25 herein. *See also* ADELE LOGAN ALEXANDER, AMBIGUOUS LIVES: FREE WOMEN OF COLOR IN RURAL GEORGIA, 1789–1879, at 36 (1991) (rapes of women of color not "even acknowledged as crimes under the Georgia criminal code").

9. As of 1991, before the Thomas nomination, 133 individuals had been nominated to the Supreme Court. *See* THE OXFORD COMPANION TO THE SUPREME COURT OF THE UNITED STATES (ed. Kermit L. Hall, 1992) at 965–71. Information about nominations first became generally available in 1916, when the Senate Judiciary Committee held public hearings and published a report on the nomination of Louis D. Brandeis, the first Jewish justice on the Supreme Court. *See* Preface to vol. I, ROY M. MERSKY AND J. MYRON JACOBSTEIN, THE SUPREME COURT OF THE UNITED STATES: HEARINGS AND REPORTS ON SUCCESSFUL AND UNSUCCESSFUL NOMINATIONS OF SUPREME COURT JUSTICES BY THE SENATE JUDICIARY COMMITTEE (Hein, 1977 & supp.) (16 volumes compiled by Mersky and Jacobstein). For an understanding of the confirmation process during the nineteenth century, the records of which can be found in the National Archives, see John P. Frank, *The Appointment of Supreme Court Justices: Prestige, Principles, and Politics*, 1941 WIS. L. REV. 172 (part I), 343 (part II); 461 (part III) [hereinafter Frank, *Supreme Court Justices*] (addressing late-nineteenth- as well as twentieth-century appointments).

While public hearings occurred in the Brandeis nomination, Brandeis himself did not testify. Harlan F. Stone was the first, in 1925, to testify on his own behalf before the Senate's Committee on the Judiciary. *Id.* at 492. According to the committee notes, the invitation was extended at 10:00 a.m., and Mr. Stone, then attorney general, appeared at 11:30; "he was interrogated by a number of the members of the Committee. The proceedings are in the form of transcript, taken by a stenographer." Special Meeting of the Full Committee on Stone Nomination, Jan. 28, 1925, Committee on the Judiciary, U.S. Senate, Minutes, 1923–25; 68th Cong.; Records of the U.S. Senate, Record Group 46, National Archives (Washington, D.C.). However, that testimony is not reproduced in the Mersky and Jacobstein compilation nor listed as available in Library of Congress holdings. Transcripts are also not readily available from the period when women's suffrage was much before the public and culminated in the passage of the

Nineteenth Amendment in 1920. Moreover, according to Mersky and Jacobstein, not all of the Senate Judiciary Committee proceedings since then have been made public.

In the later part of this century, more research materials are available. A review of hearings on Supreme Court nominees from 1960 to the present reveals that the first questioning about women's rights occurred at the Carswell hearings. *See Hearings before the Committee on the Judiciary on the Nomination of George Harrold Carswell of Florida, to Be an Associate Justice of the Supreme Court of the United States, U.S. Senate, 91st Cong., 2d Sess.* (January 27, 28, 29, February 2 and 3, 1970) [hereinafter *Carswell Hearings*].

10. *Carswell Hearings, supra* note 9, at 81 (Mink), 88 (Friedan). While Friedan noted that she was not sure she was the first from a women's rights organization to testify, she said that her presence was a "tribute to the fact that you gentlemen had begun to be aware of the importance of [women's rights] and the new voice." *Id.* at 98.

11. *Id.* at 81–82. Carswell's role in that case was quite limited; he was a member of an en banc panel that denied rehearing in Phillips v. Martin Marietta Corp., 416 F.2d 1257 (5th Cir. 1969) (en banc), in which Ida Phillips claimed that the company had violated her Title VII rights by declining to give her, a mother of children of pre-school age, a job not denied men with children of pre-school age. The Fifth Circuit concluded that the policy did not discriminate against women but was based upon "the differences between the normal relationships of working fathers and working mothers to their pre-school age children." Phillips v. Martin Marietta Corp., 411 F.2d 1, 4 (5th Cir. 1969). That decision was reversed and remanded by the Supreme Court. Phillips v. Martin Marietta Corp., 400 U.S. 542, 544 (1971).

12. *Carswell Hearings, supra* note 9, at 40–41.

13. According to one historian of the proceeding, criticism of Carswell centered on his general lack of distinction as well as his 1948 pro-segregation stance, later repudiated. *See, e.g.,* John P. Frank, Clement Haynsworth, The Senate, and The Supreme Court 103–106 (1991). Frank noted Mink's opposition, but in his view, the "real sticking points were civil rights and competence." *Id.* at 113. Frank also discussed the political context, a Democratic-controlled Senate distressed at the forced resignation of Abe Fortas, which animated the unsuccessful nomination of Clement Haynsworth (in Frank's view, unfortunately rejected) as well as that of Carswell (in Frank's view, appropriately rejected). *Id.* at xiv, 19, 28, 44, 94–95, 102–103. In May 1970, the Senate approved, with 94 affirmative votes and 6 absentees, the nomination of Harry Blackmun as an associate justice. *Id.* at 124. No questions were addressed to Blackmun about his views on women's rights during the brief one-day hearing. *Hearings before the Committee on the Judiciary, U.S. Senate, on Nomination of Harry A. Blackmun to Be an Associate Justice of the Supreme Court of the United States, U.S. Senate, 91st Cong., 2d Sess.* (Apr. 29, 1970).

14. *See Hearings before the Committee on the Judiciary, United States Senate, on the Nominations of William H. Rehnquist, of Arizona, and Lewis F. Powell, Jr., of Virginia, to Be Associate Justices of the Supreme Court of the United States,* U.S. Senate, 92d Cong., 2d Sess. (November 3, 4, 8, 9, and 10, 1971) [hereinafter *Rehnquist and Powell Hearings*].

15. She objected specifically to Rehnquist's testimony while he was in the Justice Department on the Equal Rights Amendment (ERA) and the Women's Equality Act. *Id.* at 428–29. Her criticism of Powell was premised on his failure, as a leader of the American Bar Association, to take stands on issues affecting women. *Id.* at 423–25, 428–33, 433–36. *See also* testimony of Catherine G. Roraback, president of the National Lawyers' Guild, *id.* at 460 (under Powell's leadership, the ABA was silent on equal rights for women). Barbara Greene Kilberg, of the National Women's Political Caucus, testified not about the nominees but about the absence of a female nominee (*id.* at 421–23), a topic that had been in the news in part because of President Nixon's statements that "qualified women" should be considered for the two vacancies. James M. Naughton, *Harlan Retires: Nixon Hints Poff Is a Court Choice,* N.Y. TIMES, Sept. 24, 1971, at 1.

16. In 1971, as assistant attorney general in the Nixon administration, Rehnquist had testified before the House Judiciary Committee; the testimony is somewhat ambiguous but in some respects supported the ERA. *See Federal Rights for Men and Women 1971, Hearings before Subcommittee No. 4 of the Committee on the Judiciary on H.J. 35, 208, and Related Bills,* House of Rep., 92d Cong., 1st Sess. 323 (1971) (Representative Wiggins noting that while the "administration is positively committed to the support of this constitutional amendment," it also said it was "not necessary").

    When testifying before the Senate Judiciary Committee as a nominee to be an associate justice, Rehnquist declined to state his personal view on the ERA. When asked his view on the rights of women under the Fourteenth Amendment, Rehnquist responded that it "protects women just as it protects other discrete minorities, if one could call women a minority." *Rehnquist and Powell Hearings, supra* note 14, at 163. Thereafter, noting that some of the issues were pending before the Court, Rehnquist declined to address additional questions on women's rights. *Id.* at 164.

17. According to a recent biography of Powell, when he was confronted by "a group of women's rights activists," he responded: "Ladies, I've been married for thirty-five years and have three daughters. I've got to be for you." JOHN C. JEFFRIES, JR., JUSTICE LEWIS F. POWELL, JR. 233 (1994). As Jeffries describes it, the "crucial issue was not gender but race." While Powell had resigned his memberships in all-white clubs, concern was raised about his role in the "(non)desegregation of the Richmond schools." Powell's defense was to rely on endorsements by a variety of individuals attesting to his efforts to respond calmly to the complex problems of school integration, his work with the all-black National Bar Association, and his commitment to fairness. *Id.* at 235–36.

18. *See, e.g.*, Henry J. Abraham, Justices and Presidents: A Political History of Appointments to the Supreme Court, 20–22 (3d ed. 1992).

19. *See, e.g.*, the discussion of decisions of Justice Stevens when he was an appellate judge on cases raising issues related to women's rights, as well as his attitudes toward women's rights and affirmative action, in *Hearings before the Committee on the Judiciary on the Nomination of John Paul Stevens to Be a Justice of the Supreme Court*, U.S. Senate, 94th Cong., 1st Sess. 15–17, 33–34, 56–57, 78–84 (Dec. 8, 9, 10, 1975) (NOW opposed the nomination because of his "consistent opposition to women's rights" and cited several of Stevens' rulings); the discussion of Justice Scalia's lack of interest in women's rights, in *Hearings before the Committee on the Judiciary on the Nomination of Judge Antonin Scalia, to Be Associate Justice of the Supreme Court of the United States*, U.S. Senate, 99th Cong., 2d Sess. 168–85, 207–23, 250–75 (Aug. 5, 6, 1986) [hereinafter *Scalia Hearings*] (testimony of Eleanor Smeal, president of NOW, as well as others); the discussion of Justice Rehnquist's views on equal rights in *Hearings before the Committee on the Judiciary on the Nomination of Justice William Hubbs Rehnquist to Be Confirmed as Chief Justice of the U.S. Supreme Court*, 99th Cong., 2d Sess. 114 (July 29, 30, 31, Aug. 1, 1986) (NOW testified against the nomination, and Senator Howard M. Metzenbaum noted "some concerns expressed by . . . blacks and women"), 227 (Justice Rehnquist's personal opposition to the ERA).

20. *See Scalia Hearings, supra* note 19, at 91 (also commenting that a judge should not belong to a club that "practices invidious discrimination"). Scalia resigned his membership in that club; he explained that several factors influenced his decision, including that "I was uncomfortable at doing something which, although I thought it was perfectly OK, was offensive to friends whose feelings I am concerned about." *Id.* at 105.

21. The Bork nomination was a watershed in other respects. The Senate's extensive public questioning of the nominee prompted a vigorous debate about the meaning of its constitutional obligation and about the effects of a public nomination process. This debate continues.

   One set of concerns revolves around the role of the Senate. Should its power to provide both "advice and consent" be translated to mean only "consent"? *See generally* Charles L. Black, Jr., *A Note on Senatorial Consideration of Supreme Court Nominees*, 79 Yale L. J. 657 (1970). If one believes that the Senate may take a substantive role, the next issue concerns the qualifications relevant to holding the office of judge and justice. May one ask directly about "judicial philosophy," or are "judicial temperament" and "professional competence" the only permissible topics?

   Reviewing the nominations since Bork, one finds that the question about the Senate's role seems to have been settled for the time being. The Senate asks a host of questions and the nominee responds, selectively. However, the second issue—the permissible criteria upon which to judge a nominee—remains contested. The effort to establish the legitimacy of wide-ranging senatorial evaluation is reflected in the comments of Senator Joseph R. Biden, Jr., chair of the Judiciary Committee, as he opened the confirmation hearings on Anthony Kennedy, *Hearings before the Committee on the Judiciary on the Nomination of Anthony M. Kennedy to Be Associate Justice of the Supreme Court of the United States*, U.S. Senate, 100th Cong., 1st Sess. 23 (Dec. 14, 15, 16, 1987) [hereinafter *Kennedy Hearings*] (claiming that the Senate had a constitutional right to "delve into the judicial philosophy and constitutional grounding of any nominee"). *See also* PAUL SIMON, ADVICE AND CONSENT: CLARENCE THOMAS, ROBERT BORK, AND THE INTRIGUING HISTORY OF THE SUPREME COURT NOMINATION BATTLES (1992) (advocating that the Senate take a vigorous role).

A third concern has arisen, about the effects of a vigorous and public role for the Senate. How does public questioning alter the selection process by the executive? Does it create disincentives, discouraging able individuals from being judges? What role do the press and interest groups play in the scrutiny, and is the result a caricature of an individual's substantive views? *See generally* STEPHEN L. CARTER, THE CONFIRMATION MESS: CLEANING UP THE FEDERAL APPOINTMENTS PROCESS (1994); Robert F. Nagel, *Advice, Consent, and Influence*, 84 Nw. U. L. REV. 858 (1990); Judith Resnik, *Changing Criteria for Judging Judges*, 84 Nw.U. L. REV. 889 (1990); Paul A. Freund, *Appointment of Justices: Some Historical Perspectives*, 101 HARV. L. REV. 1146 (1988).

22. *See generally* ETHAN BRONNER, BATTLE FOR JUSTICE: HOW THE BORK NOMINATION SHOOK AMERICA (1989); Martin Shapiro, *Interest Groups and Supreme Court Appointments*, 84 Nw. U. L. REV. 935 (1990).

23. *Hearings before the Senate Judiciary Committee on the Nomination of Robert H. Bork to Be Associate Justice of the Supreme Court of the United States*, 100th Cong., 1st Sess. 160–61 (Sept. 15–30, 1987) [hereinafter *Bork Hearings*]. One case that received attention was Griswold v. Connecticut, 381 U.S. 479 (1965), which involved a challenge to a statute making it a crime to prescribe contraceptives. Robert Bork had called the statute a "nutty law," and then, at the hearings, described the case as an "academic exercise." *Bork Hearings* at 114, 240–43; Stuart Taylor, Jr., *The Bork Hearings: Bork Tells Panel He Is Not Liberal, Not Conservative*, N.Y. TIMES, Sept. 16, 1987, at A1, col. 6. *See generally* Andi Reardon, *Griswold v. Connecticut: Landmark Case Remembered*, N.Y. TIMES, May 28, 1989, at 12CN, p. 6, col. 5 (describing the efforts of Estelle Griswold and Charles Lee Buxton to lobby the Connecticut legislature to repeal that law, and their subsequent arrest for operating a clinic that openly dispensed contraceptives to poor women; Yale law professor Thomas Emerson, who had argued the case, explained its import as one of the early recognitions of a constitutionally based right to privacy).

24. For example, while on the Court of Appeals for the District of Columbia, Judge Bork wrote a unanimous opinion for a panel of three judges in which that court upheld, against a challenge under the Occupational Safety and Health Act, a company policy that required women of childbearing potential to be sterilized if they wanted to hold jobs exposing them to chemicals alleged to cause harm to reproductive capacities. Oil, Chem. and Atomic Workers Int'l Union v. American Cyanamid Co., 741 F.2d 444 (D.C. Cir. 1984). Judge Bork's opinion described the company's plan as an attempt to deal with "unattractive alternatives," and wrote that rather than firing women, the company had given them "a most unhappy choice" of sterilization. *Id.* at 445, 450.

At the confirmation hearings, the question was whether Bork's discussion evidenced understanding of the stark options put to women workers: be fired, demoted, or sterilized. When questioned, Judge Bork commented that "some of [the women], I guess, didn't want to have children." *Bork Hearings, supra* note 23, at 468. *Compare* SUSAN FALUDI, BACKLASH: THE UNDECLARED WAR AGAINST AMERICAN WOMEN 450 (1991) (quoting Betty Riggs' letter to the Senate: "Only a judge who knows nothing about women who need to work could say that. I was only twenty-six years old, but I had to work, so I had no choice. . . . This was the most awful thing that ever happened to me. I still believe it was against the law, whatever Bork says"). In 1991, the United States Supreme Court ruled that, given evidence of the potential for harm to the reproductive systems of both men and women if exposed to lead, Title VII and the Pregnancy Disability Act prohibit employers from banning only women of childbearing capacity from certain jobs. *See* Int'l Union, United Auto., Aerospace & Agric. Implement Workers of America v. Johnson Controls, 499 U.S. 187 (1991).

Further, the Bork hearings also addressed an opinion by Judge Bork on sexual harassment, in which he had written about "sexual dalliance" and "sexual escapades," choosing language that could be read as making light of an atmosphere in which sexual compliance was allegedly required. Vinson v. Taylor, 760 F.2d 1330, 1330, 1332 (D.C. Cir. 1985) (Bork, J. dissenting from the suggestion for rehearing en banc), *panel opinion aff'd in part and rev'd in part sub nom.* Meritor Savings Bank v. Vinson, 477 U.S. 57 (1986).

For criticism of women's groups' opposition to Bork as unduly "personal," see CARTER, *supra* note 21, at 48–50.

25. Bork argued that the Fourteenth Amendment was addressed to race and ethnicity, not to gender, and that rules relating to race should not and could not be transposed to gender, because "our society feels very strongly that relevant differences exist and should be respected by government" (referring to single-sex bathrooms and women in combat). ROBERT H. BORK, THE TEMPTING OF AMERICA: THE POLITICAL SEDUCTION OF THE LAW 328–31 (1990).

26. *Bork Hearings, supra* note 23, at 161–62 (Bork explained that his opposition

was not energetic; he had not "campaigned" against the ERA, but he did believe it would be inappropriate to "put all the relationships between the sexes in the hand of judges").

27. *See Kennedy Hearings, supra* note 21, at 104–11.

28. *Id.* at 105.

29. *Hearings before the Committee on the Judiciary on the Nomination of David H. Souter to Be an Associate Justice of the Supreme Court of the United States,* U.S. Senate, 101st Cong., 2nd Sess. 75–76, 106 (Sept. 13, 14, 17, 18, 19, 1990) [hereinafter *Souter Hearings*]. Judge Souter responded generally to questions about women's rights with discussion of the legal tests that govern the equal protection clause and privacy. *Id.* at 53–57. Several representatives of women's organizations raised concerns about Judge Souter's views on women's rights. *See, e.g., id.* at 362–406 (testimony of Kate Michelman, executive director, National Abortion Rights Action League); 569–604, 703 (Helen Neuborne, executive director, NOW Legal Defense and Education Fund); 684–701, 708 (Eleanor Smeal, president, Fund for the Feminist Majority); 719–740 (the Honorable Sophia H. Hall, president, National Association of Women Judges). Senatorial concern about this issue is also evident in the Senate's report on the nomination; in his "additional views" on the nomination, Senator Biden noted that Souter had demonstrated a "commendable concern" for ensuring sufficient constitutional protection for women's rights. NOMINATION OF DAVID H. SOUTER TO BE AN ASSOCIATE JUSTICE OF THE UNITED STATES SUPREME COURT, S. EXEC. REP. 101–32, 101st Cong., 2d Sess. 28–30 (Oct. 1, 1990).

30. *Nomination of Judge Clarence Thomas to Be Associate Justice of the Supreme Court of the United States, Hearings before the Committee on the Judiciary,* U.S. Senate, 102d Cong., 1st Sess. 127, 144–46 (Sept. 10–13, 16, Oct 11–13, 1991) [hereinafter *Thomas Hearings*]. Thomas declined, however, to agree that statistical disparities between women's and men's participation in the workforce demonstrated such discrimination. Further, in response to questioning by Senator Edward Kennedy about discrimination in employment, Thomas noted the importance of including "minorities, women, and individuals with disabilities in the work force and to aggressively do so," but he refused to endorse affirmative action as a mechanism. *Id.* at 205–206, 234–46, 289–91. Not only did Thomas make statements endorsing "equality" and the constitutional "right to privacy" (*id.* at 127), but his supporters, such as Senator Thurmond, praised him for his "aggressive enforcement of civil rights laws and equal opportunity laws designed to protect individual rights." *Id.* at 24.

31. *Id.* at 204.

32. Richard L. Revesz, *Thurgood Marshall's Struggle*, 68 N.Y.U. L. REV. 237, 252 (1993) (also describing Revesz's own dismay when, as a law clerk for Justice Marshall, he first read of Marshall's "struggle—not his well-known struggle as a child . . . but his struggle even after he had reached

the apex of his profession." *Id.* at 261–62); Mark V. Tushnet, *From the NAACP to the Supreme Court,* chap. 2 of MAKING CONSTITUTIONAL LAW: THURGOOD MARSHALL AND THE SUPREME COURT, 1961– 1991 (forthcoming, Oxford) (manuscript on file with author).

33. *See Hearings before the Committee on the Judiciary on Nomination of Thurgood Marshall to Be an Associate Justice of the Supreme Court of the United States,* U. S. Senate, 90th Cong., 1st Sess. (July 13, 14, 18, 19, 24, 1967) [hereinafter *Marshall Hearings*]. One other note about the Marshall nomination; it was also the occasion on which a commentator remarked that women were not among those nominated to the Supreme Court. As he explained, while "asking why no Negro was appointed before, [a]n even more pertinent question is: Why hasn't a woman been appointed to the Supreme Court of the United States." *See* David Lawrence, *"Why Not a Woman on High Court?",* WASH. EVENING STAR, June 16, 1967, reproduced among other news articles attached to the statement of the "Minority Views of Mr. Erwin," opposing the nomination, in S. EXEC. REP. NO. 13, *Marshall Hearings,* Aug. 21, 1967, at 44–47. See discussion, *infra,* on efforts to delineate "women and minorities" as compared to understanding intersecting identities.

34. *See Hearings before the Committee on the Judiciary on the Nomination of Judge Sandra Day O'Connor of Arizona to Serve as an Associate Justice of the Supreme Court of the United States,* U.S. Senate, 97th Cong., 1st Sess. (Sept. 9, 10, 11, 1981) [hereinafter *O'Connor Hearings*].

35. *See, e.g., id.* at 13 (Senator Alan Simpson's comment that O'Connor was "a person who brings a real touch of class to this office"); at 23 (Senator Charles E. Grassley told O'Connor that she was "a warm, perceptive, and articulate person"); at 27 (Senator Howell Heflin described O'Connor as a "faithful wife and devoted mother"); at 35 (Senator Dennis DeConcini described O'Connor's "record as a wife and a mother [that] is commendable"); at 124 (Senator Jeremiah Denton stated that "a woman who has fulfilled the indispensable roles of wife and mother in such a successful way, and then has gone on to extrapolate into fields of professional accomplishment which would amount to, in my opinion, in sum constituting pretty much an ideal woman").

36. *Id.* at 222. West joined a panel of three members of the Arizona House of Representatives, all testifying on behalf of the nomination. West described himself as a "leading pro-life legislator" and informed the Senate Judiciary Committee that "while [O'Connor was] not a pro-life proponent while a member of the Arizona Senate, neither was she then nor to my knowledge has she ever been the friend of those who advocate the killing of innocent unborn babies." *Id.* at 221–23.

37. As one newspaper described it, abortion questions turned the confirmation into a "single-issue" event. *See New Right Loses on Judge but Gains New Zeal,* N.Y. TIMES, Sept. 17, 1981, at A20, col. 3. The combat questions

probed O'Connor's "personal position with respect to women serving in actual military combat." *See O'Connor Hearings, supra* note 34, at 87–88 (Senator Hatch); at 127 (Senator Denton). The questions may have been prompted in part by O'Connor's service, in the 1950s, on a Defense Advisory Committee on Women in the Services (*id.* at 88), and in part by the then recent Supreme Court decision upholding the all-male draft against an equal protection attack. *See* Rostker v. Goldberg, 453 U.S. 57 (1981).

While other nominees have been asked about abortion and equal rights for women, the hearings on the nominations of Stevens, Scalia, and Kennedy, as well as on the elevation of Justice Rehnquist to be chief justice, have less focus on abortion, some discussion of women's equal rights, and no discussion of women in combat—one of two "standard" questions powerful women (the other being whether single-sex bathrooms are unconstitutional).

Subsequent to Justice O'Connor's hearing, the question of abortion played a role in the hearings on some male nominees—reflective of the vulnerability of *Roe v. Wade* as a precedent. *See, e.g., Souter Hearings, supra* note 29, at 117–19, 214, 269–70; *Thomas Hearings, supra* note 30, at 36, 53, 56, 178, 218–24. *Roe v. Wade* was less central in both the Ginsburg and Breyer hearings, in part because, by then, Justices Kennedy, Souter, and O'Connor had limited but refused to overturn the case. *See* Planned Parenthood v. Casey, 112 S. Ct. 2791 (1992); Fed. News. Service, July 13, 1994, at 178 (to be published as *Hearings before the Committee on the Judiciary on the Nomination of Stephen G. Breyer to Be an Associate Justice of the Supreme Court of the United States*) (referring to the reaffirmation of *Roe* in *Casey*); *Nomination of Ruth Bader Ginsburg to Be Associate Justice of the Supreme Court of the United States, Hearings before the Committee on the Judiciary,* U.S. Senate, 103d Cong., 1st Sess. 302 (July 20, 21, 22, 23, 1993) [hereinafter *Ginsburg Hearings*] (also invoking *Casey*).

38. *See, e.g., O'Connor Hearings, supra* note 34, at 75–76.
39. The two hearings on the nominations of women provide relatively little insight into these attitudes. In the 414-page hearing record, Justice O'Connor was asked a few questions about her views on "equality for women and for many other groups" (*O'Connor Hearings, supra* note 34, at 77) (questioning by Senator Kennedy, to which she responded by noting the "situation of blacks" and the "cultural diversity" of Arizona, in which both legislature and courts were working at "trying to eliminate vestiges of discrimination"); and a few questions on affirmative action and standards of proof in discrimination cases (*id.* at 84, 148 (Senator Hatch)) and the like.

When Ruth Ginsburg was nominated in 1993, she was also queried about her general attitudes toward discrimination. Senator Kennedy asked her to describe "how your experience on gender discrimination has sensitized you on the other forms of discrimination, generally." Ginsburg responded she was "alert to discrimination" because of her experiences as a child growing up during World War II "in a Jewish family." *See Ginsburg Hearings, supra* note 37, at 139.

40. Tushnet, *supra* note 32. John Frank has argued that public attention that flows from such theatrics usefully focuses "public attention on the Supreme Court," and that it is the "everlasting possibility of rejection" that gives "vitality to the proceedings which would not be present if the Senate could not occasionally rebel." Frank, *Supreme Court Justices, supra* note 9, at 512.

41. The Ginsburg hearings departed in some respects from those of Justice O'Connor. First, while senators recognized both women as pathbreakers for women, only Justice Ginsburg had spent a good deal of her professional life primarily identified as a women's rights activist, leading the ACLU Women's Rights Project. Second, the Ginsburg hearings have relatively few references to her personal qualities. Ginsburg was many times praised for her academic and professional achievements and for overcoming discrimination against women in her own professional life. Some reference was also made to her family life, but Ginsburg was not as much located as wife and mother nor as a female presence as had been O'Connor. *See, e.g., Ginsburg Hearings, supra* note 37, at 10–11, 27, 40 (opening statements by Senators Moynihan, Leahy, and Feinstein).

The question about women being partial to other women was asked of Ginsburg; Senator Kohl questioned whether she could "shed" her life experience as an advocate for women's rights. *Id.* at 228. Ginsburg responded with the example of the attempted disqualification of another woman judge in a Title VII claim, and that if gender made one a partisan, it would make both a female and a male judge a partisan. *Id.* She also spoke of the differences between the role of judge and that of advocate. Similarly, in 1980, when she was nominated to the appellate court, Senator Metzenbaum (presumably in a friendly attempt to buffer criticism) asked Ginsburg whether her involvement in women's rights would make it "difficult to assume the responsibilities of an impartial, nonpartisan jurist." *Hearings before the Committee on the Judiciary, The Selection and Confirmation of Federal Judges,* 96th Cong., 2d Sess. 350 (1980). Ginsburg responded that, while she had worked as an advocate, the "style of work and thought" that came more "naturally" to her was of an academic, and that those attributes, considering all sides of an argument, would stand her in good stead as a judge. Further, "work as an advocate for human rights causes helps prepare one to decide cases fairly in accordance with the law even when the home crowd would not be happy with the result." *Id.*

The Ginsburg Supreme Court hearings were also congruent with the post-Bork pattern in that she was asked about her attitude toward the ERA (and responded that she supported it), and about the level of scrutiny she would apply to gender-based discrimination. *Ginsburg Hearings, supra* note 37, at 165, 193, 243, 262. Her response detailed her own role as an advocate in attempting to convince the Court to scrutinize gender-based discrimination strictly and her subsequent work on cases using the intermediary standard of review. *Id.* at 165–71. When pressed by Senator Thurmond of South Carolina about a contemporary issue, single-sex education (in the courts by way of challenges to the all-male, state-funded Virginia Military Institute and subsequently to the Citadel, the Military College of South Carolina), Ginsburg avoided a direct answer. *Id.* at 141.

The Breyer hearings are consistent with the prior precedents in that he was both queried on women's rights and expressed his commitment to women's equality. In his opening statement, for example, he said that his law school diploma refers to law "simply as those wise restraints that make men free. Women too." Fed. News Service, July 12, 1994, at 213. The first questions addressed to him by Senator Edward Kennedy, for whom he had worked on the Senate Judiciary Committee, were about his "approach in interpreting the laws against sex discrimination." *Id.* at 228. Reference was made to Judge Breyer's opinion in Stathos v. Bowden, 728 F.2d 15 (1st Cir. 1984), in which the court affirmed a finding of sex-based pay disparity. Breyer responded that women should not make "less money for doing the same thing" as men. *Id.* at 229. Senator DeConcini queried Breyer on gender equality and the Fourteenth Amendment. He responded that it was "absolutely established that gender discrimination falls within the scope of the Fourteenth Amendment" and then referred to his daughters and the barriers he was concerned they might confront as women. *Id.* at 268.

While no women's rights groups testified, the presidents of the National Bar Association, the Hispanic National Bar Association, the National Pacific Asian American Bar Association, and the Native American Bar Association presented testimony, appearing "neither to oppose nor extol" but to remind both the nominee and the Senate Judiciary Committee that the Supreme Court should "assume the mantle of leadership" to ensure equal treatment, inclusion, and "empowerment" of people of color. Fed. Doc. Clearinghouse, Congressional Testimony, July 15, 1994, at 62.

42. The comment was reported by Juan Williams, Op-Ed, *Black Conservatives, Center Stage,* WASH. POST, Dec. 16, 1980, at A21 (also describing Thomas as believing that the "worst experience of his life . . . was attending college and law school with whites who believed he was there only because of racial quotas for the admission of blacks," and quoting him as stating, "If I ever went to work for the EEOC or did anything directly connected with blacks, my career would be irreparably ruined."). During the second phase of the Thomas hearings, after Anita Hill had raised this issue, Senator Hatch noted that Hill had expressed concern about Thomas's "repeated public criticism of his sister and her children for living on welfare." Thomas said he had "no recollection of ever making a statement about my sister in any speeches. That was in one news article on December 16, 1981." *Thomas Hearings, supra* note 30, part IV, at 248.

43. Karen Tumulty, *Sister of High Court Nominee Traveled Different Road*, L.A. TIMES, July 5, 1991, at A4; Joel F. Handler, *The Judge and His Sister: Growing Up Black*, N.Y. TIMES, July 23, 1991, at A20 (letter to editor, describing Thomas as having "cruelly distorted her situation"). See also Nell Irvin Painter, *Hill, Thomas, and the Use of Racial Stereotype*, in MORRISON, *supra* note 7, at 200, 201–202 (criticizing Thomas for currying favor with conservatives by deploying the image of his sister as a "deadbeat on welfare").

44. Kimberlé Crenshaw, *Roundtable: Doubting Thomas*, 6 TIKKUN 23, 27–28 (no. 5, Sept.–Oct. 1991) ("My sense of Clarence Thomas is that he doesn't represent the much-heralded phenomenon of pulling oneself up by one's bootstraps. The story instead is how he climbed over the body of his sister—and metaphorically the bodies of the very Black women he insults with his willingness to demean us for his own political gain.").

45. *Thomas Hearings*, *supra* note 30, at part 2. King, who was a part of a panel with Marcia Greenberger of the National Women's Law Center and Judith Lichtman of the Women's Legal Defense Fund, testified that "as a black woman, it is exceedingly difficult for me to oppose the nomination of a black individual who has known great personal struggle. Nevertheless, Judge Thomas' extensive record and personal posture is so antithetical to the interests of women and blacks—especially black women—that I feel an obligation to testify against his nomination." She analyzed in detail Thomas's invocation of his sister and linked it to his failures to appreciate the economic obstacles black women faced. *Id.* at 261–62. Yard testified on a panel with Harriet Woodes of the National Women's Political Caucus, Eleanor Smeal of the Fund for the Feminist Majority, Helen Neuborne of NOW's Legal Defense and Education Fund, Anne Bryant of the American Association of University Women, and Byllye Avery of the National Black Women's Health Project. *Id.*, part 3, at 202–203 (discussing Thomas's "cruel remarks" as denigrating "people on welfare").

46. Christine Stansell, *White Feminists and Black Realities: The Politics of Authenticity*, in MORRISON, *supra* note 7 at 251, 263. Stansell also writes: "From a feminist point of view, Thomas's rendition . . . constitutes a minor scandal. . . . When Thomas was attending Yale, [his sister] was working two minimum-wage jobs to support a family." *Id.* at 260–61.

47. Dennis E. Curtis, *The Fake Trial*, 65 S. CAL. L. REV. 1523 (1992); *see also* David A. Strauss and Cass R. Sunstein, *The Senate, the Constitution, and the Confirmation Process*, 101 YALE L. J. 1491 (1992) (calling for less deference by the Senate to the president on Supreme Court nominees).

48. *See, e.g.*, Melissa Healy and Edwin Chen, *Thomas Confirmed, 52 to 48*, L.A. TIMES, Oct. 16, 1991, at A1, col. 5 ("The burden of proof has to be on the person who is making the accusation") (quoting Senator DeConcini); David G. Savage, *Thomas, Backers Try to Make Him Seem Victim*, L.A. TIMES, Oct. 13, 1991, at A1, col. 3 ("The presumption (of innocence) remains with you, judge" (quoting Senator Biden)).

49. *See* Curtis, *supra* note 47, at 1523–25.

50. *See* MAYER AND ABRAMSON, STRANGE JUSTICE, *supra* note 1, at 270–71; Charles J. Ogletree, Jr., "The People vs. Anita Hill," pp. 157–63 herein.

51. The Ad Hoc Committee on Public Education on Sexual Harassment, formed within those few days, distributed a fact sheet to each member of the Senate, detailing differences between popular perceptions of sexual harassment (such as that it was uncommon) and social science data about the phenomenon (such as congressional studies in 1981 and 1987 that found that 40 percent of female federal employees reported being sexually harassed on the job).

52. Veronica Gentilli, *The Demographic Profile of the Ninth Circuit, Working Paper of the Ninth Circuit Gender Bias Task Force*, at 3, 11 (May 1992) (these numbers include both "active" and "senior" judges). As of June 1990, in 60 of the 94 district courts, none of the life-tenured judges were women. ADMINISTRATIVE OFFICE OF THE UNITED STATES COURTS, UNITED STATES COURT DIRECTORY, at 56–338 (Spring 1990).

53. ADMINISTRATIVE OFFICE OF THE UNITED STATES COURTS, UNITED STATES COURT DIRECTORY (Summer 1991), at 5, 13, 23–24, 26–27 (those circuits were the First, Fourth, Seventh, and Eighth). By 1994, the number of federal appellate courts without any women judges had declined; only one circuit remained an all-male bench. In three of the circuits (the Second, Seventh, and Tenth), a single woman sat. *See* 22 F. 3d vii–xv, Judges of the United States Courts of Appeals (including cases through June of 1994).

54. Lee Seltman, *Appointments of Special Masters by the Supreme Court and in the Ninth Circuit: A Demographic Analysis, Working Paper of the Ninth Circuit Gender Bias Task Force* (June 1992).

55. A. Leon Higginbotham, Jr., *Seeking Pluralism in Judicial Systems: The American Experience and the South African Challenge*, 1993 DUKE L. J. 1028, 1053 [hereinafter Higginbotham, *Seeking Pluralism*]. *See also* THE ANNUAL REPORT OF THE JUDICIAL EQUAL EMPLOYMENT OPPORTUNITY PROGRAM, ADMINISTRATIVE OFFICE OF THE UNITED STATES COURTS, FOR THE TWELVE MONTHS ENDED SEPTEMBER 30, 1990, 8–9 (Preliminary Edition) [hereinafter EEO PRELIMINARY REPORT] (as of 1990, 7 percent of the active federal judiciary were people of color).

56. Leon Higginbotham, *The Case of the Missing Black Judges*, N.Y. TIMES, at A21 (July 29, 1992). *See also* Higginbotham, *Seeking Pluralism, supra* note 55, at 1054 n.97 ("The final count for all the Reagan-Bush appointments of African-Americans to the courts of appeals was 3 out of 116"). The three judges nominated were Clarence Thomas and Timothy Lewis, by President Bush, and Lawrence W. Pierce, by President Reagan. *Id.*

57. EEO PRELIMINARY REPORT, *supra* note 55. In 1993, the data collection method changed to obtain data about the intersection of gender with race and ethnicity.

58. The ease with which issues of diversity and inclusion slip through the cracks

was exemplified again in 1991 when Congress created a thirteen-person commission charged with considering the discipline and impeachment of life-tenured federal judges. The legislation dispersed the power to appoint the thirteen members to the President, the President Pro Tem of the Senate, the Speaker of the House, the Chief Justice of the Supreme Court, and the Conference of Chief Justices of the State Courts. 28 U.S.C. 332 "note"; Pub. L. No. 101–650, 104 Stat. 5124 (Dec. 1, 1990). None of them chose a woman, thereby making the National Commission on Judicial Discipline and Removal another all-male panel, of whom one was a man of color. (In 1993, after the presidential election, a woman was added to the panel.) The commission recommended that judicial canons expressly prohibit "judicial behavior that reflects or implements bias on the basis of race, sex, sexual orientation, religion, or ethnic or national original, including sexual harassment," and that each circuit not already doing so conduct studies of "judicial misconduct involving bias based on race, sex, sexual orientation, religion, or ethnic or national origin, including sexual harassment." REPORT OF THE NATIONAL COMMISSION ON JUDICIAL DISCIPLINE AND REMOVAL 152, 155 (Aug. 1993).

59. 1992 ANNUAL REPORT OF THE DIRECTOR OF THE ADMINISTRATIVE OFFICE OF THE UNITED STATES COURTS 129, Table A-1 [hereinafter 1992 DIRECTOR'S REPORT]. The number of opinions has since declined; in 1993–94, the Supreme Court issued 93 opinions. 63 U.S.L.W. 3134 (Aug. 24, 1994).

60. *Id.* at 130, Table B; at 172, Table C; and at 229, Table D.

61. EEO PRELIMINARY REPORT, *supra* note 55, at 8, Table I.

62. 1992 DIRECTOR'S REPORT, *supra* note 59, at 312, Table F.

63. EEO PRELIMINARY REPORT, *supra* note 55, at 7–8, Table I; Gentilli, *supra* note 52, at 21, Table XXV, and at 24, Table XXVII.

64. *See* John C. Holmes, *ALJ Update: A Review of the Current Role, Status, and Demographics of the Corps of Administrative Law Judges,* 38 FED. BAR NEWS & J. 202 (May 1991); 5 C.F.R. §930.203 (1990); Peter V. Lee, Sheri Porath, and Joan E. Schaffner, *Engendered Social Security Disability Determinations: The Path of a Woman Claimant,* 68 TUL. L. REV. 1477, 1507 (1994) (more recently, 7 percent of ALJs were women).

65. According to the National Center for State Courts, as of December 1991, an "estimated 8.7% of the 28,713 state court judges (2,498) [were] women." National Center for State Courts, Memorandum of Phillip A. Lattimore III (Dec. 4, 1991).

66. *See* REPORT AND RECOMMENDATIONS OF THE FLORIDA SUPREME COURT RACIAL AND ETHNIC BIAS STUDY COMMISSION, "WHERE THE INJURED FLY FOR JUSTICE" (vol. I), at 14 (1990) [hereinafter FLORIDA RACIAL AND ETHNIC BIAS STUDY I]. According to the Minnesota Supreme Court Task Force on Racial Bias in the Judicial System, as of 1992, 5 percent of Minnesota's judges were people of color. MINNESOTA SUPREME COURT TASK FORCE ON RACIAL BIAS IN THE JUDICIAL

SYSTEM FINAL REPORT, *reprinted in* 16 HAMLINE L. REV. 477, 696 (1993) [hereinafter MINNESOTA TASK FORCE ON RACIAL BIAS].

67. Among them were Joyce L. Kennard (California Supreme Court); Judith W. Rogers (District of Columbia, Court of Appeals); Julia Cooper Mack (District of Columbia, Court of Appeals); Annice Wagner (District of Columbia, Court of Appeals); Rosemary Barkett (Florida Supreme Court); Leah J. Sears-Collins (Georgia Supreme Court), and Dorothy Comstock Riley (Michigan Supreme Court).

68. *See "Clarence Thomas Easily Confirmed . . . To Appeals Court for D.C. Circuit,"* 46TH ANNUAL CONGRESSIONAL QUARTERLY ALMANAC, 102d Cong., 2d Sess. 518–519 (1990) ("nomination drew criticism from the National Council on Aging and from the Women Employed Institute," but the "anticipated fight failed to materialize"). *See also* Ethan Bronner, *Black Rightist Seen Winning Judgeship Bid,* BOSTON GLOBE, Feb. 6, 1990, at 3 ("No major liberal or civil rights group has taken a stand against Thomas"). On the opposition, see Marcia Coyle, Marianne Lavelle & Fred Strasser, *Liberals Sound Alarm on D.C. Circuit Choice,* NAT'L L. J., July 24, 1989, at 5. Those who did "raise doubts" or "deep concerns" about Thomas included the Alliance for Justice and the National Education Association. Those who were opposed included some members of Congress, some law professors, and organizations such as Women Employed Institute, voicing criticism of Thomas's role as chair of the Equal Employment Opportunities Commission. See *Hearings before the Committee on the Judiciary, Confirmation Hearings on Appointments to the Federal Judiciary,* U.S. Senate, 101st Cong., 2d Sess. 67–111, 402–404, 455–57, 458–59 (Chairman Don Edwards of the House's Judiciary Subcommittee on Civil and Constitutional Rights and Chairman Edward R. Roybal, of the House's Select Committee on Aging, opposing the nomination) (Feb. 6, 21, 27, 1990).

69. Alexander, ' "She's No Lady,' " pp. 3–25 herein, surveys this country's history of disinterest in the problems of black women, unable until recently even to stand before the law as witnesses in formal court proceedings and discredited when they told and wrote the stories of their own lives. Classical parallels are found in Amy Richlin, *Roman Oratory, Pornography, and the Silencing of Anita Hill,* 65 S. CAL. L. REV. 1321, 1327–1328 (1992) ("Attacks on the morals of women were a staple of Roman oratory and pervade Cicero's speeches"). The literary tradition is described by Carolyn G. Heilbrun in *The Thomas Confirmation Hearings, or How Being a Humanist Prepares You for Right-Wing Politics,* 65 S. CAL. L. REV. 1569, 1573 (1992) ("There is no account available to us of a woman plotting her own life, and remaining both good and in control of her own story").

70. Such efforts were aimed at eliminating discrimination in education, housing, public services, employment, and the like, and at enabling access to the processes of justice, such as permitting all races and genders to serve on

juries and prohibiting exclusions by race and gender. *See* Batson v. Kentucky, 476 U.S. 79 (1986); J.E.B. v. Alabama, 114 S. Ct. 1419 (1994); *see generally* Barbara Allen Babcock, A *Place in the Palladium: Women's Rights and Jury Service*, 61 U. Cinn. L. Rev. 1139 (1993).

71. Lynn Hecht Schafran and Norma Juliet Wikler, Operating a Task Force on Gender Bias in the Courts: A Manual for Action 1 (Foundation for Women Judges, 1986) [hereinafter Gender Bias Manual].

72. Norma J. Wikler, *Water on Stone: A Perspective on the Movement to Eliminate Gender Bias in the Courts*, 26 Court Rev. 6, 8–9 (Fall 1989). Dr. Wikler was the first director of the NJEP; Lynn Hecht Schafran is the second and current director.

73. That task force's first publication was issued two years thereafter. *See* The First Year Report of the New Jersey Supreme Court Task Force on Women in the Courts (June 1984).

74. The creation of that group came after the state's chief justice received a report from the Committee on Minority Concerns (Summer 1984) calling for a task force to study the effect of minority status on employment within the courts, juvenile justice, probation services, civil and criminal litigation, municipal courts, and courtroom atmosphere in general.

75. Conference of Chief Justices, *Resolution XVIII: Task Force on Gender Bias and Minority Concerns*, 26 Court Rev. 5 (Fall 1989).

76. *See* Judith Resnik, *"Naturally" without Gender: Women, Jurisdiction, and the Federal Courts*, 66 N.Y.U. L. Rev. 1682 (1991).

77. Clarence Thomas was its chair, and at the time of his nomination to the Supreme Court, no committee report had been made. After his elevation to the Supreme Court, District Judge June Hens Green became the chair of the Task Force of the District of Columbia Circuit on Gender, Race, and Ethnic Bias. In May of 1994, the Special Committee on Gender filed its preliminary report. *See* Preliminary Report of the Task Force of the D.C. Circuit on Gender, Race, and Ethnic Bias (May, 1994) [hereinafter, D.C. Federal Preliminary Gender Report].

78. I was a member of the Ninth Circuit's Task Force on Gender Bias; the preliminary report, issued in the summer of 1992, prompted the first day devoted to gender bias in the courts at an annual conference of federal judges and lawyers. The final report was filed in 1993 and republished in 1994; *see* The Effects of Gender: The Final Report of the Ninth Circuit Gender Bias Task Force, *reprinted in* 67 S. Cal. L. Rev. 745 (1994) [hereinafter Ninth Circuit, The Effects of Gender]. As of 1994, the First, Second, Third, Eighth, and Eleventh Circuits had also begun projects on gender and/or race and ethnicity; the Ninth Circuit had launched a study of the effects of race, religion, and ethnicity in its courts; and the D.C. Circuit had published two draft reports.

79. *See* Lynn Hecht Schafran, *Gender Bias in the Courts: An Emerging Focus for Judicial Reform*, 21 Ariz. State L. Rev. 237, 247 (1989).

80. *See* 137 CONG. REC. S9087, S9094 (June 28, 1991) (statement of Senator Bob Graham, describing eleven states that had ongoing work on race, ethnic, and minority concerns). As of 1994, the National Consortium of Task Forces and Commissions on Racial and Ethnic Bias in the Courts reported nineteen states as members.

81. Twenty-seven of those reports were the products of task forces sponsored by the judiciary and five of groups sponsored by bar associations.

82. MORRISON, *supra* note 7, at xii-xiii (quoting senator Danforth, introducing Thomas). The senator's description of the events are set forth in JOHN C. DANFORTH, RESURRECTION: THE CONFIRMATION OF CLARENCE THOMAS (1994).

83. MORRISON, *supra* note 7, at xiii.

84. *See* Painter, *supra* note 43, in MORRISON, *supra* note 7, at 200, 201–202.

85. MORRISON, *supra* note 7, at xvi (emphasis in original).

86. *See* Regina Austin, *Sapphire Bound!*, 1989 WIS. L. REV. 539, 540, 570–72 (exploring the limiting roles in popular imagery for black women, including "Sapphire," a "tough, domineering, emasculating, strident, and shrill" woman; "Mammy" as the "asexual, maternal, and deeply religious" woman (citation omitted); and "Jezebel" as a "harlot," "flaunting" sexuality). Austin calls for the reinvention of these images and roles, so that "little black girls will grow up to see the positive potential of what their mothers did and relish being Sapphires by another name."

87. MORRISON, *supra* note 7, at xvi. *See also* Kimberlé Crenshaw, *Whose Story Is It Anyway? Feminist and Antiracist Appropriations of Anita Hill*, in MORRISON, *supra* note 7, at 402. As recent history also demonstrates, racial and gender stereotyping is not confined to Supreme Court nominations but also forms the texts and subtexts for the consideration of other officials. *See, e.g.*, the withdrawal of the nomination of Lani Guinier to head the Civil Rights Division of the Department of Justice and the labeling of her as a "quota queen" by the Wall Street Journal (see Clint Bolick, *Clinton's Quota Queens*, WALL ST. J., Apr. 30, 1993, at A12, col. 9. *See also* LANI GUINIER, THE TYRANNY OF THE MAJORITY: FUNDAMENTAL FAIRNESS IN REPRESENTATIVE DEMOCRACY (1994); and the withdrawal of Zoe Baird's nomination as Attorney General of the United States, with its focus on her and her spouse's hiring of undocumented aliens as care providers for their child.

88. REPORT OF THE NEW YORK TASK FORCE ON WOMEN IN THE COURTS 5 (1986) [hereinafter NEW YORK TASK FORCE ON WOMEN]. Other state task forces have reported similar findings. *See, e.g.*, REPORT OF THE CONNECTICUT TASK FORCE, GENDER, JUSTICE AND THE COURTS 12 (1991) ("women are treated differently from men in the justice system and, because of it, many suffer from unfairness, embarrassment, emotional pain, professional deprivation, and economic hardship") [hereinafter CONNECTICUT GENDER TASK FORCE]. Adele Alexander notes how such stereotyping worked against Anita Hill, who was "suspect" as a woman who

had "never married" or had children and did not display "the emotions of outraged virtue." Alexander, " 'She's No Lady' ", p. 17 herein. See also Anita Faye Hill, "Marriage and Patronage in the Empowerment and Disempowerment of African American Women," pp. 271–92 herein.

89. REPORT OF THE NEW YORK STATE JUDICIAL COMMISSION ON MINORITIES, THE PUBLIC AND THE COURTS, vol. II at 1 (1991) [hereinafter NEW YORK COMMISSION ON MINORITIES].

90. MINORITY AND JUSTICE TASK FORCE, FINAL REPORT 181 (Washington, 1990) [hereinafter WASHINGTON MINORITY TASK FORCE].

91. FINAL REPORT OF THE MICHIGAN SUPREME COURT TASK FORCE ON RACIAL/ETHNIC BIAS ISSUES IN THE COURTS at 58, 51 (1989) [hereinafter MICHIGAN RACIAL/ETHNIC REPORT].

92. WASHINGTON MINORITY TASK FORCE, *supra* note 90, at 123 (footnote omitted). As the task force discussed, its research did not control for other variables, such as wage loss, special damages, and other medical conditions. For the view that such variables should be considered prior to concluding that racial bias is at work, see the dissents of Commissioners Sheila Birnbaum and Serene K. Nakano to the conclusions of the NEW YORK COMMISSION ON MINORITIES, *supra* note 89, at 199.

93. NINTH CIRCUIT, THE EFFECTS OF GENDER, *supra* note 78, at 786, 772.

94. *Id.* at 950.

95. *Id.* at 796–808, 811–20.

96. D.C. FEDERAL PRELIMINARY GENDER REPORT, *supra* note 77, at 75.

97. MICHIGAN RACIAL/ETHNIC REPORT, *supra* note 91, at 13. These findings echo Anita Hill's experiences. According to the Senate investigation of the disclosure of her allegations, Hill was hesitant to go forward because of "her own experience that allegations of sexual harassment are often disbelieved." In contrast, a white male Senate staffer "was confident that Hill's statements, with evidence of a contemporaneous complaint to a friend in 1981, would be credited." REPORT OF THE TEMPORARY SPECIAL INDEPENDENT COUNSEL, *supra* note 1, at 15.

98. Of thirty-two published reports on gender, fourteen use the words "gender bias" in their titles; fifteen use (sometimes in addition to the words "gender bias") one of the following terms: "fairness," "equity," "equality," "equal justice," or "gender and justice." Of ten published race and ethnic reports, six use phrases such as "minority concerns," "fairness," "justice," and "equality."

Even within the polite terms of contemporary United States discussions of this work and its official sponsorship by judiciaries, not all within the judicial system welcome the enterprise. One male federal trial judge, objecting to an inquiry about gender bias, characterized the project as "silly and degrading both to the Bench and Bar. Our profession historically is a bastion of civility and the outpost of peoples' rights, including women's rights. There may be the rare exception to conduct consistent with this tradition—but I don't need any help or this poll to deal with it when it occurs." NINTH CIRCUIT, THE EFFECTS OF GENDER, *supra* note 78, at 960. Some of the male lawyers responding to a questionnaire to which some 3,500 lawyers throughout the nine states within the Ninth Circuit replied, stated that the study of gender was "a *complete waste* of time and money," "a pile of garbage," "much ado about nothing." *Id.* (emphasis in the original). *See also* Judith Resnik, *Gender Bias from Classes to Courts*, 45 STAN. L. REV. 2195, 2207 (1993).

99. Several of the southern senators who opposed Bork understood their political debt to Jesse Jackson's voter registration campaign. *See also* BRONNER, *supra* note 22, at 286 (John Breaux of Louisiana and Wyche Fowler, Jr., of Georgia "had been elected with a minority white vote and more than 90 percent of the black vote").

100. Kimberlé Crenshaw, *Demarginalizing the Intersections of Race and Sex: A Black Feminist Critique of Antidiscrimination Doctrine, Feminist Theory, and Antiracist Policies*, 1989 U. CHI. LEGAL F. 139. *See also* Linda Greene's presentation at the 1992 Annual Meetings of the Association of American Law Schools, on Feminist Procedure, Joint Session held by the Section on Civil Procedure and the Section on Women in Legal Education, in which she discussed the absence of institutional reform litigation directed at the problems of black women.

One such organization was formed shortly after the Thomas proceedings. On November 3, 1991, a group called "African American Women in Defense of Ourselves" (AAWIDOO) provided commentary in the New York Times and described itself as a "grassroots initiative of the 1603 women of African descent" whose names were listed. *See* N.Y. TIMES, Nov. 17, 1991, Campus Life Section, 53. Thereafter, AAWIDOO "spawned loosely affiliated groups in San Francisco, New York, Michigan, New Jersey, and Philadelphia." Another organization, Ain't I a Woman Network, formed a political action committee to support Lynn Yeakel, who unsuccessfully challenged Arlen Specter. Sharon F. Griffin, *Double Struggle against Racism and Sexism Can Be Dual Burdens for Many Black Women*, SAN DIEGO UNION-TRIBUNE (Apr. 16, 1993). *See also* Margaret A. Burnham, *The Supreme Court Appointment Process and the Politics of Sex*, in MORRISON, *supra* note 7, at 290, 315–19.

101. *See, e.g.*, Florida's recent amendments to its judicial selection process, now requiring that one of the three members of the panel selecting judges must be "a member of a racial or ethnic minority *or* a woman." FLA. STAT. ANN. sec. 43.29 (West. Supp. 1993) (emphasis added).

102. This is the title of a collection of essays edited by Gloria T. Hull, Patricia Bell Scott, and Barbara Smith, ALL THE WOMEN ARE WHITE, ALL THE BLACKS ARE MEN, BUT SOME OF US ARE BRAVE (1982).

103. As of this writing, some thirty published task force reports are about bias

predicated on gender, and ten are about bias predicated on race, ethnicity, and minority status. Of the gender reports, less than a third discuss the distinctive status of being a woman of color. Those that do include ACHIEVING EQUAL JUSTICE FOR WOMEN AND MEN IN THE COURTS, THE DRAFT REPORT OF THE JUDICIAL COUNCIL ADVISORY COMMITTEE ON GENDER BIAS IN THE COURTS (California 1990), section 10 [hereinafter CALIFORNIA DRAFT GENDER BIAS REPORT]; the D.C. FEDERAL PRELIMINARY GENDER REPORT, *supra* note 77, at 75–79; FINAL REPORT OF THE MICHIGAN SUPREME COURT TASK FORCE ON GENDER ISSUES IN THE COURTS 21 (Michigan 1989) [hereinafter MICHIGAN TASK FORCE ON GENDER].

Of the race reports, almost one third devote substantial attention to the distinctive issues faced by women of color. *See, e.g.,* REPORT AND RECOMMENDATIONS OF THE FLORIDA SUPREME COURT RACIAL AND ETHNIC BIAS STUDY COMMISSION, "WHERE THE INJURED FLY FOR JUSTICE" (vol. II), at 49–60 (1991) [hereinafter FLORIDA RACIAL AND ETHNIC BIAS STUDY II] (devoting a chapter to "minority women employees and attorneys"); MICHIGAN RACIAL/ETHNIC REPORT, *supra* note 91, at 40, 42, 62, 64 ("The Status of Minority Women"); MINNESOTA TASK FORCE ON RACIAL BIAS, *supra* note 66, at 487.

Ironically, in the reports that address both race/ethnicity and gender in the same volume, the topics are kept separate. *See* REPORT OF THE FAIRNESS AND EQUALITY COMMITTEE OF THE SUPREME COURT OF IDAHO (1992), which is primarily a summary of other states' research; FINAL REPORT OF THE EQUALITY IN THE COURTS TASK FORCE (1993) at 10–18 (giving data by gender and race, but not their intersection). Further, two manuals directing the efforts on race and gender bias both urge that the inquiries be kept separate. *See* GENDER BIAS MANUAL, *supra* note 71, at 6–7; EDNA WELLS HANDY, DESIREE B. LEIGH, YOLANDE P. MARLOW, & LORRAINE H. WEBER, ESTABLISHING AND OPERATING A TASK FORCE OR COMMISSION ON RACIAL AND ETHNIC BIAS IN THE COURTS 12 (National Center for State Courts, 1993).

104. For example, most of the conclusions and summaries in these reports ignore the category of women of color, although issues specific to women of color are sometimes discussed in the body of the report. *See, e.g.,* WASHINGTON MINORITY TASK FORCE, *supra* note 90, at 8–22, 65–66; NEW YORK COMMISSION ON MINORITIES, *supra* note 89, at 165–66; CONNECTICUT GENDER TASK FORCE, *supra* note 88, at 80–83, 162. *See also* NEW YORK TASK FORCE ON WOMEN, *supra* note 88 (chaps. 2 and 3 discuss differences but do not highlight them in the findings and summaries; in contrast, the distinct problems of credibility are discussed. *Id.* at 202; *see infra* note 108).

105. Charles R. Lawrence III, speech at the USC Faculty Center (spring 1993) (discussing the interrelationships among the trials of Mike Tyson, William

Kennedy Smith, and the Hill-Thomas proceedings). See also Lawrence, "The Message of the Verdict," pp. 105–28 herein.

106. *See* Emma Coleman Jordan, *Race, Gender and Social Class in the Thomas Sexual Harassment Hearings: The Hidden Fault Lines in Political Discourse*, 15 HARV. WOMEN'S L.J. 1 (1992).

107. *See* Alexander, " 'She's No Lady,' " pp. 3–25 herein. For discussion of how legal doctrine about both sexual harassment and rape embodies questions about women's credibility, see Susan Estrich, *Sex at Work*, 43 STAN. L. REV. 813, 815 (1991) ("The focus on the conduct of the woman—her reactions or lack of them, her resistance or lack of it [familiar in the law of rape]—reappears" in the development of the law of sexual harassment).

108. These reports consider the question of credibility as part of discussions of domestic violence, sexual assault, courtroom interaction, and rights sought by women litigants under employment and federal benefits law. Many of the reports detail the specific problems faced by women testifying about sexual aggression. Illustrative is the finding of the District of Columbia that "a large plurality of respondents felt that cross-examination of victims tends to be more hostile in sexual assault cases than in other assault cases." DISTRICT OF COLUMBIA COURTS, FINAL REPORT OF THE TASK FORCE ON RACIAL AND ETHNIC BIAS AND TASK FORCE ON GENDER BIAS IN THE COURTS 119 (1992).

While we know something about the problem of credibility for the generic "woman," we know less about it in the specific context of women of color. The published reports on race/ethnic bias in the courts discuss credibility less than do gender bias reports, and the reports on gender bias in turn have not much focused on whether credibility issues differ for women of color and white women. A few gender bias reports do note that racial and ethnic bias affects credibility determinations. *See, e.g.,* NEW YORK TASK FORCE ON WOMEN, *supra* note 88, at 195–97, 202 ("Poor and minority women appear to face even greater problems of credibility"); MICHIGAN TASK FORCE ON GENDER, *supra* note 103, at 76–77.

109. Literary theory and adjudication part company on this distinction. *See* Robert M. Cover, *Violence and the Word*, 95 YALE L.J. 1601 (1986); Carolyn Heilbrun & Judith Resnik, *Convergences: Law, Literature and Feminism*, 99 YALE L.J. 1913 (1990).

110. *See, e.g.,* Jill Abramson, *Reversal of Fortune: Image of Anita Hill, Brighter in Hindsight, Galvanizes Campaigns*," WALL ST. J., Oct. 5, 1992, at 1, col. 1 (in an October 1992 poll, 44 percent of registered voters said they believed Anita Hill, and 34 percent reported believing Clarence Thomas; a year earlier, "the same poll had shown Justice Thomas believed by 47% and Prof. Hill believed by 24%").

111. One historical analogy, concerning the United States Supreme Court's disapproval of polygamy for Mormons but not members of Indian tribes, demonstrates the link between imposing regulation on groups of people

and perceiving one's kinship to them. *Compare* Reynolds v. United States, 98 U.S. 145 (1878), *with* United States v. Quiver, 241 U.S. 602 (1916). In *Reynolds*, the Court upheld the constitutionality of congressional regulation of polygamous marriages in the "territories," while in *Quiver*, the Court prohibited a state from regulating the "domestic relations of the Indians with each other." 241 U.S. at 604. As John Stuart Mill put it, polygamy, "though permitted to Mohammedans, and Hindus, and Chinese, seems to excite unquenchable animosity when practiced by persons who speak English and profess to be a kind of Christian." *On Liberty, reprinted in* THE ESSENTIAL WORKS OF JOHN STUART MILL 249, 338 (Max Lerner, ed., 1965).

112. *See* Curtis, *supra* note 47, at 1526 (likening the proceedings after Hill's accusations to "recalling the jury" that had already reached its verdict). For one account that accepted the truth of Hill's testimony but then attempted to justify Thomas's denial as appropriate to avoid "grossly unfair punishment," see Orlando Patterson, *Race, Gender and Liberal Fallacies,* N.Y. TIMES, Oct. 20, 1991, at sec. 4, p. 15, col. 2. Responses to Patterson can be found in Homi K. Bhabha, *A Good Judge of Character: Men, Metaphor, and the Common Culture* at 232, 242–49; and in Kimberlé Crenshaw, *Whose Story, supra* note 87, at 402, 422–31 both in MORRISON, *supra* note 7. Moreover, were Thomas to lose his job because of either sexual harassment or his subsequent denial of those charges, then the status of other political officials, senators included, might also be put into question. According to Mayer and Abrahamson, *supra* note 1, at 235, upon learning of Hill's accusations, Senator Metzenbaum said that, "[i]f that's sexual harassment . . . half the senators on Capitol Hill could be accused."

113. *See* Higginbotham, *Seeking Pluralism, supra* note 55.

114. A. Leon Higginbotham, *Open Letter to Justice Clarence Thomas from a Federal Judicial Colleague,* 140 U. PA. L. REV. 1005, 1010 (1992) ("Until your confirmation hearing I could not find one shred of evidence suggesting an insightful understanding on your part of how the evolutional movement of the Constitution and the work of civil rights organizations have benefitted you."). Judge Higginbotham continued his commentary on Thomas in A. Leon Higginbotham, Jr., *Justice Clarence Thomas in Retrospect,* 45 HASTINGS L. J. 1405, 1429 (1994) (criticizing Thomas' "persistently absurd and hostile anti-minority decisions").

115. Emma Coleman Jordan, *Prisoners of Sex: When Will the NAACP Get the Message that Equality Begins at Home?,* WASH. POST, Aug. 21, 1994, at C3.

116. *See, e.g.,* JUDITH GRANT, FUNDAMENTAL FEMINISM 17–21 (1993) (discussing New Left's disinterest in "politics relating to problems of sexism").

117. Explained with clarity in Alice Walker's essay, *Advancing Luna—and Ida B. Wells, in* YOU CAN'T KEEP A GOOD WOMAN DOWN (1981). White

women have been less successful in exploring their own racial prejudices. *See* Stansell, *supra* note 46, in MORRISON, *supra* note 7.

118. Painter, *supra* note 43; Crenshaw, *Whose Story, supra* note 87; both in MORRISON, *supra* note 7.

119. For proposed changes, see Gary J. Simson, *Thomas's Supreme Unfitness— A Letter to the Senate on Advice and Consent,* 78 CORNELL L. REV. 619, 649–663 (1993).

120. *See, e.g.,* Federal Death Penalty Act of 1994, sec. 60002, Pub. L. No. 103–322, 108 Stat. 1796, 1966, to be codified as 18 U.S.C. sec. 3593 (when sentencing a defendant to death, a jury must "return to the court a certificate, signed by each juror, that consideration of the race, color, religious beliefs, national origin or sex of the defendant or any victim was not involved in reaching his or her individual decision"); 1994 Resolution No. 4, Ninth Circuit Judicial Conference, Assure Fairness: Adopt General Orders Prohibiting Bias in All Forms (adopted Aug. 1994) ("urging all courts in the Ninth Circuit to adopt General Orders stating . . . that the practice of law before all the courts in the Ninth Circuit must be free from prejudice and bias in any form" and that courts' inherent powers be used to implement the "duty to exercise non-biased behavior," including "the responsibility to avoid comment or behavior that can reasonably be interpreted as manifesting prejudice or bias toward another on the basis of gender, race, ethnicity, or national origin, citizenship, pregnancy, religion, disability, age, or sexual orientation, unless relevant to an issue in the case"). *See generally* Sheri Lynn Johnson, *Racial Imagery in Criminal Cases,* 67 TUL. L. REV. 1739 (1993).

121. *See* Jody D. Armour, *Race Ipsa Loquitur: Of Reasonable Racists, Intelligent Bayesians, and Involuntary Negrophopes,* 46 STAN. L. REV. 781 (1994).

122. As Anita Hill has subsequently described, almost all who participated were relatively privileged. She is a holder of tenure at a university, and many of those who helped her shared her status. Speech of Professor Anita Hill, upon being honored by the Section on Women in Legal Education of the American Association of Law Schools, San Antonio, Texas (Jan 6, 1992). Yet, as Anita Hill has also written, her privilege did not suffice, for she came to Washington without a "patron." Hill, "Marriage and Patronage," p. 280 herein.

123. Three Democrats (Joseph Lieberman of Connecticut, Richard Bryan of Nevada, and Henry Reid of Nevada) who had been supportive of Thomas changed their votes; three other Democrats (Bob Graham of Florida, Daniel Moynihan of New York, and Robert Byrd of West Virginia), who had "hinted" support for Thomas also voted against him. "Not since Lucius Q. C. Lamar of Georgia, controversial as a Southerner while memories of the Civil War were fresh, has anyone moved into the Court with a confirmation margin as narrow as Judge Thomas's." R.W. Apple, Jr., *The Thomas Confirmation,* N.Y. TIMES, Oct. 16, 1991, at A1, col. 6.

124. *Compare* bell hooks, *A Feminist Challenge: Must We Call Every Woman Sister?*, in BLACK LOOKS: RACE AND REPRESENTATION 79, 86 (1992) (an ultimately negative reading of the events, ending with "the triumph of sexist justice").

125. *See* Leslie H. Gelb, *Untruths . . .* , N.Y TIMES, Oct. 27, 1991, at sec. 4, p. 15, col. 5 ("Washington is largely indifferent to truth. . . . Sure, politics is the natural order of things. Yes, truth is elusive. But if a free people tolerates endless untruths, darkness descends permanently"). *See also* Carolyn G. Heilbrun in *The Thomas Confirmation Hearings, supra* note 69, at 1571, 1573 (Heilbrun discusses how smear tactics were used against Anita Hill in the Thomas proceedings and notes that "[t]he object of THE SMEAR is to make the critics of your nomination stand trial instead of the nominee").

126. *See, e.g.*, David Margolick, *2 Women Take Stage and Stir Bar Meeting*, N.Y. TIMES, Aug. 10, 1992, at A10, col. 1 (Anita Hill given an achievement award, the Margaret Brent Award, from the ABA Commission on Women). Hill was the lunch speaker at the 1992 meeting of the National Association of Women Judges and received an award from the Section on Women in Legal Education of the American Association of Law Schools, San Antonio, Texas, Jan. 6, 1992.

127. *See* Isabel Wilkerson, *The 1992 Campaign: Senate Race; Where Anita Hill Is the Silent Third Candidate*, N.Y. TIMES, Aug. 31, 1992, at A1, col. 2; and *Mr. Specter's Deserved Discomfort*, N.Y. TIMES, Sept. 1, 1992, at A16, col. 1 ("Now battling for political survival, Mr. Specter carries the extra baggage of his televised cross-examination last year of Anita Hill"). However, by 1995 Mr. Specter was being mentioned as a possible Republican hopeful for the presidential election of 1996. Adam Clymer, *The 1994 Election: News Analysis; In House and Senate, 2 Kinds of G.O.P.*, N.Y. TIMES, Nov. 15, 1994, at A1, col. 3. Orrin Hatch, elected by 69 percent of the popular vote in the 1994 election, became chair of the Senate Judiciary Committee in the Republican-dominated Congress. Neil A. Lewis, *The New Congress: The Senate; New Chief of Judiciary Panel May Find an Early Test with Clinton*, N.Y. TIMES, Nov. 17, 1994, at A31, col. 1.

128. FEDERAL COURTS STUDY COMMITTEE, REPORT OF THE FEDERAL COURTS STUDY COMMITTEE 169 (Apr. 2, 1990).

129. NINTH CIRCUIT, THE EFFECTS OF GENDER, *supra* note 78; D.C. FEDERAL PRELIMINARY GENDER REPORT, *supra* note 77.

130. The First Circuit (encompassing Maine, Massachusetts, New Hampshire, Puerto Rico, and Rhode Island), the Second (New York, Vermont, and Connecticut), the Third (New Jersey, Delaware, Pennsylvania and the Virgin Islands), the Eighth (Arkansas, Iowa, Missouri, Minnesota, Nebraska, and North and South Dakota), and the Eleventh (Alabama, Georgia, and Florida) have joined the Ninth (Alaska, Arizona, California, Guam, Hawaii, Idaho, Montana, Nevada, the Northern Marina Islands,

Oregon, and Washington) and D.C. Circuits in commencing such projects. Other federal circuits are considering such work.

131. *See, e.g.*, the recent ban on peremptory challenges to jurors based solely on their gender. J.E.B. v. T.B., 114 S. Ct. 1419 (1994).

132. From the vantage point of the fall of 1994, such conflicts dominated the news. In August of 1994, Congress was persuaded to enact the Violence Against Women Act, responding to what its sponsors called the "national tragedy" that makes women the victims of violence in their homes, workplaces, and on the streets. See Violence Against Women Act of 1993, S. 11, H.R. 1133, 103d Cong., 1st Sess. (1993), enacted as Pub. L. No. 103–332, Tit. IV, 108 Stat. 1796, 1902 (1994). That bill was part of the crime package and would most likely raise incarceration rates, increase death penalties, and result in increased terms of incarceration for people of color, and especially men of color.

As Congress was working on that legislation, another black man's image dominated press reports; O.J. Simpson was accused of killing two people, his former wife, who was white, and her friend, a white male. One might have hoped that given the experiences of 1991, the public discussion would bear the freight of simultaneously understanding that gender and race informed one's views of the event. But most of the press reports gave no hint of such complexity. Rather, we were generally informed about polls of the differing attitudes of "blacks" and "whites." *See, e.g.*, Seth Mydans, *In Simpson Case, an Issue for Everyone*, N.Y. TIMES, July 22, 1994, at A16 ("the Field Poll . . . reported that while 62 percent of whites believe that Mr. Simpson was 'very likely or somewhat likely' guilty, only 38 percent of blacks agreed with them"); William Raspberry, *Judgment, Black and White*, WASH. POST, July 8, 1994, at A23 (describing as not surprising the findings of the USA Today, CNN, and Gallup poll that "blacks feel more sympathetic to Simpson than whites").

133. Jane Flax captures these tensions in her essay *The End of Innocence*, in FEMINISTS THEORIZE THE POLITICAL (Judith Butler & Joan Scott, eds., 1992). For efforts to surmount them, see Mari J. Matsuda, *Beside My Sister, Facing the Enemy: Legal Theory out of Coalition*, 43 STAN. L. REV. 1183, 1189 (1991) ("When I see something that looks racist, I ask, 'Where is the patriarchy in this?' When I see something that looks sexist, I ask, Where is the heterosexism in this?' When I see something that looks homophobic, I ask, 'Where are the class interests in this?' ").

134. BENJAMIN N. CARDOZO, THE NATURE OF THE JUDICIAL PROCESS 12–13 (Yale, 1921).

135. Catharine Pierce Wells, *Improving One's Situation: Some Pragmatic Reflections on the Art of Judging*, 49 WASHINGTON AND LEE L. REV. 323 (1992). *See also* Catharine Pierce Wells, *Clarence Thomas: The Invisible Man*, 67 S. CAL. L. REV. 117, 145–146 (1993).

136. Morrison, *supra* note 7, at xxix.

137. *Id.*

Sexual Harassment Law in the Aftermath of the Hill-Thomas Hearings

SUSAN DELLER ROSS

Anita Hill once said that she hoped history would view her as a catalyst for change. Obviously she has been, and in many ways. As the 1992 elections demonstrated, she inspired many women to run for the Senate and the House, and many other women to change their party registration or their vote. Indeed, notwithstanding the 1994 elections, it is safe to say the Congress will never be the same again. But the impact of her courageous stand has extended to other arenas as well.

Let's consider Professor Hill's impact on sexual harassment law. At the time Hill testified, a woman who had endured sexual harassment had incomplete legal remedies at best. If the harasser had acted blatantly, by firing her or demoting her for rejecting his advances, she could only recover her lost wages and get a court order against future harassment. If she had not lost her job or any pay—if she was someone in Anita Hill's position, that is—she could merely get the court order. Title VII provided no monetary damages to a woman in either situation to compensate her for the pain and humiliation she had suffered, or to punish and deter the man and provide the employer with an incentive to take effective action against harassment.

When the Hill-Thomas hearings began, Congress was considering a civil rights bill that would award monetary damages to victims of sexual harassment for the first time. But President Bush had already vetoed the bill the previous year, veto threats were circulating again, and the proponents of the legislation were convinced it was going nowhere. Then came the hearings. The air was filled, first with the sound of senators proclaiming their aversion to sexual harassment, and then with the sound of senators and Bush administration officials verbally assaulting the actual victim of sexual harassment who had come to testify. Thomas was confirmed. But in the wake of the confirmation, suddenly the veto threats evaporated and the bill became law as the Senate and the president faced the need to convince the women of the country that they were serious about taking action against sexual harassment. Now, under the new law, victims of sexual harassment *can* sue for damages—in amounts up to $300,000 per complainant, depending on the size of the employer.[1]

Lawyers in the field reported that the law quickly made a significant difference. Employers became much more willing to settle claims and began inundating groups like the Women's Legal Defense Fund for help in training employees to recognize and prevent sexual harassment. I believe that without Anita Hill's courageous appearance before the Senate Judiciary Committee we would not now have this remedy.

Another significant development enlarging the remedies for sexual harassment came from the Supreme Court itself. A high school student named Christine Franklin had sued her school under Title IX of the Education Amendments of 1972.[2] She claimed that starting in the tenth grade, one of her teachers had subjected her to continuing sexual harassment. She said that he

> engaged her in sexually-oriented conversations in which he asked about her sexual experiences with her boyfriend and whether she would consider having sexual intercourse with an older man, . . . that [he] forcibly kissed her on the mouth in the school parking lot, . . . that he telephoned her at her home and asked if she would meet him socially . . . and that, on three occasions in her junior year, [he] interrupted a class, requested that the teacher excuse Franklin, and took her to a private office where he subjected her to coercive intercourse.[3]

She also claimed that the school took no action to halt the harassment. The federal trial court had dismissed her action, saying she could not sue for damages. The case was appealed all the way to the Supreme Court and was argued shortly after Justice Thomas joined the bench.

Lawyers practicing sexual harassment law on behalf of women plaintiffs were nervous. The Bush administration's Justice Department had filed an amicus brief taking the position that Christine Franklin could not get damages under Title IX, and the Court was now solidly conservative. But in February 1992, when the decision was handed down, all nine justices ruled that Christine could sue for damages (although Justice Scalia, joined by Thomas and Rehnquist, issued a narrower opinion concurring in the judgment). And *these* damages were not even limited by the size of the institution, as were those available under the new civil rights law. Christine's lawyers and supporters were astounded but delighted. Is it not possible that the Court feared the impression that would be created if it ruled *against* a victim of sexual harassment so soon after Professor Hill's testimony? If so, we have Professor Hill to thank for this new protection for women and girls who work or study in the federally funded education programs covered by Title IX. And this full-damages remedy has wrought a sea change in the attention paid to sexual harassment issues in the education world.

Just two years after Professor Hill's testimony, the Court issued yet another unanimous sexual harassment decision, this time rejecting a narrow interpretation of what constitutes a "hostile environment." This term of art is used to distinguish sexual harassment in which a woman loses a job because she rejects sexual advances ("quid pro quo" harassment) from harassment that she endures at work (hence, "hostile environment") but that does not cost her a job opportunity.

The Court's 1993 decision concerned Teresa Harris, a woman who—like Anita Hill—was not fired or demoted for rejecting unwelcome sexual innuendo, but who eventually found the environment so unpleasant that she left. As Justice Sandra Day O'Connor described the facts:

Teresa Harris worked as a manager at Forklift Systems, Inc., an equipment rental company, from April 1985 until October 1987. Charles Hardy was Forklift's president.

The Magistrate found that, throughout Harris' time at Forklift, Hardy often insulted her because of her gender and often made her the target of unwanted sexual innuendos. Hardy told Harris on several occasions, in the presence of other employees, "You're a woman, what do you know" and "We need a man as the rental manager"; at least once, he told her she was "a dumb ass woman." Again in front of others, he suggested that the two of them "go to the Holiday Inn to negotiate [Harris'] raise." Hardy occasionally asked Harris and other female employees to get coins from his front pants pocket. He threw objects on the ground in front of Harris and other women, and asked them to pick the objects up. He made sexual innuendos about Harris' and other women's clothing.

In mid-August 1987, Harris complained to Hardy about his conduct. Hardy said he was surprised that Harris was offended, claimed he was only joking, and apologized. He also promised he would stop, and based on this assurance Harris stayed on the job. But in early September, Hardy began anew: While Harris was arranging a deal with one of Forklift's customers, he asked her, again in front of other employees, "What did you do, promise the guy . . . some [bugger][4] Saturday night?" On October 1, Harris collected her paycheck and quit.[5]

Harris then sued Forklift and lost, but pursued her case to the Supreme Court. The lower courts found that she was offended by Hardy's conduct, and that reasonable women managers would likewise be offended. Under the guidelines of the Equal Employment Opportunity Commission (EEOC), that should have been enough for Harris to win her case initially, for the federal agency had ruled that

> unwelcome sexual advances, requests for sexual favors, and other verbal or physical conduct of a sexual nature constitute sexual harassment when . . . such conduct has the purpose or effect of unreasonably interfering with an individual's work performance *or creating an intimidating, hostile, or offensive working environment.*[6]

But the lower courts ruled that even when such unwelcome behavior was directed only against women employees, and even when the behavior was offensive to Harris and would be so to other reasonable women managers, that was not enough to win a hostile environment sexual harassment case. Naturally, Charles Hardy agreed. He argued to the Court that Teresa Harris had failed to prove her job performance suffered, and had failed to prove that she was psychologically injured by his offensive behavior. Without either psychological injury or an effect on job performance, he concluded, no woman should be able to sue an employer over "merely" offensive, hostile, or intimidating sexual harassment, as the EEOC guidelines allowed. In essence, he was arguing that because Teresa Harris was a strong woman who could keep working despite his behavior, *he* had not violated Title VII.

The Court rejected this argument out of hand. It ruled that "no single factor is required" to prove a sexual harassment claim. Thus, victims of harassment do not have to prove that they became mental basket cases or stopped being productive employees in order to prevail, although evidence of either effect would obviously be relevant to their case. Justice O'Connor explained the Court's rationale:

> Title VII comes into play before the harassing conduct leads to a nervous breakdown. A discriminatorily abusive work environment, even one that does not seriously affect employees' psychological well-being, can and often will detract from employees' job performance, discourage employees from remaining on the job, or keep them from advancing in their careers. Moreover, even without regard to these tangible effects, the very fact that the discriminatory conduct was so severe or pervasive that it created a work environment abusive to employees because of their . . . gender . . . offends Title VII's broad rule of workplace equality.[7]

Harris was thus another decisive victory for working women, one that significantly strengthened the definition of illegal "hostile environment" sexual harassment.

Another change in the field of sexual harassment law is simply the volume of new cases. Despite initial fears that Professor Hill's experience would scare women out of coming forward, many women instead were inspired by her example. The EEOC reported a 60 percent increase in the volume of sexual harassment charges during the first nine months after the hearings; three years after the hearings, the number of women filing complaints was still growing.[8] Women's groups, too, reported being flooded with calls for help.

With the new attention to the issue, lawyers have tried innovative approaches to litigating sexual harassment cases. When Lori Peterson, a young attorney fresh out of law school, represented female bottlers and machinists who sued Stroh's Brewery for sexual harassment, she pointed to the role of Stroh's advertising in encouraging sexual harassment.[9] As Ronald K. L. Collins described the case in the *Los Angeles Times*,

> What the company voice says outside of the office carries into it as well. That's part of what the St. Paul women were saying when they filed a lawsuit against their employer, Stroh Brewing Co. In Stroh's "It Does Not Get Better" television ad, bikini-clad young Swedish women parachute into a male campsite bearing six-packs of beer. (Tellingly, the "Swedish bikini team" will be featured on the cover of the January issue of Playboy magazine.) Buxom women convey the same message in the company's promotional posters. The advertising fantasy is that men can have both the beer and the "broads."[10]

Peterson thus provoked discussion of the media's role in promoting the sexual objectification of women.

Some women miners made history by bringing the first class action suit charging hostile environment sexual harassment, and the judge agreed they could proceed as a class.[11] After trial, the court found that Eveleth Mines discriminated against the entire class of its women employees by "maintaining an environment sexually hostile to women." The judge relied on evidence of multiple forms of unwanted sexual innuendo and physical contact, including graffiti, photos, and cartoons that visually referred "to sex and to women as sexual objects," "verbal statements and language reflecting a sexualized, male-oriented, and anti-female atmosphere," and "physical acts that reflect a sexual motive or concern." While the judge found that both men and women sometimes cursed, he also found that only men went further and referred "to women generally in terms of their body parts." Men also made "comments to or about specific women and their sex lives, including proposing sexual relationships and discussing sexual exploits." Other examples of male behavior included pretending "to perform oral sex on a sleeping woman co-worker," touching a woman "in an objectionable manner," and presenting women with "various dildos, one of which was named 'Big Red.' " The judge concluded:

> In work places which have been traditionally male and where females constitute a small minority of the employees, employers may have an increased obligation to create environments which are safe for all em-

ployees. Whatever an employer's responsibility may be in that situation, it cannot close its eyes when confronted with sexual harassment; it has the obligation to determine the scope of the problem and take steps to alleviate it.[12]

State legislators have also been trying out new approaches. Alaska, California, Connecticut, Illinois, Minnesota, Tennessee, Vermont, and Washington have enacted "water cooler" legislation requiring employers to post in prominent and accessible locations notices informing employees that sexual harassment is illegal and telling them what to do if they are harassed.[13] California, Vermont, and Wisconsin have passed laws further defining existing prohibitions on sexual harassment; Illinois has required all businesses contracting with the state to have written sexual harassment policies; and Iowa has enacted a comprehensive prohibition covering state employees, people in the care or custody of the state, and students.[14] In another approach, employers have been required to conduct training sessions on sexual harassment and how to prevent it. California, Connecticut, Illinois, Tennessee, and Vermont have all enacted such initiatives.[15] In a sign of the impact of Christine Franklin's case, a number of other states— California, Connecticut, Iowa, Minnesota, New Hampshire, Tennessee, and Washington—have required state educational institutions to take various steps against harassment, such as adopting policies and disciplinary procedures on the subject.[16]

Anita Hill's experience has also prompted legal theorists to confront the doubly difficult issues faced by women of color. Professor Kimberlé Crenshaw has provided valuable insights into the "racialization of sexual harassment" and the "pervasive stereotypes about Black women . . . [that] shape the kind of harassment that Black women experience . . . [and] influence whether Black women's stories are likely to be believed."[17] Professor Emma Coleman Jordan has written about the combined impact of race, gender, and social class.[18] The present volume also represents an attempt to enhance our understanding of these difficult issues.[19] Eventually, new insights are bound to find their way into the law as courts learn to analyze the combined impact of race and sex on sexual harassment as experienced by women of color.

In the wake of the Hill-Thomas hearings some federal circuit courts began fine-tuning the law of sexual harassment and issued decisions that might have provided guidance to the Senate Judiciary Committee on how to conduct investigations. The Second Circuit issued a strong decision in July 1992 concerning the New York City Police Department.[20] After a woman officer reported that a male officer had sexually assaulted her brutally at gunpoint, the department refused to investigate *his* behavior but took after her with a vengeance. The court ruled that

> the relatively harsh disciplinary treatment [she] received from the NYPD when compared with the total absence of any investigation into [his] conduct, seems to us sufficiently egregious to . . . justify a jury's finding of an unconstitutional departmental practice of sex discrimination.[21]

Two months later, the Seventh Circuit decided a case brought by a harasser whose company had fired him for the harassment.[22] He sued for breach of contract and lost on a summary judgment motion after the employer presented detailed deposition testimony from the woman describing many "specific instances of sexual harassment."

> She told of [his] comments to her regarding her anatomy, of instances of unwelcome touching, and of his comments about his extramarital affairs with other women. She described these incidents in detail, relating the location, what was said, who was present, and how she felt. . . . She . . . described an incident where she had asked for a pay raise, and she remembered that he responded, " 'Well, you could be making more money if you perform favors, certain favors, on the side and you could receive bonuses' . . ." . . . She declined all of his invitations and frequently objected to his behavior, but to no avail. Instead, she testified that the frequency of his offensive behavior increased during the term of her employment.[23]

The man claimed that it was an error to decide the case on a summary judgment motion, and that he should have a trial because he had denied these allegations, thus creating a factual issue. The court responded that he was not entitled to a trial:

> In . . . his deposition, he stated that he generally denied having sexually harassed any coworker. Given his unwillingness or inability to deny the specific allegations upon direct inquiry, his few denials of the broad

accusations would not be sufficient evidence to support a jury verdict in his favor.[24]

Or consider a decision from the Third Circuit in June 1992.[25] The judges ruled that an arbitrator should not have reinstated an alleged harasser to the job from which he had been fired without a finding that he didn't do it. Even more important, the judges ruled that it was proper to require a different arbitrator to decide the case on remand, because the original arbitrator was "biased or partial towards [the alleged harasser]." The court gave some examples of the bias, including the arbitrator's characterization of the woman as " 'unattractive and frustrated,' " and his allowing questions such as " 'Would you think an average man would make a pass at a woman like that?' "[26]

In short, some courts have begun to focus on what makes an effective investigation into sexual harassment. Calling the victim names, attacking her, failing to investigate the man's behavior, and accepting the man's general denials do not, in these courts' view, constitute a good-faith attempt to resolve the matter. I hope it's safe to say that the Senate has learned these lessons too.

The evolution of the Tailhook scandal indicates just how important honest investigations can be. After twenty-six Navy women had to run the infamous gantlet of their male peers, the Navy decided to investigate. Here's a news account of what one of these women endured:

> On each of the three nights of last September's convention, investigators found, groups of officers in civilian dress suddenly turned violent, organizing with military precision into drunken gangs that shoved terrified women down the gantlet, grabbing at their breasts and buttocks and stripping off their clothes. . . .
>
> Unsuspecting women were ambushed when they walked out of the elevator and turned right down the hallway into an ocean of unrelenting arms.
>
> Among them was a 30-year-old Navy lieutenant, a helicopter pilot who was an admiral's aide at the time. As she approached a group of officers in the hallway looking for some dinner companions, one officer shouted, "Admiral's aide! Admiral's aide," while another "grabbed me by the buttocks with such force that it lifted me off the ground and ahead a step," she later told naval investigators.

Others grabbed her, too, and one man put his hands down her bra. . . .

The lieutenant kicked and punched her assailants but was overpowered. After being pawed for about 20 feet of the hallway, she managed to escape through an open door into a hotel room.[27]

By April 1992, some fifteen hundred interviews later, the Navy had found only two possible suspects, because the officers protected each other behind a "wall of silence." But then there was a new discovery. A witness interview indicating that Secretary of the Navy H. Lawrence Garrett III was at the scene had been deleted from the first report.[28] Shortly thereafter, Secretary Garrett resigned, and the Pentagon started a new investigation into how the first investigation had been conducted.[29] In the fall of 1992, the Pentagon's inspector general issued a scathing denunciation of that first attempt, finding that its major thrust was to protect the higher-ups.[30] Moreover, we learned that the man in charge of the first investigation, Rear Admiral Williams, had a rather limited opinion of women Navy pilots. A lot of them are "go-go dancers, topless dancers or hookers," he said. Now Admiral Williams, along with two fellow admirals, is also out of a job.[31]

As we have seen, the legal legacy of the hearings was substantial. Since Anita Hill's ordeal before the Senate Judiciary Committee, there has been considerable progress on the issue of sexual harassment. The law now provides a vastly improved remedy. The law has also been strengthened and clarified. More and more women have gained the courage to speak up about their experiences. Lawyers are bringing new kinds of claims to court. We are starting to focus on the double-edged discrimination faced by women of color. Some judges have begun to demand real investigations, rather than the bogus inquiries that too often carried the day in the past. High government officials have lost their jobs for their failure to investigate, and we have learned that genuine investigation requires looking into the harasser's actions and refusing to call the woman names. The voters rejected one senator for his vote on the Thomas confirmation,[32] and another narrowly escaped defeat at the polls for his version of an "investigation."[33] Indeed, the gender of the political landscape is changing as more women than ever before make their way into legislative bodies.

Anita Hill single-handedly changed American attitudes toward sexual harassment. Virtually overnight, by dint of her dignity, intelligence, and courage, she demolished the notion that sexual harassment is trivial. We can safely say that Professor Anita Hill has indeed been a catalyst for change, change that has just begun. And for that we are truly in her debt.

Notes

1. 42 U.S.C. §§1981a(a) (right to damages) and 1981a(b)(3) (limiting damages, by size of employer, to: $50,000 (for employers of 14–100 employees); $100,000 (101–200 employees); $200,000 (201–500 employees); and $300,000 (over 500 employees)).
2. 20 U.S.C. §§1681–1688.
3. *Franklin* v. *Gwinnett County Public Schools*, __ U.S. __, 112 S.Ct. 1028, 1031, 117 L. Ed. 2d 208, 215 (1992).
4. Justice O'Connor spoke obliquely here, substituting the word "sex" for "bugger," the actual term Charles Hardy had used. Brief for the United States and the Equal Employment Opportunity Commission as Amicus Curiae, at 4, *Harris* v. *Forklift Systems, Inc.*, __ U.S. __, 114 S. Ct. 367, 126 L. Ed. 2d 295 (1993) (No. 92-1168). The Justice Department brief also mentioned other examples of Hardy's sexual innuendo. For example, "a former clerical employee . . . testified that Hardy would suggest turning down the air conditioning when a female employee wore a tight shirt because of the effect of the lower temperature on the women's breasts." *Id.* at n. 3.
5. *Harris* v. *Forklift Systems, Inc.*, __ U.S. __, 114 S. Ct. 367, 369, 126 L. Ed. 2d 295, 300 (1993).
6. 29 C.F.R. §1604.11(a) (emphasis added).
7. 114 S. Ct. at 370–71, 126 L. Ed. 2d at 302.
8. Laura Blumenfeld, *One Year, A.H.*, Wash. Post, Oct. 13, 1992, at E5; Patricia Edmonds, *Year Later, Harassment's "Real to More People*," USA Today, Oct. 2, 1992, at 6A (reporting that 7,407 sexual harassment complaints had been filed with the EEOC from October 1, 1991, through June 30, 1992, compared to 6,883 for all of fiscal 1991). In August 1994, the EEOC reported that 10,532 complaints were filed in fiscal year 1992, another 11,908 in fiscal year 1993, and that there were 1,000 more complaints in the third quarter of fiscal year 1994 than there had been in the same quarter of fiscal year 1993. Telephone interview of Julie Pershan, EEOC public affairs specialist, by Jennifer Ellison, research assistant to Professor Ross (Aug. 22, 1994).
9. Doug Grow, *Stroh's and Its Ads Square Off against an Angry Young Lawyer*, Star Trib. (Minneapolis–St. Paul), Nov. 10, 1991, at 3B.

10. Ronald K. L. Collins, *Perspective on Advertising*, Los Angeles Times, Nov. 20, 1991, at B7.

11. Diane Alters, *Ruling Clears Way for 3 Women Miners to File First-Ever Class-Action Suit on Sex Harassment*, Star Trib. (Minneapolis–St. Paul), Dec. 19, 1991, at 1D; *Jenson v. Eveleth Taconite Co.*, 139 F.R.D. 657 (D. Minn. 1991).

12. *Jenson v. Eveleth Taconite Co.*, 824 F. Supp. 847, 888, 879, 880, 888 (D. Minn. 1993).

13. Alaska Stat. § 23.10.440 (Supp. 1993); Cal. Gov't Code § 12950(a)-(c) (Deering Supp. 1994) (requiring information sheet to be distributed to each employee as well); Cal. Educ. Code § 212.6 (Deering Supp. 1994) (applies to educational institutions); Conn. Gen. Stat. § 46a–54(15)(A) (1993); Ill. Ann. Stat. ch. 775, para. 5/2-105(B)(5)(b) (Smith-Hurd Supp. 1994) (policy on posting applies only to state agencies); Minn. Stat. § 135A.15 (1992) (requiring posting of policy at appropriate campus locations for students and employees at postsecondary educational institutions); Tenn. Code Ann. § 4-3-124 (Supp. 1994) (applies to entities of state government); Tenn. Code Ann. § 4-3-905 (Supp. 1994) (employers in the state to make information about state sexual harassment law available to employees through posters, brochures, or pamphlets); Vt. Stat. Ann. tit. 21, § 495h(b) (Supp. 1993); 1994 Wash. Laws 214 (to be codified at Wash. Rev. Code § 28A.640.020) (applies only to school districts).

14. Cal. Gov't Code § 12940(h)(3)(C) (Deering Supp. 1994) (clarifying that state prohibition on harassment includes sexual harassment, gender harassment, and harassment based on pregnancy, childbirth, or related medical conditions); Vt. Stat. Ann. tit. 21, § 495d(13) (Supp. 1993) (adding definition of sexual harassment); 1993 Wis. Laws 427 (to be codified at Wis. Stat. §§ 111.32(13), 111.36(1)(b), 111.36(1)(br)) (amending the existing definition of sexual harassment law to add further details); Ill. Ann. Stat. ch. 775, para. 5/2-105(A)(4) (Smith-Hurd Supp. 1994) (applying to parties to public contracts and eligible bidders); Iowa Code Ann. § 19B.12 (West Supp. 1994) (further requiring the adoption of rules, grievance procedures, and disciplinary procedures by the relevant state institutions, and guides for employees, students, and patients informing them of these rules and procedures); see also, Iowa Code Ann. § 2.11 (West Supp. 1994) (requiring each house of the state general assembly to develop prohibitions against sexual harassment and distribute such guides to its employees).

15. Cal. Penal Code § 13519.7 (Deering Supp. 1994) (requiring training sessions for law enforcement officers, and establishment of complaint guidelines for law enforcement officers who are victims of sexual harassment in the workforce); Conn. Gen. Stat. § 46a-54(15)(B) (1993) (requiring employers of fifty or more employees to have training sessions for supervisory employees); Ill. Ann. Stat. ch. 775, para. 5/2-105(B)(5)(c) (Smith-Hurd Supp. 1994) (applies only to state agencies); Tenn. Code Ann. § 4-3-1703(a)(4) (Supp. 1994) (requiring state department of personnel to help each entity of

state government in planning and holding training workshops to prevent sexual harassment from occurring); Tenn. Code Ann. § 3-13-101(a)(10) (Supp. 1994) and § 16-3-502 (Supp. 1994) (requiring legislature and allowing supreme court, respectively, to establish policy to prevent sexual harassment, hold training workshops, and establish a hearing procedure); Tenn. Code Ann. § 49-7-122 (Supp. 1994) (requiring training on sexual harassment and a hearing process for all state higher education institutions); Vt. Stat. Ann. tit. 21, § 495h(f) (Supp. 1993) (encouraging training for employees, and additional training for supervisory and managerial employees covering their specific responsibilities to take corrective action).

16. Cal. Educ. Code § 212.6 (Deering Supp. 1994) (requiring all educational institutions in California to have policy prohibiting sexual harassment of students or employees, and to make policy routinely available including by posting it at a prominent location); Cal. Educ. Code § 48900.2 (Deering Supp. 1994) (allowing suspension or expulsion from school of students above the third-grade level found by their principal to have committed sexual harassment); Conn. Gen. Stat. § 10a-55c (1993) (requiring each institution of higher education to have policy prohibiting sexual harassment, and procedures for students, employees, and others to report it and for informing victims of the outcome of resulting investigations or disciplinary proceedings); Iowa Code Ann. § 19B.12 (West Supp. 1994) (prohibiting state employees from sexually harassing either other state employees or students attending state educational institutions, and requiring rules, grievance procedures, disciplinary procedures, and guides for employees and students); Minn. Stat. §§ 126.70(2a)(8) and 126.77(1)(b)(1), (2), (7), (8) (1992) (encouraging public school districts to use curricula that address sexual harassment); Minn. Stat. § 127.46 (1992) (requiring each public school to develop a process for discussing its sexual harassment policy with students and employees); Minn. Stat. § 135A.15 (1992) (requiring posting of the sexual harassment policy, and numerous rights for employees and students who are sexual assault victims at postsecondary educational institutions); 1993 N. H. Laws 148 (creating a task force on sexual assault and sexual harassment at postsecondary institutions, with members to study the problems, coordinate resources addressed to them, and report back to the legislature and governor); Tenn. Code Ann. § 49-7-122 (Supp. 1994) (requiring training on sexual harassment and a hearing process for all state higher education institutions); 1994 Wash. Laws 213 (to be codified at Wash. Rev. Code § 28A.640.020) (defining sexual harassment and requiring each school district to adopt policy on it—including grievance procedures, remedies, and sanctions—covering employees, volunteers, parents, and students, with guidance from state superintendent of public instruction).

17. Kimberlé Crenshaw, *Race, Gender, and Sexual Harassment*, 65 S. Cal. L. Rev. 1467, 1469–70 (1992); *see also* Kimberlé Crenshaw, *Whose Story Is It, Anyway? Feminist and Antiracist Appropriations of Anita Hill*, in *Raceing Justice, En-gendering Power* 402 (Toni Morrison ed., 1992).

18. Emma Coleman Jordan, *Race, Gender, and Social Class in the Thomas Sexual Harassment Hearings: The Hidden Fault Lines in Political Discourse*, 15 Harv. Women's L.J. 1 (1992).

19. For other authors who have addressed the subject, *see generally* the symposium issue *Gender, Race, and the Politics of Supreme Court Appointments: The Impact of the Anita Hill/Clarence Thomas Hearings*, 65 S. Cal. L. Rev. 1279 (1992); *Race-ing Justice, En-gendering Power* (Toni Morrison ed., 1992); and *Court of Appeal: The Black Community Speaks Out on the Racial and Sexual Politics of Clarence Thomas vs. Anita Hill* (Robert Chrisman and Robert L. Allen eds., 1992).

20. *Sorlucco v. N.Y. Police Dep't.*, 971 F.2d 864 (2d Cir. 1992).

21. *Id.* at 873. The appellate court therefore reinstated the jury verdict in her favor, a verdict that had been set aside by the district court in response to the defendant's motion for judgment notwithstanding the verdict.

22. *Scherer v. Rockwell Int'l. Corp.*, 975 F.2d 356 (7th Cir. 1992).

23. *Id.* at 359.

24. *Id.* at 361.

25. *Stroehmann Bakeries, Inc.* v. *Local 776, Int'l. Bhd. of Teamsters*, 969 F.2d 1436 (3rd Cir.), *cert. denied*, ___ U.S. ___, 113 S.Ct. 660, 121 L. Ed. 2d 585 (1992).

26. *Id.* at 1446.

27. Eric Schmitt, *Wall of Silence Impedes Inquiry into a Rowdy Navy Convention*, N.Y. Times, June 14, 1992, at A1.

28. Eric Schmitt, *Citing Scandal, Navy Group Cancels Annual Convention*, N.Y. Times, June 18, 1992, at B11.

29. Eric Schmitt, *Navy Chief Quits amid Questions over Role in Sex-Assault Inquiry*, N.Y. Times, June 27, 1992, at A1; Eric Schmitt, *Pentagon Takes Over Inquiry on Pilots*, N.Y. Times, June 19, 1992, at A20.

30. John Lancaster, *Pentagon Blasts Tailhook Inquiry; Navy Leadership Faulted in Scandal*, Wash. Post, Sept. 25, 1992, at A1.

31. *Id.* Rear Admirals Williams and Gordon, who were respectively the commander of the Naval Investigative Service and the Navy's judge advocate general, were asked to resign, while Rear Admiral Davis, the Navy's inspector general, was reassigned.

32. Edward Walsh, *Sen. Dixon Loses in Stunning Upset*, Wash. Post, Mar. 18, 1992, at A1 (recounting how now-Carol Moseley-Braun defeated then-Senator Alan Dixon in Illinois' three-way Democratic primary, with a strong percentage of Republican women voting for her).

33. Adam Clymer, *The 1992 Elections: Congress—The New Congress*, N.Y. Times, Nov. 5, 1992, at B6 (reporting that Senator Arlen Specter narrowly won a third term with a 51 to 49 percent victory over Lynn Yeakel, a political newcomer who began her Senate race in reaction to Specter's conduct as a member of the Judiciary Committee during the Hill-Thomas hearings).

Anita Hill and the
Year of the Woman

Eleanor Holmes Norton

*F*ew private persons ever have a public effect. Anita Hill, who remains a private person, has had such an effect. Not only has she affected the political process; she has helped change the political culture. The popular shorthand for Anita Hill's impact on the political process, of course, was the designation of 1992 as "the Year of the Woman." Her impact on the political culture is more difficult to specify but is unmistakable. For example, she has certainly played a part in the willingness of men to turn to women for political change.

When men vote for women in the numbers seen in the Senate and House races of 1992, more is involved than the political process of a given election year. Something deeper is occurring in the political culture, something that allows men to see themselves very differently. Increasingly, men see themselves as people willing to be led by women. We owe this change, I believe, to more than the conventional notion that women are today's outsiders who benefit from the politics of anti-incumbency. This is surely true. It is also true that everybody who runs for office these days runs as an outsider, especially incumbents. Nonincumbent males have also been quick to rival the claims of women and argue that they too are outsiders.

Why women, therefore, and why the shift in 1992? In October

1991, when seven of us who serve in the House of Representatives walked over to the Senate to demand that Anita Hill be heard, we no more had the Year of the Woman or even politics in mind than Anita Hill did when she decided to testify during the Clarence Thomas hearings. Inevitably different things were on different minds. Two things were on mine.

First, sexual harassment was at issue, and my interest was immediate because we wrote the sexual harassment guidelines in 1980 when I was chair of the Equal Employment Opportunity Commission. I had also read dozens of cases and knew well how difficult it is for a woman to step forward, no matter how evident the abuse, especially if it is shocking or embarrassing. I felt a personal obligation to walk over to "the other body," as it is quaintly called, when it looked as though the Senate would ignore Professor Hill and go about its merry business as usual.

As a lawyer I felt another and different obligation, a responsibility to the Supreme Court. To allow the Senate to go to a vote without hearing the issue would be to allow an unchallenged taint to be passed on to the High Court itself. To do so would leave the Court tarnished. The matter had to be pursued and resolved, whatever the outcome. In a democratic society, especially one where courts are unusually important institutions, such a charge could not be buried. If it were, it would surely be exhumed one day, or perhaps every day that the Court sat. Far better to take control of the issue and dispose of it right then.

After the hearing, when the public seemed to side with Clarence Thomas, the prediction was that Anita Hill would be shunned and certainly not that she would play a large role in stimulating the Year of the Woman in American political life. Instead, we have seen an unusually rapid revisionism, one of those rare transitions when the public corrects itself instead of waiting for history to do it. Generally, the public perception of a well-known person changes only after the atmosphere itself has changed and refocusing occurs with the passage of time. The current view of Harry Truman as almost heroic is illustrative. While he was in office, Truman was one of the most unpopular presidents of the twentieth century. History and distance, however, have revised the record so radically that George Bush, a man who shared little of Truman's philosophy or style, regularly cited him with admiration.

The revised view of Anita Hill has been credited to feminists. Would that the public paid such attention to feminist leadership. America's second look at Anita Hill had a direct, remarkable source—Anita Hill herself. Her persona proved so deeply and abidingly credible that although she disappeared from view, she haunted the public imagination after the hearings until people conceded that they had been wrong.

The process engineered so ineptly by the Senate, not Anita Hill herself, was responsible for the first public reaction. The ad hoc proceeding flung together after the initial sexual harassment revelations resembled a kangaroo court to many, and they wanted to distance themselves from a spectacle they found flawed and embarrassing. The only way to achieve this distance immediately was to reject Anita Hill. The public was unwilling to "convict" in the atmosphere the Senate forum created. However, freed from the Senate's jerry-built process and from the rush of demands for instantaneous judgment, freed to think the matter through themselves, the public has embraced Anita Hill. She has prevailed.

Conscious women, of course, led the way. They sought to convert their anger into constructive action. The most obvious action to take in a political year was political rebellion against the male political establishment, especially the Senate, which had not responded to what seemed obvious to many women. A confluence of factors, however, not Anita Hill alone, led to the Year of the Woman, with Anita Hill at its center.

The Year of the Woman itself was the granddaughter of the gender gap born in the late 1970s and stillborn in the years following. The gender gap evaporated each year at the polls. The gap did not translate into significant victories even as macho presidents and other officials pursued anti-women policies and openly rejoiced at the defeat of women's issues, from the Reaganites' dance on the grave of the Equal Rights Amendment to the militant bravado of today's anti-choice zealots.

Finally, in the 1992 elections, all the pieces came together. There was a general anti-incumbency sentiment unrelated to women's issues, a search for change, and a yearning for new agents of change. Americans were ready for new blood in no small part because of a combination of the longest recession since World War II and the steady decline in the American standard of living, which had taken twenty years to strike home. There was also a specific mood of anti-incumbency, produced partly by the stalemate between the Congress and the president—"gridlock," as it is called—which provoked anxiety about the continuing failure to address major issues such as an uncompetitive economy and inflated health care costs. There was redistricting, which pointed toward new candidates, especially the record number of women of color who ran for Congress and won. There was Ross Perot, there were bounced checks at the House bank, there were twelve years of anti-government rhetoric by the Republicans, and there was cumulative disenchantment with politicians and bureaucrats. But Anita Hill provided what had been missing for a dozen years when the gender gap had repeatedly fizzled—a powerful, credible catalyst. I have said that she did not do it alone. Yet I do not believe that a Year of the Woman with the historic force and effect we have seen would have occurred without her.

Senator Carol Moseley-Braun, for example, ran only because she was pressed by women indignant at the treatment of Anita Hill. Thus, we owe the first African American woman in the Senate to Professor Hill. Patty Murray of Washington State suddenly emerged. A string of sexual harassment allegations had driven her predecessor, Brock Adams, to leave the Senate. The Anita Hill controversy focused the Washington State electorate on these allegations and on the opportunity to work from a brand-new beginning by choosing a woman for the open Senate seat. Eleven women won their Senate primaries and six were elected, tripling the number of women in the Senate in a single year. One hundred eight women won their House primaries, while only seventy had prevailed in 1990. The first Puerto Rican woman came to the House, along with six other women of color, almost tripling their representation. The number of women in Congress went up dramatically, from twenty-nine to forty-eight.

Almost as unforeseen as the appearance of Anita Hill on the political horizon, or even her subsequent public metamorphosis, has been the criticism that she has become Every Woman rather than Every Black Woman. Large numbers of black women initially did not identify with and did not believe Anita Hill. There was great confusion then and there remains some confusion now about how to respond when a black woman in a white society publicly charges a black man with abuse. Until black women and men address this confusion, it will persist. Anita Hill has made African Americans face the most dreaded of confrontations within the black community—race versus sex—in a particularly painful way. This is an encounter African Americans, who have always sought unity of purpose, do not need and do not want. As long as issues of abuse between black men and women are suppressed and left unresolved, however, we give sanction to that abuse. Thus far the burden of exposing these issues has fallen to artists such as Alice Walker and Ntozake Shange. Now the burden must be assumed by those to whom African Americans look for leadership on other matters, especially black elected officials.

It is particularly ironic that the issue of sexual harassment was brought to center stage by the testimony of a black woman. If the sexual victimization of women has been largely ignored, sexual abuse of women of color has been of even less concern. In a country where black and white often remain black and white even when they are not, it is no small matter that American women have chosen to identify not only with sex discrimination but with sexual abuse as described by an African American woman. Raped and sexually abused far more often than white women, women of color have almost always stood alone, and cross-identification has been rare. Anita Hill was the first American woman to break through the formidable barrier where sexuality and race intersect—a historical breakthrough into forbidden territory.

Nevertheless, the failure to come to grips with the racial chapter of the Anita Hill story is important unfinished business. The effect of the lethal combination of race and sexuality on the hearings and on Professor Hill's credibility has not been fully explored. There were many reasons some whites and some blacks initially disbelieved Professor Hill. It should not be surprising that the reasons were not always the same. Some of the reasons are internal to the black community, but others demonstrate that much work remains to be done among people of all backgrounds.

For African Americans, Clarence Thomas has exposed the raw reality that reliance on black skin color to the exclusion of what lies beneath it has something in common with aspects of white racism, where what counts is bloodline. As Toni Morrison has written, it is clear that "the time for undiscriminating racial unity has passed."

The Clarence Thomas hearings and his record on the Supreme Court profoundly underscore that point.

Anita Hill did not lift a finger to influence American politics. She has done the opposite. She has repeatedly shunned opportunities for "fifteen minutes of fame." Nevertheless, she has had permanent effect on American politics and on matters that go much deeper.

The Most Riveting Television:
The Hill-Thomas Hearings
and Popular Culture

ANNA DEAVERE SMITH

The other contributors to this volume have ably addressed some of the historical, political, and legal issues raised by the Hill-Thomas hearings. It is my purpose here simply to offer an impressionistic sketch of the impact of the hearings on the cultural fabric of the nation—on the media, art, and popular culture (a term I use in the broadest sense to describe any kind of creative public expression).

The Hill-Thomas hearings were one of the most watched public events in the history of television. They were in and of themselves an enormous work of theater, though one in which the two leading characters never had a scene together, as they would have in most traditional plays. When I interviewed John W. Carr, one of the witnesses for Anita Hill, and asked him how it felt to be in the room during the hearings, he said, "It was like a sporting event, intense and concentrated."[1] It is that kind of intensity, concentration, and intimate relationship with the audience that we look for in the theater.

Most observers agree that the hearings made for riveting television. Perhaps not surprisingly, the medium that brought Anita Hill, Clarence Thomas, and the Senate Judiciary Committee into our homes with such dramatic immediacy was rather reticent in addressing the issues raised by the testimony and questioning. When I began talking with people in television about the hearings and their representation, I was reminded how difficult it is for television to be political. Like the rest of the country, Hollywood was engrossed by the Hill-Thomas drama and the debate it provoked, but despite the increased level of discussion and the growing number of women in power in the television industry, most shows steered clear of the hearings themselves, and the few that broached the issue of sexual harassment did so with such delicacy that their efforts went unnoticed.

An exception was the Hill-Thomas episode of *Designing Women*, perhaps the most pointed attempt at political television.[2] It was produced by Linda Bloodworth-Thomason with remarkable dispatch, and aired just about a week after the Senate confirmation vote. A combination of documentary and sitcom, the episode cleverly mixes humor with reality throughout. One character cheers for Hill, another for Thomas. Each wears the appropriate T-shirt, "She Lied" or "He Did It." As the cast watches Thomas deny all allegations, Julia proclaims, "This man does not belong on the Supreme Court! He belongs in the national repertory theater!" Her words echoed the sentiment many had felt days earlier as they sat marveling at Thomas's performance when he delivered his infamous speech on "high-tech lynching."[3] (When I watched Thomas's speech with my friend Kristen Linkletter, one of the foremost vocal trainers of actors in the United States, we discussed the possibility of using his testimony when we teach acting.[4]) "All men are created equal," Julia goes on to remark as the televised hearings continue in the background, and Mary Jo responds, "Obviously they haven't seen Long Dong Silver." A shot of the women watching Vice President Quayle formally announce Justice Thomas's confirmation follows immediately.

In the final scene the four women are at a slumber party. Mary Jo and Julia are dressed as Bette Davis and Joan Crawford respectively. With a trademark Davis delivery, Mary Jo declares that she doesn't care whether people think she's a feminist or a fruitcake, she's going to climb a tower and yell, "Don't get me wrong, we love you, but who the hell do you men think you are!" The show segues into scenes from the hearings as everyone dances to a slow tune.

SENATOR JOHN DANFORTH: "None of us wants to discourage women from coming forward with charges of sexual harassment."[5]

JOHN DOGGETT: "She was having a problem being rejected by men she was attracted to."[6]

SENATOR ALAN SIMPSON: "And now I really am getting stuff across my transom. I've got letters hanging out my pocket from Tulsa, Oklahoma, saying 'Watch out for this woman.' "[7]

SENATOR JOHN DANFORTH: "There is a specific disorder relating to how people perceive authority figures and possible sexual interest by authority figures in them."[8]

SENATOR ARLEN SPECTER: "The testimony of Professor Hill in the morning was flat-out perjury."[9]

Finally, the confirmation and President Bush: "America is the first nation in history founded on the idea that all men are created equal." Then a shot of Anita Hill. The slumber party comes to an abrupt and moving close—a sad and bitter ending.

The effect was powerful television, and the public response was overwhelming. The CBS network received fifteen hundred calls, the largest number in its history about a single show, and the vast majority were positive. Every major women's organization in the country sent faxes applauding the episode. When I asked Linda Bloodworth Thomason's assistant for the secret of her success—she had three series on CBS at the time—he told me that she was a feminist, "but in the nicest way."[10]

In Living Color's take on the hearings was quite different.[11] The scene opens with Thomas (David Allen Grier), in his first days at the Supreme Court, serving coffee to the other justices. Whenever he is asked his opinion, he replies in Uncle Tom fashion, "I say whatever you guys say." Eventually the actress portraying Justice O'Connor suggests that Thomas relax and assures him that he'll have this job for the rest of his life. Thomas immediately puts his feet up on the table and refuses to get coffee. When questioned about his abrupt change in behavior, he says, "Five minutes ago I was a Black judge appointed by BoBo the white president. Now I'm your darkest nightmare: a Black judge with a powerful hung jury. I guess you thought you knew—ah, I guess you thought you knew Clarence Thomas." The theme to Shaft plays, and Thomas dances out with a newfound militancy as the others follow. Justice Thomas's opinions in affirmative action cases that have come before the Court since his confirmation suggest that the show was not far off the mark.

If television as a whole stepped cautiously in the aftermath of the hearings, other branches of popular culture absorbed the multitude of conflicting feelings they prompted with unprecedented speed, transmuting them into T-shirts, bumper stickers, pins, even games. For example, soon after the hearings concluded, a game called Harassment hit the toy stores.[12] It involves many different kinds of harassment, defines harassment for the players, and gives simple cases. The players must present arguments to a judge about whether or not the case is one of harassment. The judge then decides who wins. Anita Hill's case is one of the first in the game.

Such commercial artifacts reflect deeper, more important developments. For example, most of the people I spoke with about how the hearings affected their work in the arts mentioned first and foremost the creation of a community of discussion about the issue of sexual harassment. Certainly, Anita Hill's testimony and the reaction to it galvanized many women in the arts. Female performance artists and comics were quick to incorporate aspects of the hearings into their repertoires. Reno, a New York comedian, added Anita Hill to her encore. Judith Jackson included Hill in her work *Woman*, as did Robbie McCauley in her piece *Sally's Rape*. In my own work, I've added a piece called "Anita and Clarence" to my play *Identities, Mirrors, and Distortions*; another play, *Unquestioned Integrity: The Hill-Thomas Hearings*, a staging of the actual transcripts of the hearings, was performed at the Magic Theater in San Francisco in February and March of 1995.

As mesmerizing as the central characters in the drama were, the response to the hearings among women soon moved from a focus on Anita Hill and Clarence Thomas to a broad-based sense that men just didn't "get it." "Suddenly, mothers were talking to daughters, and daughters to their daughters; women talking across years; mothers saying things to their daughters they couldn't say to their husbands," noted Sarah Chrichton, assistant managing editor of *Newsweek*.[13] Women were empowered and radicalized (or re-radicalized) by the recognition, so palpable during the hearings, that men are ignorant of and insensitive to the issue of sexual harassment. As Barbara Ehrenreich put it, "Nine times out of ten, it's the male who has the power, the female who must cajole and make a constant effort to please. . . . There's hardly a woman alive who doesn't know how it feels to have her dignity punctured, her public role ripped away, by some fellow with a twinge in his groin."[14] Because of the lying and abuse Americans witnessed at the Hill-Thomas hearings, women experienced a newfound need to keep talking and to make their feelings known to those "fellows," the white men making the decisions about their lives and their children's lives.

The vibrant, if often stormy, mix of politics and popular culture was evident in the response of the Black community to the sudden emergence of Anita Hill and Clarence Thomas as pop icons of a sort. One of the main sentiments among African Americans during and after the hearings was that the whole episode was an "embarrassment to the race," and that Anita Hill, whatever the truth of her allegations, should have kept her mouth shut. Many Black women were angry at her, not because they disbelieved her, but because she had spoken out where they had kept silent. "I have been taking shit for years," they said. "Why should Anita get to talk about it?" On a *Frontline* segment that aired a year after the hearings, one Black woman said, "This should have been water under the bridge"; another said, "Oh, my God, here we go again, his penis is on television"; and several preachers declared Hill's testimony "the work of the devil." Another woman wondered why the program couldn't "pick some nice issue to go with, the Black family is falling apart, we've had a lot of conflicts on that, teenage pregnancy, we can handle that, but Black female and Black male sexual issues, I mean . . ."—and they cut her off.[15]

Until the Hill-Thomas hearings, the issue of the state of gender relations between Black women and Black men had been raised most directly, if problematically, in the arena of popular culture—that is, in rap music, which has provoked numerous controversies about the alleged misogyny of the lyrics, and of the images in rap video. In this context it is striking that Public Enemy, one of the more controversial groups, featured Anita Hill as a victim in their 1992 video *Hazy Shade of Criminal*, in a series of scenes where Black males are beaten by authority figures or harassed by judges.

In December 1991 the Studio Museum in Harlem and the Dia Foundation for the Arts co-sponsored a conference on Black popular culture organized by Michele Wallace, with Henry Louis Gates, bell hooks, Angela Davis, and Marlon Riggs among the participants. The conference poster, produced by Dia, featured a rounded box, like a TV screen, framing the famous photographs of Anita Hill and Clarence Thomas that were splashed across many front pages, with Hill looking forward and Thomas pointing his finger, as though he were addressing her. Wondering what the poster expressed from the point of view of the conference organizers, I spoke with several people at Dia and the Studio Museum in Harlem. I learned that the poster had been a source of great controversy: apparently the Studio Museum had not been consulted about the use of these images to advertise the conference, and did not want the poster circulated. The museum's director, Kinshasha Holman Conwill, found the juxtaposed photographs of Hill and Thomas "in some ways a very painful image to evoke," and wondered why Dia had not selected an image more appropriate to the theme of the conference—film directors Spike Lee or John Singleton, for example.[16] It turned out, however, that the decision about the poster had been made not by Dia but by Michele Wallace, who is African American. Dia, according to Wallace, had originally wanted to use a very innocuous image of race, but she had chosen Hill and Thomas because she wanted to create an opportunity to look at Black feminist issues in relation to Black male demands, to look at Black political needs in relation to the Reagan-Bush years, and to look at the emergence of Black conservatives. Wallace considered the Studio Museum's response to the poster a kind of censorship.[17]

Interestingly enough, the images of Clarence Thomas and Anita Hill ended up in another art gallery, this time as part of a show at the Whitney Museum, Black Male: Representations of Masculinity in Contemporary American Art. The images were not rendered by an artist, however. They were again two photographs juxtaposed so that Thomas and Hill seem to be facing each other—the drama that never happened. The photographs of Thomas and Hill, and others that document real life and recognize personality, remind us of how eloquently real life speaks to us. The Hill-Thomas hearings represented more than words can express. The dramatic action of the hearings tells us much more than was said. In fact, part of our fascination, part of our obsession with the hearings (as now with the O. J. Simpson trial), was that we knew the words were not enough. We kept watching to hear the whole story. We kept watching in hopes that the unspoken would be spoken.

Normally art tells us what we don't know. The news tells us what we should know, or what is known by some and not by others. Art tells us more than what we know. It tells us what we could know, or looks at our dreams. In the case of the Hill-Thomas hearings, the arts have a lot of catching up to do. Even after four years, we are left, as artists, relatively speechless about this remarkable drama that played out in real life. More than one person has said that the Hill-Thomas hearings pointed to a great lack in our language: the fact that we find it difficult to speak about race and gender at the same time. As artists, we find ourselves in front of an armoire filled with old clothing for old characters, a costume shop designed for certain kinds of men, certain kinds of women, certain types of acceptable behavior, without prediction that these men and women and this behavior would ever go out of fashion. Our dramas were satisfied with the old ways, our lyrics were satisfied with the old tunes, and suddenly the nation stopped everything to watch the news. It would be interesting to check box office receipts on the weekend of the hearings to see how many people failed to make it to the theater. I am reminded of a movie producer who told me she called up major Beverly Hills restaurants during the Los Angeles riots, half a year after the hearings, just to see who would have the audacity to stay open and serve food. The adage "The show must go on" doesn't apply when life is the show.

Playwright Aishah Rahman has written an allegorical play, *Only in America*, in response both to the Hill-Thomas hearings and to David Mamet's popular and critically acclaimed play *Oleanna*, which had an Off Broadway run in New York a year after the hearings, played in regional theaters, and was made into a movie. *Oleanna* is about a student who accuses a teacher of sexual harassment—unjustly, it seems, from what we see on stage—thereby causing him to be denied tenure and lose his house. At the end of the play the teacher hits Oleanna and throws a chair at her. I'm told that at some performances audience members applauded when she was hit. When I tried to determine if *Oleanna* was written as a result of the Hill-Thomas hearings, I learned that David Mamet had turned in his first draft in October 1991. It is unlikely, then, that he wrote the play as a direct response to the hearings, but it may be that they had an effect on subsequent drafts. In any case, *Oleanna* became an important part of the cultural, social, and political dialogue that was more widely articulated as a consequence of the Hill-Thomas explosion. Aishah Rahman's play seeks to advance that dialogue.

Only in America has four characters: a woman named Cassandra who represents Anita Hill, a man named Oral who represents Clarence

Thomas, an African American cleaning woman, and a white woman speech therapist. Cassandra cannot speak. When she tries, she speaks a language all her own. She can understand, but she cannot respond. Oral, on the other hand, is extremely verbal. The cleaning woman speaks in scat, and the white therapist treats Cassandra. For Rahman, the play is a journey into speech. She herself seems to be on that journey too. She is having difficulty finding a producer, and cites a letter from a major Off Broadway theater that called the play "oracular and spectacular" but "too out there for our audiences." She says *Only in America* is about people who cannot be seen and cannot be heard, and that Cassandra, for her, represents Black women in particular, who cannot speak or can be killed for it when they do. "The louder you speak, the less you are heard," she says.[18]

The idea that the Black woman is muted is not a new one. It is explored by many of the contributors to this volume and takes many forms. For instance, Harvard psychiatrist Alvin Poussaint, whom I interviewed for my series *On the Road: A Search for American Character*, told me he felt that the Hill-Thomas drama should not have been played out in a public arena, that the problems between Black men and women should be dealt with in private since the public air is dangerously racist.[19]

Another person I interviewed for *On the Road* was Charles Ogletree, an attorney on Anita Hill's team, whose views were very different from Alvin Poussaint's. Ogletree felt that it was important for Anita Hill to come forward, as strongly as possible. The Hill-Thomas hearings were a perfect subject for *On the Road*, since one of the goals of the series is to document changing relationships between men and women and among races in current times. In the series, I portray the people I interview, verbatim, in one-woman shows. To me, everyday speech has poetry, and for this reason all the interviews are titled and given in the cadence spoken. I performed Ogletree's remarks at the Crossroads Theater in New Brunswick, New Jersey, in a workshop production of a piece called *Dream*. An excerpt follows.

　　　　Not

. . . and I was willing to step forward
and say
"I believe you
I'm gonna ask you some tough questions

and ask you to do some difficult things like
take a polygraph test."
My sense was
Anita Hill needed to live beyond
that weekend.
She needed to in some sense
establish a permanent
legacy,
and one way to do that
would be to say
"I'm gonna do
what
no one,
what none of the other critical
parties in this
debate have been willing to do
I'm gonna subject myself to scrutiny for the rest of
       my life
by submitting my allegations
to close examination
with the polygraph
and
I'm gonna live with those results."
And that's the ultimate
that's the moment when a relationship
between a lawyer and a client
changes
because it was not just a lawyer
client relationship
it was a relationship
of
a trusted friend
uh
a counselor
adviser
a strong critic
saying
that there are consequences that could be very negative
if this fails

and you don't have to do this
but it could make
all of the difference in the world
not at the hearings,
it might not change the votes
but in terms of the public's perception
they will always remember
she was willing to sit down
uh
in this very hectic
weekend
and have
an FBI agent
who worked for the government
who trained all the FBI polygraph examiners
who
had a scrupulous reputation
subject
who believed Clarence Thomas
uh
having heard the first day's testimony
subject her to some very personal
intrusive
uh
and specific questions.
I was there pre test and post test
it's just between the examiner and examinee
under very very precise circumstances
what I was doing
was wondering why my feet were so wet and my suit
            was wet . . .
It was like
waiting for a jury to come back from a
            murder case . . .
those moments
put you in the twilight zone where there's no help
there's no rescue
you just wait for the decision
and I was there saying

God I hope it works out this time
uh
it's like
in my criminal trials I would wait to hear
only one word that would be
the word to me that I wanted to hear
was *not*
the rest of it is irrelevant
once the jury said "not"
right
my client and I *(bangs heels of his hands together)*
were gone
said we don't need to hear any more
thank you
uh
I didn't want to hear "not guilty"
and think "well did they say 'guilty' or
just"
I listen for
"not"
that's the word
and it's that kind of focus
and I was outside the door waiting
oh yes, oh yes
and she was still in the room she was filling out
          some papers
and it's kind of like I remember
going through childbirth and
going through all the systems
and when the doctor returned
our son,
we went through all the
the Lamaze
method and the doctor would come
turn around and say
"It's a boy"
or "a girl"
the doctor's joy in telling you
what you have a son or a daughter

but this guy just kind of looked
in a passive way
and it took him about four or five minutes to tell me
  that she passed
he was explaining dah dah dah dah dah
and I asked him "well what happened?"
and he says
"Oh
She's telling the truth, she passed overwhelming
there was no evidence of deception"
and I was just sitting there
just lifeless for a moment
it was one of the greatest moments of
joy in my life
to see this
whole process
in my judgment
in some sense
establish Anita Hill's credibility
and then
everything else seemed irrelevant
the vote
the debate
seemed irrelevant
because
I was representing a client
and here was
a kind of independent objective instrument
telling me that
Anita Hill told the truth.
The external system
would never have told me that
even if
Anita Hill
if they had voted against Clarence Thomas
people would still be upset at Anita Hill
as the messenger!
She was the messenger and that was not going to
  change.[20]

When I did some interviews about the hearings for a play I wrote and presented in December 1991, *Identities, Mirrors, and Distortions* (also part of *On the Road*), I was particularly moved by the words of John Carr, a lawyer at Simpson Thacher & Bartlett, and a friend of Anita Hill's who testified in her behalf at the hearings. In the show I performed him giving this explanation of his involvement in the hearings:

The Best and the Brightest

I wrote Anita Hill
Anita Hill's people called me
and asked if I would testify. . . .
and I thought
hey
if the whole world is gonna turn
and ask you to demonstrate . . .
that you're not lying
and I remember you telling me this nine years ago—
It was just an expression of support
for someone who was about to get
creamed . . .
and so
once she said through the people
"we'd like you to do this"
then I felt
then all this other sort of "it's your duty
and it's
service to the right thing" . . .
at that same time
it was that question of "Well
what's it gonna cost you?
you know what's the price you're going to have to pay?"
And that analysis was very quickly
small
by comparison to the price she was going to pay . . .
You may well
be able to remember a conversation you had with
     someone ten years ago

although you may or may not be accurate in your memory
compared to a tape recording
but you will remember
something
and you may not remember anything
else
about the person the place the time
just these things they fit in your mind
and they stay
and there certainly are a few of those memories
that I have
one of which is
this telephone conversation
and it goes less to the fact that she was being
hara—
you know
less to the fact that
I was sensitive to the fact that she was being
        harassed and more to the fact that
it was the head of the EEOC.
I mean
it just you know
this is a brother *(like a song)*
he was in a position of power
these notions of people sort of having the public trust
to do a job
I
I don't know if I would ever want to accept
        that burden but it seems to me if you do
then you really can't
pardon the phrase
screw around.
And that happened. . . .
I mean keep in mind
I'm very much
I'm very big on thoughts
like "let's not air our dirty laundry
let's look out for the group
over the individual"

I'm real keen on those concepts
but let's not be
moral and intellectual midgets
let's not
for broad
stroke principles
or concepts or emotional feelings
not confront real issues. . . .
when this guy came out and started talking about
     high tech lynching
and sexual stereotypes I'm sitting here saying
"What
is he talking about?
Why is he making a speech about how pissed off he
     is about the way
they are treating him?
Why don't we deal with the issues?"
And you think about it for a second and you say
"Is this really some raw emotional
outbreak
or did some guys get together in a conference room
     and say
this is the theme and this works
and this is the way to write that
yeah high tech high tech
that's a good term yeah"
and in a perverse way . . .
I find that fascinating
I can appreciate the aesthetic of what I think
was a managed process
these are people
being the best that they can be
you know this is the best and the brightest I guess.[21]

Perhaps the most comprehensive explanation I have found of the Hill-Thomas hearings and the way in which they themselves were theater is this one, from Donald Bogle, a film historian and critic also featured in *Identities*.

Riveting

. . . What I found really interesting,
in terms of perceptions,
when he talked about uppity
being an uppity
Black
and this was a high tech
lynching
and bringing in race
with all this
and the business of a stereotype
of an African American
male—
what I found interesting of course
was that
he went through all of this thing
as if they were seeing him
as this sort of
brutal Black buck
but
what he didn't deal with
is that
earlier for them
for Orrin Hatch and Strom Thurmond
and Alan Simpson I mean these
very you know
right wing figures
and particularly this Strom Thurmond—
I mean coming from the
South *(bit of melody)*
and *his* history
in *their* world
in the world of *images*
he becomes the friendly *(declining inflections)*
          conciliatory
agreeable
congenial
Uncle Tom.

This is who he *is*
for them!
And when Anita Hill
testified
what I found *fascinating,*
I mean
she was so poised
and so intelligent
and so eloquent
and so *real* a person
and not
a stereotype—
so that when she's there
talking—
there was a moment
where the camera
went from Anita Hill
and you saw this this
wide shot of this this panel
and you looked at Orrin Hatch
and Strom Thurmond
and in an instant
their faces
dropped
as they they
heard what she was saying
and you knew
whether they were going to deny it
to themselves
that they realized she spoke the truth.
And then there was another thing of perception
in the minds of these white men
their friendly Uncle Tom
is really
when he leaves their presence
and shuts the door
he's a *buck!*
You know Uncle Tom has this *penis*
and he may have a big penis
according to what Anita Hill is telling them

so they've got a *buck* on their hands
and *worse*
he has one of their women!
Up there!
So
for an instant
I mean in the world of *images*
this is what they were confronted with.
But it becomes
that whole thing
has to be a series
of denials
for all those people
in order to survive.
Clarence has to *completely* deny
anything
Anita Hill has said
so he says he never listened (*a little melody throughout*)
the wife
we assume
just completely denies
anything
by never saying
"Well Clarence *could* something have happened
that she misinterpreted?"
And Orrin Hatch and Thurmond and the others
they too have to deny
that
Anita Hill is
the possibility she's
speaking the truth.
They have to deny the possibility of truth there.
So what they concoct
are the worst of stereotypes about women—
that this is a woman with real delusions
real fantasies
then she's sort of depicted
as a woman scorned
and so
there are all these

things that they resort to
and they do resort to to
stereotypes to avoid
a truth
and they didn't find one for her.
I think that's one of the problems—
that's why they had to create a stereotype for her.
See the stereotypes are these little boxes
that that just sit there and they have to put her
in there.
She's not a tragic
mulatto.
She's not a mammy.
She's not a high strung
strumpet.
She's not
this sort of Jezebel.
She's not this this
loud
bawdy
Sapphire.
She's none of those!
This is a poised educated woman. . . .
Now the interesting thing about *him*
in terms of something *real*
when he did come in in the morning
when he was first there
there was something real about him
his face
you could see the tension
and you did feel here is a man
his whole life
in this
in these moments to come
everything that he's worked for
could go.
And I must admit when I looked at him
I felt for him
I mean
there's something

human
there
you
just
"Oh my God"
and they all are there
the whole nation
is watching
this
and of course
this is
an African American man sitting there
so you do feel something for him.
And then when she came in I said
"Oh well he's done for
because there's no way
anyone could doubt what this woman is saying
he's finished."
And then he comes back in prime time
and he's geared for prime time
and he really gave
a shrewd, clever
a well crafted performance
and of course
he injects race in too
because
Uncle Tom will do anything to save himself! *(laughing heartily)*
He was a man at that point who was cornered.
And I think there was a kind of real element there
in terms of fighting to save himself
and to say whatever
he could
and
it's almost as if
you know many people felt
that he was so much more honest
there
than he had been during the initial
hearings
where he really didn't say

anything
so he did get to the point
where you got to a *real* element
but the *real* element
it may indicate what he
I mean there's much there about himself that he did
    not know
because all along you know he said that race did
    not matter
and suddenly
he uses it
and this saves him.
Maybe on some level *maybe* on some level
he believed it
but I think at that point
there does become something real there
even though what he's saying
and his denials
may not be real
what's real is the
survival tactic
and the will to live
and not to uh
not to
go under.
I thought it was
it was *riveting* television
there was so much that was totally un
expected there were twists and turns
it was live
it wasn't taped
television
so at any moment
something could happen . . .[22]

The Hill-Thomas hearings were popular culture. They significantly raised the ante on what I could call "speechfulness." To use Aishah Rahman's phrase, they were a "journey into speech" for the muted issue of sexual harassment. They also put new scene partners on stage for the first time—the partners of race and gender. The hearings have pushed artists to render these issues. They make us concoct new images of men and women, new images of ourselves in race. They urge us to reevaluate power dynamics. During the hearings, the silence and the masks that protect power were more awesome, more grandiose, more epic than ever. They were at work again, a year and a half later, during the nomination of Lani Guinier. She has said that she was silenced. In response to that silence, she is still speaking. Earlier I said that art has not prepared us for this, but in fact there have been such plays, plays that laid the groundwork, in form if not in content, for tackling the relationship of silence to speech. I am referring to the type of play written by Harold Pinter, who says that speech is a strategy to cover nakedness. I am thinking of the plays of Samuel Beckett or Adrienne Kennedy, where the visual behavior of characters is orchestrated as carefully as the language. These are plays in which words are not enough, the epic theater of Bertolt Brecht, where truth lives in irony, or the grand puppetry of the Bread and Puppet Theater, which would need a space like a cathedral to capture the grandness of the senators who conducted the hearings.

We have a problem in the American theater, one that can perhaps be traced to the Vietnam War, according to Peter Zeisler, former executive director of the Theater Communications Group.

> I don't think we should have a purely political theater, but we have an apolitical theater now. . . . I think it started going downhill with the Vietnam War, when suddenly, every day on television, you got images that the theater couldn't provide. That was the first time television became testimony to our time. The theater has never found out how to react to the television documentary.[23]

In this day of minute-to-minute televised coverage of controversies, and of the charismatic individuals who embody them, how do we who study the science of performance compete? Perhaps we can merely take lessons. Perhaps we must look more closely at the relationship of speech to silence. The power and charisma of Anita Hill's remarks at the symposium chronicled by this book were in relationship to the relative silence she kept in the year following the hearings. The room around her rang with the hunger of the ear of the audience, electric with excitement, to hear the unspoken. Few theatergoers, few gallery roamers, few concert attendees give such silence, such expectation, to professional artists. The Hill-Thomas hearings, as well as other dramas of our time, have tested stereotypes and made them pale. Few plots have as many twists and turns. There is no character in the canon of characters who could represent Clarence Thomas or do justice to Anita Hill.

Notes

1. John W. Carr, interview by author, New York, N.Y., October 29, 1991 (tape recording on file with author).
2. My account of this episode is based on notes taken at the time I viewed it.
3. *Nomination of Judge Clarence Thomas to Be Associate Justice of the Supreme Court of the United States, Hearings before the Committee on the Judiciary, United States Senate* (Committee Print Draft), 102d Cong., 1st Sess., October 11–13, 1991, 147 [hereinafter *Hearings*].
4. We also discussed using Anita Hill's testimony as a reference in acting classes, because of her simplicity, her self-control, the economy of voice and movement.
5. See *Hearings*, 212.
6. See *Hearings*, 90.
7. See *Hearings*, 235.
8. Unidentified news clip.
9. See *Hearings*, 214.
10. Interview by author, October 1992.
11. My account of this episode is based on notes taken at the time I viewed it.
12. TDC Games, Inc., created by TDC creative director Sandy Bergeson and TDC president Larry Balsamo. See also T. J. Howard, "Play Harassment: It's Only a Game," *Chicago Tribune*, August 9, 1992.
13. Sarah Crichton, telephone conversation with author, October 1992.
14. Barbara Ehrenreich, "Women Would Have Known," *Time*, October 21, 1991, 104.
15. My account of this segment is based on notes taken at the time I viewed it.
16. Kinshasha Holman Conwill, telephone conversation with author, October 1992.
17. Michele Wallace, telephone conversation with author, October 1992.
18. Aishah Rahman, telephone interview with author, November 1994.
19. Alvin Poussaint, interview by author, March 1992 (tape recording on file with author).
20. Charles Ogletree, interview by author, March 1992 (tape recording on file with author).
21. Carr interview, *supra* note 1.
22. Donald Bogle, interview by author, New York, N.Y., November 21, 1991 (tape recording on file with author).
23. Peter Zeisler, interview by author, *American Theater*, July 1995.

Marriage and Patronage in the Empowerment and Disempowerment of African American Women

Anita Faye Hill

Reallocation of power is what confronting racism is about. Throughout the history of this country, African Americans have sought to obtain those things which lead to economic, political, and social power. African American women share with Black men the goal of attaining power, but often we seek it in ways culturally dictated by our gender. Black women also differ from Black men in that the power we seek is denied us because of both our race and our gender. We have sought education, employment, marriage, family, and other group associations, including religious affiliations, in efforts to centralize ourselves in a society that often views us as marginal[1] and our experiences as unessential to the definitions of race and gender.[2]

In ways that cannot be measured but that the essays in this collection attempt to explore, my dual status as Black and as female impaired my ability to present my story to the Senate Judiciary Committee and later to the public. Because of my gender and because of my race, I was then and continue to be on the fringe of what defines the African American community and the community of women.

On October 6, 1991, the press carried reports about the conduct to which I had been subjected by President George Bush's nominee to the Supreme Court, Judge Clarence Thomas. On October 11, 1991, I testified in further detail about this conduct, which I considered relevant to Thomas's competence to hold the position of associate justice of the Supreme Court. The exact sequence of events that led to the publication of my story and to my testimony at a public hearing remains a mystery to me.[3] Yet this much I do know. After inquiries from Senate staffers, I made a statement to the Judiciary Committee. I was assured that my statement would be confidential, used only for purposes of the investigation of Judge Thomas and for the committee's consideration. I never anticipated that once I issued the statement to the committee, I would have no power to control this information about my own experience, its use or its handling. Without my knowledge the statement was apparently leaked to members of the press, who then contacted me for comment and verification. After the press coverage I was contacted by and ultimately subpoenaed to appear before the Judiciary Committee for a public hearing.

The decision to hold a hearing about the charges, and in particular a public hearing, was made by the Senate. I had no control over the forum, its focus, its procedures, or its quality, even though it purported to be a hearing about my experience with sexual harassment. The entire structure was set by the Senate committee, the definitive insiders, and I, clearly an outsider, was forced to explain myself. Against this backdrop, it should come as no surprise that the investigation into my statement and the "fact-finding" hearing quickly turned into a "fake trial," in the words of Dennis Curtis.[4] Because of the clearly political focus of the individual senators and the absence of any established rules of procedure, the burden of proof shifted to me. I had to prove myself worthy to speak before the committee; to prove, beyond any doubt, that my testimony was true; and to prove that my experience should matter to the Senate in its capacity to advise and consent on Supreme Court nominations.

In short, I was required to validate myself and my experience within the experiential realm of the members of the Judiciary Committee. The fact that the senators were all men, all White, all powerfully connected, all insiders, and that I, with no political connections, was a dual outsider by virtue of race and gender, made the likelihood of my success remote—and all the more so as I had only two and a half days to prepare for the hearing.

In going before the committee I came face to face with a history of exclusion from power. Notwithstanding many advances over the past three decades, it is hard to deny that as a group African Americans, and in particular African American women, at best can only associate with or approach power. Power and prestige are only given to African American women by license, not ownership, and that license is easily revoked. I cite my treatment by the Judiciary Committee as an example of the limits of power achieved through education or employment. At the beginning of the hearing, as for the previous ten years, I was viewed as a person holding a position of relative social respectability, a law professor at a state university. The rhetoric used to discuss my claim of harassment made my credentials irrelevant. Through their "cross-examination," the senators attempted to show their power in relationship to my powerlessness. In the end I was characterized as a contemptible threat, a vindictive pawn of radical feminists, a victim of erotomania, someone to be viewed at best with pity, at worst with disdain.[5]

The ease with which I was transformed from respected academician to malicious psychotic in the eyes of the public illustrates the tenuousness of my association with power. In sum, my license to speak before the committee as a credible witness was revoked by the tribunal and the process. I was cast as just another African American woman who was not to be trusted to describe her own experiences truthfully and who had no place in the decidedly political arena of the moment. To paraphrase Adele Logan Alexander's discussion, I was no law professor; I was a "niggress."[6]

My reality was so different from that of the members of the Senate Judiciary Committee that they found it incomprehensible.[7] They failed or refused to relate to almost every dimension of my race and gender, in combination with my education, my career choice, and my demeanor. Senators Simpson and Specter epitomized this incomprehension. They could not understand why I was not attached to certain institutions, notably marriage, which has traditionally defined the relationship between men and women, and the patronage system, which has often defined the relationship between African Americans and Whites. Because they misunderstood the nature of sexual harassment, the senators raised questions about my sexuality.[8] Because they were unaccustomed to issues presented without official endorsement, they searched for the senator who might have been the sponsor of the claim.

In examining the Judiciary Committee's response to my testimony, it is useful to borrow the terminology of some legal philosophers and literary critics. Through questioning on the first day of the hearing, the senators attempted to "deconstruct" my "narrative," and in the days that followed, to "construct" their own "narratives" to explain what had occurred. Richard Delgado has argued that "narratives are powerful means for destroying mindset—the bundle of presuppositions, received wisdom, and shared understandings against a background of which legal and political discourse take place"; but narratives can also be used, perhaps even more effectively, to maintain prevailing mindsets, as Charles R. Lawrence points out in his discussion of the "Master Narrative," and that is how they functioned during the hearing.[9] Indeed, many senators were simply maintaining a point of view they held even before they heard my testimony, as Charles J. Ogletree notes.[10] Because my narrative did not comport with their mindset, their assumptions about what was true and real, it had to be reconstructed—a task they undertook with assistance from the press, Thomas supporters, and Thomas witnesses. The senators claimed they had no experience with the kind of behavior I described. Thus, rather than entertain the idea that I was telling the truth, they concluded that I must be lying, and concocted an explanation based on their understanding of race and gender relationships.

According to the reality of the committee, "women are married, or have been, or plan to be, or suffer from not being."[11] In the senators' narrative, therefore, I was single because I was unmarriageable or opposed to marriage, the fantasizing spinster or the man-hater.

According to the reality of the committee, every opposition is politically motivated. In the senators' narrative, therefore, I was part of a left-wing conspiracy to "Bork" the Thomas nomination.

According to the reality of the committee, every Washington outsider worthy of interest has a patron to confer legitimacy at official proceedings like the hearings and to navigate the corridors of power. Clarence Thomas had such a patron in Senator Danforth. The fact that I had none, and chose to speak for myself, aroused suspicion. In the senators' narrative, therefore, I was acting at the urging of Democrats who opposed Thomas or as an agent for radical feminists.

According to the reality of the committee, sexual harassment is a rare phenomenon, and in the few instances where it does occur outside the imaginations of delusional or vindictive women, it is committed only by depraved, easily identified males. In the senators' narrative, therefore—because Thomas was not identifiably depraved, and despite the scientific data about the prevalence of sexual harassment in the workplace and the rarity of false claims—I was the spiteful, spurned woman who was suffering romantic disappointment or the pathetic erotomaniac who was so deluded as to actually believe what she said.

According to the reality of the committee, my career success as an African American and as a woman had nothing to do with my qualifications and everything to do with the myth of the double advantage enjoyed by women of color.[12] In the senators' narrative, therefore, I was aloof and ambitious, an incompetent product of affirmative action and an ingrate who betrayed the man who had done me a favor by hiring me.

According to the reality of the committee, and of much of society, women, particularly African American women, cannot be trusted to tell the truth in matters concerning sexual misconduct. In the senators' narrative, therefore (within the framework first introduced by Freud to explain female patients' stories of incest), my story became a fantasy fueled by desire for the object of the story, "stuff . . . from the moon" and at the same time "stuff" from *The Exorcist*.[13]

It was this reconstruction of me—a portrait of a dangerous, unbelievable, ambitious, disappointed woman—that the senators used to justify the warning to "watch out for Anita Hill." The portrait was further reinforced by the retelling of the stories of Janet Cooke and Tawana Brawley by some commentators and editorial writers.[14] Various senators and their collaborators struggled to place me as far outside the norms of proper behavior as they could, painting me as simultaneously prudish yet lewd, easily duped yet shrewd and ambitious, fantasizing yet calculating, pathetic yet evil.[15]

The irrelevance of the narrative the senators constructed would have been apparent had they taken an honest look at the workplace and power relationships and explored the assumptions their insider status made invisible to them. Other contributors to this collection have written about some of these assumptions and their impact on African Americans and women. On the issue of sexual harassment, for instance, Susan Deller Ross has discussed its pervasiveness and the difficulty of bringing forth and pursuing charges; Adele Logan Alexander has delineated the multilayered reality of Black women's lives and the stereotypes against which they must struggle.[16] Had the senators availed themselves of the information on the nature of sexual harassment prepared for them by experts in the social sciences like Dr. Louise Fitzgerald, instead of excluding it from the record, they might have recognized the seriousness of sexual harassment as a social problem. Had they or their staffers even a rudimentary familiarity with the case law on sexual harassment, they would have understood that the language and behavior I described are common in many modern work settings and that the standards and procedures adopted by the committee were neither legally acceptable nor helpful in getting to the truth. Had the senators paid more than perfunctory attention to gender issues, as Judith Resnik explains, they might have understood the relevance of Thomas's behavior and views on gender subordination to his fitness to serve on the Supreme Court.[17] Had they been aware of the complex resonance of a claim of sexual misconduct raised by a Black woman, they might have stopped trying to invent a stereotypical and untrue portrait of me against which I was forced to defend myself.

The hearings indeed brought to the surface many negative preconceptions about African Americans in general and African American women in particular (though the senators' concerns about stereotyping were confined to negative stereotypical assumptions about Black males[18]). In the limited space of this paper I want to focus on two strategies that Black Americans, especially Black women as outsiders, have adopted to attain insider status in the face of these preconceptions: patronage and marriage. I want to address the cultural and social price one may pay for rejecting those institutions as the basis of one's identity. Specifically, I argue that my unwillingness to establish an association with power through marriage and patronage reduced my credibility in the eyes of the Senate Judiciary Committee and the public. Finally, I assert that Black women must claim our experiences and develop a sense of power based on the value of those experiences.

Patronage

One of the ways African Americans associate with power is by acquiring a patron, or in some cases having a patron imposed on them.

Patronage, seemingly a universal concept, has had some peculiar manifestations in African American history. It has been argued that patronage in the slave South was part of the slaveholder's paternalistic vision of himself as an "authoritarian father," and that Blacks shared or endorsed this vision—ideas perhaps impossible to verify in the context of slavery.[19] Whether the active or the passive interpretation more accurately describes the interaction between African Americans and Whites, patronage is part of the history of race relations in this country.

During slavery African Americans relied on the patronage of slaveholders for their very survival, both physical and economic. The slave codes stipulated that slaves could not leave a plantation without permission, and that if they did, any White person finding them could turn them over to public officials. When insurrections were rumored, vigilante committees randomly murdered and lynched African Americans, both slave and free, both male and female.[20] In some states the codes were more elaborate and severe than in others. In Georgia, for example, "slaves could not travel outside Savannah or their own plantation without a ticket or letter from their master. Nor could they travel in groups of more than seven slaves without a 'white person.' They could not carry firearms during the week without . . . the supervision of a white person."[21] Thus, the patronage system was injected into the culture by statute.

Since the only penalties against killing a slave were tied to interference with the slaveowner's property rights, it was incumbent on slaves outside the plantation to establish their owners' patronage. Those who could not were presumed to be runaways, and since there were no penalties for killing runaways, proof of patronage became crucial. Physical survival compelled slaves to seek the protection of their owners. And for both the enslaved and the free African American, economic survival often depended on patronage as well. Slaves had no right to interest in property, whether real, personal, or intellectual. Slaves could not own the expression of their ideas. "Slaves could not 'buy, sell, or exchange any goods, wares, provisions, grains, victuals, or commodities' of any sort without a special license." Slave inventors were initially prohibited from applying for patents in their own names or even in the name of their owner, but in 1861 the Confederate Congress passed a provision allowing a patent to be issued to the owner if he "took an oath that his slave had actually invented a device."[22] Even early slave narratives had to be sanctioned by or "told to" a White patron; without a patron the text was assumed to have no validity.[23]

Vestiges of the patronage relationship between African Americans and Whites can be seen in recent stories of African Americans who have been stopped by law enforcement officials, questioned, and even arrested because they were alone in White neighborhoods and could not explain why they were there. Derrick Bell, in *And We Are Not Saved*, describes the sense of powerlessness experienced by a young African American military officer who wandered into an unfamiliar area. Ultimately his military uniform persuaded a state trooper that he was not the suspect wanted by local law officials. Later in life, a respected attorney and law professor, the man relives this experience when he has to invoke the name of a law school dean and a university president before a police officer will let him counsel a woman stopped for speeding. His patronage is established by professional associations and by dress, but he bitterly resents that it remains a necessity of his existence.[24]

For many individuals the struggle to attain power begins with seeking education and powerful associations, but for African American women, because of our unique history, established institutions and networks take on greater significance as we attempt to overcome society's negative presumptions about us. Despite apparent gains and the myth of the double advantage, Black women are overrepresented in service occupations: private household worker, cook, housekeeper, welfare aide, and other jobs that offer little autonomy and are subject to high levels of personal control by individual employers.[25] Not only is it harder for Black women to attain certain educational, workplace, social, and cultural positions of status, but when we do, we are not rewarded commensurately. According to the 1989 census figures, Black women earned 60.9 cents for every dollar earned by a White male, compared to 68.5 cents earned by White females. Moreover, the difference in earnings cannot be explained by education alone. In 1985 the Census Bureau reported that differences in education, labor force experience, and commitment accounted for only 14.6 percent of the wage gap between women and men.[26]

In modern educational training and professional life, the role of the patron cannot be underestimated. No matter how impressive their credentials, individuals of all races, female and male, need sponsors in business and mentors in academia. Inside the beltway, patronage is part of the political culture and is critical to political survival. The political patrons of Washington, D.C., sponsor bills, programs, and individuals. It is understood that as the patron goes, so goes the beneficiary.[27] At least one commentator has attributed some of the problems in Lani Guinier's failed nomination as assistant attorney general for civil rights to her lack of a patron. "On Capitol Hill," Mark Shields remarked, "it's better to have one tiger than a hundred pussycats—in other words, one legislator who feels that his or her fate, fortune, or future is tied to her cause. Lani Guinier lacked that."[28]

Patronage in education, politics, and the professional sphere helps to establish an individual's relationship to the powerful, though it may not confer insider status. For African American women, the ultimate outsiders, participation in patronage relationships is crucial. However, the patronage system can be a double-edged sword. For a Black woman who attempts to make it on her own, whatever her class or position, refusing a patron can be as harmful as having one can be beneficial. And aligning herself with the wrong patron, one who harbors negative presumptions about race or gender can be even more devastating.

The story of Sofia in Alice Walker's *The Color Purple* vividly illustrates the problem of refusing patronage. In a key scene, two White characters, the Mayor and his wife, Millie, encounter Sofia, her friend the prizefighter, and Sofia's children on the street. "All these children. . . . Cute as little buttons though . . . and such strong teeth," says Millie. She looks at Sofia and the prizefighter, at his car and Sofia's wristwatch, remarks that Sofia's children are "so clean," and asks if Sofia would like to be her maid. Sofia emphatically rejects the offer: "Hell no." In response, the Mayor strikes Sofia, and then she knocks him down. In the ensuing fight Sofia is brutally beaten by six policemen. She is later imprisoned.[29]

In prior passages Walker has made it clear that Sofia is no stereotypical "lazy Black." Sofia enjoys work. She is seen working in the fields, cleaning and cutting shingles to repair the roof. What Sofia rejects is not the work of being the maid for the Mayor and Millie but their patronage and their patronizing behavior toward her and her children.

Sofia's refusal is viewed as a threat to her would-be patrons; to contain that threat she has to be beaten and imprisoned both physically and psychologically. It seems she also poses a threat to other Blacks who feel a stake in the patronage system. When Sofia's father-in-law, a man who "know he colored," is sent as an envoy to plead with the sheriff to allow Sofia visitors, he agrees with the sheriff's description of Sofia as crazy, tries to excuse her on the grounds that she comes from a crazy family, and adds that the sheriff "know how women is."[30] In sum, when Sofia challenges the patronage system, White society punishes her, and in response her family must disavow her behavior to assure those in power that Sofia is wrong (crazy) and that the system is correct.

Most evident from the televised Judiciary Committee hearings was the fact that I sat in that hearing room without a patron on the panel. That image still resonates. My sin was not simply that I did not have a patron. Nor was it simply that I rejected patronage offered to me, since none was offered. My initial sin in the eyes of the senators was that I dared to come to the body on my own, that I did not actively pursue patronage at the outset. No senator, either Democrat or Republican, acted on behalf of my right to speak before the committee. None was sought. As Judith Resnik notes, I was allowed to speak only after public pressure made it nearly impossible for the Senate to ignore my statement.[31] I and then the public challenged the senators' system.

As the process continued and I prepared for the "fact-finding" hearing, my counsel and I did not focus on getting a key senator to act as my advocate; instead we relied on the weight of my testimony and the fairness of the process as we thought it should be. Again I unwittingly denied the patronage system, which is an entrenched part of Washington's political culture. In refusing to rely on this system, I implicitly questioned it and posed a challenge to those invested in it. The response was to strike back at me, the challenger. Even neutral commentators have criticized my counsel for not having organized in more political terms.[32] I thus wandered into Washington, D.C., without a patron or even a proper letter of introduction, and with no apparent explanation of how I came to be there; like the slave who wandered off the plantation, I was without my papers, so to speak. Though I was able to gain a forum without the patronage of a committee member, it quickly became clear that I would be punished for my temerity as Senator Simpson threatened me with "plain old

Washington variety harassment" for raising the issue of sexual harassment,[33] and as the senators struggled to regain the control and power they perceived they had lost during the events that led to the second round of hearings.

Marriage

Marriage, as described by Simone de Beauvoir, is a form of patronage, but a distinct form. In *The Second Sex* de Beauvoir says that "for girls marriage is the only means of integration in the community" and that it is a joint enterprise with man as "the economic head through which woman gets some share in the world as her own." Of marriage in America, de Beauvoir writes, "A single woman in America . . . is a socially incomplete being even if she makes her own living; if she is to attain the whole dignity of a person and gain her full rights, she must wear a wedding ring."[34] In other words, marriage provides a way for a woman to establish her social, economic, and cultural insider status.

More recently Susan Faludi has debunked some of the many myths about modern marriage and shown th power of marital status as a social weapon used against single working women. Faludi traces the characterization of the single woman as "social misfit" from the Victorian press into the 1980s. She cites *Newsweek*'s unbalanced coverage of two conflicting stories about the demographics of marriage in the United States. An unpublished study that foretold "The Spinster Boom" was given greater play than a contradictory Census Bureau study because the former confirmed "impressions [the editorial staff] already had" that single women, among other things, "are more likely to be killed by a terrorist" than to marry. *Newsweek* went on to give further space to the lamentable plight of the single woman.[35]

As insightful as de Beauvoir's and Faludi's observations are, they are based on the White American model of marriage and its role in American culture. That model is helpful in that it is the model many slaves and freedmen and their descendants were urged to follow, but marriage in this country has also been a "peculiar institution" for African Americans.[36] Though marriage between slaves was prohibited in some states and not legally recognized in others, historians believe that "the slave family was a viable institution."[37] Despite formal and informal opposition, African Americans embraced marriage as an institution during slavery. After the Civil War, former slaves sought to legalize unions made during slavery and to establish new marriages. Nevertheless, the model of a marriage with the husband working outside the home and the wife working only in the home was irrelevant to the slave experience, and has been largely irrelevant to the situation of many African Americans ever since. For them, the economic struggle was and is a shared experience.[38]

Work patterns among African American couples were not the only point of deviation from the White American model of marriage. In some instances African American attitudes about female subordination in marriage differed from the model as well. Though some freedmen urged their brethren "to get the woman in the proper place" for the good of the race, others advocated the full partnership of women in the struggle for equality.[39] Some African American women preferred the traditional concept of marriage because it exempted them from the double duty of working outside and within the home, while others, unaccustomed to domination by a male partner during slavery, were not disposed to "subordination to masculine authority" in the post-slavery period.[40] At times the insistence on male dominance within the African American marriage took on a physical expression in the form of wife beating.[41]

Derrick Bell captures the ambivalence about marriage in today's African American community in a chapter of *And We Are Not Saved* entitled "The Race-Charged Relationship between Black Men and Black Women: Chronicle of the Twenty-Seven-Year Syndrome." The female protagonist of Bell's book, Geneva Crenshaw, rejects the ideals of patriarchy as an answer to problems in Black female-male relationships, though the author seems to embrace them. He describes a disease contracted only by Black women who have achieved above-average educational or professional status. Those afflicted by this disease, the Twenty-Seven-Year Syndrome, fall into a sleep and awaken after four to six weeks to find that they have lost their professional skills and have to be retrained for the workplace. No cure is found, but the disease can be prevented if a woman in the susceptible category marries a Black male before reaching the age of twenty-seven. "Women who were or had been married to, or who had received a serious offer of marriage from, a black man, seemed immune to the strange malady."[42] Though Geneva Crenshaw makes compelling arguments against the author's choice of solutions to the problem of the Twenty-Seven-Year Syndrome, in the end Bell argues that maintaining "traditional" male-female relationships is crucial for African Americans and ultimately necessary to achieve racial justice.[43]

Along with its obvious benefits, the difficulties of modern marriage have been widely publicized. Despite these difficulties, those who reject traditional marriage as an institution based on female-to-male subordination have been criticized from within and outside the African American community, and some analysts and public officials have suggested that many social and economic problems would be solved if women married before having children. They have even placed the responsibility for urban violence and unrest, delinquency, crime, and drug use on single mothers, who bear two out of three African American children, according to recent census statistics. Orlando Patterson, for one, argues that the problems of young Black males are largely attributable to their mothers.[44] For all the debates, marriage continues to reflect a measure of social and economic success within the Black community. Though only one in four Black females below the age of forty is married, marriage is still equated with sexual desirability and sexual preference.[45]

During the Judiciary Committee hearings, as the legal burden of proof was either ignored, misunderstood, or deliberately misstated, it was left to me to prove myself politically and socially acceptable. Much was made in the press of the fact that I was single, though the relevance of my marital status to the question of sexual harassment was never articulated. Some of this attention was provoked by the insinuations of Clarence Thomas, Senator Simpson, and journalist William Safire. Simpson tried to discredit my claim by referring to my sexual "proclivities," and Safire later elaborated upon the phrase.[46]

In raising questions about my marital status, the senators were apparently attempting to establish a relationship between marriage, values, and credibility. The scrutiny of my marital status caused people to wonder in an uninformed way why I, a thirty-five-year-old Black woman, had chosen to pursue a career and to remain single—an irrelevant shift of focus that contributed to the conclusion that I was not to be believed. This conclusion about credibility not only required a leap of logic but an ignorance of the facts of my existence. Though neither logic nor facts should have been forgone by the committee, both were. As the youngest of thirteen children, I have long embraced family values. The extended family is part of our tradition, as it is for many African Americans. Though we respect marriage, being single does not exile me from my family and its values, or from African American culture. Nor does being single in today's America equate with the rejection of values, traditional or otherwise. Linking credibility in questions of sexual harassment to marriage presumes that single women are not sexually harassed or that they should carry an extra burden of proving that they are. Marital status should never be a factor in assessing anyone's veracity, but the hearing turned into an exercise in measuring veracity by social and political clout. And as both de Beauvoir and Faludi point out, marriage is a symbol of power for many.

If my lack of a husband preoccupied certain members of the committee and the press, there was another dynamic at work in the African American community. To some Blacks, neither the truth of my claim nor the illegality of harassment mattered; the central issue was that I had violated a spoken or unspoken norm of the African American community—what Emma Jordan calls "gag order" placed on African American women who suffer abuse at the hands of African American men.[47] In the eyes of some, a declaration of such abuse diminishes the Black community in relation to the White community. This violation damned me in the eyes of many Blacks whose profound experiences of racism have led them to ignore within our own community what we find intolerable when committed by others against us. Because I seemed to break the racial solidarity rule, some in the African American community attempted to reconstruct me as a pawn of radical feminists, even though I had no contact at all with "the feminists" before the hearings. Though mostly concerned with what they viewed as the political problems I created by coming forward, partisan detractors eventually exploited my breach of the norm of the African American community in their efforts to discredit me. I had disrupted the regrettably politicized process *and* created community disharmony by giving harmful testimony against the president's nominee, a Black judge.

A passage from Zora Neale Hurston's *Their Eyes Were Watching*

God perhaps best illustrates my feelings when I came before the Judiciary Committee, having challenged the norms of that body, of society, and of the Black community. Hurston's protagonist, Janie, has also committed a list of sins according to the standards of her community. Ultimately her transgressions involve the legal system as well, when she is tried for the murder of her third husband, Tea Cake, an act committed in self-defense. Hurston describes Janie's trial as follows:

> The court set and Janie saw the judge who had put on a great robe to listen about her and Tea Cake. And twelve more white men had stopped whatever they were doing to listen and pass on what happened. That was funny too. Twelve strange men who didn't know a thing about people like Tea Cake and her were going to sit on the thing. . . .
> Then she saw all of the colored people standing up in the back of the courtroom. . . . They were all against her, she could see. So many were there against her that a light slap from each one of them would have beat her to death.[48]

Janie recognizes her dual role. First she has to prove that she has operated within the constraints of a legal system that was not established with her and her experiences in mind, and then she has to prove herself and her acts socially acceptable to a community concerned with its own established norms of behavior. Likewise, before a Senate committee that understood neither the experience nor the law of sexual harassment, I was forced to make my case. And before a community that cared less about gender subordination and harassment than about a definition of racial survival driven by racism, I had to atone for my sin of "bringing down a brother."

Though Janie strikes the reader of *Their Eyes Were Watching God* as an individual who wrestles for control of her life and destiny, in the end she is judged under circumstances beyond her control. For deviating from certain societal expectations, Janie is first tried by a court made up of those who cannot relate to her experience and then ostracized by her peers who will not. Though Janie is ultimately forgiven and brought back into the fold, the pain of the initial rejection and distrust of her story remains with her and with her community.

Through Whose Eyes, in Whose Voice: The Telling of African American Women's Stories

As the hearings came to a close, many commentators expressed concern that women would be less likely to file harassment claims because of the committee's harsh treatment of me and the dismissal of my complaint. The commentators were wrong; ironically, the hearings had the opposite effect as record numbers of women came forward with sexual harassment complaints in their aftermath.

Ultimately the committee's characterization of me as just another woman who was to be viewed with immediate skepticism allowed other women to relate to me and my experience. Though the senators claimed to be shocked by the possibility of the behavior I described, many working women of color and White working women knew the scenario well. Many had had similar experiences, some much more egregious; most had never complained, as the senators were sure they would have if the harassment had really occurred, and even fewer had documented it, except in memory. The senators' incredulous reaction painfully reminded women of that incongruous, though typical, gender-biased response to any woman who reports a sexual assault: "It couldn't have happened. What did you do to provoke it?" And while the racial implications of the senators' incredulity were not fully explored by the press, they did not escape many Black women.

Just as the members of the Senate Judiciary Committee told their narratives about the experience of harassment, so did those of us who were outsiders to the political maneuvering that marked the hearing. Our narratives were often in conflict with the senators' and were often unspoken in all but the most private of conversations. Since the hearings, we have begun to tell the stories of those "whose voice and perspective—whose consciousness (and experiences)—have been suppressed, devalued and abnormalized."[49] And finally we have begun to go public with those stories. Adele Logan Alexander has shown how pervasively and effectively African American women have been silenced.[50] Now it is our responsibility to share our own narratives lest the world conclude that our unique experiences do not count in defining what it means to be a woman or what it means to be African American. In seeking to understand gender, our history, our received wisdom, and our shared perceptions must not be omitted or lost in the outpouring of other voices. In describing the impact of race and racism on the African American community, our peculiar pain must be acknowledged if the story is to be complete. We must claim the right to speak of both race and gender. We must not contribute to our own trivialization by remaining silent about our existence. Any achievement of real power for all African Americans and for all women requires no less.

The imagery presented by the hearings has given us new impetus and opportunity to refute the stereotypes that are part of our culture and that were reinforced by the scene in the Judiciary Committee hearing room. We can now stop deluding ourselves about how far we have come on race and gender issues and take a good long look at where African American women are and how we got here. We can make the examination without the filter of old sexually charged stereotypes and modern myths about the political and cultural benefits of our dual status. We can replace the stock images with new ones that do not depend on association with power in some of its traditional forms.[51] We can tell our stories.

One of the most poignant expressions of the beginnings of our willingness to share our narratives was an advertisement taken out by African American women from all over the country in various publications, including the *New York Times*.[52] The women's statement called attention to the painful part of our history that perpetuates the abuse and demeaning of African American women in general, and in particular when they raise claims of sexual misconduct. The women vowed that they would not "tolerate this type of dismissal of any one Black woman's experience or this attack upon our collective character without protest, outrage, and resistance." Their piercing observations are a clarion call for African American women to introduce our narratives into the discourse that ultimately defines the normative universe in which we reside.[53] A group of African American men also issued a statement warning against the misuse of the history of Black people for political gain, and asserting that the committee's failure to "thoroughly investigate Professor Hill's claim" would be a fundamental insult to all Black women.[54] I would add that it was an insult to the African American community and the community of all women.

Ironically, we must share our history, through narrative, with the often resistant African American community as well as the larger American society. Yet I believe that our credibility as a community turns on our willingness to address wrongs within as well as outside it. Equality begins at home.[55] Racial equality cannot be gained at the expense of gender equality. Reallocation of power is what including African American women in the confrontation with racism is about.

Notes

1. Kimberlé Crenshaw, "Demarginalizing the Intersection of Race and Gender in Antidiscrimination Law, Feminist Theory, and Antiracist Politics," 1989 *Chicago Legal Forum* 139.
2. Angela Harris, "Race and Essentialism in Feminist Legal Theory," 42 *Stanford L. Rev.* 581 (1990).
3. See the accounts in Timothy Phelps and Helen Winternitz, *Capitol Games*, 229–33 (1992); and Jane Mayer and Jill Abramson, *Strange Justice: The Selling of Clarence Thomas* (1994), chap. 12, "The Leak."
4. Dennis E. Curtis, "The Fake Trial," 65 *So. Calif. L. Rev.* 1523 (1992).
5. Senator Simpson claimed to have devastating information about me yet later refused to make the information public or be more specific about it. See "The Thomas Nomination; Senator Simpson Refuses to Make Public Letters He Says Criticize Hill," N.Y. *Times*, October 14, 1991.
6. Adele Logan Alexander, " 'She's No Lady, She's a Nigger,' " p. 18 herein.
7. This parallels the experience of many women of color who are met with confusion and disbelief in the professional world. See Constance Baker Motley's essay in Goldman and Gallen, *Thurgood Marhsall: Justice for All*, 162 (1992).
8. See note 46, *infra*.
9. Richard Delgado, "Storytelling for Oppositionists and Others: A Plea for Narrative," 87 *Michigan L. Rev.* at 2413 (1989); Charles R. Lawrence, "The Message of the Verdict," pp. 107–11 herein.
10. Charles J. Ogletree, "The People vs. Anita Hill," pp. 143–44 herein (citing statements by Senators Hatch and Simpson on October 8 indicating that they did not believe me).
11. Simone de Beauvoir, *The Second Sex*, 474 (1953).
12. See Pamela Smith, "We Are Not Sisters: African American Women and the Freedom to Associate and Disassociate," 66 *Tulane L. Rev.* 1467 (1992).
13. Recall from the hearings that Senator Hatch accused me of inventing my story based on a passage from *The Exorcist*. Senator Simpson described my

testimony in the following manner: "And the stuff we listened to, I mean, you know, come on—from the moon." *Nomination of Judge Clarence Thomas to Be Associate Justice of the Supreme Court, Hearings before the Committee on the Judiciary*, 102d Cong., 1st Sess. (Committee Print Draft), October 11–13, 1991, at 191–92, 235.

14. See Dickerson, "Why Is Anita Hill Out to Get Judge Thomas?" *Atlanta Constitution*, October 11, 1991, at A12. Janet Cooke is a journalist who invented characters in a prize-winning story that was published as nonfiction. Tawana Brawley accused law enforcement officers of a grotesque and racially motivated sexual assault and abduction. Investigators later concluded that the accusation was false. Cooke and Brawley are both African American women.

15. See Patricia J. Williams, "The Bread and Circus Literacy Test," *Ms.*, January–February 1992.

16. Susan Deller Ross, "Sexual Harassment Law in the Aftermath of the Hill-Thomas Hearings," pp. 228–41 herein; Alexander, pp. 3–25 herein.

17. Judith Resnik, "From the Senate Judiciary Committee to the Country Courthouse," pp. 177–227 herein.

18. See the statements of Senators Hatch and Simpson, *Hearings, supra* note 13, at 187–89, 235.

19. See Herbert G. Gutman, *The Black Family in Slavery and Freedom, 1750–1925* (1976).

20. See Franklin and Moss, *From Slavery to Freedom*, 6th ed., 122–25 (describing the slave codes throughout the South) (1988).

21. A. Leon Higginbotham, Jr., *In the Matter of Color: Race and the American Legal Process—The Colonial Period*, 258 (1978).

22. *Id.*

23. See, e.g., Harriet Jacobs, *Incidents in the Life of a Slave Girl* (1861), which was sponsored by white abolitionist Lydia Maria Child.

24. Derrick Bell, *And We Are Not Saved: The Elusive Quest for Racial Justice*, 181–84 (1987).

25. See National Committee on Pay Equity, "The Wage Gap: Myths and Facts," reprinted in Rothenberg, *Race, Class, and Gender in the United States*, 129–36 (1992).

26. *Id.* See also Staff Report, United States Commission on Civil Rights, *The Economic Status of Black Women: An Exploratory Investigation* (1990).

27. See Phelps and Winternitz, *supra* note 3, for a discussion of John Danforth's role as Clarence Thomas's patron.

28. Mark Shields, *MacNeil/Lehrer News Hour*, PBS, June 4, 1993.

29. Alice Walker, *The Color Purple*, 75–76 (1982).

30. *Id.* at 77–79.

31. Resnik, p. 178 herein.

32. See Phelps and Winternitz, *supra* note 3, at 306: "What Hill really needed was a political advance team, but there had been neither the time nor the inclination to assemble one."

33. *Cong. Rec.*, Senate 14545–46, October 8, 1991.
34. De Beauvoir, *supra* note 11, at 477–80.
35. Susan Faludi, *Backlash: The Undeclared War against American Women*, 95–101 (1991).
36. See generally Gutman, *supra* note 19, who dismisses the impact of African history and tradition on slave culture and on the slave marriage and family.
37. See Franklin and Moss, *supra* note 20, at 127 (citing John Blassingame and Herbert Gutman).
38. Franklin and Moss suggest that the stability of the slave marriage "depended on the extent to which the couple had an opportunity to work together and live together so that through common experiences they could be drawn closer together." *Id.* Ironically, Aburdene and Naisbitt report that the collaborative couple that works as a team on an economic enterprise is "making creative partnerships a new paradigm for the 21st century." *Megatrends for Women*, 165 (1992).
39. Paula Giddings, *When and Where I Enter: The Impact of Black Women on Race and Sex in America*, 58 (1984).
40. *Id.*
41. *Id.* at 64.
42. Bell, *supra* note 24, at 199.
43. Other scholars disagree. See Angela Davis, *Women, Culture, and Politics*, 75 (1989): ". . . to focus myopically on family problems as the basis for the oppression of the Afro-American community—as if setting the family in order will automatically eradicate poverty—is to espouse the fallacious 'blame the victim' argument."
44. Orlando Patterson, "The Crisis of Gender Relations among African Americans," pp. 56–104 herein.
45. See Davis, *supra* note 43, 75–76.
46. William Safire, "The Plot to Savage Thomas," *N.Y. Times*, October 14, 1991; and "About Men: Cordialities and Crushes," *N.Y. Times Magazine*, November 3, 1991, 18. In both pieces Safire mentions Senator Simpson's references to information about my "proclivities" received in "letters and faxes." Safire goes further than Simpson to explain that the term "was used sneakily—to hint at homosexuality," and goes on to admonish Simpson that "if he has evidence that the accuser's sexual preference is related to her reluctance to bring a charge of sexual harassment, let him make the case or shut up." Safire's remarks were read as veiled approval couched in the form of a reprimand of Simpson. Interestingly, Safire not only assumed that Simpson had information but also presumed the validity of the unsworn "letters and faxes" and of Simpson's conclusion about my sexual preference. At the same time, Safire expressed complete disbelief in my sworn testimony and statements.
47. Emma Coleman Jordan, "The Power of False Racial Memory," pp. 37–55 herein.

48. Zora Neale Hurston, *Their Eyes Were Watching God*, at 89 (1937; reprint, 1978).
49. Delgado, *supra* note 9, at n. 29.
50. Alexander, pp. 3–25 herein.
51. Many who believed me were persuaded by my association with traditional values, education, middle-class economic status, and religion. The significance of these factors for them has not gone unnoticed by me. Their significance for me is that they illustrate that like most people, I am not a monolithic stereotype. The stereotype of the superwoman is just as unyielding and unrealistic as that of the welfare queen. The image of the African American woman I hope for will reflect the multiple dimensions of our lives.
52. Reprinted in Chrisman and Allen, eds., *Court of Appeal: The Black Community Speaks Out on the Racial and Sexual Politics of Thomas vs. Hill*, 292 (1992).
53. See generally Cover, "The Supreme Court Forward: Nomos and Narrative," 97 *Harvard L. Rev.* 40.
54. Statement of Concern of African American Men, October 13, 1991 (on file with the author).
55. In the summer of 1995 a group of African American women protested the endorsement of violence against Black women symbolized by the tickertape homecoming parade planned for convicted rapist Mike Tyson. Though many in the community decried the women's protest as "Black male bashing," eventually they were heard. The parade was cancelled.

POSTSCRIPT

Though the events of October 1991 are long past, the headlines bring continuing reminders of the issues raised during the hearings. These issues are far from resolved—nor can they be resolved until the nation engages in an honest conversation about race and gender of the kind this volume seeks to foster.

The essays gathered here offer perspectives and analyses that go beyond their occasion. For instance, Charles R. Lawrence's essay gives the reader a framework to assess not only Mike Tyson's imprisonment but his release from prison in 1995. A year prior to his release, appearing before the parole board, Tyson protested his innocence: "I'll die before I admit my guilt. I am not a rapist." But one news analyst commented that although "Tyson seems to have changed, transformation isn't enough." These words seem to confirm Lawrence's observation that no matter what Tyson does, his face will always represent the face of a rapist. The public's voyeuristic interest in the O. J. Simpson trial prompts one to wonder if this is the fourth act of Lawrence's "three-act morality play," or perhaps a new drama unfolding according to the dictates of the Master Narrative.

One wonders, too, whether Representative Maxine Waters might have been responding to the Senate handling of the October 1991 hearing when she reprimanded her Republican colleague Representative Peter King during a House Banking Committee hearing on Whitewater in 1994. "You're out of order. Shut up," she admonished in response to King's especially harsh questioning of Margaret Williams, Hillary Clinton's chief of staff, a black woman. Waters, also a black woman, later remarked, "The time is out when men can intimidate and badger women." For her comments, Representative Waters' House floor speaking rights were suspended for thirty seconds. Perhaps the assessment of black women's status found in the title and further described in the text of Adele Logan Alexander's essay still holds true in the minds of some.

Ruth Bader Ginsburg's confirmation to the Supreme Court was a significant event in the history of the judicial selection process as Judith Resnik describes it. It was as much a non-event in terms of public interest. It lacked the "riveting drama" discussed by Anna Deavere Smith in her essay. Though the nomination involved a gender issue—Justice Ginsburg is the second woman to sit on the United States Supreme Court—it failed to pique the nation's interest. Perhaps the inattention can be ascribed to the absence of the "intersectionality" of race, sex, and gender as analyzed by many of the contributors.

In reading of the ouster of former NAACP executive director Benjamin Chavis by the NAACP board, one is reminded of Robert L. Allen's discussion of the role of gender bias in the African American community. Can it be that the equality-minded Chavis is a product of socialization into the same gender attitudes and behaviors as other males? Can the concept of equality be compartmentalized, or must it be all-encompassing?

Emma Coleman Jordan's chronicle of lynching reminds us of the lamentable use of vigilante force throughout the history of this country. Read this essay in the context of the hearings, and understand the role that historical events play in creation of modern political dramas. Read this essay against the backdrop of the resurgence of paramilitary and armed separatist groups and the tragedy of the Oklahoma City bombing, and it is also instructive. Its sobering message is that lawlessness tacitly or openly approved by the government can be turned against that very government as well as against ethnic and racial minorities.

Eleanor Holmes Norton's assessment that the 1992 political reaction to the issue of sexual harassment was a spontaneous and unpredictable result of many combined factors was bolstered by two events following the hearings. News stories told of multiple charges of sexual harassment against Senator Robert Packwood, a Republican with a reputation for supporting women's issues, and a single charge of sexual harassment by Paula Jones against President Bill Clinton, who owes his election to strong support from women voters in the Year of the Woman. Congresswoman Norton, like any experienced politician, knows that the political ax is double-edged and swings both ways. The gendered political ax is no different. Notwithstanding the backlash of the 1994 elections, when men switched party affiliation and voted for conservative candidates in record numbers, Norton is correct: politics has been forever changed by the 1991 hearings and the 1992 election outcome.

The legal issue of sexual harassment has been forever changed as well. Susan Deller Ross's essay chronicles sexual harassment law as it has evolved since the hearings. She discusses as well the impact of public sentiment about the hearings on the development of the law. Perhaps this sentiment had something to do with Rena Weeks' $7,500,000 jury award for sexual harassment she suffered at the hand of a partner of the law firm where she worked. This award—the largest in the history of the issue—parallels the broader public impatience with the lack of institutional response to complaints of harassment. (The law firm had been advised of the harasser's behavior yet took no measures to stop it. The firm fired the harasser only after he committed an unrelated ethical infraction.)

Though the law has changed along with public sentiment, the Packwood case shows that the Senate still finds it difficult to develop a process whereby powerful men are held accountable in the face of credible accusations. Ironically, members of the Judiciary Committee aligned themselves with a minority of their colleagues in attempting to shield Packwood from the scrutiny of the Senate Ethics Committee, which was investigating the harassment charges.

Reluctance to hold those in power accountable is not limited to the Senate; in some cases the private sector has similarly lagged behind public feeling on the issue. Corporate action in the face of harassment charges sometimes sends a double message. News reports about John Buldoc, a W. R. Grace Corporation executive whose resignation was accepted after five female employees accused him of sexual harassment, sounded promising to those working to rid the workplace of the problem. However, in accepting his resignation rather than forcing him to leave, the board offered Buldoc a lucrative settlement. Moreover, the reports alluded to allegations that the sexual harassment charges were used as a ploy and that the real differences between the board and Buldoc had little to do with the charges. Whether the arena is corporate headquarters or the halls of the Senate, women, who lack institutional power and support, face formidable obstacles when the colleagues and supporters of those accused judge their claims of sexual harassment. Often the handling of such claims leaves the impression, as in the Grace situation, that the accused men are rewarded rather than punished for their behavior.

The events that make the headlines will continue to remind us of the hearings of October 1991. It is the hope of all the contributors to this volume that our work will continue to shed light on those events.

June 1995   —Anita Faye Hill

CONTRIBUTORS

Adele Logan Alexander   Author of the critically acclaimed *Ambiguous Lives: Free Women of Color in Rural Georgia, 1789–1879* (1991), Adele Logan Alexander graduated from Radcliffe College and holds a Ph.D. in American history from Howard University. She wrote the introduction to *The Guide to Black Washington: Places and Events of Historical and Cultural Significance in the Nation's Capitol* (1990) and, among other writings, has contributed essays to *Black Women in America: An Historical Encyclopedia* (1993), *Picturing Us: African American Identity in Photography* (1994), and *Stepping Out of the Shadows: Alabama Women, 1819–1990* (1995). Professor Alexander teaches history at George Washington University.

Robert L. Allen   Writer, teacher, and community activist, Robert L. Allen is senior editor of the *Black Scholar*, Dr. Allen is a graduate of Morehouse College and holds a Ph.D. in sociology from the University of California at San Francisco. He is co-editor of *Court of Appeal: The Black Community Speaks Out on the Racial and Sexual Politics of Clarence Thomas vs. Anita Hill* (1992), and of *Brotherman* (1994), a collection of stories and essays by and about African American men.

A. Leon Higginbotham, Jr.   Former chief judge of the United States Court of Appeals for the Third Circuit, A. Leon Higginbotham received his bachelor's degree from Antioch College in 1949 and his LL.B. from Yale University in 1952. He is the author of the widely praised *In the Matter of Color: Race and the American Legal Process in the Colonial Period* (1978), and the co-author, among many other articles, of "De Jure Housing Segregation in the United States and South Africa: The Difficult Pursuit of Racial Justice"

(1990) and "The Hughes Court and the Beginning of the End of the 'Separate But Equal' Doctrine" (1992).

Anita Faye Hill Professor of law at the University of Oklahoma College of Law, Anita Faye Hill received her B.A. from Oklahoma State University in 1977 and her J.D. from Yale University Law School in 1980. Her writings include articles on bankruptcy, commercial law, and sexual harassment, among them "Sexual Harassment: The Nature of the Beast," *Southern California Law Review* (1992). Since the Thomas confirmation hearings of 1991, she has given numerous lectures and presentations on race and gender issues in American law and society.

Emma Coleman Jordan Professor of law at Georgetown University, Emma Coleman Jordan is an expert on financial services and commercial law. She received her B.A. from San Francisco State University (1969) and her J.D. from Howard University (1973), where she was editor in chief of the *Howard Law Journal*. She has written numerous articles and book chapters in the fields of financial services and civil rights, and is the author of "Race, Gender, and Social Class in the Thomas Sexual Harassment Hearings: The Hidden Fault Lines in Political Discourse, *Harvard Women's Law Journal* (1992). Professor Jordan served as a legal advisor to Anita Hill during the Hill-Thomas hearings. In 1994 she was the recipient of the NAACP's first Ida B. Wells Award for courageous civil rights advocacy.

Charles R. Lawrence III Professor of law at Georgetown University, Charles R. Lawrence received a B.A. from Haverford College in 1965 and a J.D. from Yale University in 1969. He co-authored *The Bakke Case: The Politics of Inequality* (1979), and has written numerous articles in the areas of public education and race relations, including "Cringing at Myths of Black Sexuality," *Southern California Law Review* (1992). Among other honors, he has been awarded the National Black Law Students Association's Paul Robeson Service Award (1978) and the W. K. Kellogg Foundation National Fellowship (1982–85).

Julianne Malveaux Economist, writer, and lecturer, Julianne Malveaux holds a Ph.D. in economics from the Massachusetts Institute of Technology. Her syndicated column appears nationally in various papers through the King Features Syndicate. She also contributes to

Essence and *Ms.* magazines, *USA Today*, and the *San Francisco Sun Reporter*. In addition, she is the author of *Sex, Lies and Stereotypes: Perspectives of a Mad Economist* (1994), and the co-editor of *Slipping Through the Cracks: The Status of Black Women* (1986).

Eleanor Holmes Norton Congresswoman for the District of Columbia, Eleanor Holmes Norton holds a B.A. from Antioch College (1960), an M.A. in American Studies from Yale University (1963), and an LL.B. from Yale Law School (1964). She has been on leave from her position as a labor law professor at Georgetown University Law Center since winning a seat in Congress. Former chair of the Equal Employment Opportunity Commission, she co-authored *Sex Discrimination and the Law: Causes and Remedies* (1975), and is an authority in the fields of labor law, employment discrimination, and sex discrimination.

Charles J. Ogletree, Jr. Professor of law at Harvard University and director of the Harvard Law School Criminal Justice Institute, Charles J. Ogletree has written widely on criminal justice issues and is a nationally known speaker on the criminal justice system, youthful offending, and violence in America. He received his bachelor's degree in 1974 and his masters degree in 1975, both from Stanford University, and his J.D. from Harvard Law School (1978), where he served as special projects editor of the *Harvard Civil Rights–Civil Liberties Law Review*. Professor Ogletree is a board member of the National Legal Aid and Defender Committee, and chair of the Southern Prisoner's Defense Committee. He was a member of Anita Hill's legal team during the Hill-Thomas hearings.

Orlando Patterson Professor of sociology at Harvard University, Orlando Patterson is an authority on race, nationalism, and ethnicity. He received his B.S. in economics from London University and his Ph.D. in sociology from the London School of Economics (1965). He is the author of *Ethnic Chauvinism: The Reactionary Impulse* (1977), *Social Death: A Comparative Study* (1982), and *Freedom in the Making of Western Culture* (vol. 1), which won the National Book Award for nonfiction in 1991.

Judith Resnik Orrin B. Evans Professor of Law at the University of Southern California Law Center, Judith Resnik teaches procedure, federal courts, feminist theory, and large-scale litigation. She holds a

B.A. from Bryn Mawr College (1972) and a J.D. from New York University (1975), and is the author of *Procedure* (1988, with Robert M. Cover and Owen M. Fiss) and of numerous articles about federal courts, adjudication, and feminism. Professor Resnik was a member of the Ninth Circuit Gender Bias Task Force, the first in the nation to consider the effects of gender on federal adjudication. She has served as chair of the Section on Women in Legal Education of the American Association of Law Schools, testified before congressional committees, and argued in the United States Supreme Court on behalf of a local Rotary Club's right to admit women. During the week of October 7, 1991, she provided legal assistance to Anita Hill. In 1993, she received the Florence K. Murray Service Award from the National Association of Women Judges.

Susan Deller Ross   Professor of law at Georgetown University Law Center, Susan Deller Ross teaches courses in equal employment opportunity, family, gender, and international and comparative law on the rights of women. She is director of both the Sex Discrimination Clinic and the Women's Law and Public Policy Fellowship Program at Georgetown; co-chaired the Gender Committee and co-authored its *Final Report* (1995) for the D.C. Circuit Task Force on Gender, Race, and Ethnic Bias; and served as project consultant and editor for the Women Judges' Fund for Justice's *Judicial Training Materials on Child Custody and Visitation* (1991) and *Spousal Support* (1991). Other publications include *The Rights of Women* (3d ed., 1993) and *Sex Discrimination and the Law* (1975). She has participated in major legislation and litigation on gender issues, including numerous cases before the Supreme Court. Professor Ross received her J.D. from NYU Law (1970) and her B.A. from Knox (1964). She was a member of Anita Hill's legal team during the 1991 hearings.

Anna Deavere Smith   Actor, teacher, writer, and performance artist, Anna Deavere Smith is the creator of a theatrical series entitled *On the Road: A Search for American Character*. The series includes *Fires in the Mirror: Crown Heights, Brooklyn, and Other Identities*, and *Twilight: Los Angeles, 1992*, both of which won Obies and numerous other awards. Her play *Piano* received the 1991 Drama-Logue Award for Playwriting. She has appeared in the movies *Dave*, *Philadelphia*, and *The American President*, and is Ann O'Day Maples Professor of the Arts at Stanford University.